W9-BMO-666

"Too often books on prayer offer practical advice but are almost entirely devoid of sound exegesis, or they demonstrate sound scholarship but make no attempt to connect to everyday life. David Crump does a splendid job of bridging the gap between exegesis and application in this stimulating book on petitionary prayer. One does not need to agree with all of Crump's conclusions to benefit from his careful study of the biblical text, his attention to biblical theology, and his theological synthesis that speaks to our contemporary situation."

Thomas R. Schreiner, James Buchanan Harrison Professor of New Testament, The Southern Baptist Theological Seminary

"By limiting his focus to petitionary prayer, David Crump is able to deal thoroughly with the kind of prayer that raises the most problems for believers and unbelievers alike. In this work, he has made accessible a wealth of recent New Testament scholarship while engaging in a theological critique of the most revered 'prayer warriors' of the last two centuries—a bold move that is both refreshing and long overdue."

Sharyn Dowd, professor of New Testament, Baylor University

"This is not just another book about prayer. David Crump has achieved a very satisfying blend of exegetical analysis and theological reflection in a volume that provides insightful and, at times, challenging perspective on the tough questions. His presentation of the biblical teaching on prayer is very helpful and needs to be heard."

Clinton E. Arnold, professor and chairman, department of New Testament, Talbot School of Theology

Knocking
on Heaven's Door

*A New Testament Theology
of Petitionary Prayer*

David Crump

Baker Academic
Grand Rapids, Michigan

Published by Baker Academic
a division of Baker Publishing Group
P.O. Box 6287, Grand Rapids, MI 49516-6287
www.bakeracademic.com

Printed in the United States of America

Library of Congress Cataloging-in-Publication Data
Crump, David, 1956–
    Knocking on heaven's door : a New Testament theology of petitionary prayer / David Crump.
        p.   cm.
    Includes bibliographical references and index.
    ISBN 10: 0-8010-2689-X (pbk.)
    ISBN 978-0-8010-2689-8 (pbk.)
    1. Prayer—Biblical teaching. 2. Bible. N.T.—Theology. I. Title.
  BS2545.P67C78 2006
  248.3′2—dc22   2006010807

For Terry,
who prays for me

Contents

Acknowledgments

I have the good fortune of teaching at a college that is not only serious about scholarship but is generous in providing the institutional support necessary for its accomplishment. My work on this manuscript would have taken much longer to complete were it not for the teaching relief I enjoyed through a Diekema research fellowship (2002–3) and sabbatical leave (2003–4) granted to me by Calvin College. For this, I am grateful.

Introduction

When Prayer Becomes a Burden

The young woman entering my church office was a stranger to me, but it took only a moment to discern that she had been crying for a long time. Her sobs were more groans than sighs, deep groans that rumbled upward from the wellspring of a fractured heart. I sat waiting and praying, asking for wisdom. After a few moments, she told me why she had come to my door.

Only the day before, her best friend had died of cancer in the prime of life, leaving behind a husband and several small children. But this young woman now found herself mourning not one but two shocking deaths, for she discovered that her own Christian faith had begun to die soon after her friend.

Both women had attended the same church. Once the cancer was diagnosed only a few months earlier, their pastor had organized an around-the-clock, 24-hours-a-day, 7-days-a-week prayer vigil. He told everyone that they would storm the gates of heaven, claim their sister's healing in the name of Jesus, and if they only had enough faith, then they would prove that the God who brings healing is still more powerful than the devil who breeds cancer.

So the church prayed.

Now, this broken, deflated woman stared at me through swollen eyes and asked, "Pastor, why did God lose? How can the devil be more powerful than Jesus?"

My friend's son had just been released from the hospital because there was nothing more to be done. The twelve-year-old wanted to return home in order to spend his last few days of life sleeping in his own bed. The boy's grief-stricken father, a local pastor and community leader, had always believed in God's power to heal the sick and had led his family (friends and church members included) in fervent prayer for many years, asking that Jesus would heal his son's leukemia. There were brief periods of remission, but overall the boy's condition only deteriorated.

Late one night a group of men from the church knocked on the family's front door. A spokesman stepped forward and announced that they had been sent to deliver a message from God: the boy was dying because his father lacked faith. That was why God had refused to answer the family's prayers: my friend was not praying faithfully enough. God had told them that if the family would allow the group's leader to lay his body down over the boy, shielding him from the family's unbelief, and then pray once more for his recovery, he would be healed. My stunned friend stepped in between them and the bedroom door, blocking their march into his son's room, and angrily insisted that they leave his home immediately. As they reluctantly turned and walked out, the group's leader looked over his shoulder and said, "You are now responsible for your son's death."

My friend buried his twelve-year-old child later that year. He also left the pastorate.

My wife and I had been dependent upon prayer to pay the bills from the very beginning of our married life. For a seven-year period, while we started a family and I pursued graduate studies, we never knew the possible sources of all the income needed for next month's expenses. We learned to pray daily for regular, monthly miracles.

Eventually, I began to sense God's nudging me to pursue doctoral work overseas, a project that would involve the daunting task of relocating our young family to a foreign country with no savings, no regular income, and no prospects of financial support once we arrived. This would not be the first time we had done something that friends and neighbors might describe as crazy, but it certainly was on a much larger scale. So, I did something I had never done before; I asked God for a very specific sign—a fleece, if you will, much like Gideon's (Judg. 6:36–40). My wife, Terry, and I began to pray for a financial sign. We often received anonymous financial gifts to buy groceries and keep the bills paid, so we needed to ask for something noticeably out of the ordinary. We prayed that if the Lord wanted us to move overseas, then he needed to send us

$2,000, above and beyond our normal expenses, to begin a travel fund within the next four weeks. My wife and I kept this prayer to ourselves and waited to see what would happen.

About two weeks later, I walked into town to check our post office box. As I opened the small metal door, I could see a bulging white envelope lying on top of the junk mail. There was no identification of any kind. When I opened the flap, all I saw was a thick bundle of cash! In fact, there was $1,000 in cash, all in twenties. No name. No note.

I raced home to show my wife. We knelt together and thanked the Lord for his Gideonesque gift and then promptly reminded him that this was only half of what we were asking for. He needed to send at least one more miraculous thousand within the next two weeks before we could interpret this gift as a signpost directing us to move overseas. To make a long story short, before those two weeks were over, we had received two more substantial gifts from distant friends (who knew nothing of our plans), bringing the four-week total to almost $2,500. We gratefully interpreted these windfalls as God's answer to our prayers and began making preparations to embark upon a marvelous adventure in exercising the same type of faith in Great Britain.

Like most of us, I periodically receive alumni newsletters from the various schools I have attended over the years, updating me on the unfolding life stories of old friends and casual acquaintances. It is always a shock when you hear that someone you know, someone in your own age bracket, has been diagnosed with a terminal illness. In this instance, the news was particularly unsettling because it was an instructor for whom I had been a research assistant. We had once worked closely together, so the news grabbed my attention. His prognosis was bleak.

One month later, in the next edition, my former teacher had written his own reply to the school's announcement. Confidently professing the biblical promise that "the prayer of a righteous man is powerful and effective," he was claiming that his disease would be removed through the power of faith. In fact, as testimony to the reality of God's miraculous response to the power of believing prayer, he had declined all medical treatment. His healing would give glory to God and God alone.

Several months later, the same college newsletter announced my instructor's death from cancer.

I believe in the possibility of miracles, but I am also wary of whose stories I believe. There are, after all, many imposters even within the church.

I once had a good friend who had grown up in central Africa. Her parents were missionaries in the bush, and she was well acquainted with primitive living conditions. I knew her as a sane, well-adjusted woman, not prone to fantasy or exaggeration. Yet, on more than one occasion, I heard her tell the story of how her family's vehicle had once run out of gas on a long cross-country trip. Her father had underestimated the length of the journey, leaving them stranded in the blistering African sun miles away from anywhere. While his wife and three children tried to find some refuge in the vehicle's shade, the young father prayed, knowing that his miscalculation had placed his family in a life-or-death situation. The spare gas canisters were empty, but they did have a large canister of water. Raising the water to heaven, he confessed his foolishness and asked the Lord to perform a miracle in order to save his family. He then poured it all into the gas tank. After loading up the family and climbing into the driver's seat, he turned the ignition. The newly baptized engine roared to life, enabling them to drive nonstop to the next village, where they promptly told anyone who would listen about their Lord's miraculous answer to their desperate prayer.

September 11, 2001, will be remembered as the day that international terrorism successfully planted its harpoon in the American landscape. Almost three thousand men, women, and children, from eighty different nations, lay entombed in the six stories of smoking rubble that was once the twin towers of the World Trade Center. As the dust settled and the rescue efforts progressed and total strangers held hands to cry out to God, the apparently random stories of miraculous escapes and seemingly arbitrary heartache began to circulate through the media.

One woman shared the story of how an unexpected delay had caused her to miss the train she normally rode into the city. Claiming that it was a sovereign act of God's mercy, she was immensely grateful to have been spared by "divine providence."

Another person, a father who was originally scheduled to have the day off, wanted to make a quick trip to the office in order to tie up some loose ends before returning home to spend the rest of the day with his family. Catching an early morning train that delivered him to the office at just the wrong moment, he was caught in an elevator when the first plane tore through tower number one. His grieving widow now asks friends who want to pray with her, "Why? Why did God let him get on that train, that day of all days? How can I ever pray again?"

—∞—

Life is filled with mystery, and, much to our chagrin, claiming to know God does not shed any light upon certain dark recesses of our world. In fact, God often appears to cast a very long, very dark shadow, a shadow that can conceal more than we like to admit. Perhaps one of wise King Solomon's more astute observations is found in the introduction to his own prayer recorded in 2 Chron. 6:1: "The LORD has said that he would dwell in a dark cloud." God shows himself in darkness. He invites us to meet in a place where he cannot be seen. Divine self-revelation may obscure as much as, if not more than, it illuminates.

Nothing brings a feeble human being face to face with spiritual co-nundrums as quickly as prayer, especially petitionary prayer. For many, balancing the prospect of a divine response to our cries for help against the disappointment of heavenly silence in the face of our suffering tips the religious scales in favor of skepticism, atheism, and renunciation. Knocking on heaven's door, asking for an audience with the cosmic king, and then making our requests clearly known is a mysterious enough activity for those of us consigned to inhabit the physical limitations of flesh and blood. But then tracing answers through the fabric of life's chaos, drawing even tentative lines of heavenly connection between the pleas of human uttering and the course of subsequent history—that is a prophetic role for which few of us seem to be qualified. Admittedly, there are always those eager to claim the prophetic mantle, but my experience with life suggests that the longer you live and the more you pray, the less prone you are to give quick, self-assured answers. This is not to deny the possibility of answers; it is merely to acknowledge that nothing in this life, including the realm of the spirit, is automatic, and precious little is ever self-evident. Putting a coin in slot A does not immediately guarantee a Snicker's Bar from chute B, especially when the pocket accumulating my spare change belongs to God. The Creator also has his own purposes, which may include sending me something totally unexpected through chute G once I have surrendered the requisite number of quarters.

Prayer comprises the interface between human frailty and divine power. Yet, connection and comprehension are two very different things. Trying to peer from our world into that other domain is a bit like opening your eyes underwater. It is possible to see, somewhat, but not easily, not far, and not without considerable distortion. Light is refracted, distances are difficult to judge, size is deceptive, sticks appear to bend at the surface, brilliant underwater colors vanish when raised to the surface. We may be able to explore both worlds, but it is painfully apparent that we are better suited for the one than the other. This should not stop us from trying to understand how the two realms relate; it ought, however, to curb our human penchant for dogmatism, replacing heavy-handed solutions with a healthy dose of humility and a very gentle touch.

Practicing petitionary prayer raises a complex set of questions for those who think about what they are doing: How can we know if a request is appropriate? Are there proper and improper ways to ask? How do our concerns intersect with God's designs? Can prayer change God's mind? If so, under what conditions will God adjust? Does God always answer? How do I know when God responds? How do I learn to connect my changing circumstances to my specific prayers? Are any of these concerns illegitimate?

As we might expect, different church traditions have arrived at differing solutions. Some sincere believers insist that any request will be granted if the person praying only has enough faith. One popular writer contends, "If you have faith, you will not fail; if you fail, it is a sign that you do not have faith."[1] Others claim that persistence is the key ingredient, so that answers are guaranteed for those who never quit: "Persistence in prayer meets all the requirements that are necessary to get prayers answered."[2] Yet, the reality of seemingly unanswered prayer cannot be ignored, leaving hopeful petitioners to nurse their unresolved disappointments by either (1) questioning the sincerity of God's concern, (2) doubting the value of prayer altogether, (3) silently accusing themselves as unfaithful failures lacking either stamina or faith or both, or (4) weaving together some spiritually tenuous fabric made of all three.

Others, unwilling to abandon their personal commitment to the value of prayer or the reality of God's love, stake their faith to an opposite extreme. For these people, prayer was never intended to influence heaven or to move God to action. Prayer is purely for our sake; petition is God's tool for shaping an individual's will to the divine pattern. Confronting the requests that apparently go unanswered teaches us to stop praying for our own selfish wants, to stop placing our misguided hopes in our own persistence, even to stop asking altogether. Genuine prayer, this position argues, is finally learned when the believer surrenders all personal interests and simply sighs, "Your will be done."[3] Yet, for many

1. C. L. Allen, *Prayer Changes Things: How to Tap Man's Powerhouse of God's Strength* (New York: Revell, 1964), 55.

2. J. R. Rice, *Whosoever and Whatsoever When You Pray* (Murfreesboro, TN: Sword of the Lord, 1970), 74.

3. Such convictions, sometimes associated with extreme forms of Calvinism, have a long lineage in modern Protestant liberalism. For example, see Friedrich Schleiermacher's

of the faithful this answer leans precipitously toward the edge of fatalism and makes the invitation to "present your requests to God" (Phil. 4:6) sound like a sadist's invitation to a heavenly prank. There must be some way to honor the sovereignty of God's will within the context of a truly reciprocal relationship where the believer's concerns make a real difference to God.

Attempting to unravel this Gordian knot of practical theology is the goal of this book. More specifically, *Knocking on Heaven's Door* will approach the theological and practical questions raised in petitionary prayer by studying the relevant New Testament evidence. Other dimensions of communion with God such as praise, lament, and thanksgiving will not be the focus of attention, nor will the Old Testament contribution to such a discussion, except as it offers essential background to understanding the New Testament documents themselves. The task at hand is very specific: to construct a New Testament theology of petitionary prayer. With this end in view, chapters 1–2 examine the New Testament passages that highlight the pivotal role of faith in effective petition, while chapters 3–4 investigate the parables of Jesus that focus on persistence in answered prayer. Chapters 5–7 study the Lord's Prayer, Jesus's paradigm for faithful petition, highlighting God's eschatological design for the world and how divine intent can coexist with the invitation to "present your requests to God." Chapter 8 uncovers the characteristically Johannine perspective on human petition and divine sovereignty. Chapter 9 excavates the petitionary prayers of the early church, at least as they are portrayed in the book of Acts. Chapters 10–12 grapple with the complexities of apostolic petition and intercession as they are worked out in Paul's ministry as church planter and letter writer. Chapter 13 explores the uniquely ethical perspective on the hindrances to Christian petition discovered in the General Letters and the book of Revelation. Finally, chapter 14 synthesizes the numerous observations arising from these biblical materials in order to construct a normative theology for Christian petition today, including the complex interrelationships between personal faith, persistence, divine sovereignty, and individual requests.

Every investigator brings his or her own collection of assumptions to a study such as this. Those assumptions form the tinted spectacles

---

sermon "The Power of Prayer in Relation to Outward Circumstances," in *Selected Sermons of Schleiermacher* (ed. M. F. Wilson; New York: Funk & Wagnalls, 1890): "If our prayer does not have the effect of moderating the wish that it expressed, of replacing the eager desire with quiet submission, the anxious expectation with devout calmness; then it was no true prayer, and gives sure proof that we are not yet at all capable of this real kind of prayer" (48–49). Ostrander offers an excellent discussion of how late-nineteenth- and early-twentieth-century Protestant liberalism, following in Schleiermacher's footsteps, removed petition from the realm of legitimate prayer; *Life of Prayer*, esp. 97–115.

through which we all view our world. It is only fair that I try to describe, as best as I can, the particular tint that my assumptions give to my worldview. First, I confess that my theological preferences tend toward the Reformed end of the spectrum. While my goal is to allow the biblical text to speak for itself, unencumbered by any interpretive bias, I confess the possibility of personal blind spots.[4] Like any believer, however, I also trust that faithful Bible study will eventually reshape mistaken assumptions, even Reformed ones.

Second, I believe that the Old and New Testament Scriptures are not only ancient documents that illuminate the life of Israel and the first-century Christian church, but that they are also the divinely inspired word through which God speaks today. When these texts are properly interpreted, we learn about God's truth, truth that becomes authoritative for both the belief and the practice of God's people. This means (or, at least, ought to mean) that the disciplined, precise, exegetical study of Scripture should be a primary concern for every Christian without exception, even if the believer has never attended seminary or graduate school. Ideally, every believer needs (and should want) to know how to read the Bible as accurately and insightfully as possible. Consequently, I will assume that even though my readers may not all possess the necessary expertise to conduct such precise analysis themselves, we all are, nonetheless, interested in knowing what questions of language, grammar, literary context, and so on are at stake when a specific interpretation of any biblical passage is offered. With this in mind, many readers may find some of the following interpretation to be a bit complex, but I encourage all to persevere. How else do any of us learn new truths or expand our horizons? Sound theology can be constructed on only a solid foundation. Even the best-built missile will be sent astray when lifting off from a misshapen launchpad. Misinterpretation can lead only to mistaken theology, and mistaken theology produces misunderstanding and misbehavior.

On the other hand, I should also alert my more academic readers that I have worked to avoid compartmentalizing the existential, pastoral significance of my exegesis from the technical processes leading to my conclusions. The flora and fauna of real-life experiences are deliberately interwoven throughout the academic discussions of translation variants and theological alternatives. This is no accident. Although the scholar, seminarian, or graduate student may think it unusual to discover such popular material sharing the same page with the more familiar word studies and higher criticism, I hope that my academic readers will

---

4. See the classic discussion by Bultmann, "Is Exegesis without Presuppositions Possible?"

give equal attention to both aspects of my hybrid presentation. Rudolf Bultmann was fond of reminding the New Testament academy of the inevitable errors that arise whenever theological reflection is isolated from what he called "the act of living." For all his own serious theological errors, and I believe he had many, on this score Bultmann was absolutely correct, and he offers us a prophetic warning. My method in this book is one man's attempt to steer clear of that hermeneutical, theological faux pas. We repeat a timeworn methodological mistake when we separate the task of theology from its existential outworkings in faith.[5]

Unfortunately, the largest portion of the literature on prayer is dominated by popular "folk theologies" rooted in anecdote and personal experience, with only a thin veneer of biblical, theological window dressing added after the fact to lend an air of authority to previously held opinions. I am continually amazed at how many books on prayer offer nothing more than the author's personal convictions—whether well-worn platitudes or eccentric assertions fueled by an overactive imagination—without any serious attempt to rigorously engage the biblical text and demonstrate how theology arises from the Scriptures. This can only make for bad theology and frustrating, even damaging, experiences at prayer. To the extent that the field of modern biblical studies encourages a strict separation between the academic task of interpretation and the practicalities of real-life application, we academics must share a large portion of the blame for the absence of any theological sophistication in most popular works on prayer. The methodological segregation between intellectual engagement with the ancient text, on the one hand, and the practical embrace of modern living, on the other, is a colossal mistake with crippling consequences for both church and academic guild. The academy's reluctance to make space for the expression of personal experience in our theologizing creates both a sterile theology devoid of life (thereby keeping it out of the hands of a wider audience) and a myopic life devoid of the deeper insights made possible by good theology.

Finally, I trust that my method will also clarify the difference between telling a story in order to establish a theological assertion bereft of bibli-

5. Bultmann, *Theology of the New Testament*, 2.240: "When revelation is conceived as an arrangement for the impartation of teachings, these teachings have the character of the objectifying thought of science, a kind of thought which dims their existential reference to living into a mere object of thought. . . . *Such a procedure leads to the misunderstanding that theology, conceived as the 'right teaching,' is the object and content of faith*" (emphasis added). Nowhere is this truer than in one's theology of prayer. If only more of Bultmann's critics and students alike would take this central tenet of his work to heart! His insistence on unifying the act of knowing with the act of living is a much-neglected jewel in biblical scholarship.

cal foundation and telling a story to illustrate a theological conclusion arising out of sound interpretation. The distinction is vital but seemingly unknown in much popular literature.

I hope that by taking the time to pursue a detailed study of the New Testament, readers will find that a deeper understanding of the Bible will generate a more profound commitment to personal prayer. The mind and the heart can cooperate in this venture. The biblical writers were firmly convinced that genuine faith will seek understanding and that deeper understanding inevitably yields a more galvanized faith. In this instance, faith raises the faithful to pray; a discerning, well-grounded faith compels the faithful to continue in concerted prayer long after ill-informed hangers-on have abandoned hope and turned away. May this study so transform both the author and the reader that we will learn to "always pray and not give up" (Luke 18:1).

All Things Are Possible for Those Who Believe

Jesus Curses the Fig Tree

I was teaching an evening class for new members at my church, introducing young Christians to the importance of Bible study, prayer, and community relationships. Even though Gary was not a new believer, he had recently left another neighborhood church and was interested in learning more about the distinctives of mine. His questions offered a variety of opportunities for us to compare the different philosophies of ministry, theology, and biblical interpretation exemplified by the two. Of particular concern to Gary was his ongoing struggle with a long-term, debilitating illness that severely limited his ability to function. He had prayed for healing numerous times with a variety of church leaders and knew that his eventual recovery was assured, if he would only persist in faithfully claiming it. How did he know this? Mark 11:23–24 told him: "I tell you the truth, if anyone says to this mountain, 'Go, throw yourself into the sea,' and does not doubt in his heart but believes that what he says will happen, it will be done for him. Therefore I tell you, whatever you ask for in prayer, believe that you have received it, and it will be yours."

The power of faith could turn the impossible into reality for anyone willing to take the risk of true, believing prayer. Asking God for the impossible was not something to be taken lightly by the faint of heart, but neither was it out of the question for the true believer. Receiving the desired answer, no matter how unlikely, was only a matter of time for anyone who persisted in refusing all doubt. Consequently, even though Gary had been suffering and praying for years, his insistence that he had, in fact, already received his healing ensured that one day complete physical health would be restored.

Gary's reading of Mark 11 is not unusual. I have heard similar claims about the promised power of believing prayer many times. And, at least on a surface reading, if the student pays no attention to the context of Jesus's words and knows nothing about the historical and religious backgrounds to his claims, they do appear to offer something of a blank check to any petitionary prayer that can honestly be signed with the pen of mountain-moving faith. For many of us, however, such claims raise more questions than they answer. What about those who never see their long-requested, long-awaited miracles? Are they simply left to intuit heaven's silent indictment? Does the absence of a miracle accuse the one who prays of insufficient faith? Any attempt to explain the interrelationships between prayer, faith, and divine response in the New Testament must begin by taking a serious account of Mark 11 and its Gospel corollaries.

Synoptic Parallels

Similar statements about the power of faith appear in several different settings within the Synoptic Gospels.[1] Their relationships may be visualized this way (the following translations are my own):

Matthew	Mark	Luke
Then coming to Jesus privately the disciples said, "Why weren't we able to cast it out?" He said to them, "Because of your little faith. For truly I say to you, if you have faith like a grain of mustard seed, you will say to this mountain, 'Move from here to there,' and it will move; and nothing will be impossible for you." (17:19–20)	His disciples asked him privately, "Why weren't we able to cast it out?" And he said to them, "This kind cannot be driven out by anything except by prayer." (9:28–29)	

1. I assume the current scholarly consensus regarding Markan priority (Mark is the earliest Gospel) and the Two-Source Hypothesis (Matthew and Luke used Mark and a now-lost source called Q) as explaining the origins of the Synoptic Gospels; for an introduction to these questions, see Stein, *Synoptic Problem*. I use the designation Q to simply identify material shared by Matthew and Luke without prejudging the question of whether it designates oral and/or written tradition(s).

Matthew	Mark	Luke
		The Lord said, "If you had faith the size of a mustard seed, you could say to this mulberry tree, 'Be uprooted, and be planted in the sea,' and it would obey you." (17:6)
Answering them Jesus said, "Truly, I say to you, if you have faith and do not doubt, you will not only do what has happened to the fig tree, but even if you say to this mountain, 'Be taken up and thrown into the sea,' it will happen. And whatever you ask in prayer, believing, you will receive." (21:21–22)	[Jesus answered,] "Truly, I say to you, whoever says to this mountain, 'Be taken up and thrown into the sea,' and does not doubt in his heart, but believes that what he says will happen, it will be done for him. Therefore I say to you, whatever you ask in prayer, believe that you have received it, and it will be yours." (11:23–24)	

Since our interest lies primarily in understanding how to interpret each saying within its own Gospel context, there is no need for us to investigate the complex question of possible relationships between the different versions of Jesus's words.[2] We can simply read them as they stand in Matthew, Mark, and Luke.

Luke's saying has no particular relationship to prayer. Within its Lukan context (17:3–10) it is concerned with the faith needed to repeatedly forgive an offending brother or sister. In response to Peter's astonishment over this expectation, Jesus identifies such faith as a requirement of true discipleship. Forgiving repeated offenses is not a matter of faith's volume but of its authenticity, as is indicated by the comparison to a mustard seed. The lesson is not that we must "believe and not doubt" in order to receive the impossible, but that we demonstrate that we believe *at all* by a willingness to repeatedly forgive a repentant offender.[3] Great faith is precisely what is not required in this instance.

2. I tend to agree with those who argue that Luke preserves the original Q version of the saying, which Matthew also inserted into his own account of the exorcism recorded in Mark 9:14–29 (∥ Matt. 17:14–21). But Matthew also assimilated this Q saying to his own version of the Markan "mountain-moving" saying from Mark 11:23–24 (∥ Matt. 21:21–22). Consequently, we have a doublet in the Gospel tradition regarding the power of faith and the miraculous.

3. See my discussion of this text in *Jesus the Intercessor*, 129–30.

Matthew 17 also uses this mustard-seed saying independently of any reference to prayer. Although we might assume that prayer played some role in the disciples' failed attempt to exorcise a demon-possessed boy, it is not explicitly stated in the passage, and Matthew omits Jesus's summary statement from the parallel in Mark 9:29—"this kind can come out only by prayer"—which is certainly an odd step to take had he wished to link the quality of faith to the efficacy of prayer (chapter 2 will address these questions further when discussing Mark's version of the story). Matthew instead uses the saying about mustard seed faith to implicitly accuse the disciples of unbelief in their failure to exorcise the epileptic boy.

Consequently, our search for an explicit connection between faith and prayer leaves us with Jesus's teaching offered in the wake of his cursing the fig tree (Mark 11:23–24 ‖ Matt. 21:21–22), where the power of faith free of doubt is apparently connected to the outcome of petitionary prayer.

Mark's Composition

Jesus's cursing of the fig tree has raised more than a few eyebrows. English philosopher Bertrand Russell, author of *Why I Am Not a Christian*, claims that the distinct lack of virtue demonstrated in Christ's outburst was one of the reasons he considered Jesus a lesser figure than Buddha or Socrates.[4] Even among those more sympathetic to the New Testament, such words as "unedifying," "problematic," "objectionable," "nonsense," and "irrational and revolting" are not unusual,[5] especially in light of Mark's observation in 11:13 that "it was not the season for figs." Jesus's treatment of an unproductive fruit tree certainly raises questions for any curious reader, particularly in its noticeably longer Markan version.

Most notable in Mark's rendition is the way that Jesus visits the fig tree twice over a period of two days, as opposed to once in Matthew's account. The initial cursing (Mark 11:12–14) precedes Jesus's demonstration in the temple (11:15–19), unlike Matthew, where it follows. The withered tree is then rediscovered the next morning (11:20–21), and the incident is used as an occasion for instruction on prayer (11:22–26). The four units of Markan material can be visualized like this:

4. Bertrand Russell, *Why I Am Not a Christian and Other Essays on Religion and Related Subjects* (New York: Allen & Unwin, 1957), 19.

5. These five evaluations may be found, respectively, in Losie, "Cursing of the Fig Tree," 3; Cranfield, *Mark*, 354; Nineham, *Mark*, 299; Manson, "Cleansing of the Temple," 278; and Bundy, *Jesus and the First Three Gospels*, 425.

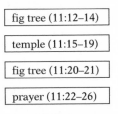

The result of Mark's arrangement is called an intercalation,[6] a term used to describe Mark's habit of interweaving two different stories together in such a way that each helps to interpret the other, thereby creating a "narrative sandwich" that looks something like this: A[1]-B-A[2]. The first (A[1]) and second (A[2]) halves of the same story are separated by Mark's insertion of an altogether different story (B). The result is a blending of the two narratives so that by the time a reader completes A[2] the details of story B become integral to interpreting the entirety of story A.[7]

Initially, Mark's intercalation associates Jesus's temple demonstration with his cursing of the fig tree by inserting the temple scene between the two segments of fig tree material. Then 11:22–26 expands this material into a *double* intercalation. Instead of three sections (A[1]-B-A[2]), Mark creates four interlocking sections (A[1]-B[1]-A[2]-B[2]), yielding several results simultaneously. First, not only do the two fig tree units (A[1] and A[2]) come to bear upon the interpretation of the intervening temple scene in B[1], but the temple scene (B[1]) and Jesus's teaching about prayer (B[2]) are associated and brought mutually to bear on the interpretation of the withered fig tree in A[2]. Imagine lines of interlocking interpretive influences like this:

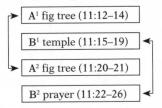

6. Kio, "Prayer Framework in Mark 11," 323–24; J. R. Edwards, "Markan Sandwiches"; and Stein, "Cleansing of the Temple," 127–28. Stein offers a long list of additional examples.

7. For another example, see Mark 8:14–30. The disciples' initial spiritual blindness (A[1] in 8:14–21) is overcome by Peter's eventual confession of Jesus as Messiah (A[2] in 8:27–30); separating those two moments is the intervening story of Jesus restoring sight to a blind man (B in 8:22–26). Why does Mark interrupt his narrative about the disciples with this story about a blind man? Mark's method gives the miracle a dual purpose. It not only describes Jesus's ability to effect physical healing; it also becomes a metaphor describing Peter's spiritual healing. Peter's confession becomes analogous to the blind man's healing; his profession of faith is the miraculous gift of supernatural insight.

The significance of this thematic interweaving will become clear as the study progresses.

Jesus and the Temple

The debate continues over what Jesus hoped to accomplish by attacking the money changers and traders in the temple precincts, and there is little hope that the question will be resolved anytime soon.[8] The options may be roughly divided between two schools of thought: either the historical Jesus was condemning the temple and/or Israel, predicting its eventual destruction,[9] or he was protesting the impieties of the current temple leadership/priesthood, enacting a symbolic cleansing indicative of the need to restore the temple to its proper service.[10] In either case, whatever Jesus's original intent, most scholars agree that Mark intended his readers to interpret Jesus's behavior in light of the first option: Jesus offers a prophetic warning of the eventual doom that will soon overtake the temple, its priesthood, and even Israel itself.[11]

The condemned fig tree, withered from the roots up, is emblematic of the temple. This is the point of Mark's intercalation, sandwiching the temple scene between the cursed and then withered tree. The cursing of the tree is symbolic of the temple's condemnation. Mark has a substantial Old Testament precedent for this association, since the fig tree is a favorite prophetic symbol for the people of Israel. The barren and withered fig tree, depicting an apostate nation soon to be overrun by its enemies, is a common Old Testament image (Isa. 28:4; 34:4; Jer. 8:13; Hosea 2:12; Joel 1:7, 12; Amos 4:9; Nah. 3:12; Hab. 3:17). Quite often the locus of Israel's faithlessness is its abuse of the temple services, such that it was not unusual for the prophets to associate withered fig trees with warnings of the temple's destruction. In fact, the passage quoted in Mark 11:17 is just such a text. Jeremiah condemns Judah for

8. Of course, some skeptics believe that the story is unhistorical; for example, see Seeley, "Jesus' Temple Act." Evans provides a helpful response to such criticisms; see *Mark*, 165–71.

9. The primary representative of this view today is E. Sanders, *Jesus and Judaism*, 61–76.

10. Evans is a consistent advocate of this position; see his "Jesus' Action in the Temple" (*CBQ*); "Jesus' Action in the Temple" (*SBLSP*); and "Jesus and the 'Cave of Robbers.'"

11. This observation has become a commonplace. Cranfield, *Mark*, 356–57, notes that this interpretation can be traced back to the fifth-century commentary on Mark written by Victor of Antioch; see also Robin, "Cursing of the Fig Tree," 279, who quotes Adolf Schlatter; Nineham, *Mark*, 299; Hooker, "Traditions about the Temple," 7; idem, *Mark*, 261; Losie, "Cursing of the Fig Tree," 12; C. Marshall, *Faith as a Theme*, 160; Stein, "Cleansing of the Temple," 123–25; and Evans, *Mark*, 152–54.

hypocritically thinking that temple attendance would expunge the guilt of her idolatry:

> Hear the word of the Lord, all you people of Judah who come through these gates to worship the Lord. . . . Reform your ways and your actions, and I will let you live in this place. Do not trust in deceptive words and say, "This is the temple of the Lord, the temple of the Lord, the temple of the Lord!" . . . But look, you are trusting in deceptive words that are worthless. . . . Has this house, which bears my Name, become a den of robbers to you? (Jer. 7:2–4, 8, 11)

The lengthy judgment oracle continues, and eventually Jeremiah incorporates a variety of conventional images, including the withered fig tree:[12]

> I will take away their harvest, declares the Lord.
>   There will be no grapes on the vine.
> There will be no figs on the tree,
>   and their leaves will wither.
> What I have given them
>   will be taken from them. (Jer. 8:13)

Warnings about an apostate temple and images of barren fig trees are an easy prophetic association. Since the temple is the heart of the nation, there is no confusion in applying the fig tree to both temple and nation. As one goes so goes the other, and so too goes the priesthood and its temple leadership. Prophetic judgment oracles typically warned of what would happen if Israel refused to repent. Consequently, they were, first, calls to national renewal before they were forecasts of eventual destruction. If we keep this prophetic pattern in mind, made explicit by Mark's references to Jeremiah and Isaiah, perhaps we can view the ongoing debate over the precise significance of Jesus's action as an unnecessary distinction. Any cleansing that Jesus performed would have entailed both a call to restoration and a threat of impending disaster should the required repentance fail to materialize. A call for cleansing implied the threat of judgment, and eventual judgment assumed a prior call to restoration.[13] Perhaps a similar conclusion applies to the debate over the exact object of Jesus's condemnation, whether temple, priesthood, or Israel. The prophetic heritage suggests that the representative nature of the temple and its priestly leadership make it impossible to separate the

12. For additional examples of fig tree imagery applied to the condemnation of the temple see Hosea 2:11–12; 9:10–17; Amos 4:4–13. These judgments are not elicited by the temple services per se, but by Israel's apostasy and subsequent abuse of the temple.
13. This suggestion is also made by Hooker, "Traditions about the Temple," 17–19.

fate of the nation from that of its worship center.[14] Be that as it may, the interpretation thus far has at least explained how Mark's intercalation relates Jesus's temple appearance to the divided fig tree episode.

The Fig Tree, Temple, and Prayer

Yet, Mark creates a double intercalation. The disciples' eventual rediscovery of the withered tree (11:20–21 = A[2]) becomes the occasion for Jesus's teaching on the effectiveness of believing prayer (11:22–26 = B[2]). This new association transforms Jesus's curse into an example of petitionary prayer, and the withered tree becomes its miraculous result. The injunction "have faith in God" (11:22, in B[2]) now alludes to Jesus's words in 11:14: "May no one ever eat fruit from you again" (A[1]). Jesus has spoken in faith, and the fig tree turns into an example of effective prayer from someone who believes that anything is possible with God. Jesus's miracle takes on a dual symbolic significance because Mark associates the fig tree with *both* the temple *and* the lesson on prayer. Rather than debate which of these associations is more authentic or germane, we ought to follow Sharyn Dowd's insight in recognizing that Mark's double intercalation deliberately creates a dual role for the fig tree: negatively, the withered tree symbolizes the eventual destruction of the Jerusalem temple; positively, the tree also represents the power of prayer offered in faith.[15]

One more result of Mark's composition should be recognized before we can make proper sense of faith's role in effective prayer. The twofold significance of the fig tree further associates the rejection of the temple (B[1]) with the prayers of the Christian community (B[2]). The fig tree becomes a "metaphorical clamp to hold [these] two ideas together."[16] Jesus condemns the temple for its failure to become "a house of prayer for all nations" (Mark 11:17, quoting Isa. 56:7). While historians continue to debate the existence and legitimacy of a priestly sponsored marketplace providing money changers for the obligatory temple tax and livestock approved for sacrifice,[17] as far as the Markan Jesus is concerned,

14. Telford observes that prophetic warnings of national punishment were often expressed in relationship to an apostate temple; *Barren Temple*, 135.

15. Dowd, *Prayer*, 37–40.

16. Ibid., 53.

17. The issues in this discussion are far from resolved; see Eppstein, "Historicity of the Gospel Account"; Buchanan, "Symbolic Money-Changers?"; Evans, "Jesus' Action in the Temple" (*CBQ*); idem, "Jesus' Action in the Temple" (*SBLSP*); idem, "Jesus and the 'Cave of Robbers'"; Hamilton, "Temple Cleansing and Temple Bank"; and Neusner, "Money-Changers in the Temple."

a market's location in the Court of the Gentiles is symptomatic of the temple leaders' failure to fulfill their divinely ordained responsibilities. Their hostility toward Jesus, repeated challenges to his authority, and failure to recognize his messiahship (Mark 11:18, 27–33; 12:12–40) are entirely in keeping with the spiritual failure that Jesus now diagnoses in their mismanagement of the temple. His allusion to Jeremiah's "den of robbers" equates the priesthood of Jesus's generation with the apostate priests condemned by the prophet. Jesus is not contrasting external ceremonialism (i.e., sacrifice, temple, priesthood per se) against personal devotion (i.e., prayer), as some commentators suggest.[18] He is condemning a corrupt leadership that failed to ensure that all of God's house is equally available to all of God's people.[19] The priesthood's corruption, exclusivity, and opposition to Jesus are symptomatic of the same spiritual malaise. Like the fig tree in full leaf but devoid of fruit, the temple, bustling with priestly activity, was all show, with no true fruit for God.[20] Consequently, the Jerusalem temple, which was supposed to be functioning as a house of prayer for Jew and Gentile alike, would soon be destroyed (Mark 13) and replaced by a new community of prayer to be drawn from all nations (11:22–26).

This connection between temple and prayer would have been crucial to Mark's readers, an association not unique to ancient Judaism.[21] The temple was God's dwelling place, the home of the divine shekinah; thus, Jewish prayer was typically offered toward the capital city, as its efficacy was increased, if not guaranteed, by the recognition that Yahweh communed with his people at Mount Zion. Solomon's dedication prayer for the first temple (1 Kings 8:22–61) emphasized the direct connection between Yahweh's inhabiting the temple and the efficacy of Israel's prayers:

> Hear the cry and the prayer that your servant is praying in your presence this day. May your eyes be open toward this temple night and day, this place of which you said, "My Name shall be there," so that you will hear the prayer your servant prays toward this place. Hear the supplication of your servants and of your people Israel when they pray toward this place. (1 Kings 8:28b–30a)

---

18. Schweizer, *Mark*, 233, says that Jesus is condemning Jewish legalism. Sabbe, "Cleansing of the Temple," 336, has Jesus reacting against "external religion."

19. Losie, "Cursing of the Fig Tree," 12; and Hooker, *Mark*, 263–64.

20. Evans, *Mark*, 154; and Geddert, *Mark*, 266.

21. See the helpful discussion of the relevance of temples to prayer in Dowd, *Prayer*, 45–54.

This essential connection between temple and prayer is reiterated throughout the passage (8:33, 35, 38, 42, 44, 48). Religious literature produced during the period of the second temple, the temple known to Jesus, continued to affirm the vital relationship between temple and prayer. In fact, so important was this connection that the Roman destruction of the temple in AD 70 caused some rabbis to wonder if prayer was still possible for Israel. The temple's destruction meant the withdrawal of God's presence. For example, Rabbi Eleazar (early second century) surmised that since the temple had been the chief means of approaching God, its loss meant that the gates of heaven had been closed:

> Rabbi Eleazar said: From the day on which the Temple was destroyed, the gates of prayer have been closed, as it says, "Yea, when I cry and call for help, He shuts out my prayer" (Lam. 3:8). R. Eleazar also said: Since the day that the Temple was destroyed, a wall of iron divides between Israel and their Father in Heaven. (Babylonian Talmud, tractate *Berakhot* 32b)[22]

Obviously, Judaism eventually found a way to overcome this problem, since prayer's role in Jewish liturgy continued to flourish. At the time, however, it presented an ominous religious crisis for many of the faithful. Some rabbis insisted that, although the divine presence had removed itself from the ruined temple site, it still dwelled among the people in the synagogues and in the houses of study.[23] A similar solution—that the community of the faithful could replace the temple—had already been suggested before the temple's destruction by at least one group of first-century Jewish sectarians. The majority of scholars today agree that this solution was proposed by the Essene communities represented by Qumran, the home of the Dead Sea Scrolls. They, like Jesus, believed that the Jerusalem priesthood was apostate and that the temple services were unclean. Their remedy was to view their own community as a new spiritual temple replacing the old.[24] They were assured that God heard their prayers because they were offered within the new human temple of the believing community.

Jesus's warning of the temple's impending destruction required a solution to the inevitable question of prayer's future feasibility. What

---

22. Quoted in Dowd, *Prayer*, 48. See also Heinemann, *Prayer in the Talmud*, 19–20.

23. Heinemann, *Prayer in the Talmud*, 21.

24. Gärtner, *Temple and the Community*, esp. 16–46; Juel, *Messiah and Temple*, 159–68. For example, the *Rule of the Community* (1QS) 9.3–5 describes the obedience and devotion of the Qumran community replacing temple sacrifice: "They shall atone for guilty rebellion and for sins of unfaithfulness that they may obtain lovingkindness for the Land without the flesh of burnt offerings and the fat of sacrifice. And *prayer* rightly offered shall be as an acceptable fragrance of righteousness" (Vermes, *Complete Dead Sea Scrolls*, 110, emphasis added).

assurances could the disciples have that God would continue to hear the prayers of his people? Mark composed this Jerusalem material with Jesus's answer in view. The assembly of Jesus's followers is destined to become the true house of prayer for all nations; they become the new temple.

Moving Mountains

This circuitous route to the meaning of Mark 11:22–24 reminds us that there is often more to reading and interpreting Scripture than first meets the eye. Passages should not be wrenched out of context, and the correct understanding of literary contexts is tied to a proper understanding of historical contexts. Though the task of historical understanding may seem difficult at times, it results in clearer, more accurate interpretation of the Bible, making it well worth the extra effort involved. In fact, such work is unavoidable for any serious student of God's word who is genuinely interested in knowing and responding to what God asks of us. With this end in mind, we have one more "mountain" of historical background to climb before we are in a solid position to explore Mark's theology of petitionary prayer. The spectacle of mountains performing back flips into the Mediterranean Sea is a dramatic depiction of God's doing "whatever we ask" in prayer (11:24), if we believe and do not doubt (11:23). But how are we to understand this imagery? Several suggestions are offered to explain such hyperactive landscape.

First, W. R. Telford observes that the phrase "one who moves mountains" is a technical term in rabbinic literature that describes a teacher who has so mastered the intricacies of torah that he is able to resolve otherwise insoluble legal conundrums.[25] Here as elsewhere, however, literary context must determine historical relevance, and since Mark's lesson on moving mountains is associated with faith and prayer, not teaching or questions of torah, this particular suggestion, though interesting, can be set aside.

Second, Telford and many others argue that the mountain being moved is not only a metaphorical representation of the power of faith; it also refers to the temple mount, Mount Zion, which will symbolically be removed when the temple is destroyed by Rome.[26] Thus Jesus highlights

25. Telford, *Barren Temple*, 110–15.
26. Ibid., 115–19. Isa. 2:2 and Mic. 4:1 identify the mountain with the temple. See also Hooker, "Traditions about the Temple," 7–8; and idem, *Mark*, 269. Some, such as Gundry, *Mark*, 649–53, argue on the basis of Jesus's itinerary from Bethany to Jerusalem that the mountain in question must be the Mount of Olives. Traditionally, this is the more com-

the contrast between old and new; the failed house of prayer in Jerusalem will be removed to make way for the new house of prayer embodied in the community of his disciples.

Third, Dowd argues that the removal of this mountain should be interpreted against the background of ancient debates regarding the limits of divine power. Today we ask whether it is hypothetically possible for God to create a stone too large for him to lift. In the ancient world an analogous question was whether God could create a mountain too heavy for him to move. God's ability to dislodge mountains was figurative language asserting his power to do the impossible.[27] Mark highlights this conviction elsewhere by reminding the reader that "all things are possible with God" (10:27; 14:36).

So, which of the two remaining possibilities, the second or third, offers greater insight into Jesus's words? I suggest that we hold onto both.[28] After all, Mark's intercalation makes the fig tree a symbol of both the destruction of the temple and the power of believing prayer. For similar reasons, the mountain is associated with both the destruction of the temple and the power of believing prayer. Why must we choose?—especially since the interlocking lines of thematic influence associate the prayers of the believing community (11:22–26) with both the Jerusalem temple, now being replaced with the disciples (11:15–19), and the miraculous effects of Jesus's cursing the fig tree (11:20–21). The disciples' speaking to this mountain (11:23) is analogous to Jesus's having faith in God and speaking to the fig tree (11:14, 21). The interconnections may be diagrammed like this:

$$\text{fig tree} \; \rightarrow \; \text{temple cursed} \; \rightarrow \; \text{mountain moved}$$
$$\updownarrow$$
$$\text{fig tree} \; \rightarrow \; \text{power of faith} \; \rightarrow \; \text{mountain moved}$$

---

mon interpretation; see the list of names provided by Telford, *Barren Temple*, 124n48; and Evans, *Mark*, 188. The first-order question, however, concerns the results of Mark's compositional method, not the historical facts of geography. In all probability, the fig tree was also located nearer the Mount of Olives than Mount Zion, but this did not prevent Mark from associating both tree and mountain with the Jerusalem temple.

27. Dowd (*Prayer*, 69–94) marshals an abundance of literary evidence establishing this position, and it certainly appears to be corroborated by the other New Testament appearances of the metaphor where it highlights the limitless possibilities of divine power (Matt. 17:19–20; 21:21; 1 Cor. 13:2).

28. Dowd insists that we must choose between these options and energetically rejects the first two in favor of the third. Once we are convinced, however, that Mark created a dual reference for the fig tree, I fail to understand why he could not have done the same with this mountain imagery.

In other words, the very same divine power that Jesus invoked to curse the barren tree and prophetically described as the agent of the temple's destruction remains available to praying disciples. The mountain's dual significance yields two important lessons for Mark's readers.

First, it provides considerable comfort to a persecuted Christian community to be assured that its primary opponents will not be allowed to permanently hinder the progress of community life. Initially, opposition to the church arose from the Sanhedrin spearheaded by the priesthood and its temple leaders (Acts 4:1–22; 5:17–42; 6:12–15; 7:54–60; 22:5; 23:1–4, 14–15; 24:1; 25:15; 26:10, 21), but it eventually came to include the synagogue at large (8:1–3; 9:23, 29; 12:1–4; 13:45, 50; 14:2–5, 19; 17:5–9, 13; 18:6, 12–17; 19:9, 33; 20:3; 21:27–36; 23:12–15; 24:9; 25:7, 24). Although Jesus's disciples can anticipate that the hostility vented against their Savior will continue to be directed toward them (Mark 13:9; Matt. 10:17; Luke 12:11; 21:12), the temple's destruction will continually symbolize the ineluctable power of the disciples' faith in God—the God who sent Jesus as their Messiah—to overcome any and all opposition. The final outcome of this "war of faith waged against the mountain of unbelief" is not in doubt.[29] Jesus inaugurated the age of fulfillment in which the coming of God's kingdom demands the removal of every obstructionist mountain and the raising of every intervening valley (Isa. 40:3–5; 45:2; 49:11; 54:10; Zech. 14:4–5); the cosmic forces now establishing the eternal reign of the divine king are forever available to Jesus's followers. Success is assured by their faith in him.

The second lesson flows from the first. Faith in Jesus puts the disciples in touch with the miraculous power of God. We are invited to pray in the confidence that all things remain possible for our Creator. No request is ever too great. No need is beyond the reach of God's ability. The same power by which Jesus healed the sick and was finally raised from the tomb is available to Christ's new community, so we have no reason to hesitate in believing that miracles are still possible. Anyone who places arbitrary, naturalistic limits on what a disciple can reasonably expect of God in this world should stop to consider whether that person's God is the same deity that Jesus turned to when he said to the fig tree, "May no one ever eat fruit from you again" (Mark 11:14).

Two Conditions

Jesus does, however, appear to place two conditions on God's answers to such prayers: faith and forgiveness. A thorough search into

29. C. Marshall, *Faith as a Theme*, 169.

the role of forgiveness will be reserved for later in this study when we look at the question of hindrances to prayer. For now it is enough to observe that Mark's insistence on forgiveness is reiterated at several points in the Gospels (Matt. 6:12, 14–15; 18:35; Mark 11:25; Luke 6:37; 11:4; 17:3–4). Mark's emphasis, however, is not that forgiving others is a condition to the general effectiveness of a disciple's prayers, but that extending forgiveness is a condition for the community's being forgiven of its own sins.[30] We must be careful not to universalize something that originally had a very specific application. Jesus says, "Forgive so that your Father in heaven may forgive you," not "so that your Father may hear your prayers at all." Extending forgiveness may be one of the terms for receiving forgiveness, but there is no clear indication that it conditions all possible access to God's power. The person who prays does not need to be perfect in this regard before confidently approaching God with a request.

The question of faith, on the other hand, certainly is crucial to Jesus's teaching. Its significance is highlighted by the threefold repetition "have faith in God" (Mark 11:22), "does not doubt . . . but believes" (11:23), and "whatever you ask . . . , believe that you have received it" (11:24). Clearly, faith is essential to answered prayer, but in precisely what way is faith related to petition? Furthermore, what is faith? How is it defined? How may we recognize it when we see it? Or must we simply wait to see if our prayers are answered and then draw our own conclusions?

Mark 11:22 opens a Pandora's box of complex questions about faith. First, this verse is noteworthy because the expression translated "have faith in God" is unique in the New Testament.[31] Jesus exhorts disciples to place their faith in God's power, remembering that the outcome of prayer is dependent on divine not human ability. Precisely *what* the disciple is to believe about the power of God is that "with him all things are possible" (10:27; 14:36).[32] The disciple is told to believe, first, *"that* what he says happens" (11:23), and, second, *"that* you have received" "whatever you asked for" (11:24). Generally, in the Synoptic Gospels the language of faith signifies trust or confidence in the power of God demonstrated

30. Dowd, *Prayer*, 126.

31. Ibid., 60; and Evans, *Mark*, 186. The anarthrous phrase "of God," used as an objective genitive after *pistin* (as in Mark 11:22), occurs nowhere else in the New Testament. Although there are several points where questions of translation arise, understanding the verb "have" as imperative rather than indicative and reading the noun "God" as an objective rather than a subjective genitive is the most common, straightforward reading of the sentence. Dowd, *Prayer*, 59–63, surveys the various alternatives, finally settling on "have faith in God."

32. The two affirmations of faith following in Mark 11:23–24 make this definition explicit by specifying the content of faith in their two respective *hoti* ("that") clauses.

through Jesus and/or his disciples (Matt. 8:10, 13; 9:28–29; Mark 2:5; 5:34, 36; 10:52; Luke 1:45; 17:19; cf. Acts 27:25; Rom. 4:17–21).[33] The injunction to "believe that" specifies the particular exhibition of power now requiring faith.

In other words, Christian prayer presupposes the adoption of a very specific worldview affirming that if certain prayers are not answered, it is not because the requests are beyond God's ability. When we pray, we must come to God confidently believing that "with him all things are possible"; he is the Creator who can restart whatever has stopped, terminate whatever has begun, or redirect anything in process. Faith in this context requires that we embrace the conviction, especially in prayer, that God can still work miracles.

Potential answers are not conditioned by the volume or strength of our faith. This is apparent for two reasons. First, translations that make Mark 11:22 a conditional statement, *"if* you have faith in God," are following the weaker textual variant, probably influenced by Luke 17:6, and creating numerous grammatical problems within the sentence.[34] Also, the phrase following in Mark 11:23 begins with "amen" or "truly," and it is virtually unparalleled for Jesus's amen statements to appear as the second clause (apodosis) in a conditional sentence. Consequently, Jesus did not say, *"If* you have such faith, *then* your prayers will be answered." Rather, he makes a straightforward exhortation, "Have faith in God! Pray. You will be answered!" The volume or quality of faith is not at issue.[35]

Neither does the reference to doubt in Mark 11:23 establish a proviso between possible answers and the quality of one's faith. Jesus says, "Do not doubt, but believe." The adversative "but" serves to link the two verbs ("doubt" and "believe") as alternatives. The command is "not A but B." In other words, choose. You can have A *or* B, doubt *or* faith, but not *both* simultaneously. In this context, there is no suggestion of variable qualities of faith infected by greater or lesser degrees of doubt. Rather, believing and not doubting are equivalent to each other.[36] To have faith is to refuse to doubt. The phrase "not doubt" is not intended to describe

33. Bultmann, "Πιστεύω," 206.

34. Metzger, *Textual Commentary*, 92.

35. Although an imperative may serve a similar purpose in an implicitly conditional statement, as in, "Hurry! You'll miss the train," it remains an ambiguous construction that must be read in context.

36. Schweizer, *Mark*, 234; and Dowd, *Prayer*, 64. This is not to deny that degrees or levels of faith may exist in the Christian life; note Jesus's accusations against the disciples as having "little faith" (Matt. 6:30; 8:26; 14:31; 16:8; Luke 12:28). The apostle Paul also refers to those who possess the "gift" of faith (1 Cor. 12:9). My point is that there is no connection between the degree of faith, on the one hand, and the efficacy of petitionary prayer, on the other.

an especially strong faith, a faith strong enough to see miracles, as opposed to a weak faith that is haunted by doubt and cannot see miracles. Rather, eschewing doubt is the very definition of faith; a faith willing to ask for miracles, however tentatively, is the faith that will one day see miracles. The doubter suspects that God does not have the power to do the impossible; allowing these doubts to shape one's behavior is to reject the worldview promoted by Jesus. Consequently, the doubter fails to pray—or at least refuses to ask God for miracles, for the impossible. After all, many people pray daily, but they have no real confidence in God's ability or his willingness to act in ways that transcend the natural order of things. Yet, according to 11:22–24, such prayers are not prayers of faith but of doubt, which is the antithesis of true faith. Prayers that allow no scope for at least the possibility of the miraculous are prayers made in unbelief.

Are There Any Guarantees?

I would be remiss to ignore two promises guaranteeing God's affirmative response to faithful prayer in Mark 11:23–24. In each verse, the possibility of miraculous answers to any and every prayer is apparently held out to anyone who asks in faith: "*Whoever* says to this mountain, 'Rise up and be thrown into the sea' and does not doubt in his heart but believes that what he says will happen, *it will be done for him*. . . . Whatever you ask in prayer, believe that you have received it, and *it will be done for you*" (my translation). Do not these words assure us that, as long as the request is made with genuine faith, anyone (whoever) is free to ask for anything (whatever) and that person is guaranteed a positive response from God? It certainly sounds that way.[37] Caveats intended to moderate such a wholesale promise have already been unmasked as illegitimate readings of the passage. There are no conditional (if/then) clauses, no evaluations of greater or lesser faith (with or without doubt), only a straightforward promise that God will continue to perform the impossible for those who believe and ask. Yet, it is a simple fact of life that many people have desperately sought supernatural intervention in their lives only to be sorely disappointed. How are we to understand Mark's seemingly blanket assurance that prayers for miracles will always receive positive answers? Several factors must be taken into consideration.

37. For example, see J. R. Rice, *Whosoever and Whatsoever When You Pray* (Murfreesboro, TN: Sword of the Lord, 1970): "If one has faith in God, 'whosoever,' that is, anybody in the world, may ask for 'whatsoever,' anything he desires, and in answer to faith, receive it" (10); "one who believes when he prays, may receive whatsoever he desires" (13).

First, perhaps the simplistic nature of the saying is a rhetorical device intended to heighten the seriousness of cultivating undying faith in divine possibilities, particularly in the face of the natural human tendency to disbelieve. The specific concrete images of mountains and fig trees have been made into metaphors for the broader promise that God is still at home in his world, living, moving, and even rearranging the furniture regularly. Just as the promise of moving a specific mountain, as demonstrated by the withering of a particular fig tree, is actually an illustration of how ubiquitous a disciple's expectation of the miraculous should be, so too the apparent guarantee of every mountain being moved by any and every prayer is actually an encouragement never to stop looking for miracles, no matter how many rocky peaks we have been forced to climb. Cynicism is the enemy of faith, the root rot of prayer.

Second, the emphatic assurances of Mark 11:23–24 are made with the future tense of the verb "to be." While it is not unusual for the future ("it will be") to be used as an imperative ("it must be"),[38] and this in fact is the standard way of reading these verses, they can also be read for what they are, the future tense. Perhaps Mark intends to remind his reader that the final fulfillment of all God's miraculous promises still awaits the consummation. After all, the entire context for the continuing promise of potentially miraculous intervention is the inbreaking of the eschatological kingdom, the arrival of the end of the age with Jesus, and his impending showdown in Jerusalem. Jesus's own death demonstrates that sometimes the mountain first crushes before it is removed. It will be gone, but not just yet. Miracles do not always happen precisely as we had hoped. Oftentimes the promises of faith approach as tenuous shapes poised on the horizon of a distant eschatological tomorrow. Our requests have been heard and answered, but the arrival of pertinent answers is subject to the oddly bifurcated time frame of God's "already/but not yet" kingdom[39]—Jesus has come, but he is yet to come; Jesus brought the end, but we await the end; Jesus brought salvation, but we wait to be fully saved. Pray for miracles, believing that your petitions have been heard and that God has already responded, but some answers arrive more quickly than others—some in our lifetimes, others at the end of the age.

38. Zerwick, *Biblical Greek*, 94 §280.

39. The phrase "already/but not yet" has become shorthand for describing the all-pervasive eschatological (end-time) tension running throughout the New Testament; disciples live in the middle of two overlapping realities. On the one hand, Jesus has already inaugurated the kingdom of God, salvation is a present reality, the old is gone, the new has come. On the other hand, the kingdom has yet to arrive fully, salvation is still a future hope, and the old nature continues to struggle against the new. See the classic treatments in Kümmel, *Promise and Fulfilment*; and Cullmann, *Salvation in History*.

I know that some will balk at these suggestions, insisting that the verbs retain their imperatival sense and that this is a promise of answers given now! This view, however, leaves us with the perennially pestering questions of apparently unanswered prayers and of miracles that never arrive. How can the supposed assurances of Mark 11:23–24 be made to fit the average believer's real-life experience? How many of us can honestly say that we have literally received every miracle we have ever requested? Did our desperation make any difference?

Final answers to such questions require that we first look at the interactions between faith, prayer, and the divine will, especially as they unfold throughout the ministry of Jesus. His life offers the greatest example of human existence directed by faith in God's ability to perform the impossible. It is also the subject of our next chapter.

Conclusion

No, I did not try to explain all of these interpretive issues to my friend, Gary, as he shared the thinning optimism of his prayers for healing with my evening Bible study class. Perhaps I should have, but I doubt it. He was continuing to pray; he still believed in God's power to perform miracles, and I had no way of knowing what God's future plans might entail. I would have been more inclined to confront his misreading of Mark 11:23–25 had I detected some whiff of spiritual exhaustion or a cancerous cynicism concerning prayer in general, for those are the principal dangers of the typical misunderstanding that Gary brought to this passage. Prayer is not magic, and there is no blanket promise, no faith formula, to guarantee God's granting any and every petition *if only* the one praying will *believe*. I trust that this chapter has made that much clear.

According to Mark 11:12–26, prayer is the expression of faith, and faith is the only means of relationship with God. The way a person talks with God and what one is willing to venture as petition reflect on the reality or the illusion of that person's faith commitment. The unbelieving temple establishment of Jesus's day was replaced by (and finds fulfillment in) the tenacious community of believing disciples—you and me, members of the Christian church—who will never surrender true faith in Jesus Christ, never give up believing that the Father of our Lord has made us members of the eschatological family of God. No amount of opposition from any source, religious or secular, will be able to hinder the ever-expanding circle of salvation engulfing this world through the invincible kingdom of God and its residents, the church. The principal living expression of such faith is the continuous offering of petitions that our heavenly Father work in those ways that only God can work, to do the things that only God can do, knowing that each new moment may easily provide the fresh unfolding of another long-awaited miracle. We may not be able to predict particular outcomes, but we do live as those who know that our heavenly Father "is able to do immeasurably more than all we ask or imagine" (Eph. 3:20).

2

I Believe, Help My Unbelief

Prayer, Faith, and Miracles

As quick as we are to raise querulous questions about the numerous prayers that seem to go unanswered, the average person is less likely to complain about the unanticipated miracles that occasionally take the person by surprise. But, for those who continue to insist that seemingly unanswered prayers are due to a lack of faith, are we also to assume that unexpected answers are due to an overabundance of faith? Not likely. What, then, about those instances where the delighted recipient had no expectations of any kind?

My friend, Chris, wore the look of a world-weary religiosity that can sometimes descend upon the children of professional Christians. She had spent her childhood in Southeast Asia, the daughter of missionaries, and had absolutely no interest in returning to anything even remotely resembling that life as an adult. The tropical jungles had left her with a mysterious souvenir, a skin rash of unknown origin that had so far defeated every medical treatment. It simply came and went as it pleased, much to my friend's embarrassment and discomfort. One Sunday morning she asked our adult education class if she could tell us the most amazing story about what had happened to her during the week. We could tell by her smile and enthusiasm (both somewhat unusual for her) that, whatever it was, it had to be good.

Chris had been doing housework one afternoon with the television on as background noise. A televangelist appeared on the screen, and rather than switch the channel as she would normally, my cynical friend decided to watch for whatever entertainment value the show might provide. At one point the man began his so-called healing segment by describing the various illnesses suffered by members of the viewing audience. Suddenly, Chris heard a description of what sounded very much like her skin disease. She left her ironing and took a few steps toward the television. Describing a young woman's plight with years of ineffective, expensive medical treatments, he asked that she now place her hands upon the television screen as he prayed for her recovery. Chris did not believe in miracles, was convinced that men like this were charlatans, and had never before felt any particular need to lay hands on a television set. Yet, something inside her said, "Try it. What have you got to lose?" So she put her hands on the television screen, carefully matching her fingers to his. He began to pray. Chris said she never felt anything, no tingling, burning, or chill, but when she opened her eyes, the rash was gone. She pulled up her sleeves and showed us her arms.

Over the years, I periodically checked with Chris to see if the rash ever recurred. She insisted that it had not. She never did become a great fan of televangelists or faith healers, and while her own jaded outlook on life may have softened over the years, it never really left her. Yet, she knew that she had been miraculously healed, even though at the time of the miracle she had no expectations and no faith whatsoever that such a thing could ever happen for her. God had apparently decided to work in her life quite independently of her own expectations.[1]

In chapter 1, I demonstrated that, according to Mark 11:12–26, Jesus's encouragement to pray for miracles does not construct any straightforward cause-and-effect relationship between the quantity or quality of a praying disciple's faith and the efficacy of the petition being offered. This issue now needs to be examined more thoroughly throughout the Gospels, for the ambivalent relationship between faith and miracle is an essential ingredient to the theological background informing this preliminary observation about petitionary prayer in the New Testament. The absence of a miracle does not require the absence of sufficient faith; neither does the presence of a miracle necessarily assume the presence of substantial faith. People who pray with heroic faith may never see

---

1. Sadly, my friend's life came to a tragic conclusion several years ago when she committed suicide. Not even miraculous answers to prayer can guarantee peace and contentment.

their requests answered, at least in this life. Whereas, those who offer timorous prayers with minuscule faith may sometimes witness miracles beyond their grandest imaginations. The wild card, so to speak, in the entire process is one overriding factor: the will of God. This chapter thus attempts to integrate this new ingredient in three stages: first, we will examine the relationship between faith and miracle throughout the Gospels; second, the healing of a demon-possessed boy in Mark 9:14–29 will provide an explicit discussion of the relationship between prayer, miracle, and meager faith; and, third, Jesus's own prayer in Gethsemane offers the quintessential instance of how God's will may easily contravene the repeated petitions of a man who firmly believed in his heavenly Father's ability to perform the impossible.

Faith and the Gospel Miracles

The most exhaustive examination to date of the Gospel miracle accounts, *The Miracles of Jesus* by H. Van Der Loos, straightforwardly states this unavoidable conclusion: to examine the relationship between faith and the miracles of Jesus is to be struck by its absence.[2] There simply is no consistent correlation between the apparent faith or unbelief of a miracle's beneficiary and Jesus's performance of a miraculous act. There are tendencies, but nothing perfectly consistent. B. Gerhardsson's analysis of miracles in the Gospel of Matthew offers some particularly helpful insights in this regard by observing a distinction in the Synoptic Gospels between what he calls "therapeutic" and "nontherapeutic" miracles.[3] The first category involves acts of personal healing and restoration; the second designates what are traditionally called the nature miracles. The nontherapeutic miracles are demonstrations of divine power performed for the benefit of the disciples, yet they are neither preceded nor followed by evidence of the disciples' faith. In fact, just the opposite. When confronted by Jesus's stilling of the storm (Mark 4:35–41 ‖ Matt. 8:23–27 ‖ Luke 8:22–25), the feedings of the multitudes (Mark 6:35–44 ‖ Matt. 14:13–21 ‖ Luke 9:12–17; also Mark 8:1–10 ‖ Matt. 15:32–39), and Jesus's walking on the water (Mark 6:45–52 ‖ Matt. 14:24–33), the evangelists make it clear that Jesus performed these miracles *in spite of* the disciples' *lack of faith*. Not only do the disciples neither expect nor ask for any miracles, but the miracles themselves are highly uncertain in their outcome. Only once is there any suggestion that the miracle advanced the

2. Van Der Loos, *Miracles of Jesus*, 264, passim.
3. Gerhardsson, *Mighty Acts of Jesus*. To my knowledge, Gerhardsson was the first to make this distinction.

disciples' faith (Matt. 14:33); more often than not the disciples remain perplexed and uncertain as to what to make of their experience. Jesus repeatedly chides them for their obtuse inability either to exercise trust in his power or to perceive the inner significance of his acts.[4] When miracles are performed for the disciples, they are neither the result nor the (predictable) agent of faith.

Therapeutic miracles, on the other hand, are performed for outsiders who by and large approach Jesus in search of a miracle. Jesus never turns these people away and always performs what they ask, even when the request comes from a Gentile, the outsider par excellence (Mark 7:25–30 ‖ Matt. 15:21–28).[5] The apparent lesson of the therapeutic miracles is that Jesus freely responds to the faith of any and every true seeker; those in need are encouraged to bring their burdens to him as the agent of God's eschatological kingdom. These miracles become the tangible expression of the wholeness available to the subjects of that kingdom, a wholeness made visible by the healing of a paralytic (Mark 2:1–12 ‖ Matt. 9:1–8 ‖ Luke 5:17–26), the raising of Jairus's daughter (Mark 5:21–24, 35–43 ‖ Matt. 9:18–19, 23–26 ‖ Luke 8:40–42, 49–56), the healing of a hemorrhaging woman (Mark 5:25–34 ‖ Matt. 9:20–22 ‖ Luke 8:43–48), and the restoration of hearing to the deaf (Mark 7:32–37 ‖ Matt. 15:29–31) and sight to the blind (Mark 8:22–26; 10:46–52 ‖ Matt. 20:29–34; Luke 18:35–43).[6] These miracles are demonstrable evidence that the kingdom of God is being inaugurated here and now by Jesus as the agent of divine mercy (Mark 6:53–56 ‖ Matt. 14:34–36). The miracles are not symbols pointing toward some spiritual reality located elsewhere; they are earthly demonstrations of divine power that simultaneously share in the new reality being depicted. Each healing is—at least in part—the actual arrival of salvation. "They are rather like . . . moving images"[7] of the kingdom's unfolding, playing themselves out upon the stage of history. It is not surprising, then, to observe that

4. Ibid., 62. Gerhardsson's study offers a valuable modification of the seminal work on this subject by Held, "Matthew as Interpreter." Held ably demonstrates that Matthew redefines Mark's "absence of faith" as "little faith" in his own depiction of the disciples (292). In order to consistently advance his thesis that faith is key to *all* Matthean miracles, he must, however, redefine the nature miracles as "epiphanies" rather than miracles (282n2). This is not an argument but semantic juggling.

5. Held, "Matthew as Interpreter," 283–84, 291. It is interesting that Matthew's examples of faith are always outsiders, never disciples. Held's observation that Matthew portrays requests for healing as "prayers" and faith in miracles as "praying faith" is an important insight (281–82, 284–91).

6. For good discussions on the apologetic value of miracles as visible demonstrations of the kingdom's real presence, see Nicol, *Sēmeia in the Fourth Gospel*, 113–24; Latourelle, *Miracles of Jesus*, 282–98; and Held, "Matthew as Interpreter," 284.

7. Nicol, *Sēmeia in the Fourth Gospel*, 119.

no such seeker, however meager his or her faith, is ever turned away disappointed.[8]

Not even this pattern of miracle-producing faith, however, is perfect. Gerhardsson himself admits that one cannot expect to find faith as a theme among the exorcisms (Mark 1:23–28 ‖ Luke 4:33–37; Mark 5:1–20 ‖ Matt. 8:28–34 ‖ Luke 8:26–38; also Matt. 12:22–24 ‖ Luke 11:14–16);[9] they display the divinely ordained and unsolicited triumph of God's power over the forces of evil. But this theme of divine sovereignty extends itself to other therapeutic miracles as well, where Jesus performs miracles quite independently of any apparent faith: the healing of Peter's mother-in-law (Mark 1:30–31 ‖ Matt. 8:14–15 ‖ Luke 4:38–39), the healing of the man with a withered hand (Mark 3:1–6 ‖ Matt. 12:9–14 ‖ Luke 6:6–11), the raising of a widow's son (Luke 7:11–15), and the healing of a crippled woman (13:10–13).[10] These miracles have nothing to do with a petitioner's faith and everything to do with the purposes of God. Yes, Jesus asks for faith and responds to faith, but he does not limit himself to the parameters of faith. He remains free to exercise kingdom power wherever and whenever he pleases, whether within or without the confines of another's convictions.

The ambiguity inherent within the faith-miracle relationship is never far off in any of the Gospels, but it becomes particularly explicit in John. A consensus exists within Johannine scholarship that this Gospel critiques both the value of miracles in promoting faith, as well as the value of any faith that seeks after or is dependent upon miracles.[11] Any faith motivated to seek displays of power is portrayed as the inadequate faith typical of the vacillating multitudes. Genuine disciples should expect to grow beyond the phenomenological fixations of "sign seekers" (John 2:23–24; 4:48; 6:2, 14, 26, 30, 66; 12:37; 20:29).

The unpredictability of the popular response to the miracles in John is explained by their parabolic function as signs. The Johannine signs are similar to the Synoptic parables; one might even define them as *enacted* parables.[12] They "exert no incontrovertible power before which all must

8. Luke-Acts is distinctive in giving a greater role to the place of miracles in the production of faith and the birth of the early church; see Achtemeier, "Lucan Perspective."

9. Gerhardsson, *Mighty Acts of Jesus*, 48.

10. Luke retains both of Mark's examples and adds two further instances of his own. Elsewhere I demonstrate how Luke's theology of divine sovereignty influenced his redactional work, including the subordination of petitionary prayer to the divine will. The evidence of these miracle stories is precisely in line with those earlier observations; see *Jesus the Intercessor*, 128–36.

11. Nicol, *Sēmeia in the Fourth Gospel*, 99–106; Lohse, "Miracles in the Fourth Gospel," 64–65; and Kysar, *John*.

12. The concept of not just the Johannine signs, but of all Gospel miracles functioning as enacted parables is not new; see Richardson, *Miracle-Stories of the Gospels*, 57; Van Der Loos, *Miracles of Jesus*, 246; and Blomberg, "Miracles as Parables."

bow, but rather, like [Jesus's] preaching, consistently provoke a double reaction (7.40f.; 9.16; 10.19; 11.45f.)."[13] For those already predisposed toward faith, the miracle becomes a means of divine revelation (2:11; 4:26–53; 9:1–38; 11:1–45), but for those inclined toward skepticism and hostility, the miracle merely provides another occasion for offense (10:25; 12:10–11, 37; 15:24). Thus miraculous signs do not persuade as much as they confirm one's predispositions. Furthermore, according to 12:39–40 (alluding to Isa. 6:9–10) that personal predisposition is correlated to a divine decision:

> He has blinded their eyes
>   and deadened their hearts,
> so they can neither see with their eyes,
>   nor understand with their hearts,
>   nor turn—and I would heal them.

The role of God's sovereignty in the outworking of Jesus's miracles, particularly as sovereignty relates to a miracle's intersection with personal faith, is explained by way of Isaiah's ministry to apostate Israel. The Father hardens the hearts of the Son's opponents. The relationship between miracle and faith cannot be fully explained apart from God's own intentions as he works within the hearts and minds of Jesus's audience. John's reference to Isaiah highlights the functional equivalence of these signs with Jesus's parables, since the same text is used by the Synoptic Gospels to explain the double reaction typically elicited by those stories (Mark 4:12 ‖ Matt. 13:13 ‖ Luke 8:10). The crowds respond to the parables just as they respond to Jesus's miracles: many have faith; many more do not. Neither reaction takes the Father by surprise. Of course, a question remains concerning the order of the relationship between an individual's will (to believe) and the divine will (to harden): which is the cause, and which is the effect? Does Isa. 6:9–10 explain the initial cause of the leaders' hostility toward Jesus? Or is it describing God's reaction to their hostility? In either case, it is sufficient for our purposes merely to observe that unbelief (whatever its ultimate cause) often precedes the miraculous. While Jesus certainly calls for faith and regularly performs miracles in response to faith, there is no exclusive relationship between the two. He is not limited by faith. The Gospel writers carefully insist that *faith itself is not the cause of miracles*. God is. Extraordinary demonstrations of divine activity are not rooted in the power of faith per se, as if personal convictions could purchase authority over the disposition of heavenly intervention into world affairs.

13. Lohse, "Miracles in the Fourth Gospel," 73.

Every possibility for the miraculous is grounded solely in the character of God as the merciful Creator who closely attends to the requests of his creatures and providentially meets the needs of those who possess sufficient faith to turn to him.[14]

Healing the Epileptic Boy

"The story of the demon-possessed boy [Mark 9:14–29] provides a dramatic example of a miracle that is given in response to a request made in unbelief."[15] It is equally important, however, to observe that the disciples' inability to cure the boy is finally explained, not by an absence of faith, but by an absence of prayer (9:29). The concerns of both faith and prayer are clearly distinguished as lessons to be learned by two different segments of the audience. The problem of unbelief is addressed as Jesus converses with the boy's father (9:21–24); the problem of neglected prayer is confronted in conversation with the disciples (9:28–29).[16]

The parallel accounts in Matt. 17:14–21 and Luke 9:37–43 eliminate the issue of prayer and refocus Jesus's verdict in their own ways. Unlike Mark, Matthew highlights that the disciples fail because of their lack of faith. He does this, first, by omitting Jesus's conversation with the boy's father[17] and, second, by linking the quantification of the disciples' "little faith" with the saying about moving mountains (Matt. 17:20c). The Matthean Jesus assures his disciples that nothing is impossible for those who possess faith the size of a mustard seed. Consequently, the comparative value of the mustard seed defines the disciples' "little faith" as very little indeed—in fact, it is smaller than a mustard seed![18] Consequently, the disciples are shown to fail because they exercised no faith whatsoever. The shock value of Jesus's verdict becomes apparent in the disciples previously performing such miracles quite successfully (Mark 6:7–13, 30 ‖ Matt. 10:7–11, 14 ‖ Luke 9:1–6, 10). It is their past

14. "Believing does not imperil the freedom and majesty of him to whom it is directed, but recognizes them and remains faithful by submitting to his will"; Adolf Schlatter, quoted in Held, "Matthew as Interpreter," 287n2; see also 283–84, 288.

15. Dowd, *Prayer*, 110.

16. This feature of Mark 9:14–29 is one of the elements that suggest to many that Mark's narrative is a conflation of two originally separate miracle stories; see Bultmann, *History of the Synoptic Tradition*, 211; Nineham, *Mark*, 242; and Achtemeier, "Miracles and the Historical Jesus." My failure to take account of this shift in the story line explains my earlier interpretation of Mark 9 in *Jesus the Intercessor*, 129–30, an interpretation I now modify.

17. Held, "Matthew as Interpreter," 188–89, 271–72.

18. Held insinuates this observation, but his thesis prevents him from drawing the necessary conclusion; ibid., 295.

success that provides the basis for the disciples' present surprise (Mark 9:28 ‖ Matt. 17:19). What is the explanation? Had they become overly impressed with themselves? Were they relying on methodology and incantation like the average magician?[19] Did they forget to trust God, thinking that divine power was permanently at their disposal to use whenever, wherever they pleased?[20] Mark and Matthew offer different answers to these questions. The Markan Jesus directs his disciples to the role of prayer, whereas Matthew's version highlights the necessity of faith. Yet, Matthew's point is not to quantify the amount of faith needed in order to perform miracles successfully; rather, he emphasizes that even the smallest degree of faith, as small as a grain of mustard seed, will be allowed to witness the miraculous signs of God's kingdom.[21] Matthew finally uses the mountain-moving saying in the same way as it is used in Mark 11:22–26 (see chapter 1).

Luke's version of the story is removed even further from Mark's. Luke drops the remarks on faith altogether as he eliminates both conversations with the boy's father and the disciples. The only remaining reference to faith is found in Luke 9:41 as Jesus condemns this "unbelieving and perverse generation." If this comment is intended to accuse the disciples of faithlessness, it is an exceedingly oblique reference. First, whom does Jesus accuse: the disciples, the father, the crowd, the father and the crowd, the disciples and the crowd, or all three groups?[22] The answer is far from clear. Second, if Luke's version of the accusation is aimed in whole or in part at the disciples, then they are not accused of inadequate faith but of a complete lack of faith. In other words, as representatives of an "unbelieving and perverse generation" they failed to perform the miracle because they had no faith at all. If that is the case, Luke agrees with Matthew. Jesus is not quantifying the requisite level of miracle-working faith; he is calling for the exercise of any amount of faith.[23]

19. For evidence of magic within Second Temple Judaism, see Morgan, *Sepher ha-Razim*; Naveh and Shaked, *Amulets and Magic Bowls*; idem, *Magic Spells and Formulae*; Kee, "Magic and Messiah," 128–31; Schäfer, "Jewish Magic Literature"; and Schiffman and Swartz, *Hebrew and Aramaic Incantation Texts*. Even though the extant physical evidence dates from late antiquity, there is ample evidence to suggest its roots in the pre-Christian era.

20. For a variety of such suggestions, see Swete, *Mark*, 191; Cranfield, *Mark*, 301; and Geddert, *Mark*, 224.

21. Schweizer, *Matthew*, 353; Hagner, *Matthew*, 1.505–6; and Keener, *Matthew*, 442.

22. See Fitzmyer, *Luke*, 809, for representatives of the various options.

23. Fitzmyer (ibid., 807) also observes how strange it is, given Luke's interest in prayer, that he omits Mark's reference to prayer as the means of exorcism (Mark 9:29). This lacuna is certainly curious, although I suggest that Luke's consistent disassociation of prayer's outcomes from the value of faith helps to explain its omission here. Luke so thoroughly excises faith from the passage that he could have conceivably retained Mark's prayer reference without posing any threat to his overarching view of prayer and divine sovereignty; see *Jesus the Intercessor*, passim. Luke's rewriting ensures that this healing of a demon-

Help My Unbelief

While none of the Synoptic authors use the healing of the epileptic boy to correlate either the quantity or the quality of faith to the effectiveness of petitionary prayer, we must examine Mark's particular method more closely.

A careful reading shows that Jesus's condemnation in Mark 9:19 is not directed at the disciples; he is addressing the crowd, including the scribes and the father.[24] Elsewhere in the Synoptics, "generation" invariably denotes Jesus's opponents, never his followers (Mark 8:38; 13:30; Matt. 23:36; 24:34; Luke 11:51; 16:8; 17:25; 21:32).[25] This generation's unbelief is expressed in its cynical pursuit of miracles, not as demonstrations of the kingdom's power within their own lives but as evidence subject to their scrutiny (Mark 8:12; Matt. 11:16; 12:38–39; 16:4; Luke 7:31; 11:29). Jesus refuses to submit himself to such cynical evaluation, and his designation of the crowd, including the scribes and the father, as "an unbelieving generation" indicates that the demon-possessed boy was not brought to Jesus out of altruistic motives. It is commonly suggested that the father's confession of unbelief (Mark 9:24) is the result of the disciples' earlier failure; their inability to heal the boy caused the father's conviction to weaken.[26] In light of 9:19, however, Jesus identifies the father as a member of the hostile generation now searching for evidence to discredit him. This is further confirmed, first, by the way in which the father steps forward as the representative spokesman for the crowd (9:17) and, second, by the hesitant nature of his conditional request, "If you can . . . , take pity [lit., have mercy]" (9:22). These words are more than the tentative query of a man with faltering faith; it is, at least in part, a test. Of course, seeing his son healed would be a wonderfully unexpected benefit, but the man has allowed his helpless child to become the bait in a cynical trap set to discredit Jesus.

---

possessed boy is transformed from a miracle highlighting the lessons of faith into a miracle single-mindedly exemplifying Jesus's divine power and compassion (Achtemeier, "Miracles and the Historical Jesus," 474; Fitzmyer, *Luke*, 807), a transformation thoroughly in line with Luke's view of both prayer and divine mercy.

24. See the analysis in Dowd, *Prayer*, 118n109; and Cook, *Structure and Persuasive Power*, 230. At 9:15 the crowd's attention shifts from the nine disciples to Jesus and his inner circle. The larger group of disciples does not reappear until 9:28. For other perspectives see Cranfield, *Mark*, 301 (9:19 condemns the disciples, not the crowd); Gundry, *Mark*, 489 (9:19 condemns the father and the crowd, not the disciples); and C. Marshall, *Faith as a Theme*, 117 (9:19 condemns both the disciples and the crowd, including the father).

25. Held, "Matthew as Interpreter," 191n2; he then goes on to argue (192) that Matt. 17:17 is the sole exception.

26. Gundry, *Mark*, 490–91; C. Marshall, *Faith as a Theme*, 117; Evans, *Mark*, 52; and Geddert, *Mark*, 223.

As with his other exorcisms, Jesus confronts the power of evil and liberates its oppressed victim without requiring any expression of prior faith (9:25–27). In this instance, however, he also takes advantage of the father's candor ("help . . . my unbelief") to offer a lesson on the relationship between faith, or the lack thereof, and miracles. Gaining a clearer understanding of this lesson requires that we first answer two questions: Whose faith is at issue in 9:23? What is the father requesting in 9:24?

All Things Are Possible for the One Who Believes

Jesus's crucial statement in Mark 9:23 is thoroughly ambiguous: "All things are possible for/by the one who believes" (my translation). We already discovered in chapter 1 that the language of unlimited possibilities is the Synoptic Gospels' standard method for describing the miracle-working power of God (Mark 10:27 ‖ Matt. 19:26 ‖ Luke 18:27; see also Luke 1:37; Mark 14:36). That God is able to perform the impossible is beyond doubt as far as the Gospel writers are concerned. Furthermore, precisely whose faith is able to engage this divine power? Is Jesus referring to the faith of the petitioner (the boy's father) or to the faith of the miracle worker (Jesus himself)?[27]

This question is due to the uncertain meaning of the dative "for/by the one who believes," which can be translated in two different ways: (1) "for," meaning "on behalf of the one who believes," or (2) "by," meaning "through the agency of the one who believes." Is Jesus saying, "God can do anything for the believing person" (#1)? If this is the proper translation, then Jesus is encouraging the father to trust in God's power to answer his request. Or is Jesus saying, "There is nothing that cannot be done by the person of faith" (#2)? In this case, Jesus is asserting the value of his own faith and promising a positive outcome to the impending miracle.[28]

27. The first half of 9:23 also has a problem. Various early copyists, failing to realize that Jesus was repeating the father's words ("if you can . . .") in order to challenge the man's skepticism (i.e., "as far as this 'if you can' is concerned . . ."), inserted the verb "to believe," thereby altering the subject of the verb "can" from Jesus to the father; see Metzger, *Textual Commentary*, 85. Consequently, the Byzantine text reflected in the AV reads: "If you can believe, all things are possible to him who believes." This is an evident adulteration of the original text. Held, "Matthew as Interpreter," 190n3, argues that this insertion ought to be retained as an appropriate clarification of Jesus's intent; it is illegitimate, however, to allow one's thesis to override the text-critical evidence in this way.

28. For a discussion of the options, see Cranfield, *Mark*, 302–3; C. Marshall, *Faith as a Theme*, 118–19; and Geddert, *Mark*, 223–24. The ambiguity of *tō pisteuonti* in 9:23 can be resolved without reference to the *pistis Christou* debate in Pauline studies; for an introduction to the debate, see Hays, *Faith of Jesus Christ*.

I find myself agreeing with C. Marshall's argument that the narrative's logical flow indicates that Jesus intended the second meaning, but the father's response indicates that he mistakenly understood the first.[29] Jesus strongly affirms his ability to perform the impossible through his faith in the power of God; the boy's father, however, hears this assurance as a challenge to bolster his own meager convictions. Perhaps the ambiguity is deliberate, for the resulting double entendre certainly serves to advance the dramatic story line. Jesus presents himself as the model of authentic faith, the one whose depth of trust and conviction allows him confidently to ask that the Father now make all things possible.[30] The story's irony turns on the father's misunderstanding of these words. His confession of weak, inadequate faith (9:24) demonstrates the peripheral role played by a petitioner's convictions. Actually, the father's faith is more than weak and uncertain; it is associated with the dishonorable, cynical motives of the scribes and the sensationalist sign-seeking of the unbelieving crowds. Yet, the healing miracle is granted nonetheless, not because of anyone's faith but because of God's mercy made available through the faithfulness of Jesus.

Mark's insight into the peripheral role of faith is further highlighted once the father's statement in 9:24 is clarified. He exclaims, "I do believe; help . . . my unbelief!" These words are commonly taken as a request for greater faith, that is, "overcome my unbelief by increasing my faith!"[31] On this reading, the father seeks some divine augmentation of his faltering conviction so that the desired miracle may proceed. His admission of inadequacy, however, actually establishes an important contrast between the powerful faith of the miracle worker and the impotence of the faithless seeker, a common image in ancient stories where a group of ineffectual followers become a literary foil highlighting a master's power.[32] Jesus allows this contrast to stand. He does not take issue with the father's admission, nor does he attempt to supplement what the father lacks. "Nowhere is there any indication that the father's faith ultimately rose above its ambiguity."[33] He remains meager in faith even as he witnesses his son's restoration! This man's failure to ever exercise sufficient faith is central to the story's final resolution.

---

29. C. Marshall, *Faith as a Theme*, 118–19.

30. Gundry disagrees, arguing that Jesus is not made a model of faith but is simply presented as unique in power (*Mark*, 499, 501). His argument, however, fails to convince. Why must the two lessons be mutually exclusive? Why cannot they stand together?

31. Nineham, *Mark*, 244; Schweizer, *Mark*, 188–89; Taylor, *Mark*, 399–400; and Evans, *Mark*, 52.

32. Bultmann, *History of the Synoptic Tradition*, 211; and Achtemeier, "Miracles and the Historical Jesus," 480.

33. Achtemeier, "Miracles and the Historical Jesus," 480.

In fact, the father's words are not a request for more faith but a rearticulation of his search for a miracle. In other words, the apparent request for faith is actually another request for the boy's healing: "Help me to believe *by healing my son!*"[34] The narrative's vocabulary makes this evident. The father comes initially asking that Jesus have pity and "help us," which is clearly a request for healing. His petition in 9:24 is similar: "help me." The renewed admission of his need for help reiterates his request for a miracle. He is not making an additional request ("increase my faith"); he is repeating the only request ("heal my son"). Greater faith was not a prerequisite for Jesus's response. The boy's healing was a gift of mercy from the man of perfect faith who always believes that all things are possible with God. The father's disappearance from the story—we are not told if the healing effected a change of heart—further focuses the spotlight upon Jesus and his preeminence as *the* man of faith, the conduit of God's power and mercy.

This Kind Cannot Be Driven Out by Anything except Prayer

Mark 9:28–29 relays the private conversation between Jesus and the disciples; such explanatory conversations behind closed doors are a common feature of Mark's style (Mark 4:10–12; 7:17–23; 10:10–11). In this instance, it provides Jesus an opportunity to explain prayer's role in miracle-working while also disassociating the miracle from the disciples' faith. By addressing these two subjects separately and applying the consequent lessons to two different audiences, Mark effectively demonstrates that the disciples' problem was not their lack of faith, any more than the father's problem was a lack of prayer. Jesus's faith was the only faith that mattered. The disciples' failure was their neglect of prayer. Jesus offers no evaluation of whether they prayed with weak faith or faith "the size of a mustard seed"; they simply failed to pray at all. The implication is that prayer alone, any prayer offered with any degree of faith, would have been sufficient to meet their needs.[35]

Perhaps their past success at exorcisms throughout Galilee (Mark 6:7–13, 30), something that undoubtedly began tentatively with a deep sense of prayerful dependence on God, had eventually misled the disciples to presume too much. Mistakenly assuming that the power to exorcize was now inherently theirs, the self-confident disciples applied proven methods that had worked many times before, thereby forgetting

---

34. Dowd, *Prayer*, 114 (emphasis added).
35. Whether "this kind" refers to a particular sort of demon or to exorcisms in general as opposed to other sorts of miracles is an interesting question, but its answer does not affect the conclusions of this study; see Schmid, *Mark*, 176; and Gundry, *Mark*, 501.

that they were only God's instruments with no more inherent power
than the poor boy now writhing in the dirt. The power of God, like
the creative muse, must humbly be sought afresh with each new visit
to necessity's well. It is far too easy for miracles to be misconstrued if
they are believed to be dependent upon a disciple's ability to muster
the necessary level of faith or expertise; "there is no room for human
achievement; all that [one] can do is be receptive to the action of God."[36]
This is where the disciples had failed; their obstacle was not the father's
unbelief but their own sense of self-sufficiency that led them to forget
prayer.

The seemingly natural tendency to mistakenly search for some way
of linking the efficacy of prayer with qualitative demonstrations of
individual faith has an ancient history. A textual variant to Mark 9:29
adds the words "and fasting" to the end of the sentence: "This kind can
come out only by prayer and fasting." Similar additions were also made
to the texts of Matt. 17:21; Acts 10:30; and 1 Cor. 7:5, but none of these
later glosses about fasting constitute the original readings.[37] They are
reflections of later church practice being read back into the biblical
text. Fasting quickly became an important ingredient of pious, faithful
behavior in the early Christian community; it was particularly crucial
to any attempt at performing the miraculous. Yet, its addition to Mark
9:29 indicates a serious misreading of Mark's intent and moves the interpretation in exactly the wrong direction. Lack of effort or inattention
to human agency was not the disciples' problem. What they lacked was
a willingness to confess themselves powerless in their turning to God.

Faith and Prayer in Mark 9:14–29

Before concluding this chapter with a look at Jesus's prayer in Gethsemane, a brief summary of the conclusions reached thus far might be useful. Three observations on Mark 9:14–29 are particularly significant.

First, while Jesus asks for faith among those who request miracles
and condemns as faithless those who disingenuously seek miracles
as tests, he does not demand faith as the nonnegotiable prerequisite
for his performance of miracles. A petitioner's faith is important but
not essential to God's response. Believing in Jesus's ability to actually
perform the signs of the kingdom is an important act of personal trust
and obedience that always yields significant benefits for the faithful,[38]

36. Schweizer, *Mark*, 189.

37. Taylor, *Mark*, 401; Fee, *First Epistle to the Corinthians*, 272n17; Barrett, *Acts*, 1.517–18;
and Metzger, *Textual Commentary*, 35, 85, 331, 488.

38. O'Connor, *Faith in the Synoptic Gospels*, 83–110; and Held, "Matthew as Interpreter," 279.

but God remains free to exceed the limited—or even nonexistent—expectations of those who find it difficult or impossible to believe. At times, for reasons known only to himself and God, Jesus is more than willing to be moved by even the most hesitant request born of the most marginal faith.

Second, Jesus is the paradigm of faithfulness. He is the one whose faith makes all things possible with God. Mark's depiction of Jesus, not only as the perfect believer, but as the perfect believer whose faith enables him to exercise God's miracle-working power, is a crucial feature of this study. Others note this dimension of Mark's Christology and conclude that it is unique among the Synoptic Gospels.[39] P. Achtemeier asserts, "This implication about the source of Jesus's power [his faith] found little support in the continuing theological and Christological reflections of the primitive church, as its absence in other Gospel traditions clearly shows."[40] Although evidence of such hesitation may be available from the postapostolic church, later chapters of this study will show that there is considerable evidence, at least from the evangelists Luke and John, that the image of Jesus as the ideal man of faith and prayer is an essential ingredient of Gospel Christology.[41] This observation also lays the groundwork for additional theological statements in the New Testament describing Christ's role as mediator/intercessor (Rom. 8:33–34; Heb. 7:25; 1 John 2:1–2). Whatever effectiveness our prayers enjoy with the Father, the New Testament makes it clear that their efficacy results from Christ's own faithful mediation on our behalf.

Third, Jesus makes it clear that some things may be accomplished only through prayer. Not only is the Father free to grant miracles for those who lack faith; he is also free to withhold miracles from those who lack prayer. Strictly speaking, miracles do not happen because we pray; they happen because God chooses to hear our prayers and graciously respond. Divine power is no more intrinsic to prayer than it is to faith, but just as faith demonstrates dependency upon God, so too a life devoid of prayer reveals an attitude of independence and self-sufficiency. Just as God delights in responding to human dependency, he will not force miracles on those who are convinced they have no need. The Gospels clearly teach that sometimes God will lovingly give us gifts that we never had the faith to seek, but Mark also asserts that at other times we do not have because we do not ask (cf. James 4:2).

39. Held, "Matthew as Interpreter," 190; and Achtemeier, "Miracles and the Historical Jesus," 480–81.
40. Achtemeier, "Miracles and the Historical Jesus," 481.
41. Crump, *Jesus the Intercessor*, passim.

Jesus's Prayer in Gethsemane

Mark 14 and its parallels provide the most starkly emotive scene anywhere in the New Testament. Jesus's agonized prayer in the Garden of Gethsemane groans a surprisingly candid depiction of the natural human aversion to suffering and death now erupting full force in the life of the Son of God.[42] Knowing the gruesome demise awaiting him (Mark 8:31–33 ‖ Matt. 16:21–23 ‖ Luke 9:22; Mark 9:9 ‖ Matt. 17:9; Mark 9:30–32 ‖ Matt. 17:22–23 ‖ Luke 9:43–45; Mark 10:32–34 ‖ Matt. 20:17–19 ‖ Luke 18:31–34), Jesus experiences an overwhelming internal conflict over his own willingness to follow the Father's plan any further. He kneels before a fork in the road and is well aware of his options, seriously wrestling with the possibility that death may not be necessary after all.[43] The Gospels give no indication that Jesus's torment resulted from some supernatural awareness of sin's impending burden.[44] In fact, such unwarranted speculations, however piously motivated, actually detract from the full force of the narrative. The Synoptic Gospels describe a man who is "alarmed" (Mark 14:33), "troubled" (Mark 14:33 ‖ Matt. 26:37), "distraught" (Matt. 26:37), "grieving so deeply that it feels as if he might die of the pain" (Mark 14:34 ‖ Matt. 26:38),[45] "in agony" (Luke 22:44), and producing "sweat . . . like drops of blood falling to the ground" (22:44).[46] These are the gut-wrenching emotions of a man reluctantly confronting his impending mortality.[47] At this moment, Jesus participates

42. Jesus's reaction is very much in line with the Old Testament attitude on death as a horrible aberration in God's creation; Brown, "Passion according to Mark," 118–19.

43. See also Green, *Death of Jesus*, 260.

44. For one such suggestion, see Schwartz, "Jesus in Gethsemane."

45. Brown, *Death of the Messiah*, 155–56, surveys the various suggested meanings of this phrase, finally opting for something akin to "so sorrowful that it's killing me."

46. Elsewhere, I thoroughly argue for the authenticity of Luke 22:44; see *Jesus the Intercessor*, 117–23. Neyrey ("Absence of Jesus' Emotions," 153–59; idem, *Passion according to Luke*, 52–53) argues that Luke's omission of Mark 14:33–34 with its allusions to Pss. 42–43 is an attempt to avoid negative Hellenistic connotations to the word *lypē*. The word being omitted, however, is *perilypos*, which is used in Mark 14:34 ‖ Matt. 26:38; see Green, "Jesus on the Mount of Olives," 32–33.

47. "Jesus' agony in the garden . . . was a plague and embarrassment to patristic and medieval interpreters. Few narratives in the New Testament were so inimical to received Christological assumptions"; Madigan, "Ancient and High-Medieval Interpretations," 157. Madigan offers a helpful overview of the extreme lengths to which ancient interpreters were willing to go in order to ensure that the philosophical/theological notions of divine omnipotence, omniscience, impassibility, the unity of the divine will and obedience, and the Christian ideal of *apatheia* ("passionlessness") would not be compromised by a straightforward reading of the Gethsemane story. Unfortunately, such attempts to force the biblical narrative into the confines of traditional theological categories continue today; for a contemporary example, see Blaising, "Gethsemane"; see also Baldwin, "Gethsemane." Space does not permit a detailed evaluation of such interpretations, typically arguing

in the ancient Old Testament tradition of the lament psalms, where the righteous sufferer, complaining of apparent abandonment, confronts God and pleads—cajoles, accuses, demands—that God abide by his own covenant promises. In fact, Jesus expresses his grief by drawing upon the vocabulary of Pss. 42:6, 11 and 43:5—lament psalms describing the righteous person's despondency over the painful, inexplicable withdrawal of God's presence.[48]

Perhaps the unanticipated power of Jesus's sudden doubts account for a certain degree of this emotional upheaval. Does Jesus find himself caught slightly off guard by the unexpected depth of his hesitation? Until now, the Gospels have portrayed him as the perfectly obedient servant of God, the one who will embrace his destiny no matter how horrific, never pulling back in any attempt to avoid God's plan. Yet, pulling back is precisely what Jesus now considers, at least according to the Synoptic Gospels (compare John 12:27). Were this the case, perhaps another segment of Jesus's agony is fomented by disappointment in himself. Not only must he wrestle with the human fear of torture and death, he must face these fears as a conflicted human being who is also the Son of God now seriously considering other options. That Jesus is perfectly aware of his tenuous position in Gethsemane is highlighted by Luke's distinctive emphasis on the necessity of prayer to avoid temptation (Luke 22:40, 46).[49] "The spirit is willing but the flesh is weak" describes Jesus's *own* personal struggle as well as the existential calculus confronting his disciples.[50] The Gospels never suggest that Jesus endured obediently

---

that Jesus prays to avoid premature death in the garden; compare Robson, "Meaning of Christ's Prayer," for a refreshing nineteenth-century corrective to this tendency. Blaising's admission to protecting certain theological priorities (333) and the tortured nature of his exegesis are typical features of such arguments, which offer their own immediate critique. The common urge to harmonize the Gospel accounts also robs each evangelist of his own voice, ignoring essential components of the New Testament text. The key methodological question at issue is what constitutes the proper starting point for theology? Should it be constructed on the basis of biblical exegesis or derived from certain philosophical/theological presuppositions. I do not deny that exegesis and theology must coexist in mutually corrective reciprocity, but it is in interpreting the biblical data that we discover revelation. The theological articulation of that revelation's meaning and significance must always serve the text, never dominate it.

48. See Freed, "Psalm 42/43," 65; and Derrett, "Sleeping at Gethsemane." Experiencing grief "unto death" occurs in the New Testament only here in Mark and Matthew but is often found in the Old Testament (Judg. 16:16; 1 Kings 19:4; Jon. 4:9; Sir. 51:6; see also Ps. 107:18; Isa. 38:1; 39:1; Sir. 4:28; 18:22; 34:13; 37:2; *Testament of Joseph* 3.9; 4 Macc. 14:19). Kiley also makes an interesting argument for the formative influence of the lament found in Ps. 116, one of the Hallel songs sung at Passover (cf. Mark 14:26), upon Mark's Gethsemane narrative; see "Lord, Save My Life," 655–59.

49. See the discussion in *Jesus the Intercessor*, 167–70.

50. Brown, *Death of the Messiah*, 158–62, 198–99, agrees that this language must be applied to Jesus's own experience of temptation as well as to that of the disciples. But it

because of something unique in his nature or identity.[51] His agony was no illusion intended for popular consumption. Jesus survived private temptation by applying the same strategy required of any other human being wrestling to follow God: devotion to prayer. The disciples fail in their moment of crisis and eventually deny Jesus because they slept when they should have prayed. Jesus continued to obey his Father, even to the point of death, despite his having seriously entertained other options, because he persisted in prayer.[52]

Father, All Things Are Possible for You

Jesus's Gethsemane prayer broadly follows a threefold pattern typical of Jewish deathbed prayers:[53] (1) statement of confidence ("if it is possible/all things are possible"), (2) request ("remove this hour/cup"), and (3) surrender ("not my will . . . but yours"). We will examine each segment in turn.

Jesus's initial "if it is possible" (Mark 14:35 ‖ Matt. 26:39) immediately recalls the words of the epileptic boy's father in Mark 9:22: "If it is possible, help us." Unlike that man, however, Jesus is not expressing doubt over God's power; he is asking about divinely approved alternatives. Jesus distinguishes himself by immediately affirming the conviction that "all things are possible [for God]." This particular phrasing, which appears in only Mark's version of Gethsemane (14:36), evokes the earlier portrait unique to Mark 9:23 where Jesus displays perfect faith in God's power to perform the impossible—a portrait now reaffirmed in this nocturnal glimpse of anguish and despair. Luke 22:42 further clarifies the issues at stake by rephrasing the prayer as "if you are *willing*." In other words, it is not a question of God's ability but of divine desire.[54] Ironically, by

---

would be a mistake to import the notion of "flesh" as "sinful nature" into this text. Flesh and spirit denote the whole human being considered from two different vantage points. Flesh simply designates human frailty, not sinfulness, particularly when confronted with demonic attack; see K. Kuhn, "New Light on Temptation," 95. Applying this adage to Jesus does not undermine any Christian notion of Christ's sinlessness; it merely portrays Jesus as affirming his complete humanity.

51. Kelber, "Mark 14:32–42," 178: "Mark does not seem disturbed that the near-lapse of Jesus might conflict with the divine status of the Son of God. . . . Jesus did, after all, not succumb to his 'temptation.'"

52. Kelber, ibid., 182–87, perceptively elaborates how Jesus's final embrace of his passion is contrasted with the disciples' ongoing failure to understand the necessity of the cross.

53. Daube, "Prayer Pattern in Judaism."

54. Elsewhere I investigate Luke's redactional activity in the Gethsemane material and demonstrate how it conforms to his overarching theology of divine sovereignty. "As far as Luke is concerned, it is only possible for the will of God to be fulfilled. . . . If it *were* God's will that this cup pass from Jesus, *it would do so*" (emphasis original); see *Jesus the Intercessor*, 122.

probing the flexibility of God's will in this way, Jesus effectively confirms both his absolute faith in divine power as well as the genuineness of his own desire to find some other way to achieve God's purposes. For him to say that "all things are possible for God" is as much a request as it is a statement; in other words, "Since you can do anything, save me from this moment!"[55]

The moment to be escaped is "the hour" at which Jesus must "drink this cup."[56] This hour is the moment of eschatological fulfillment (Mark 14:41 ‖ Matt. 26:45)[57] that must be accomplished by Jesus's drinking from the Father's cup of judgment and suffering (Mark 10:38–39 ‖ Matt. 20:22–23; Mark 14:23–24 ‖ Matt. 26:27–28 ‖ Luke 22:20; compare John 18:11; Rev. 14:10; 16:19; 18:6; Isa. 51:17, 22; Lam. 4:21; Ezek. 23:32–34).[58] Jesus never questions or abandons God's final objective, but he does probe for a way to accomplish salvation for God's people that does not require his death.[59]

Finally, through prayer Jesus discovers an internal confirmation of the passion's necessity, and turmoil gives way to resolve. Both Mark and Matthew highlight the protracted nature of Jesus's struggle by noting a threefold repetition of the prayer and his repeated discovery of the sleeping disciples.[60] All three Synoptics depict Jesus's final surrender at the end of this lonely wrestling match: "Not what I want, but what you want" (Mark 14:36 ‖ Matt. 26:39 ‖ Luke 22:42). As if to remove any possibility of confusion, Matthew reworks Jesus's first prayer, recorded in 26:39, and offers a second, slightly revised version in 26:42: "My Father,

55. Evans, *Mark*, 413.

56. Holleran demonstrates how "cup" and "hour" refer to the same events; *Synoptic Gethsemane*, 27–28.

57. This theme of the eschatological hour (or "the right time") is most thoroughly developed by John's Gospel (2:4; 4:21, 23; 5:25, 28; 7:6, 30; 8:20; 12:23, 27, 31; 13:1; 16:32; 17:1).

58. Cranfield, "Cup Metaphor," 137–38, demonstrates that the cup refers, not simply to suffering, but to suffering as the result of God's wrath against sin. M. Black, "Cup Metaphor," 195, takes issue with this, contending on rabbinic backgrounds that the metaphor merely refers to suffering. The entire Gethsemane narrative is, however, so highly attuned to the Old Testament that Cranfield is certainly correct.

59. "Mark is not directly saying that Jesus attempted to completely drop out of his royal ministry and to abandon his messianic role altogether. He is . . . begging for a reprieve from the death warrant which in his own testimony had been imposed upon him"; Kelber, "Mark 14:32–42," 177. Jesus must now align his will and emotions with his previous instruction, knowing that to remove suffering from messiahship is to become unfaithful. The Old Testament regularly portrayed human prayer as influencing, even altering, God's purposes; see Brown's discussion of Moses (Exod. 32:10–14), Hezekiah (2 Kings 20:1–6), David (2 Sam. 15:25–26), and Judas Maccabeus (1 Macc. 3:58–60) in *Death of the Messiah*, 166–67.

60. Attempts to discover some evolutionary development in Jesus's attitude within the three moments of prayer are invariably forced; see Kelber, "Mark 14:32–42," 178–79.

if this cannot pass unless I drink it, may your will be done" (my translation). The second half of this petition ("may your will be done") is taken
literally from the third petition of the Lord's Prayer (6:10).[61] In this way,
Matthew presents Jesus as the perfect exemplar of all that he has taught
regarding both faith and prayer. He asks no one to do what he has not
first done himself.[62] Jesus finally surrenders unreservedly to the will of
God, even after learning that this requires his torture and death.[63] He demonstrates that prayer, even petitionary prayer, is not only about offering
requests to God, but more important, it is about hearing God's response
and allowing him to realign our wills according to his design.

Everything Is Possible for the One Who Believes—or Is It?

Jesus survives his time of testing and finally emerges from this long,
dark tunnel just as he entered—the perfectly obedient servant who places
absolute trust in God and is certain of the Father's ability to do all things
for those who pray. He continues to meet each of the criteria for miraculous responses to prayer set forward in Mark 9 and Mark 11. First, Jesus
believes in God's ability to perform the impossible. Second, he boldly asks
God to act on his behalf. Certainly, this is enough to guarantee Jesus the
positive response predicted in 11:24: "Whatever you ask for in prayer,
believe that you have received it, and it will be yours"! But, apparently,
this is not the case, for Jesus has introduced a crucial new ingredient to
his recipe for genuine, effective prayer: *the will of God*.

Sometimes prayer results in stretching the faith of those who pray
as they risk asking for a miracle that only God can perform. At other
times, prayer elicits heavenly gifts that would not otherwise be granted.
But overseeing all of these circumstances is the notion that God always

61. Senior, *Passion Narrative*, 112; idem, *Passion of Jesus*, 81–82; Green, *Death of
Jesus*, 260; and Brown, *Death of the Messiah*, 176–77.

62. Some might object that the interpretation offered here sacrifices too many ingredients essential to the orthodox confession of Christ's divinity. I show throughout that
this need not be the case. Furthermore, I argue that my interpretation retrieves essential
features of Christ's full humanity that traditional orthodox interpretation often sacrifices
to its own detriment. The Jesus who weeps in Gethsemane is more than able to experience
profound empathy with anyone wrestling with pain and doubt.

63. Rabbinic scholar J. Heinemann argues that Jesus's disposition of complete surrender to God's will is a "fundamental novelty," unlike anything found in ancient Judaism;
see *Prayer in the Talmud*, 186–87; idem, "Background of Jesus' Prayer," 86–87. He goes on
to argue that Jesus's attitude "constitutes a serious blow to the value of prayer . . . [and]
reduces the very possibility of prayer to absurdity." In making this argument, however,
Heinemann assumes that abject surrender is all that is ever involved in Christian prayer,
overlooking the other components discovered thus far in our study, such as the invitation
to pray for miracles, the possibility that our prayers can influence God, and the warning
that some gifts are granted only after we pray for them.

remains free to say no to any request that conflicts with his plan. Apparently, according to Jesus, prayer can and does influence God—but only within certain boundaries. All things are possible, but all things are not permissible. Nothing is beyond God's ability, but some things are outside God's purposes. The decisive question for each and every person who prays becomes, do I place (at least) as much (if not more) faith in the goodness of God's intentions as I do in God's ability to move mountains? Will I be equally happy to receive either response? Answering yes to this question is to possess the sort of faith that truly makes *all* things possible. Indeed, effective petition ventures into the tenuous realm of flickering, halfhearted faith as we risk a serious engagement with God's invitation to ask for miracles, but such petition must also risk abandoning its own requests once it becomes evident that heaven's gates are shut tight against them (the possibility of persuading God through persistence is addressed in chapters 3–4). "The appropriate prayer . . . can only be determined in the process of praying."[64] We learn to pray by praying.

Jesus's struggle in Gethsemane is uncomfortably paradigmatic. He demonstrates that prayer may involve deep feelings of abandonment, even as God remains extraordinarily close. His agony illustrates how prayer is as much a means of divine correction as it is an avenue for human request. His conversation with the Father becomes the environment for his instruction, not because he is incarnate but because he is a human being like any other who seeks to discern the mysterious ways of God. As the writer to the Hebrews says, "During the days of Jesus' life on earth, he offered up prayers and petitions with loud cries and tears to the one who could save him from death, and he was heard because of his reverent submission. . . . He learned obedience from what he suffered" (5:7–8) (see chapter 13). The uncomfortably stark power of this particular dramatic moment is preserved in the Gospel writers' insistence that human suffering is part and parcel of God's plan: "The scene is terrible, not because Jesus must suffer, but because his suffering is the will of the God who is powerful enough to prevent it. . . . The God who wills to move the mountain does not always will to take away the cup. Those who belong to Jesus' true family do the will of God, whether it involves miracles or suffering."[65]

64. Tupper, "Providence of God," 588.
65. Dowd, *Prayer*, 158.

3

Persistent Prayer

The Parable of the Friend at Midnight

Over the years I have collected an array of books that explore the histories of various awakenings, revivals, missionary ventures, and social-reform movements that have arisen in the English-speaking world, describing such phenomena as the first and second Great Awakenings, the Welsh and Cambuslang revivals, the abolitionist movement, and the creation of America's first institutions of higher learning, to name just a few. I have always derived great personal benefit from reading biographies of the men and women who rose to leadership in these groundswells of social and cultural transformation, the preachers, evangelists, circuit riders, social reformers, educators, and missionaries who pursued a divinely inspired vision of the future. One feature that virtually every spiritual biography and history of revival share in common is the crucial role played by petitionary prayer. People asked God for miracles and trusted him to answer, believing that God alone could accomplish the many insuperable tasks standing between their dreams and reality. Nineteenth-century preacher and social reformer George Müller is one such inspirational figure. Müller became a household name in his own lifetime, not only because of the numerous orphanages he founded throughout England, but for the widely circulated accounts of his remarkable prayer life. He supported his orphanages entirely through prayer. Müller never advertised or campaigned for funds but insisted on divulging his needs only to God. He would pray specifically and persistently until his orphans' material needs were satisfied, often quite miraculously.[1]

Such living paradigms can have a profound influence in shaping popular ideologies. The notion that effective prayer is synonymous with persistent prayer became deeply entrenched within certain strains of English and American devotional literature, drawing inspiration from figures such as Müller. The distinctive emphasis in this "piety of persistence" was not simply that faithfulness required continual prayer in all circumstances. Continual prayer itself was not the main lesson to be learned. Rather, the central lesson involved the discovery that genuine persistence consists in asking repeatedly for the same thing over and over again until it is eventually granted, regardless of the time elapsed or the circumstances involved. The implied distinction between persistence as continual prayer and persistence as repetitious prayer is pivotal to a great deal of popular theology, and almost without exception biblical evidence for the necessity of repetition is found in the parables traditionally called the parables of the persistent friend (Luke 11:5–8) and the persistent widow (18:1–8).[2]

Furthermore, the true efficacy of repetition is commonly linked to the emotional urgency undergirding such prayer. The deeper the passion, the more powerful the prayer. Repetition alone is not sufficient; repetition bathed in emotional fervor, however, can make prayer an unstoppable force. Such writers describe prayer in terms of wrestling with God, finding the urgency to prevail, winning the victory, and learning to "pray through." Those who pray like this are known as "prayer warriors," whose tears produce spiritual victory.[3] "A requisite for effective prayer is intensity of thought and emotion. We must pray with overwhelming

1. See R. Steer, *George Müller: Delighted in God* (Wheaton, IL: Shaw, 1981). To illustrate the continuing influence of Müller's life story, see W. L. Duewel, *Mighty Prevailing Prayer* (Grand Rapids: Francis Asbury, 1990), who quotes Müller, without citation, as a paradigm for persistent prayer: "It is not enough to begin to pray, nor to pray aright; nor is it enough to continue to pray for a time; but we must patiently, believingly, continually pray until we obtain an answer" (81).

2. For only a few examples, see C. G. Finney, *How to Experience Revival* (ed. E. E. Shelhamer; Springdale, PA: Whitaker, 1984), 55; S. D. Gordon, *Quiet Talks on Prayer* (New York: Revell, n.d.), 116; E. M. Bounds, *The Necessity of Prayer* (1929) (repr. in *The Complete Works of E. M. Bounds on Prayer* [Grand Rapids: Baker, 1990]), 39; B. Monroe, "Unlocking the Power of Prayer," *Fundamentalist Journal* 2, no. 10 (1983): 28–30, 39; D. Holman, *Conquest through Prayer* (Hazelwood, MO: Word Aflame, 1988), 87–88.

3. Holman, *Conquest through Prayer*, 27; H. Lockyer, *How I Can Make Prayer More Effective* (Grand Rapids: Zondervan, 1960), 38.

desire."[4] "No prayer is more godlike than agonizing prayer. . . . You are never more Christlike than when you are prevailing in prayer wrestling and prayer agony. . . . God's cause will suffer unless you fulfill your role in this holy partnership. How willing are you to learn to prevail?"[5]

Various theological explanations are typically offered to explain the need for such emotional, repetitious prayer. Sometimes the time elapsed in repetition is said to allow for a process of spiritual maturation: "Perseverance can often have the effect of clarifying and segregating in our minds deep-seated desire from fleeting whim."[6] Repetition catalyzes a purification process within the person praying. Some concerns diminish while others intensify as we repeat our requests time and again, such that our passion becomes more focused. Other writers insist that persistence is a strategy of spiritual warfare; the prayer warrior attacks satanic forces with a holy onslaught of continuous petition until eventually prevailing over the forces of darkness, clearing a pathway for God's unfolding purposes.[7] Occasionally, the emphasis on prevailing over evil is combined with God's own desire to stretch the believer's faith. We have already seen how easily popularized treatments of prayer link its effectiveness to the quality of the petitioner's faith. Insisting on the long-term repetition of a request becomes another way for God to strengthen feeble faith until it becomes a faith large enough to move mountains. As S. D. Gordon says, "The faith that believes that God *will* do what you ask is not born in a hurry."[8]

A final factor shaping this theology of repetition was the intellectual environment of burgeoning modernism surrounding the nineteenth-century birth of this new genre of devotional literature. Many writers reflect a mechanistic worldview in which "spiritual principles" are part and parcel of the numerous laws of nature dictated by the Creator. The law of repetitious persistence is merely one of the many divine laws operative in the created order, regulating the spiritual world as well as the

4. C. H. Richmond, "Your Prayer Can Shake the World," in *Prayer: Its Deeper Dimensions*, by Alan Redpath et al. (Grand Rapids: Zondervan, 1963), 53.

5. Duewel, *Mighty Prevailing Prayer*, 223, 226, 228; for further examples, see R. A. Torrey, *The Power of Prayer and the Prayer of Power* (New York: Revell, 1924); D. M. Dawson, *More Power in Prayer: How to Pray Effectively* (Grand Rapids: Zondervan, 1942); Bloesch, *Struggle of Prayer*, 72: "Prayer is not simply petition, but strenuous petition."

6. C. C. Mitchell, "The Case for Persistence in Prayer," *Journal of the Evangelical Theological Society* 27 (1984): 168; idem, "Why Keep Bothering God? The Case for Persisting in Prayer," *Christianity Today* 29.18 (1985): 33–34.

7. Gordon, *Quiet Talks on Prayer*, 116–24; Dawson, *More Power in Prayer*, 120–21; R. Humbard, *Praying with Power* (Grand Rapids: New Hope, 1975), 15–16, 74; Duewel, *Mighty Prevailing Prayer*, 18, 58–66.

8. Gordon, *Quiet Talks on Prayer*, 157–58 (emphasis original); also Duewel, *Mighty Prevailing Prayer*, 60–63.

physical. "Prayer works on God's laws just as sure as the law of gravity."[9] For whatever reason, God made repetitious prayer one of those laws that regulate prayer's effectiveness. Although few writers go so far as to say that repetition is required to get God's attention, many come very close. For example, E. M. Bounds, one of evangelicalism's most honored and prolific devotional writers, says: "We must not only pray, but we must also pray with great urgency, with intentness and with repetition. We must press our prayers upon God."[10]

Others compare the process to that of a child asking his or her father for a certain something "again, again, and again" until finally the father relents.[11] Elijah's prayer for rain is a favorite example (1 Kings 18:42–46); he asked repeatedly that God would end the drought punishing the apostate land of Israel. After the seventh request, the rains came. "What if he had only prayed six times?"[12] Had he stopped, the rains could not have come. No one makes this type of argument more fervently than nineteenth-century revivalist Charles Finney, who laments over the untold "millions in hell" because lackadaisical Christians failed to pray for their souls with sufficient urgency and repetition.[13] It is as if our prayer requests hang in a cosmic balance, each prayer adding another pebble to the positive side of God's equation. Only when enough requests, offered with sufficient passion, tilt the scale toward heaven's preferred option is salvation able to take its next step forward. Thus stopping even one prayer short may send a potential saint to perdition or stymie one component or another of God's plan. I cannot help but wonder if it is not appropriate to ask this brand of theology exactly how many prayers and tears are generally required to move God?

Certainly, Finney and his ecclesiastical descendants represent the extreme end of this particular theological spectrum, but most extremes find a taproot somewhere in the commonplace. The belief that repetition—not simply the continual disposition of prayerfulness, but the specific repetition of certain requests over and over again—somehow empowers petitionary prayer is widespread in many sectors of the modern church, but is this, or any of the other explanations outlined above, the obvious lesson to be learned from Jesus's parables in Luke 11 and Luke 18? Whether there is any practical, spiritual value in these suggestions will be discussed later in our study; we must first determine whether

9. Humbard, *Praying with Power*, 76; also Duewel, *Mighty Prevailing Prayer*, 19.

10. Bounds, *Purpose in Prayer* (1920), reprinted in *Complete Works*, 321.

11. Holman, *Conquest through Prayer*, 146.

12. Ibid., 146. Actually, a careful reading of the text indicates that seven is the number of times the servant runs to see if the anticipated storm clouds are yet visible. There is no self-evident lesson on repetition.

13. Finney, *How to Experience Revival*, 57.

these lessons are self-evident in the biblical text. To answer that question, this chapter will explore the promises offered in the parable of the friend at midnight (11:5–8), together with the attached sayings on prayer that follow (11:9–13). Chapter 4 will then examine Luke's parable of the persistent widow (18:1–8).

The Midnight Visitor

Luke's parable (11:5–8) is unique to his Gospel, whereas the following instructions on petition (11:9–13) are shared with the Gospel of Matthew (7:7–11). Both writers apparently found the lessons on asking/seeking/knocking (Matt. 7:7–8 ‖ Luke 11:9–10) and the generous father (Matt. 7:9–11 ‖ Luke 11:11–13) already associated with the Lord's Prayer in their tradition (Matt. 6:9–13 ‖ Luke 11:1–4), which makes it clear that the asking under discussion is petitionary prayer.[14] Luke's additional parable about a friend's late-night request for help fits this theme quite nicely, augmenting his generally recognized interest in prayer:

Matthew	Luke
	Then he said to them, "Suppose one of you has a friend, and he goes to him at midnight and says, 'Friend, lend me three loaves of bread, because a friend of mine on a journey has come to me, and I have nothing to set before him.' Then the one inside answers, 'Don't bother me. The door is already locked, and my children are with me in bed. I can't get up and give you anything.' I tell you, though he will not get up and give him the bread because he is his friend, yet because of the man's *anaideia* he will get up and give him as much as he needs." (11:5–8)
Ask and it will be given to you; seek and you will find; knock and the door will be opened to you. For everyone who asks receives; he who seeks finds; and to him who knocks, the door will be opened. (7:7–8)	So I say to you: Ask and it will be given to you; seek and you will find; knock and the door will be opened to you. For everyone who asks receives; he who seeks finds; and to him who knocks, the door will be opened. (11:9–10)

14. Although this connection is less obvious in Matthew than in Luke, it is convincingly demonstrated by Guelich, *Sermon on the Mount*, 356–60, 377–79.

Matthew	Luke
Which of you, if his son asks for bread, will give him a stone? Or if he asks for a fish, will give him a snake? If you, then, though you are evil, know how to give good gifts to your children, how much more will your Father in heaven give good gifts to those who ask him! (7:9–11)	Which of you fathers, if your son asks for a fish, will give him a snake instead? Or if he asks for an egg, will give him a scorpion? If you then, though you are evil, know how to give good gifts to your children, how much more will your Father in heaven give the Holy Spirit to those who ask him! (11:11–13)

Luke intends that the householder represent God, and the friend coming to ask for help stands for anyone coming to God in prayer. Nearly every commentator can agree on at least this much.[15] That is, however, as far as the agreement goes. Further interpretation turns on two elements that continue to be hotly contested: the correct meaning of the Greek word *anaideia* (traditionally translated "persistence" in 11:8) and the identity of the one to whom *anaideia* applies—is it a characteristic of the sleeping householder or the inquiring friend?

At various points in the story, it is unclear who is designated by the masculine pronoun. The parable contains three characters: the sleeping householder, the neighbor who asks for bread, and the traveler whose unexpected visit precipitates the request. In most instances, it is not difficult to identify the person being referred to, but at the point most decisive for interpretation, the meaning is completely ambiguous.[16] The story's logic may be charted this way:

11:5	go to him	householder
	say to him	householder
11:6	set before him	traveler
11:7	he will answer	householder
11:8	he will not get up	householder
	to give him anything	petitioner
	because he is	?
	his friend	?
	because of his anaideia	?

15. Although some, such as Waetjen, "Subversion of 'World,'" argue for a very different pre-Lukan context that had nothing whatsoever to do with prayer; he sees the lesson as challenging social norms. Our concern, however, is with Luke's purposes.

16. Although many fail to comment on this, I. Marshall, *Luke*, 465, explains the problem clearly: "The two διά phrases [in 11:8] are ambiguous. Does the first mean 'because the man in the house is a friend (active) of the man at the door' or 'because the man at the door is a friend (passive) of the man in the house'?"

he will give	householder
whatever he needs	petitioner

Because "the friend" being approached in 11:5 is the sleeping house-holder, the audience is being asked to identify with the petitioner looking for bread.[17] This does not, however, solve the problem of identifying the friend in 11:8. Since friendship is mutual, either party, the householder or the petitioner, could conceivably be designated by the phrase "he is his friend," leaving the quality of *anaideia* unattached and waiting for a home. Although many writers tackle this problem, more than one convinced that the matter was settled once and for all, the ongoing debate demonstrates that the question is hardly answered to everyone's satisfaction.[18] My own conclusion is that deciding who Jesus describes as possessing *anaideia* can be settled only after the word has been properly defined; with that information in hand, the reader may then decide to whom the quality most properly belongs. So, what is the meaning of *anaideia*?

Persistence or Shamelessness?

Words do not have meanings as much as they have uses. Words mean what we use them to mean. Definitions are simply a matter of convention; meaning changes over time because conventions are determined by evolving popular usage. For example, when a seventeenth-century noblewoman entered a ballroom, she would have been pleased to hear that suitors held their breath and described her appearance as "awful," for they meant that she was awe-inspiring, beautiful, and majestic. I do not, however, recommend that anyone offer this particular compliment today, unless one is ready to duck.

Reading an ancient book such as the Bible, a book originally composed in another language, is complicated even further because someone else, a translator, has already decided for us what the words mean.

---

17. The antecedent of the verb "to go" is "you," not "friend." Thus the "friend" referred to in 11:5 is the man sleeping. The listeners are to understand themselves as the surprised host seeking help from a sleeping neighbor. An awkward shift in subject from second person ("you") to third person ("he") in the Greek complicates the translation; see K. Bailey, *Poet and Peasant*, 124–25; and Fitzmyer, *Luke*, 911.

18. *Anaideia* is a quality of the sleeping householder according to Fridrichsen, "Exegetisches zum Neuen Testament"; Jeremias, *Parables of Jesus*, 158; K. Bailey, *Poet and Peasant*, 128; I. Marshall, *Luke*, 465 (after allowing for either possibility); Scott, *Hear Then the Parable*, 89–90; Nolland, *Luke*, 622–26; and Green, *Luke*, 445–50. *Anaideia* is a quality of the petitioner according to Fitzmyer, *Luke*, 912; L. Johnson, *Luke*, 178; Herzog, *Parables as Subversive Speech*, 196 (if I understand Herzog correctly; he appears to change his position inexplicably in 212–14); and Young, *Parables*, 45–48.

Every translation involves a certain component of interpretation as the translator chooses from among a variety of possible definitions. Most of the time, the process is fairly straightforward. Occasionally, however, it requires a judgment call. For example, the Greek word *anōthen*, used in John 3:3, can be translated either "again" or "from above." This raises a question for the translator: Does Jesus tell Nicodemus that he must be "born again" or that he must be "born from above"? Different translators make different decisions.

Very rarely, a translator will encounter a word that appears only once in the entire Bible, in which case there are no other instances or contexts for comparison.[19] Discovering how this word was used requires reading other ancient literature, determining how the word is used in these nonbiblical texts, and then making a decision about whether the biblical writer intended to use the word in the same way. That final decision is an interpretive judgment that could possibly be influenced by how the translator has already learned to read that particular story. None of us are entirely free of such preconceptions. The translator's challenge is to prevent these unavoidable presuppositions from tainting the evidence gathered while studying a word's usage outside the Bible. The historical interpretation of the Greek word *anaideia* in Luke 11:8 is an excellent example of how difficult this process can be.

One point that can be stated categorically is that the traditional translation of *anaideia* as "persistence" is incorrect and should be consigned once and for all to a short paragraph among the historical oddities of biblical (mis)interpretation. Lexical analysis of *anaideia* in ancient literature proves conclusively that it was never used to denote persistence until Christian writers appropriated the word for themselves under the obvious influence of Luke 11:8. When Luke wrote his Gospel, the word had a decidedly negative sense, referring "to people who have no proper sense of shame and willingly engage in improper conduct,"[20] freely disregarding all commonly accepted social norms. Words such as

19. Such a word is called a *hapax legomenon*, meaning that it is used only once in the New Testament.

20. Snodgrass, "*Anaideia* and the Friend," 506. See also Levinson, "Importunity?"; Derrett, "Friend at Midnight"; Jeremias, *Parables of Jesus*, 158–59; K. Bailey, *Poet and Peasant*, 119–33; Rickards, "Translation of Luke 11.5–13"; A. Johnson, "Assurance for Man"; Catchpole, "Q and 'The Friend at Midnight'" (but see 413, where "persistence" reappears by way of Luke's redaction); Scott, *Hear Then the Parable*, 88–90; Herzog, *Parables as Subversive Speech*, 202; Green, *Luke*, 445–50; and Waetjen, "Subversion of 'World.'" One possible exception is the Septuagint version of Jer. 8:5, which may be translated "perpetual apostasy." The phrase *apostrophēn anaidē*, however, could just as easily read "shameless apostasy"; see K. Bailey, *Poet and Peasant*, 126; and Snodgrass, "*Anaideia* and the Friend," 511.

shamelessness, impudence, and immodesty are typical synonyms.[21] Yet, this created obvious difficulties for early Christian interpreters. If this disparaging sense of the word was applied to the sleeping householder, God was turned into a shameless character reluctant to hear his people's prayers. On the other hand, what could possibly be shameless about a neighbor asking for help in the middle of the night, or believers bringing their requests to God? The Old and New Testaments alike regularly encourage God's people to confidently offer petition to their heavenly Father. The negative space left by this interpretive impasse was eventually filled by the apparent implication of persistence found in the following verses (11:9–10; "ask, seek, knock"), despite the parable itself suggesting nothing about asking persistently.[22] The midnight visitor does not knock but "calls out," as would any fellow villager, and the householder does not delay but rises.[23] Regardless of the sleeping man's motivation or disposition, there is no need for his breadless friend to repeat his request. Nevertheless, the contextual associations between 11:5–8 and 11:9–10 eventually won out over the seemingly inappropriate sense of shamelessness. The possible implications of 11:9–10 became the established meaning of 11:5–8 (ask repeatedly). Thus the parable of a midnight visitor was transformed into the parable of the persistent friend.

In 1934 German scholar Anton Fridrichsen confronted the need to reinterpret the parable in light of proper linguistic evidence. Since *anaideia* cannot mean persistence, who is described as shameless and why? His solution, though also seriously flawed, was a significant step forward in the history of interpretation and gained a sizable following over the years; it is found in many modern commentaries.[24]

Fridrichsen began by deciding that *anaideia* must be a quality of the sleeping householder, which meant that he also must explain how God is shameless in answering prayer. Seeking to avoid the troublesome theological implications of this reading, he transformed the negative

21. Snodgrass, "*Anaideia* and the Friend," 507, offers a long list of words in whose company *anaideia* typically appears: rashness, insolence, recklessness, injustice, disorderliness, licentiousness, coarse behavior, wantonness, cowardice, lies, pollution, negligence, crudeness, derangement, wickedness, unchastity, effrontery, ignorance, obscene conduct, harshness, treason, lawlessness, self-willed, and wastefulness.

22. This "creeping persistence" can be seen in the Latin versions, where *improbitatem* ("wickedness, impudence") is eventually replaced by *importunitatem* ("importunity, persistence"); see K. Bailey, *Poet and Peasant*, 127nn43–44; and A. Johnson, "Assurance for Man," 127.

23. In this ancient village setting a stranger would knock, while a friend would shout; K. Bailey, *Poet and Peasant*, 128; and Young, *Parables*, 45–46.

24. Fridrichsen, "Exegetisches zum Neuen Testament"; see Jeremias, *Parables of Jesus*, 158; I. Marshall, *Luke*, 465; A. Johnson, "Assurance for Man," 130–31; Scott, *Hear Then the Parable*, 91; Nolland, *Luke*, 623, 626; and Green, *Luke*, 445.

quality of shamelessness into a positive quality of "seeking to avoid shame." Fridrichsen justified this rereading by reconstructing the ancient Middle Eastern expectations regarding communal hospitality.[25] The late-night traveler was a guest not only of his particular friend but of the entire community; if the host were unable to feed his guest properly, the entire village would have been humiliated. The shame of the surprised host, now desperately combing the neighborhood for bread, would have been shared by the stingy householder, ruining his reputation as well. Word would inevitably spread throughout the community and the surrounding countryside; the sleeping neighbor had been too lazy to rise and help to preserve the honor of the village. In order to avoid such shame, the householder responds, preserving both his honor and that of his neighbor. Even though the lateness of the hour overwhelms his natural sense of neighborly goodwill, he, nevertheless, can be trusted to do what is right, to meet his responsibilities as a dependable member of the community. In other words, according to Fridrichsen, the parable assures us that the person who prays can always count on God to listen faithfully and to preserve the divine honor by responding appropriately to our requests.

Although no one contests this reconstruction of the parable's ancient cultural context, Fridrichsen's interpretation depends on a crucial shift in the meaning of *anaideia*, which is highly suspect. *Anaideia* is transposed from a negative quality (lacking a proper sense of shame) into a positive characteristic (a desire to avoid shame). Although K. E. Bailey offers a noteworthy attempt to justify this redefinition, his argument ultimately fails.[26] There is no reason to (re)interpret *anaideia* as the admirable quality of behaving in such a way as to avoid shame. This

25. Followed by Jeremias, *Parables of Jesus*, 158–59, and expanded in detail by K. Bailey, *Poet and Peasant*, 121–24. For a thorough discussion of the literature covering this sociocultural background, see Herzog, *Parables as Subversive Speech*, 199–203.

26. K. Bailey, *Poet and Peasant*, 130–32. *Anaideia* is formed from *aidōs* plus the *alpha* privative. *Aidōs* can mean either a sense of shame (a positive attribute) or bearing shame (a negative attribute). *Anaideia* properly negates the first definition, yielding the sense "being without a proper sense of shame." When the translator of the Aramaic tradition (which had no comparable word to cover both "sense of shame" and "bearing shame") rendered the original saying into Greek, however, he mistook *anaideia* to be the negation of the second sense of *aidōs*. This second definition plus the *alpha* privative yields the meaning of "the avoidance of shame." There are, however, several problems with Bailey's argument. Aside from its highly speculative nature, arguments based on etymology are always tenuous; meaning is determined by usage, and in this instance the consistent usage is overwhelmingly negative. Most important, Bailey's argument finally makes *anaideia* synonymous with the first definition of *aidōs*. Seeking to avoid shame (*anaideia*) is the same thing as possessing a proper sense of shame (the first definition of *aidōs*). Why did not the translator simply use *aidōs* and allow the context to dictate which sense was most appropriate?

suggestion is as lexically inappropriate as was the old language of persistence. *Anaideia* cannot mean "a desire to avoid shame" any more than it meant "persistence." We are forced to read the story as an account of someone—whether householder or petitioner—who behaves shamelessly. But since it is strange to consider God shameless in answering prayer, it seems necessary to attribute shamelessness to the breadless host. What would this entail?

Shameless Prayer

Although the context requires that *anaideia* be applied to the petitioner rather than to the sleeping householder, it is often objected that, given the social expectations of the time, no ancient villager would have been judged shameless in asking a neighbor for help, regardless of the hour. Thus shamelessness cannot describe the petitioner any more than the householder. Is it really so unthinkable, however, that the midnight caller could be considered shameless by the disturbed householder? Two additional features of the parable have a bearing on how we answer this question.

First, it is generally admitted that the introductory formula "which of you" in 11:5 begins a rhetorical question that expects a negative response: "No one, of course!"[27] The rhetorical question encompasses the whole of 11:5–7.[28] Consequently, the characters' outrageous behaviors (the householder refusing assistance, the petitioner's shamelessness) are not seriously offered as realistic possibilities, but as the dramatic components of an outrageous story.[29] Jesus asks this question with his tongue firmly planted in his cheek.

Second, the story is not intended as a comparison but as a contrast. It offers an a fortiori argument (from the lesser to the greater), or what the ancient rabbis called *qal wahomer* (light and heavy). This is a common storytelling technique. The sleeping householder is not like God; he is precisely unlike God. If the householder fails to respond out of friendship alone (Outrageous! Impossible!), how much more may God be counted on to respond promptly out of unfailing love and devotion. The technique is explicitly repeated in Luke 11:13 (‖ Matt. 7:11): "If you

27. Fitzmyer, *Luke*, 911; Nolland, *Luke*, 624; Scott, *Hear Then the Parable*, 87; and Young, *Parables*, 45.

28. I. Marshall, *Luke*, 464.

29. For example, Waetjen's entire argument hinges on determining why the householder is not moved by friendship alone and why the petitioner is judged to be shameless. Such questions misunderstand the rhetorical nature of Jesus's question; see "Subversion of 'World,'" 708–16.

who are evil know how to give good gifts to your children, *how much more* can your heavenly Father be counted on!" That is a fortiori logic. Similarly, Jesus's parable implicitly asks, "If this householder responds only out of a begrudging sense of duty, how much more can your heavenly Father be counted on to respond freely!"

We are now in a position to understand the place of shamelessness in Luke's story. Actually, it was entirely possible for ancient neighbors to be considered shameless in asking for assistance if they asked inappropriately or at an inopportune moment. Regardless of the ancient social mores concerning village honor and hospitality, these men and women were still human beings with typical human emotional responses to trying situations. B. Young cites a humorous rabbinic story about proper methods of borrowing that sheds considerable light on Jesus's parable:

> Rabbi Acha said: One woman is clever at borrowing, and another woman is not clever at borrowing. The woman who is clever at borrowing goes to her neighbor, and though the door is open, she knocks at it, and says, "Peace be to you. How are you? How is your husband? How are your children? Is it convenient for me to come in?" The neighbor says: "Come in, what do you require?" The visitor says, "Have you such and such a utensil that you can give me?" The neighbor answers: "Yes." The woman not clever at borrowing goes to a neighbor, and though the door is closed, she opens it, and says to her, "Have you such and such a utensil?" The neighbor answers, "No."[30]

Social norms are always pliable, no matter how deeply entrenched. It is perfectly possible that the householder, rudely awoken from a sound sleep in the middle of the night, together with his wife, children, and assorted livestock, would be less than enthusiastic in answering his neighbor's call. Yet, because of his friend's impudence, his shameless, immodest willingness to raise a ruckus in the middle of the night regardless of what others might think, the householder will give his unruly friend whatever he needs.

The parable has nothing to say about persistence or the power of asking repeatedly. The shameless neighbor asks but once. His request is heard and answered, albeit grudgingly. By remembering that we are dealing with an a fortiori argument, we can deduce Jesus's lesson: if this sleeping neighbor responds to his friend's shamelessness, how much more may we depend on God not only to hear our prayers promptly and to respond freely, *but to never consider our coming shameless*! There is no such thing

---

30. *Leviticus Rabbah* 5.8 (a midrashic commentary on the book of Leviticus); see Young, *Parables*, 46.

as an inopportune moment with God, nor an inappropriate manner of approach. "God . . . is not offended or dishonored by conduct that honor/shame culture considered hateful. There is a 'good shamelessness.'"[31] We are extended an open invitation to enter God's presence, bringing our needs at any time of the day or night, regardless of our disposition or manner of request, knowing that our Father always hears us the very first time. Herein lies the twofold lesson of Luke's parable of the midnight visitor: (1) God is always graciously disposed to hear every request; and (2) we are free to approach at any time without hesitation.

Ask, Seek, Knock

The larger context of Luke 11:5–13 is now established. Rather than allowing misplaced inferences from 11:9–13 to color our reading of Luke's parable, we can allow a proper understanding of the parable to set the stage for interpreting what it means to ask, seek, and knock. Many try to bolster the traditional persistence argument by pointing out that the main verbs in Luke 11:9 (Matt. 7:7) may be read as the continuous present tense: "keep on asking, keep on seeking, keep on knocking." Although this is technically possible, it is not necessarily the obvious way to translate the sentence. In fact, the context of invitation and assurance now evident in the preceding parable indicates that Luke 11:9–10 naturally continues the same theme. Greater emphasis should fall on the future tenses in the next verse—"it will be given, you will find, it will be opened"—that now provide every prayer, even those offered only once, with a solid guarantee. God always hears; he always responds. Your needs *will* be met. Your search *will* lead to solutions. In other words, never hesitate to bring your requests to God. Whatever the question, ask it! Whatever the need, present it!

Naturally, this interpretation raises several questions of its own. In previous chapters we discovered that, contrary to much popular opinion, Jesus never describes faith as a means to guarantee that we will always get exactly what we request in prayer. We are invited to have faith enough to look for miracles, but the overarching consideration is always God's plan, as Jesus's own prayers in the Garden of Gethsemane dramatically demonstrate. Ask in faith, but then trust in God's wisdom and goodness to do what is best. How do these earlier observations from chapters 1–2 fit with the apparent lessons now emerging from Luke 11:9–10 (and

---

31. Waetjen's vital observation is, unfortunately, blunted by his relocation of its significance to a hypothetical reconstruction of the pre-Lukan tradition; "Subversion of 'World,'" 717.

Matt. 7:7–8)? Is there a contradiction here? Once again, I realize that I am arguing against a long-standing interpretive tradition. Numerous writers insist this passage demonstrates that if we will only ask fervently enough, with sufficiently emphatic passion, we will eventually receive whatever we request. Our problem is not simply the absence of repetition, but an absence of passion, a neglect of fervor—we simply need "to keep on asking!"

Frankly, I believe that this particular misunderstanding of prayer is even more damaging than the misplaced emphasis on receiving what we want through persistence. Neither faith, persistence, nor passion can guarantee us anything. The solution to the possible contradiction alluded to previously becomes readily apparent by reading the next block of teaching in Luke 11:11–13 (|| Matt. 7:9–11). In fact, I suspect that heading off this potential error is the very reason that Luke 11:9–10 and 11:11–13 were placed together as they are in both Matthew and Luke. Loving fathers are known for protecting their children, wanting nothing but the best for the sons and daughters who depend on them for survival. Such fathers will give their children only good things. If a son asks for food to eat, will his father offer something useless (a stone) or even dangerous (a snake or a scorpion), instead? Of course not![32] How much more, then, can we depend on our heavenly Father to give us only good gifts in response to our prayers? But more than that, if in our youthful foolishness we unwittingly ask for something dangerous, will God grant that request? If a father will not give snakes or scorpions to children who ask for bread, can God be expected to supply dangerous snakes and poisonous scorpions to ignorant children who foolishly ask for them? I know that the text does not become this explicit, but it is the logical consequence of the argument at work.[33] The strength of Jesus's a fortiori reasoning leads inevitably to this conclusion.

Good parents do not necessarily provide everything a child asks of them, even if they are able to do so. My son, Aaron, grew up with a healthy fascination for all things reptilian. Over the years he kept a variety of snakes, iguanas, and monitor lizards in his basement bedroom. There was a time when he would frequently—repetitiously and passionately—ask if he could have our permission to branch out and keep venomous snakes; he thoughtfully suggested beginning with a rattlesnake or a cobra before graduating to pit vipers. He would also gleefully regale us with stories printed in the letters section of his monthly reptile magazine recounting how Burmese pythons had been known to swallow family pets and

32. Both Matt. 7:9 and Luke 11:11 introduce this rhetorical question with the same phrase introducing the question in Luke 11:5. Thus, this question also demands a negative reply.

33. See the more extended argument in Crump, *Jesus the Intercessor*, 131–34.

attempt to devour their sleeping masters whole. I am not sure how he thought this might help his cause, but do you think my wife and I ever gave our son a rattlesnake, let alone a cobra or pit viper?

Luke's particular commitment to the sovereignty of God's good intentions accounts, I believe, for a vital distinguishing feature found in 11:13: "If you then, though you are evil, know how to give good gifts to your children, how much more will your Father in heaven give *the Holy Spirit* to those who ask him!" Matthew's version arrives at the destination we have been prepared to expect: "How much more will your Father in heaven give *good gifts* to those who ask him!"[34] In Matthew, good fathers can be expected to give good things. In Luke, the best Father can be expected to give only the very best, the Holy Spirit, to all his praying children. No one in Luke's text has specifically requested the Holy Spirit; the children have asked only for fish and eggs. Deciding what constitutes the best gift, however, is a prerogative assumed completely by God. Not only will he not give harmful things to children who ask for good gifts; not only will he refuse to give harmful things to children who unknowingly request harmful gifts; but now he insists on giving only the best even to those who fail to request it! What is good and appropriate is for God alone—not the petitioner—to determine, and no amount of insistence can change that. By specifying the gift of the Spirit in this way, independently of any specific request, Luke highlights that prayer is not a guaranteed means of acquiring whatever we want, whether by repetition or urgency. Rather, petitionary prayer is a means by which God gives whatever he has decided is most necessary,[35] and Luke knows that the Holy Spirit is the gift par excellence, making all others pale in comparison. We can relax and trust our heavenly Father to answer our prayers—sometimes with affirmation, at other times with silence, often with responses we never anticipated—because we can have absolute confidence in his absolute commitment never to damage but only to bless the children he loves.

Conclusions

The book *Mighty Prevailing Prayer* tells the moving story of an Oregon man called Praying Payson, a man who

34. It is probably impossible to determine which Gospel writer preserves the original tradition and which has edited this part of his material, although most modern writers opine that Luke altered his source. Fortunately, our ability to read Matthew and Luke as they stand does not depend on knowing the answer to this question. See Woods, *"Finger of God,"* 197–203.

35. I show elsewhere how the verb "to ask" in Luke 11:13 became synonymous with "to pray"; *Jesus the Intercessor*, 133–34.

prevailed mightily in prayer. After his death he was found to have calloused knees. By the side of his bed, where he wrestled in prayer day after day, were two grooves worn into the hard boards as he moved back and forth on his knees in prayer. It is said that in his prayer wrestling he at times groaned as if he were dying, but such mighty groanings were then followed by tremendous spiritual transformations [in others].[36]

Sometimes such stories are inspirational, whether by their power to convict or to encourage. They motivate us to more earnest prayer because we see the possibilities experienced by someone else. If him, why not me? But, at other times, the same story can become extremely manipulative, whether intentionally or unwittingly. There is a profound difference between an example of what might be and a paradigm of what must be. If the author intends for us to read the story paradigmatically, as an illustration of all proper prayer, what are its implications? God grants the petitions of those who pray with continual groans. What, then, are we to conclude when our petitions seem empty? First, we have not prayed persistently enough. Second, we have not prayed with sufficient anguish. If we had prayed "correctly," like Praying Payson, we too would see stunning, miraculous transformations.

My experience tells me that books about prayer are often better at conjuring guilt than motivating piety. Not that I have anything against guilt per se. Guilty people ought to feel their true guilt appropriately, but there is a difference between true guilt and false guilt, just as there is a difference between example and paradigm. True guilt is rooted in a correct understanding of personal sin—something that is derived from good theology, which in turn is informed by a true interpretation of Scripture. I suspect that the implied lessons of a Praying Payson, on the other hand, illustrate how counterproductive well-intentioned but ill-informed theology can be. Hopefully, a more appropriate reading of the parable of the midnight visitor will help to redress this mistake.

Persistent prayer is an essential component of the Christian life. The apostle Paul describes his own experience of wrestling in prayer (Rom. 15:30; Col. 2:1; 4:12). Yet, is there a biblical basis for the formula long-term repetition + sufficient fervency = positive response? No. It is impossible to construct such an equation from the materials found in Luke 11:5–13. (The next chapter will show the same for Luke 18:1–8.)

My point is not to dissuade anyone from praying persistently or passionately, nor is it to discount the useful pastoral observations that many have made about the power of long-term petition to challenge personal priorities, to inculcate greater patience, or to deepen superficial faith.

36. Duewel, *Mighty Prevailing Prayer*, 222.

We need, however, to distinguish practical benefits that may vary from person to person from theological norms that apply to all prayer everywhere. The truth of Luke 11:5–13 is that God is the ideal parent who hears every child's request the first time and promises to respond at the right moment, in the best possible way. Therefore, ask anywhere, anytime, in tears or dry-eyed, continually or briefly, passionately or calmly; when it seems convenient; when it appears impossible. Just ask! You are always heard because you are always loved.

4

Patient Prayer

The Parable of the Widow and the Judge

The companion passage to the parable of the midnight visitor (Luke 11:5–13) is the story of the persistent widow and the unjust judge found in Luke 18:1–8. Together these two parables comprise the traditional double-barreled argument for the value of repetition in energizing Christian prayer. Jesus seemingly makes the lesson crystal clear at the outset: "Jesus told his disciples a parable to show them that they should always pray and not give up" (18:1). He then tells the story of a gutsy lone widow who overcomes the slow-moving grindstones of city hall by tenaciously insisting that she have her day in court. The indifferent bureaucrat in charge of her case is eventually motivated to take the proper action only because the woman becomes a nag; she makes herself too irksome for him to bear any longer (18:5). The parable's conclusion then transforms her badgering into a metaphor for our persistence in prayer (18:7). In other words, if God fails to respond the first time, come back again, and again, and again, until he does. Like this widow, disciples who persist in asking are those who find their prayers answered. Chapter 3 referred to the abundant supply of literature offering this lesson as the self-evident significance of the parables of both the midnight visitor and the persistent widow; there is no need for further documentation here.

The previous chapter, however, also disclosed that this popular reading of Luke 11 seriously misses the mark. So, the question begs to be asked, if one barrel misfired, what about the other? Initially, at least, the popular reading of the widow's plight certainly appears more promising. Unlike the parable of the midnight visitor, Luke 18 clearly invokes a lesson about persistence, whatever that may be. After all, the judge relents only to avoid further harassment. But what exactly is the significance of that observation? The praying disciple is certainly encouraged not to give up, but the question remains: not to give up on what: petition, asking repeatedly, prayer of any sort? What, *specifically*, is the preferred alternative to quitting? Is the parable a blanket invitation to launch an assault against heaven for any and every cause that claims our interest? Is the sky the limit for those with sufficient energy to persevere, or is there such a thing as an illegitimate prayer request? If so, how are legitimacy and illegitimacy determined?

What about the unjust judge? What does he model about the divine judge to whom we persistently pray? For instance, what is God's disposition toward our requests? Certainly, he cannot be as apathetic toward his people as this judge is toward the widow! But, then, what lesson is to be learned from her persistence and his initial lack of interest? In what way does repetition gain God's attention? Is he theoretically willing to give anything to the person brave enough to ask, as long as she asks often enough? Many interpreters read the parable in this way, but it puts this parable immediately at odds with the lessons learned from the parable of the midnight visitor. In Luke 11:9–13 the heavenly Father gives only good gifts to his praying children, the good things he has already determined to be in their best interests. Is Luke now adding an unexpected twist—God *usually* will give you only good things, but if you are persistent, he may become weary enough to grant your request for a poisonous snake, after all? I suspect not. Finding more satisfying answers to these questions, however, requires that we first locate the parable within the larger context of Luke's Gospel.

Waiting for the Son of Man

The parable of the persistent widow concludes a more extensive segment of material united by a concern for the coming of the Son of Man.

The entire unit encompasses Luke 17:20–18:8.[1] Its unifying theme is the anticipation of the parousia, the final return of the resurrected Jesus. Luke's conclusion to the parable in 18:8b, "When the Son of Man comes, will he find faith on the earth?" binds the lesson of this parable to Jesus's earlier description of the Son of Man's surprising appearance at the end of time: "The Son of Man in his day will be like the lightning, which flashes and lights up the sky from one end to the other" (17:24). Both sections are also characterized by the disciples' yearning for a long-delayed denouement: in 18:7 God's chosen ones have waited "day and night" for an answer to their requests; while in 17:22 they "long to see one of the days of the Son of Man, but . . . will not see it." There is also a suffering theme in both sections. The persistent widow is a portrait of the people of God seeking relief from oppression, forced "to cry out" repeatedly for justice inexplicably withheld (18:7–8). Similarly, Jesus warns that his disciples will "long to see one of the days of the Son of Man" (17:22) because they now follow in the master's footsteps, "suffer[ing] many things and being reject[ed] by this generation" (17:25). Lastly, when their deliverance finally arrives, it appears "quickly" (18:8), so quickly in fact that, just as in the days of Noah and of Lot, people will go about their normal day-to-day affairs, only to be tragically overwhelmed by a judgment for which they are unprepared (17:26–29). These four connective themes demonstrate that the parable in 18:1–8 cannot be properly interpreted apart from the apocalyptic message of 17:20–37. The parable of the judge and the widow is not a parable about prayer simpliciter; it is not concerned with generic principles relating persistence to efficacious prayer per se. This is first and foremost a parable about waiting, waiting appropriately and effectively, for the eventual, surprising return of Christ. The question is, how does a disciple maintain vigilance while waiting for a long-delayed but inevitable instant that will sneak up on everyone like the proverbial thief in the night?

The particular features of the story are important: the widow/elect repeatedly appeal to the judge/God over an extended period of time during which an adversary (or "this generation" in 17:25) appears unjustly victorious. The prayers offered are not requests for food—eggs and bread or other "good things"—mentioned in Luke 11. These petitioners are imploring the heavenly judge for a cosmic reprieve from unrelenting injustice at the hands of their enemies. In this instance, context is everything. The widow represents the desperate pleas of God's people

1. "There is a fairly broad recognition that the natural section here runs from 17:20 to 18:8. . . . The final unit 18:1–8 is bound to the large central unit (17:22–37) by the inclusion of 18:8b with its reference to the coming of the Son of Man"; Nolland, *Luke*, 851.

struggling against the insidious temptation to think themselves abandoned by their long-awaited Lord.

How Long Will He Keep Them Waiting?

Luke 18:1–8 bristles with major interpretive questions at each juncture in the story. For our purposes, three questions need to be addressed: (1) How is the judge intended to portray God in 18:2–4? (2) What finally motivates the judge to respond in 18:5? (3) How should we understand Jesus's rhetorical question in 18:7?

The first question is the easiest to answer since there is almost universal agreement that, as in the parable of the midnight visitor, this parable turns on an a fortiori argument. God is not being compared to but contrasted against the unjust judge.[2] The logic is this: if even this incompetent judge who disregards both divine and humane concerns will eventually respond, how much more can you count on your just, faithful God to hear your prayers? A particularly evocative passage from the Old Testament Apocrypha is generally recognized as important literary background against which Jesus positions his story:[3]

> Do not try to bribe him with presents, he will not accept them,
>   do not put your faith in wrongly motivated sacrifices;
> for the Lord is a judge
>   who is utterly impartial.
> He never shows partiality to the detriment of the poor,
>   he listens to the plea of the injured party.
> He does not ignore the orphan's supplication,
>   nor the widow's as she pours out her complaint.
> Do the widow's tears not run down her cheeks,
>   as she accuses the man who is the cause of them?
> Whoever wholeheartedly serves God will be accepted,
>   his petition will carry to the clouds.
> The prayer of the humble pierces the clouds:
>   and until it does, he is not to be consoled,

2. Plummer, *Luke*, 414; Jeremias, *Parables of Jesus*, 156; Cranfield, "Parable of the Unjust Judge," 300; Catchpole, "Son of Man's Search," 89–90; I. Marshall, *Luke*, 670; Fitzmyer, *Luke*, 1177; Scott, *Hear Then the Parable*, 187; Hicks, "Parable of the Persistent Widow," 221–22; Bovon, "Apocalyptic Traditions," 388; Stagg, "Luke's Theological Use of Parables," 227; and Young, *Parables*, 58.

3. The Wisdom of Jesus Son of Sirach (also known as Ecclesiasticus) was composed originally in Hebrew during the first quarter of the second century BC and was translated into Greek toward the end of the same century; see Nickelsburg, *Jewish Literature*, 55–65; and Collins, *Jewish Wisdom in the Hellenistic Age*, 23. K. Bailey, *Through Peasant Eyes*, 128, provides a good comparison of the similarities and differences between Sirach and Luke.

> nor will he desist until the Most High takes notice of him,
>   acquits the upright and delivers judgement.
> And the Lord will not be slow,
>   nor will he be dilatory on their behalf. (Sir. 35:11–19 NJB)

The merciless judge in Jesus's parable is a deliberate antitype to Israel's heavenly judge, although there is some measure of similarity insofar as both may try their petitioners' patience. Even Sirach's petitioner "is not to be consoled, / nor will he desist until the Most High takes notice of him." In other words, it is entirely possible that the just God who immediately hears all requests may nevertheless delay his response for reasons known only to himself.[4] Consequently, the stubbornness of Jesus's widow is not an exemplary model of how persistence moves God to action, for the Lord never ignores a widow's complaint (Sir. 35:14). Rather, her persistence is part and parcel of an exaggerated scenario highlighting its dissimilarity to the disciple's relationship with God. Jesus's point is that praying disciples need not depend on repetition to gain God's attention. Although they too are often kept waiting, it is not because their requests require further repetition before being heard or that God is uninterested in their plight; it is because the heavenly judge has determined that, for the moment, for whatever reason, they need to wait. Luke's Jesus is not enjoining repetitious prayer but patient prayer.

Second, if God is not moved by persistence or repetition, what finally causes him to intervene? An answer to this second question hinges on the translation of the word *hypōpiazein* at the end of 18:5. The most common English rendering has the judge fearing that, if he does not eventually answer the widow's complaint, she will "weary him" or "wear him out" (AV, RSV, NEB, NIV, NRSV, CEV) by her persistence.[5] While this is still

4. In this way, the contrast between God and judge is not absolute—an observation that will become significant as the interpretation proceeds. This is, however, typical of any meaningful contrast. If the two items juxtaposed were utterly dissimilar, the juxtaposition would not constitute a contrast but a non sequitur communicating nothing. Overlooking this necessary linguistic feature of contrast accounts for the error of those (few) interpreters who contend that the parable's explanation is based in the positive *comparison* of God to the unjust judge. See Derrett, "Law in the New Testament," 179, who advances his argument by claiming that the judge's "lack of respect for man" (18:2, 4) is actually the positive trait of "judging with impartiality." Few follow him in this regard. See also Goetz, "On Petitionary Prayer," who argues that circumstances only appear unjust for those who lack faith in divine sovereignty.

5. I. Marshall, *Luke*, 673, itemizes the four possible ways of translating 11:5b. *Hypōpiazein* literally means "to strike under the eye," "to give a black eye to" (compare Paul's metaphorical use of the word in 1 Cor. 9:27). Although most English translations adopt the weakened metaphorical sense "to wear out"—following the ancient Syriac, Georgian, and Arabic versions (Jeremias, *Parables of Jesus*, 154; K. Bailey, *Through Peasant Eyes*, 136)—it is very difficult to document this usage elsewhere; see Nolland, *Luke*, 868.

the translation that most readers find in their Bibles, the majority of researchers agree with J. Nolland's translation: "Yet, because this widow is a bother to me, I will vindicate her, so that her coming does not utterly shame me."[6] The judge's problem is not weariness but honor; he is concerned about his reputation.[7] His persistent neglect of this woman's case creates an occasion for increasingly forward, shameless behavior as she violates the social norms of public deportment.[8] Eventually, the judge's neglect will make him the object of ridicule as well. Although his action is as self-serving as his previous inaction, at least it is shaped by legitimate social expectations meant to safeguard a proper (albeit belated) response. Unlike revenge, justice may not be a dish best served cold, but at least cold justice is better than no justice. By finally fulfilling his responsibilities, he puts an end to their embarrassment as well as her suffering.

While there is good reason for the traditional association of Luke's two parables in the history of interpretation, seldom has the connection been drawn along the particular lines of honor and shame. For example, because many interpreters fail to understand *anaideia* as a characteristic of the petitioning friend (11:8), the similarity between the midnight petitioner and the persistent widow (18:3), both of whom are compelled to behave somewhat shamelessly, is typically overlooked. Furthermore, some interpreters argue that *hypōpiazein* accomplishes for this unjust judge what Fridrichsen and his followers suggested that *anaideia* achieves for the sleeping householder: they both seek to avoid

6. Nolland, *Luke*, 865.
7. It is not a difficult step from "striking a blow to one's face" to the metaphorical "striking a blow to one's honor." See the convincing evidence assembled by Derrett, "Law in the New Testament," 190–91; also Catchpole, "Son of Man's Search," 89; Fitzmyer, *Luke*, 1179 (while adopting the traditional English translation, he admits that the figurative meaning is possible); Hicks, "Parable of the Persistent Widow," 218; Sellew, "Interior Monologue," 248; Nolland, *Luke*, 868; and Herzog, *Parables as Subversive Speech*, 230. Some object to this translation on the grounds of the judge's "disregard for men" in 18:2, 4, claiming that this entails lack of interest in what others think of him. Showing disregard for others (the judge's demeanor in 18:2, 4), however, is quite different from others showing disregard for you (what the judge hopes to avoid in 18:5). K. Bailey, *Through Peasant Eyes*, 132, argues that 18:2 and 18:4 describe the judge as "not ashamed before people," demonstrating that he is unable to feel shamed himself (136). Unfortunately, by always making the Syriac and Arabic versions the final arbiter of Greek definitions, Bailey builds his often insightful literary analyses on a very dubious lexical foundation.
8. Ideally, a woman ought to have been represented by a male relative; in any event, for a woman to repeatedly show herself in public, and to remain so vocal, would have been shameful for all involved. See Derrett, "Law in the New Testament," 186; Scott, *Hear Then the Parable*, 187; Eddy, "Transformed Values"; and Herzog, *Parables as Subversive Speech*, 228.

shame.[9] I demonstrated in chapter 3 why this suggested parallelism cannot work, since *anaideia* has nothing to do with either the avoidance of shame or the sleeping householder. Consequently, whereas both the sleeping householder and the unjust judge are contrasted with God, the shame dynamic in 18:5 highlights that they are also contrasted with each other: while the householder has no reason for shame, the judge has every reason to be ashamed. Consequently, any satisfying interpretation of 18:1–8 must give some account of God's honor as he hears, but seemingly fails to respond to, the oft-repeated petitions of his people. If in Luke 11 there is no need for the praying person to experience shame in approaching God any time of the day or night, what does Luke 18 intimate about divine honor as God delays responding to the disciples' requests?

The third question awaiting an answer is the proper rendering of the rhetorical question in 18:7, often referred to as the *crux interpretum* of the passage. I. H. Marshall itemizes nine possible interpretations of this verse.[10] Recognizing the similarity between Luke's parable and Sirach's description of God as judge offers the greatest assistance in finally deciding how to translate Luke 18:7.[11] The sentence ought to

9. Jeremias, *Parables of Jesus*, 158; and Catchpole, "Son of Man's Search," 89.

10. I. Marshall, *Luke*, 674–75. The literature is vast and complex; space limitations prevent me from thoroughly justifying all of my conclusions. Three principal issues are involved: (1) how to translate the word *makrothymein*, which could mean (a) "to wait patiently," (b) "to be forbearing," or (c) "to be dilatory, slow"; (2) whether to punctuate the verse as one sentence or two; and (3) whether "them" refers to the elect or their opponents. Hicks, "Parable of the Persistent Widow," 219, conveniently assembles a list of the most common English translations, which I expand:

Moffatt	will he be tolerant to their opponents?
RV	and he is longsuffering over them
AV	though he bear long with them
RSV	will he delay long over them?
NRSV	will he delay long in helping them?
ASV	and yet he is longsuffering over them
NIV	will he keep putting them off?
NEB	while he listens patiently to them
NEB margin	while he delays to help them
CEV	won't he be concerned for them?

11. Sir. 35:19b, which is nearly identical to the final clause in Luke 18:7b, places the verb *makrothymein* in parallelism with *bradynein* ("to hesitate, delay, be slow"), indicating that it is best to translate *makrothymein* similarly. See Plummer, *Luke*, 414; Fitzmyer, *Luke*, 1180; and the additional literature cited by Jeremias, *Parables of Jesus*, 154nn9–10. Interpreting 2 Pet. 3:9 also depends on the background found in Sir. 35; see Freed, "Parable of the Judge and the Widow," 54.

read: "Will not God vindicate his elect who cry out to him day and night, even though he is slow to act for them/even though he keeps them waiting?"[12] Jesus finally interprets the parable, offering a word of assurance, encouraging God's people to remember that while their prayers may appear to be in vain, they wait because of God's timing, not because of God's neglect. The heavenly judge hears every petition immediately, and he always rules justly; sometimes, however, the timing remains mysteriously his own, leaving petitioners waiting and wondering.

Defending God's Honor

Luke 18:1–8 is referred to as the parable of the unjust judge and the persistent widow because both figures play an equally important role in determining its meaning. Attempts to focus on one character over the other reflect the outdated notion that parables can make only one point.[13] Recent developments in parable research have shifted to a more sensible position in which the parable's lessons are related to the number of major characters in the story.[14] Luke 18:1–8 conveys at least two primary lessons, with details revolving around its two main characters, located as they are within the framework of eschatological expectation and the delay of the parousia.

12. Plummer, *Luke*, 414, who also observes that strict grammar requires "them" to refer to the elect; Jeremias, *Parables of Jesus*, 154–55; I. Marshall, *Luke*, 675; and Hicks, "Parable of the Persistent Widow," 220.

13. The parable focuses on the judge according to Arndt, *Luke*, 377; Jeremias, *Parables of Jesus*, 156 (arguing that Jesus's interpretation in 18:6–8a focuses on the judge, whereas Luke's reinterpretation in 18:1 shifts to the widow); Derrett, "Law in the New Testament," 179, 191; Catchpole, "Son of Man's Search," 89–90; Craddock, *Luke*, 208; Hedrick, *Parables as Poetic Fictions*, 193, 201; and Goetz, "On Petitionary Prayer," 96–99. The parable is about the widow according to Jülicher, *Die Gleichnisreden Jesu*, 2.286–90; Herzog, *Parables as Subversive Speech*, 225–32; Freed, "Parable of the Judge and the Widow," 50; Eddy, "Transformed Values," 125; Schottrof, *Lydia's Impatient Sisters*, 101; Bovon, "Apocalyptic Traditions," 388; Reid, *Choosing the Better Part?* 192; idem, "Godly Widow," 31–33. The parable has a dual reference to both the judge and the widow according to Manson, *Luke*, 200–201; I. Marshall, *Luke*, 670–71; Fitzmyer, *Luke*, 1177; Danker, *Jesus and the New Age*, 296; Tiede, *Luke*, 304–6; Stein, *Luke*, 444; Nolland, *Luke*, 871; Hicks, "Parable of the Persistent Widow," 221–23; Green, *Luke*, 637; and Lieu, *Luke*, 139.

14. "Each parable makes one main point per main character"; Blomberg, *Interpreting the Parables*, 163; see also his explanation of Luke 18:1–8 as "a two-point parable" (271–74). Blomberg offers a good survey of the history of parable interpretation. The popular notion that Jesus's parables make only one point was first asserted by nineteenth-century German scholar Adolf Jülicher who was (quite rightly) reacting against the antihistorical excesses of traditional allegory. Unfortunately, as often happens in history, he went from one extreme to another.

The unjust judge initially ignores the widow's pleas, procrastinates for a considerable period, and then finally acts only to preserve his public reputation. In this regard, he is unlike our heavenly judge, who always hears our requests and never ignores a disciple's cries even though he too may delay inexplicably. This characteristic of divine slowness follows a long-standing Old Testament tradition in which God's purposes, though deliberate and assured, often unfold at a tortoiselike pace (at least, it can feel that way to us). The lament psalms are replete with the cries of faithful men and women who trust in God's promises but, nevertheless, find their faith stretched to the breaking point by God's apparent lack of interest:

> I say to God my Rock,
>   "Why have you forgotten me?
> Why must I go about mourning,
>   oppressed by the enemy?"
> My bones suffer mortal agony
>   as my foes taunt me,
> saying to me all day long,
>   "Where is your God?" (Ps. 42:9–10)

> Awake, O Lord! Why do you sleep?
>   Rouse yourself! Do not reject us forever.
> Why do you hide your face
>   and forget our misery and oppression?
> . . . .
> Rise up and help us;
>   redeem us because of your unfailing love. (Ps. 44:23–24, 26)

These are faithful people who continue to pray despite heaven's doors seeming to be tightly shut against them. Eventually, the wicked begin to malign God's character, since by all appearances his inaction is decidedly faithless. Does not God's slowness illustrate what the wicked already know, that God is a mean-spirited liar who cannot be trusted (Isa. 5:19; Jer. 17:15)? In the face of such accusations, God's people are grieved by both their own abandonment as well as the salacious taunts of blasphemers:

> Help us, O God our Savior,
>   for the glory of your name;
> deliver us and atone for our sins
>   for your name's sake.
> Why should the nations say,
>   "Where is their God?"
> Before our eyes, make known among the nations
>   that you avenge the outpoured blood of your servants. (Ps. 79:9–10)

The faithful grieve not only for themselves, but for the reputation of their God, who has become an object of public scorn.

God's frequent reply is that he will eventually act, and when he does it will be both to redeem his people and to vindicate the honor of his name (Ps. 115:1–3; Isa. 52:1–6; 64:1–5; Jer. 14:21; Ezek. 20:41–44; 38:14–39:8; 39:21–29). Nevertheless, his timing is his own and will neither be stretched nor forcibly abbreviated by any considerations other than his own. The great God of Abraham, Isaac, and Jacob remains forever committed to claiming the honor and glory due his holiness, and when the time is right, he will ensure that every divine action is praised as faithful and just. In this respect, God and the judge are somewhat alike. Both keep their petitioners waiting. Both finally act to preserve their reputation. Unlike the judge, however, God's eventual response is motivated by a two-pronged passion: the honor of his name and the love of his people.

A cardinal feature of Old Testament lament is the final inclusion of a statement of confidence whereby the psalmist reaffirms devotion to the Lord. In spite of all appearances, the author will not surrender trust in God, and a principal means of demonstrating such faithfulness in the face of darkness is to persist in presenting his needs before heaven's throne. Thus Jesus's widow is typical of the faithful psalmist:

> O Lord, how many are my foes!
>   How many rise up against me!
> Many are saying of me,
>   "God will not deliver him."
> But you are a shield around me, O Lord,
>   my Glorious One, who lifts up my head.
> To the Lord I cry aloud,
>   and he answers me from his holy hill. (Ps. 3:1–4 NIV margin)

This Old Testament man of prayer knows by faith that God will answer even though there has, as yet, been no answer. He believes that he is not abandoned even though, by all appearances, he is completely abandoned. He trusts that God hears his every word even though there is no visible evidence that God cares, much less hears. Like the widow, the psalmist perseveres.

Will the Coming Son of Man Find Faith on the Earth?

For over two thousand years the Christian church has waited for Jesus's return, an event known as the parousia. For some in the early church, this unexpected delay raised serious doubts about the truth of the Gospel. As early as the New Testament letter called 2 Peter, some were complaining—"scoffing" we are told—that the more time that passed without a parousia, the more unreliable became the Gospel promises (2 Pet. 3:3–4). These skeptics needed to be reminded that the Son's return was not "slow" (*makrothymein*) because God was a sluggard; it was slow because God mercifully lengthened the opportunity for repentance and faith ("with the Lord a day is like a thousand years"; 3:8–9).

Luke's Jesus warned his disciples, "The time is coming when you will long to see one of the days of the Son of Man, but you will not see it" (Luke 17:22). Throughout the ages the faithful have cried out, "Maranatha!" Come, Lord. Come! For centuries, the saints have patiently raised their eyes to heaven while enduring the persecutions of Nero and executions under Chairman Mao. Whether living through the brutality of Domitian, Trajan, Lenin, Stalin, Pol Pot, or some unnamed tyrant yet to come, God's faithful people have always set their eyes on Jesus, refusing to surrender their belief in the value of prayer, the reality of God's answers, or the certainty of their eventual deliverance. This is no less true of disciples who may be fortunate enough to live free of political oppression but wrestle nonetheless against the destructive forces of death, disease, social ostracism, and the sinful status quo.

Do not be fooled by the passing of time. Jesus guaranteed that his disciples will be vindicated (Luke 18:8a). Evil will be eradicated. Justice will overflow like a rushing river covering the earth as the waters cover the sea, as the prophets declared (Amos 5:24; Isa. 11:9). It will happen "quickly/suddenly" (Luke 18:8a),[15] in the blink of an eye, like a thief in the night (2 Pet. 3:10), catching many unprepared in their lethargy, surprised in their indolence (Luke 17:26–35). What is the solution? How do you maintain proper preparedness? Prayer.

Jesus offers advance warning. He has already described the Son of Man's criterion for faithfulness at the final day. He will see faithfulness wherever he finds disciples praying. "When the Son of Man comes, will he find faith on the earth?" (Luke 18:8b).[16] Who is faithful? The persistent

15. The phrase *en tachei* may mean either "quickly, suddenly" (some also suggest "unexpectedly") or "soon, shortly" depending on how *makrothymein* is translated. I opt for the first meaning. The point is not that the Son of Man will return soon after only a short elapse of time, but that when he does return, the events involved will transpire suddenly. For a survey of the literature, see I. Marshall, *Luke*, 676; and Hicks, "Parable of the Persistent Widow," 220, especially n. 57.

16. The use here of "faith" (*pistis*) with a definite article is unusual and is occasionally taken to mean "the Christian faith." This is not, however, how Luke uses the word "faith" elsewhere (Luke 5:20; 7:9, 50; 8:25, 48; 17:5, 6, 19; 18:8, 42; 22:32; Acts 3:16 [twice]; 6:5, 7; 11:24; 13:8; 14:9, 22, 27; 15:9; 16:5; 17:31; 20:21; 24:24; 26:18). Given its context, "the faith" is most readily understood as faithful endurance that prays while waiting; I. Marshall, *Luke*, 676.

widow who refused to abandon her request. Who will be welcomed into the kingdom of God at Christ's return? All who never stopped praying in the darkness, who never allowed God's apparent absence to overwhelm their prayerful quest for God's presence. This is what Luke means when he says, "Jesus told his disciples a parable to show them that they should always pray and not give up" (18:1).[17] The lesson is one of patient faithfulness in spite of appearances. God seems to be dead. We talk to him anyway. God seems not to hear. We bare our souls anyway. Prayer is not made more efficacious by repetition.[18] Praying more often does not hasten Christ's return, any more than infrequent prayer retards God's timing.[19] This prayer has nothing whatsoever to do with repetition as such or with our ability to influence God's schedule. The point is this: will I continue to bring my life before God in prayer when all tangible, empirical—and even all personal, experiential—evidence demands that I abandon prayer as worthless?

Conclusions

Gospel parables should not be pulled out of their literary contexts and read as isolated units. Floating independently, the story is free to become all things to all readers. Whether the interpreter is a nineteenth-century devotional writer, an advocate of social-historical reconstruction, or a feminist applying the hermeneutics of suspicion makes little difference.[20] The outcome remains basically the same. The parable

17. The word "always" (*pantote*) answers the question "for how long?" by responding, "All the time."

18. One can only hope that this tenacious misinterpretation will soon be laid to rest once and for all; for a similar observation, see Green, *Luke*, 638–39.

19. Very few go to the extent of advocating this interpretation, but see Arndt, *Luke*, 377: "To me the answer to the question why the final triumph has not yet occurred is clear. The Christians have not prayed enough, hence the day of final redemption has not yet come. . . . Jesus himself declares the final redemption may be far off because there is not enough earnest prayer for its coming." This is exactly the connection that Jesus does not make!

20. Some locate the parable within their own particular social reconstructions, turning it into a story of liberation as the kingdom of God overturns oppressive social norms; see Scott, *Hear Then the Parables*, 187 (the widow represents the kingdom of God coming shamelessly to change the world); Benjamin, "Persistent Widow" (the widow represents Jesus, who persistently protests against the rich and powerful in defense of the poor); and Herzog, *Parables as Subversive Speech*, 231 (the widow represents all the oppressed, who must rise up and challenge the status quo). Reid, looking to "unmask sexist presuppositions," understands the widow to represent God overthrowing sexist cultural expectations; see "Godly Widow," 31–33. Via reads the parable against a backdrop of Jungian psychology, finding a story that uncovers "the various aspects of human estrangement"; see "Parable

becomes a wax nose molded into whatever creative shape the reader's imagination prefers. The final canonical context must remain decisive for interpretation. Luke's setting tells us that the parable of the unjust judge and the persistent widow is not about the power of repetitive prayer to move God, any more than it is about the church's mission to overturn oppressive social structures or the validation of Jungian psychology—regardless of the intrinsic value of such things. The overarching dynamic of a beleaguered disciple waiting for vindication by her Lord returning on the clouds requires a more disciplined reading.[21] This story confronts the desperate, pastoral situations arising any time that prayer remains unanswered. Will we stop believing? Will we give up on prayer? Consequently, the parable also resoundingly shuts the door against any suggestion that increased repetition is the solution to our problems.

The young woman mentioned in this book's introduction, draped over a chair in my office weeping because her dearest friend had died that night, faced just such a challenge. No doubt, her pastor would suggest that the church had not started to pray early enough, that they had not pleaded earnestly or forcefully or frequently enough. Yet, she had begged God for healing, desperately, persistently, shedding tears night and day while fasting and renouncing any and all earthly pleasures, if only God would restore her friend's health. Had she been flogged in a communist prison, her pain could not have been more palpable. But the young mother had died, and now my visitor found herself trapped in the parenthetical position of waiting blindly between the ages. Trapped between a spiritual rock and an eternal hard place, would she continue to believe in the ancient Gospel promises of a Father who saves each of our tears in his bottle, of a Savior whose coming will redeem all our waiting? I feared that my visitor was teetering on the precipice, ready to let go of prayer as she slowly toppled into the darkness. When the Son of Man comes, will he find her praying?

I pray that he will.

---

of the Unjust Judge." Such authors simply reaffirm my belief in allowing the canonical context to be the final arbiter in interpretation.

21. Canonical context must also determine which historical background material is relevant to interpretation. For example, Young argues that the Son of Man's search for faith is synonymous with a quest for repetitious prayer. He does so by way of rabbinic stories that, he believes, show first-century Judaism's definition of faithful prayer as repeated prayer; see *Parables*, 60–65. The problem, however, is that none of the rabbinic parallels share anything like the eschatological expectancy demanded by Luke's context.

Theological Reflections on Prayer
in the Synoptic Gospels

Now is an apt moment to take an intermission from exegesis in order to (1) summarize the various conclusions gleaned thus far from our study and (2) begin to organize them into a theological composite, like fitting together the puzzle pieces of a jigsaw landscape. Chapters 1–4 examined all the Synoptic passages where Jesus could conceivably be understood to place some constraint on the effectiveness of petitionary prayer. Theoretically, this study could have begun at several different points of introduction, but I selected these parts of the Synoptic tradition, as opposed to Paul's letters, for example, as providing the most fundamental entry point to the church traditions developed elsewhere in the New Testament.[1] The life and teaching of Jesus were *the* catalyst to the development of the early church and its theological reflection. Second, I started with the question of apparent petitionary constraints partly because of the overwhelming significance

---

1. Although Paul's letters antedate the Gospels and all four Gospels were composed in dialogue with the developing circumstances of early Christian communities, there is no good reason to disallow the fundamental contours of the Gospels as arising from the historical Jesus. For example, the tradition-history of Luke 18:1–8 is quite contentious. Many argue that it is a patchwork collection of variegated traditions emanating from Jesus, the early church, and Lukan editing. A few, such as Linnemann, *Parables of Jesus*, go so far as to call the entire pericope a wholesale invention of the church. Catchpole, on the other hand, no naïve stranger to critical reconstruction, firmly defends both the integrity and the authenticity of the entire passage, excluding only Luke's editorial introduction (18:1); see "Son of Man's Search," 102–4. Similar examples could be offered for nearly every passage in the Synoptic Gospels. What one scholar labels unauthentic, another affirms as fundamentally reliable.

that these questions have exercised in the history of Western prayer literature and partly because they focus attention on a discreet set of texts that delineate a clearly identifiable starting point for the study.

Specifically, the two constraints under discussion are what I will call the "amoral conditions" of faith and persistence. Later, we will examine various "moral conditions" found primarily in other portions of the New Testament, where personal behavior, sin to be specific, exercises some bearing over God's willingness and/or ability to answer prayers affirmatively. Some, undoubtedly, disagree with this distinction between moral and amoral conditions, arguing that any component of Christian obedience, including faith, must necessarily be included among the responsibilities of personal ethics. I believe, however, that the exegetical results demonstrate that neither faith nor persistence has any relative bearing on the value of a disciple's petitions to the Father, unlike such inappropriate attitudes as selfishness (James 4:3) or a disregard for others (1 Pet. 3:7). The constraints of faith and persistence are absolute conditions in the sense that each distinguishes true discipleship from false, not gradations of strong discipleship from weak. First, anyone who turns to God with any degree of faith in the Father's contemporaneous power to perform miracles prays with authentic faith. On the other hand, praying to a God purportedly bound by the laws of nature or physics[2] means that we no longer truly pray at all. Similarly, authentic Christian prayer persists, regardless of how deafening the silence, not in the insistent demand for any particular answer, but in the unswerving conviction that God's answers, whatever they may be, are only a matter of time. To abandon prayer is, thus, to abandon faith. True faith is revealed in a persistent openness to the normalcy of the supernatural, knowing that the Father's ultimate miracle will be Christ's return on the clouds of heaven.

In the course of uncovering these two points of theology, several additional observations were made that will exercise considerable significance in the pages ahead.

Perhaps the principal theological observation thus far concerns the Gospels' portrait of Jesus as the preeminent man of prayer. Mark 9:23 portrays Jesus of Nazareth as the man of faith par excellence, one for whom anything is possible because he always prays with unadulterated confidence in his Father's ability to move mountains (11:23). Not only is the demon-possessed boy exorcized (9:25–27) and the fig tree eventually withered (11:21–22), but all opposition to the coming kingdom is finally removed as Jesus, the perfect man of prayer, obeys his Father to the

2. Or, I might add, the historical-critical principles of skepticism, analogy, and correlation.

bitter end. The pivotal qualities of both faith and persistence are exemplified most profoundly as this story unfolds. Jesus is the ideal disciple. Granted, Matthew does not contribute to this particular aspect of Jesus as a man of prayer—he has other items on his christological agenda—but Mark, the earliest of the Gospels, introduces the image in its essential form: all things are possible for the historical Jesus because he is the quintessential man of faithful prayer (1:35–39; 6:46; 9:23–29; 11:17, 24; 14:32–39). The Gospel of Luke elaborates this aspect of the tradition until it becomes a central component of his Christology: Jesus is *the* praying Messiah, the Son of God, the prophet like Moses, the successful servant, the heavenly intercessor who accomplishes all that has been asked of him because he inhabits an Edenic atmosphere of uninhibited divine communion generated by perfect prayer.[3] The Synoptic Gospels do not explain the miraculous dimensions of Jesus's earthly existence through a doctrine of incarnation, as if he were God in disguise walking among humanity.[4] We must look to Paul (Phil. 2:6–11) or John's Gospel (John 1:1–18) for clear expressions of the life of Christ as the story of God in the flesh. Luke prefers to present Jesus as ideal humanity, the Son of God as second Adam (Luke 3:38), expressing utter dependence on the heavenly Father by means of prayer—human prayer finally prayed as God had always intended. This is the historical foundation for Christ's postresurrection role as the church's heavenly intercessor now seated at the right hand of God (Acts 7:54–60; Rom. 8:34; Heb. 7:25; 1 John 2:1). We can pray because Jesus prayed. Because Jesus prayed, Christ continues to pray. Because Christ continues to pray, we are able to pray with complete confidence.

The Synoptic Jesus also clearly teaches that the God who answers prayer remains free to accomplish his own purposes with or without our petitions. On the one hand, God chooses to perform some things only in response to our prayers. Mark explains that the disciples failed to exorcize the demon-possessed boy because none of them took the time to ask God for a miracle (9:29). Apparently, some matters remain contingent on our willingness to believe, to risk, to ask. God's freedom extends so far as to declare his people and their faith decisive factors in determining the exact contours of how his work will unfold throughout the twists and turns of history. Something as intrinsically beneficial as a child's deliverance depended on someone first having faith to pray. On

3. Luke accomplishes this through a variety of materials describing Jesus's own prayer habits. Since chapters 1–4 focused on parenetic materials addressing the disciples' prayers, most of the specific Lukan instruction does not require closer investigation here; see Crump, *Jesus the Intercessor*, passim.

4. As important as they may be, the Matthean and Lukan birth narratives fall short of anything resembling the Nicene Creed; see Crump, "Virgin Birth."

the other hand, God's grace remains perniciously free to seep through history's crevices and erupt even in those recesses never visited by either faith or prayer. This reminds us of Jesus's nontherapeutic miracles and many of his healings. God is free to work the miraculous for those who would never think to ask, just as he may withhold miracles from those who knew they should ask but never did.

God's response to prayer is shaped, not simply by what we request, but by his concern for his own divine honor and by his accomplishing what he knows to be the good. The Father makes himself entirely available to any and every plea from the people he loves, yet his eventual response is not determined by any measurable quality in the human condition as much as it is shaped by his divine determination to grant only the best of all gifts for his children. Prayer is never a blank check. The same God who is free both to withhold and to grant the things we never request is also free not to grant exactly what we do request, especially if our petitions miss the mark of either his goodness or honor. Our Father may act immediately or wait for the end of time. He may deny my petition as unwittingly suicidal, defer responding until a more appropriate moment, or reinterpret my needs entirely, deconstructing my ignorant, fleshly vision according to his own eternal panorama of grace flowing beyond measure. Nothing illustrates this aspect of God's freedom to respond as he chooses quite as profoundly as Jesus's prayers in Gethsemane. There the perfect man of prayer, who has complete confidence in God's ability, takes the risk of probing his Father's willingness to accomplish salvation while sidestepping the cross. The Father turns to his beloved Son and says no.

Jesus invites us to pray with the assurance that our prayers make a genuine difference. Our requests can influence God. But we are also told that our petitions interact with a mysterious realm of divine freedom that oftentimes obscures any apparent connection between the initial request and subsequent answers. Consequently, faith involves not only trusting in God's miraculous power but trusting that God is always responding to my prayers in his own inimitable way, regardless of whether I can see how to connect all the dots. But I must be careful not to use this observation as a pretense for slyly reintroducing the coercive claims of my own will to believe. This is not a new avenue for suggesting that I will get whatever I want after all, if only I believe that it has already been granted. Rather, it is to say that I will always get what I most need, exactly when I most need it, provided I have risked asking, have the eyes to see, and have the patience to wait. For many of us, some answers will be revealed only when the Son of Man finally appears from heaven. Will faith endure long enough to see that day?

Finally, Mark simply but unavoidably introduced the concept of the church as God's new temple (11:15–25). The community of disciples now constitutes that place where "all nations" are gathered together as God had always intended, regardless of race, color, or nationality. The temple was the locus of God's presence on earth. It was the point at which the King of heaven "touched down" so that his people might approach as closely as possible. The presence of the divine shekinah in the inner sanctum of the holy of holies was God's pledge to hear his people's prayers, to meet their needs, and to faithfully shield them in the promises of the covenant. Now those declarations of covenant faithfulness are realized around the globe among all those who look to the resurrected Jesus as their victorious King. Just as it was the godly king's responsibility to restore the Jerusalem temple after periods of Old Testament apostasy (see Josiah, Hezekiah, Judas Maccabeus),[5] so Jesus triumphantly entered the temple precincts to proclaim the arrival of God's kingdom and to cleanse the temple once again (Mark 11:15–18). Having been soundly rejected by the priesthood, however, his royal restoration took the form of an entirely new temple altogether—his people.[6] God's shekinah now dwells in the universal church. The international community of Christian faith is the earthly crossroads at which eternal power invades the world. This is why the prayers of the church matter, for we are "being built into a spiritual house to be a holy priesthood, offering spiritual sacrifices acceptable to God through Jesus Christ" (1 Pet. 2:5). The Father hears every prayer, just as he inhabits every praying heart that yearns to offer up a life of sacrificial service.

5. Hiers, "Purification of the Temple," 82–90; Runnalls, "King as Temple Builder"; and Evans, *Mark*, 178–79.

6. See Ezek. 40–48; *1 Enoch* 90.28–29; and *Psalms of Solomon* 17.30–33 for the belief that the Messiah's task included the construction of a new temple.

Praying to the Son's Father

The Lord's Prayer, part 1

Reciting the Lord's Prayer, whether kneeling in a sanctuary or seated at the family dinner table, and laying a personal claim to all that those words convey is the irrevocable birthright of every follower of Jesus Christ. Unfortunately, recitation and appropriation are often closely related strangers. How many of us know the words but fumble over the meaning of well-worn phrases repeated, sometimes hypnotically, week after week? For much of her childhood, my wife was deeply confused over why she asked God "to lead a snot into temptation." Because the AV is most commonly used for public recitation in our churches, I had my children memorize the King James version of the Lord's Prayer. Imagine my chagrin when I first heard my son pray, "Our Father, Art, in heaven; Hollowood is your name." Entirely on his own, my young son had deciphered the deeper meaning of God's full name; he is actually someone called Art Hollowood.

Of course, young children offer the most memorable and extreme examples of liturgical foot-in-mouth disease, but these stories also raise the question of whether the average adult understanding of the Lord's Prayer is any more accurate. With such questions in mind, the next three chapters will examine the Lord's Prayer in order to position its theology in relation to the other prayer teaching found throughout the Gospels. Given the overwhelming volume of literature available on this prayer, I confess that I have little new to add to the discussion, a discussion carried on much more thoroughly by many others. My goal is simply to explain, for those not familiar with it already, how the Lord's Prayer should be interpreted in light of its Jewish ancestry and then to integrate those insights into the broader New Testament theology of prayer now under construction.

The Lord's Prayer

Matthew may offer a glimpse of his familiarity with Jewish prayer habits when he introduces the Lord's Prayer as a model rather than a fixed formula; Jesus says to the disciples, "Pray like this" (6:9).[1] Perhaps this turn of phrase also helps to explain how a prayer, so sacred to the Christian church that it was often repeated only in secret in order to remain safeguarded from outsiders, has managed to come down to us in three slightly different versions (my translations):[2]

Matt. 6:9–13	Luke 11:1–4	*Didache* 8.2
Our Father in heaven,	Father,	Our Father in heaven,
may your name be sanctified,	may your name be sanctified,	may your name be sanctified,
may your kingdom come,	may your kingdom come.[3]	may your kingdom come,

1. Heinemann, *Prayer in the Talmud*, 63; Brown, "Pater Noster," 180; and Davies and Allison, *Matthew*, 1.599. Whether he knew it, Tertullian (second century AD) certainly reflects the practice of the ancient synagogue when he explains that we are free to include personal requests at the end of the Lord's Prayer; *On Prayer* 10.

2. The *Didache*, or the Teaching of the Apostles, is generally dated to the late first or early second century, although Jeremias (*Prayers of Jesus*, 84) and Brown ("Pater Noster," 177n4) place it as early as AD 50–70. Most contemporary scholarship follows Jeremias's opinion (85–93) that Luke preserves the more original form of the prayer, while Matthew retains the more original vocabulary. Others remain sympathetic, however, to Burney's argument (*Poetry of Our Lord*, 112–13) that Luke ("the mutilated version") abbreviated the original Matthean form; see Lohmeyer, *Lord's Prayer*, 27–31. As far back as Origen (*Prayer* [trans. J. J. O'Meara; New York: Newman, 1954], 66), some suggested that the Gospel versions are two different prayers; even Jeremias admitted this possibility (91). But few go so far as O'Neill ("Lord's Prayer") in suggesting that Matthew and Luke are two entirely different collections of as many as nine different prayers of Jesus. It seems clear that the *Didache* is following the prayer in Matthew, although with its own characteristics.

3. One ancient tradition substitutes the words "may your Holy Spirit come upon us and cleanse us," although few today accept its originality; see Leaney, "Lucan Text of the Lord's Prayer"; and Nolland, *Luke*, 610.

Matt. 6:9–13	Luke 11:1–4	*Didache* 8.2
may your will be done,		may your will be done,
on earth as it is in heaven.		on earth as it is in heaven.
Give us today our daily bread.	Give us each day our daily bread.	Give us today our daily bread.
Forgive us our debts,	Forgive us our sins,	Forgive us our debt,
as we also have forgiven our debtors.	for we also forgive everyone who sins against us.	as we also forgive our debtors.
And lead us not into temptation,	And lead us not into temptation.	And lead us not into temptation,
but deliver us from evil.[4]		but deliver us from evil.

All of Luke's prayer is contained in Matthew's, making the first evangelist the more comprehensive of the two. Matthew's version also divides into two equal segments, both comprised of three petitions united by parallel grammatical constructions:

address	first set	second set
our Father	may your name	give us
	may your kingdom	forgive us
	may your will	deliver us

These observations lead many to suggest that Matthew augmented the received tradition to better serve the liturgical and theological purposes of his Gospel.[5] Whether this is the case, these features make Matthew's version of the Lord's Prayer the better candidate for our attention. Consequently, the rest of this chapter will examine Matthew's opening address, "Our Father who is in heaven." The first set of petitions will be explored in chapter 6, and chapter 7 will examine the second set of Matthean requests.

Abba, Father

A former acquaintance used to deliberately address all of his prayers to "daddy" because he once heard a preacher explain that this is the

4. The doxology, "for yours is the kingdom and the power and the glory forever, amen" (the *Didache* omits "the kingdom"), is a liturgical addition not original to the Gospel; see Metzger, *Textual Commentary*, 130–31.

5. For helpful studies in the relationship between Matthew's prayer and his theology, see Finkel, "Prayer of Jesus in Matthew"; Gerhardsson, "Matthean Version of the Lord's Prayer"; Garland, "Lord's Prayer"; and Kiley, "Lord's Prayer and Matthew's Theology."

proper translation of the Aramaic word *'abbā'*, the word that Jesus used to address God as Father. I must confess that listening to my friend pray sometimes set my teeth on edge; I knew, however, how meaningful the word was and all that it conveyed to him, so I never had the heart to tell him that his pastor, though sincere, was sincerely mistaken. Unfortunately, he was not alone in promulgating a widespread misconception about *abba*.

The source for this popular misunderstanding is German scholar Joachim Jeremias (1900–1979).[6] His extensive research into the original language of Jesus and its theological significance led him to conclude that not only was Jesus unique among first-century Jews in praying to God as Father, but that he did so by exclusively using the Aramaic word *abba*, an intimate, informal address typical of young children (hence my friend's "daddy").[7] Despite *abba*'s appearing only once in the Gospel tradition (Mark 14:36), Jeremias cemented these conclusions as the cornerstone of his scholarship, asserting that his discovery offered the key to understanding all of Jesus's ministry and proclamation.[8] Jeremias's work, however, failed to withstand the tests of time and reexamination; the *abba* legacy needs to be dislodged once and for all.[9]

6. See the debate over the value of Jeremias's work in Meyer, "Caricature of Joachim Jeremias"; and E. Sanders, "Defending the Indefensible."

7. This misconception persists despite Jeremias's own attempt to correct it (*Prayers of Jesus*, 62): "One often reads (and I myself believed it at one time) that when Jesus spoke to his heavenly Father he took up the chatter of a small child. To assume this would be a piece of inadmissible naivety. . . . Even grown-up sons addressed their father as abba." For a thorough correction, see Barr, "*'Abbā* Isn't Daddy." Greek had other words to convey the nuance "daddy" (*papas, pappas, pappias, pappidion*), yet they never appear in the Bible. Whatever Jesus said, it is always translated by the normal adult word for father (*patēr*), a strange consistency indeed if Jeremias's thesis were true (Barr, "*'Abbā* Isn't Daddy," 38).

8. See Jeremias's "Kennzeichen der ipsissima vox Jesu"; "Abba" (*TLZ*); "Abba" (*ZNW*); *Central Message of the New Testament*; *Abba*; *Prayers of Jesus*; and *New Testament Theology*. Here is a typical summary from *Prayers of Jesus*, 57: "In the literature of early Palestinian Judaism there is no evidence of 'my Father' being used as a personal address to God. . . . For Jesus to address God as 'my Father' is therefore something new. . . . Of course, there are instances of God being addressed as 'pater' (Father) in the milieu of Hellenistic Judaism. But this is under Greek influence. . . . We can say quite definitely that there is *no analogy at all* in the whole literature of Jewish prayer for God being addressed as Abba" (emphasis added). Jeremias's argument has several crucial features: (1) the evidence is limited to Palestinian sources "free" of Greek influence such that any appearance of "Father" becomes suspect as a Hellenistic intrusion; (2) descriptions of God's fatherhood are irrelevant; God must be addressed as Father; (3) corporate references to "our Father" are disregarded; and (4) the significance of praying to God as "Father" is confused with the purported meaning and significance of *abba*. Not only is each of these premises a significant error in Jeremias's method, but the fourth feature provides the fatal flaw in his logic.

9. See Vermes, *Jesus the Jew*, 210–13; Fitzmyer, "Abba and Jesus' Relation to God"; Barr, "*'Abbā* Isn't Daddy"; idem, "*Abba*, Father"; Davies and Allison, *Matthew*, 1.600–603; Mawhinney, "God as Father"; VanGemeren, "Abba in the Old Testament?"; D'Angelo,

There can be no doubt that the fatherhood of God was vital to Jesus's self-understanding and therefore central to his entire ministry; neither can there be any doubt that Jesus held a very particular, unique apprehension of what that fatherhood meant for him personally, but it is confusing and misleading to assume that the legitimacy of these theological assertions depends on the viability of Jeremias's (or anyone else's) understanding of the word *abba*. Jesus's use of *abba* need not have been extensive or unique for God's distinctively intimate fatherhood to remain central to his life and teaching.[10] The questions of *abba* and divine fatherhood are two related *but separate* issues. Once the church is willing to shed the presumption that Jesus's uniqueness is somehow defined in terms of an "advance" over inferior Judaism (see the excursus at the end of this chapter)—in this instance, by the revolutionary introduction of *abba* into prayer—we are more liable to rest content with the simple recognition that Jesus's uniqueness is found in his person—not in a peculiar vocabulary, but in his personal identity.

Our Father in Heaven

T. W. Manson's classic treatment of God's fatherhood in Jesus's teaching remains as true today as when it was first written: "When Jesus spoke of God as Father he was not presenting a new and revolutionary doctrine for men's acceptance; but rather taking up into his teaching something that had been part of the faith of prophets, psalmists, and sages for centuries."[11] To call God Father entailed several equally important components in the ancient world:

"Theology in Mark and Q"; idem, "*Abba* and 'Father'"; and Charlesworth, "Caveat on Textual Transmission."

10. Many writers apparently fail to recognize the logical flaw in Jeremias's argument when he identifies (a) Jesus's use of *abba* with (b) his distinctive understanding of God's fatherhood. Charlesworth ("Caveat on Textual Transmission," 9–10), for example, is typical when he assumes that by disproving *a* he simultaneously disproves *b*. This is to commit the mirror image of Jeremias's error. In addition, all of Jeremias's key pieces of historical evidence have been undermined: (1) he claims that the Hebrew word for "my father" (*'ābî*) was thoroughly replaced by the Aramaic *'abbā'*, yet extant evidence of the first-century use of *'abbā'* remains quite rare and cannot be demonstrated before the second century (Schuller, "Psalm of 4Q372," 78); (2) the Dead Sea Scrolls (4Q372 1.16) now provide an example of what Jeremias was looking for—a Palestinian prayer from Second Temple Judaism that addresses God as "my Father" (Schuller, 67–79); and (3) Jeremias errs by ignoring the extensive Hellenization of Palestine when he neglects the numerous Jewish prayers in Greek that address God as Father.

11. Manson, *Teaching of Jesus*, 93. See also the fine survey of how deeply embedded was the fatherhood of God in early Judaism by Oesterreicher, "Abba, Father!"

1. *God is the Father-Creator.* Plato refers to God as "the maker and father of this universe" (*Timaeus* 28c), reflecting a common conviction
   in Hellenistic society.[12] Both Testaments agree with this ubiquitous
   perception, as long as Yahweh alone is acknowledged as God. The
   God of Abraham, Isaac, and Jacob is the Creator of the universe and
   all its inhabitants, the source of all life—not as progenitor, but as
   author—including humanity: "Is he not your Father, your Creator,
   / who made you and formed you?" (Deut. 32:6); "for in him we
   live and move and have our being. . . . We are his offspring" (Acts
   17:28). Consequently, humanity's proper response is to acknowledge
   complete and utter dependence. We owe the Creator everything;
   our abundance is an interest-free loan; everything that sustains life,
   offers meaning, and announces the prospects of a new day comes
   to us as a gift of the Father-Creator's mercy.

2. *God is the Father-King.* Historically, it is no exaggeration to say that
   every father was king of his castle, no matter how quaint. Similarly,
   the king was considered a father to his people, responsible for
   the protection and prosperity of the kingdom divinely entrusted
   to him. A similar reciprocal relationship between fatherhood and
   kingship is reflected in Yahweh's relationship with Israel: "A son
   honors his father, and a servant his master. If I am a father, where
   is the honor due me?" (Mal. 1:6). It is not difficult, therefore, to see
   how the privilege of lordship follows from the irresistible power
   wielded by one who creates *ex nihilo.* Our Lord God is not only
   the fatherly provider but also the sovereign ruler who commands
   the dispersion of angel-hair nebulae light years beyond the Milky
   Way while simultaneously directing the braided streams of human
   history: "Who is he, this King of glory? / The LORD Almighty— / he
   is the King of glory" (Ps. 24:10). This same King declared himself
   Father to every Davidic descendant seated on Israel's throne, simultaneously making himself the Father-King of the nation: "He
   said to me, 'You are my Son; / today I have become your Father'"
   (2:7). Consequently, to call God Father is to unconditionally pledge
   allegiance to his eternal kingship. Both the fifth and sixth benedictions of the Tefillah[13] address God as "our Father, our King,"[14] while

12. See Harner, *Understanding the Lord's Prayer,* 28–37, for a thorough discussion of
ancient extrabiblical backgrounds.

13. Discussions of these important rabbinic prayers, their role in Jewish prayer, and
their possible relevance to the Lord's Prayer may be found in the excursus at the end of
this chapter.

14. Jeremias's attempt to dismiss these as "additions" is more an assertion than an
argument; as with so much of his evidence, Jeremias forces the material to fit his conclusions (*Prayers of Jesus,* 26n59). He does, however, point out additional, early references

the designation "son" is generally reserved for covenant members demonstrably committed to wholehearted obedience.[15] A wide variety of texts, illustrated by intertestamental passages such as *Jubilees* 1.24–25[16] and *Psalms of Solomon* 17.26–27,[17] describe the realization of this filial relationship in the eschatological dawn of the kingdom when the Messiah finally leads an obedient nation of "sons" before God's throne.[18]

3. *God is the Father-Redeemer.* "You, O LORD, are our Father, / our Redeemer from of old is your name" (Isa. 63:16). Finally, Yahweh is the Father who adopts new children and goes to the most outrageously extravagant lengths to rescue them when they need help: "This is what the LORD says, Israel is my firstborn son, and I told you, 'Let my son go, so he may worship me'" (Exod. 4:22). The covenant created a new family, a family centered around grateful devotion to the deliverer. God fused his mercy to his covenant partner, freed Israel from slavery, and invited the nation to rest in his fierce devotion: "'Is not Ephraim my dear son, / the child in whom I delight? . . . / Therefore my heart yearns for him; / I have great compassion for him,' / declares the LORD" (Jer. 31:20).

The Father's election of a new nation determined that this paternal relationship was, first of all, a corporate feature of salvation-history. Here is the conceptual precedent behind the frequent collective address "Our Father." Far from making him remote or impersonal, specifying God as "our Father who is in heaven" highlights the preciousness of this filial relationship above all others.[19] Furthermore, Yahweh's fatherhood over the nation did not militate against a more personal intimacy, nor did it

---

to "our Father, our King" in the Talmud and the second morning blessing before the Shema (24–25).

15. 1QH 9.35: "You are a Father to all the sons of your truth" (Vermes, *Complete Dead Sea Scrolls*, 284). The necessity of obedience for sonship is especially highlighted in the rabbinic literature; see Jeremias, *Prayers of Jesus*, 18–19.

16. "Their souls will cleave to me and to all my commandments. And they will do my commandments. And I shall be a father to them, and they will be sons to me. And they will all be called 'sons of the living God.' And every angel and spirit will know and acknowledge that they are my sons and I am their father in uprightness and righteousness. And I shall love them" (Charlesworth, *Old Testament Pseudepigrapha*, 2.54).

17. "He will gather a holy people / whom he will lead in righteousness. . . . / For he shall know them / that they are all children of their God" (Charlesworth, *Old Testament Pseudepigrapha*, 2.667).

18. Moore, *Judaism*, 2.208–9; and Zeller, "God as Father," 119.

19. Moore, *Judaism*, 2.203–5. I am not aware of any dispute over Jeremias's claim (*Prayers of Jesus*, 16, 34) that Johanan ben Zakkai (ca. AD 50–80) offers the first rabbinic instances of the designation "heavenly Father," admitting that its popularity in the Gospel tradition indicates the adoption of a title already in popular circulation.

prevent individualized pietistic approaches to the Father-Redeemer from developing. Referring to God as "my Father" (or "Father" with a more individualistic flavor) occurs in prayers composed during times of persecution when the need for personal deliverance was felt most acutely:[20]

He said, "My Father and my God, do not abandon me to the hands of the nations." (4Q372 1.16)[21]

O Lord, Father and Master of my life,
    do not abandon me to their designs,
    and do not let me fall because of them. (Sir. 23:1 NRSV; cf. 23:4)[22]

I cried out, "Lord, you are my Father;
    do not forsake me in the days of trouble,
    when there is no help against the proud." (Sir. 51:10 NRSV)

If . . . you turn back to me with a whole heart and say, "Father," I will heed you as a holy people. (*Apocryphon of Ezekiel*, fragment 2)[23]

You, Lord, are a sweet and good and gentle father.
What father is as sweet as you, Lord? (*Joseph and Aseneth* 12.14–15)[24]

The tenderness, authority, intimacy, and unconditional demands of God's fatherhood were regularly expressed in every strain of first-century Judaism, quite apart from the word *abba*. Both Hebrew *'āb* and Greek *patēr* served the purpose equally well. Also, the significance of God's fatherhood in Judaism and the Old Testament is multidimensional. A common mistake in certain strains of contemporary interpretation is the tendency to evaluate Jesus's teaching about divine fatherhood in light of

20. Exploration of this connection is particularly helpful in D'Angelo, "Theology in Mark and Q"; and idem, "*Abba* and 'Father.'" For additional references to God as Father in Second Temple Judaism, whether individually or corporately, see Zeller, "God as Father"; Finkel, "Prayer of Jesus in Matthew," 152–68; Schuller, "Psalm of 4Q372," 75–78; D'Angelo, "Theology in Mark and Q," 151–53; O'Neill, "Lord's Prayer," 19; and Charlesworth, "Caveat on Textual Transmission," 6–8.
21. Schuller, "Psalm of 4Q372," 67–79. The translation is from Vermes, *Complete Dead Sea Scrolls*, 530.
22. Jeremias says, "Here, and only here, God is addressed by a writer from ancient Palestinian Judaism as 'my Father'" (*Prayers of Jesus*, 28). He then, however, dismisses the wording on the basis of a much later Hebrew paraphrase!
23. Translation from Charlesworth, *Old Testament Pseudepigrapha*, 1.494. It is hard to imagine that anyone following this advice would not have supplied a personalized (if silent) "my" to this attribution.
24. Translation from Charlesworth, *Old Testament Pseudepigrapha*, 2.222.

a modern focus on psychological well-being and a quest for emotional connection between parent and child.[25] While this is a perfectly appropriate task for the pastoral application of Jesus's teaching, it makes for highly anachronistic exegesis. Jesus was not a family therapist; his teaching was not a therapeutic technique for healing the psychic wounds inflicted by either distant fathers or negligent mothers, both of which can be problematic. It is equally inappropriate to label Jesus's teaching an unfortunate remnant of ancient patriarchy, as if this actually explained anything. Both Jesus and ancient Israel inhabited a world replete with powerful female deities. Patriarchy alone never deterred either the rise of female gods or the use of female imagery in a god's description.

We need to guard ourselves against importing anachronistic personalized concerns into biblical exegesis. My experience in pastoral counseling reminds me that fathers are not the only parents that children can grow to resent. If, for some reason, Jesus had referred to God as "heavenly mother" or even as "heavenly being," he would merely have replaced one set of complications with another. For every praying Christian who experiences "intense alienation" over the words "Our Father,"[26] there is another gripped with profound consolation by hearing these very same words. Each of us carries our own private history wherever we go, complete with smiles as well as skeletons, even when meeting with God. The pathway to genuine spiritual and emotional well-being does not include excising God's fatherhood from Christian theology, but ensuring that it is understood correctly, taught sensitively, and explored therapeutically whenever necessary. Otherwise, whatever our intentions, we only normalize brokenness and withhold from others the full measure of the Spirit's healing power.

God's fatherhood brings grace, mercy, salvation, forgiveness, and unending, unconditional love, but our Father in heaven also stands over us as the holy Creator, the uncontestable, irresistible, cosmic sovereign,

---

25. In my opinion, much of the modern critique of fatherhood language operates on this level; for various approaches to the ongoing debate, see M. Daly, *Beyond God the Father: Toward a Philosophy of Women's Liberation* (Boston: Beacon, 1973); R. R. Ruether, *Sexism and God-Talk: Toward a Feminist Theology* (Boston: Beacon, 1983); C. Mangan, *Can We Still Call God "Father"? A Woman Looks at the Lord's Prayer Today* (Wilmington, DE: Glazier, 1984); R. M. Frye, "On Praying 'Our Father': The Challenge of Radical Feminist Language for God," *Anglican Theological Review* 73 (1991): 388–402; J. Cooper, *Our Father in Heaven: Christian Faith and Inclusive Language for God* (Grand Rapids: Baker, 1998); J. Miller, *Calling God "Father": Essays on the Bible, Fatherhood, and Culture* (New York: Paulist Press, 1999); and M. M. Thompson, *The Promise of the Father: Jesus and God in the New Testament* (Louisville: Westminster John Knox, 2000).

26. Juel, "Lord's Prayer," 56. It is completely unwarranted to assert that "in the present moment it seems that the designation of God as Father has become flat, without contours, depth, or texture"; see Thompson, *Promise of the Father*, 157.

free to command us at the drop of a falling star. Any address to "our Father who is in heaven" must conceive the whole of God engaging the whole person—heart, mind, and will—eliciting a broad spectrum of responses: love, thankfulness, and gratitude, but also submission, obedience, and adoration.

Yet, Christianity is not completely identical with Judaism. Jesus did introduce a radically new component: himself.

Jesus the Son of the Father

The newness of Christian prayer is rooted in the uniqueness of Jesus's relationship with God. He used the same vocabulary as his contemporaries, but he harnessed familiar language to portray an unprecedented reality, a conviction arising from the depths of his own unique religious experience. Jesus was the one and only Son of the Father. Not only did Jesus claim to know God in a way that no one else ever could, but he offered himself as the only avenue for others to experience God's fatherhood themselves. Although it is true that he distinguished "my Father" from "your Father," never associating himself with the disciples in praying "our Father," the Lord's Prayer nevertheless authorizes Jesus's followers to approach God precisely as he approached God.[27]

Appreciating the value of Jesus's father language requires that we go beyond specific designations and examine the substance of his teaching about God the Father and how that relationship determined Jesus's own behavior. A crucial passage for this task is Matt. 11:25–27 ‖ Luke 10:21–22, a text sometimes dubbed "the Johannine lightning bolt" because of its similarity to language otherwise unique to John's Gospel.[28] Here Jesus coordinates the vital aspects of fatherhood, sonship, revelation, and prayer in a fashion that sets them apart as key to illuminating the significance of Jesus's invitation for others to call God Father:[29]

27. Those commentators who want to rename the Lord's Prayer the "Disciples' Prayer," as if Jesus could not repeat these words, miss this important point.

28. For a thorough examination of this passage, particularly in its Lukan version, see Crump, *Jesus the Intercessor*, 49–75. For its bearing upon the Lord's Prayer and a defense of its authenticity, see Manson, *Teaching of Jesus*, 109–13; and Fitzmyer, "Abba and Jesus' Relation to God," 36–37.

29. Manson, *Teaching of Jesus*, 94–100, and Jeremias, *Prayers of Jesus*, 29–57, remain the standard surveys of Jesus's father language. Barr thoroughly deconstructs Jeremias's implication that all of Jesus's references to Father may be traced back to *abba* ("'Abbā Isn't Daddy," 42–47). It is impossible to know if *abba* was Jesus's exclusive, periodic, or merely occasional word for father.

I praise you, Father, Lord of heaven and earth, because you have hidden these things from the wise and the learned, and revealed them to little children. Yes, Father, for this was your good pleasure. All things have been committed to me by my Father. No one knows who the Son is except the Father, and no one knows who the Father is except the Son and those to whom the Son chooses to reveal him.

Jesus characteristically prays to God as Father. The sole exception is Jesus's prayer of desperation from the cross (Mark 15:34), which is easily explained by his adherence to the language of Ps. 22:1. More telling than the reference to God as Father, however, is Jesus's self-identification as (the) Son.[30] This particular Son is *the* Son who shares a peculiar, reciprocal relationship with *his* Father. Their mutual intimacy and rapport are both unique and exclusive—"no one knows who the Son is except the Father, and no one knows who the Father is except the Son." No previous Son of God, whether wise man, prophet, or charismatic wonder-worker, could make this claim.[31] Jesus stands alone. Consequently, when Jesus invites the disciples to pray "our Father," he is able to transform an exclusive relationship into an open invitation. All those who obediently follow Jesus may now be embraced within the continuous current of divine love enveloping the Father and the Son as one.

Furthermore, in line with Jewish teaching, Jesus identified God's fatherhood with the roles of King and Creator. His Father is "Lord of heaven and earth," and Jesus submits to the Father's lordship as no one else could, for he obeys perfectly. The pivotal instance of this hard-won surrender is found in Jesus's Gethsemane prayer: "Abba, Father, . . . everything is possible for you. Take this cup from me. Yet not what I will, but what you will" (Mark 14:36). The privilege of sonship entails absolute submission to the ineluctable decisions of heaven; this one and only Son sustains an uninterrupted, unadulterated yielding to the Father's impress on his life. By their inclusion in this new Father-Son relationship, disciples not only take that yoke upon themselves but are imbued with the knowledge of its possibility.

Finally, Jesus thanks his Father for making him the sole revealer. The Father has revealed and concealed both their identities among those

30. Whether "the son" is read as a title or as a generic use of the Semitic article does not alter the final significance of the relationship. Jeremias's comparison with father-son/master-apprentice metaphors (*Prayers of Jesus*, 45–52) is frequently taken as grounds for dismissing any christological significance from these words. That conclusion does not, however, follow; neither was it Jeremias's intent: "Jesus bases his authority on the fact that God has revealed himself to him like a father to his son. 'My Father' is thus a word of revelation. It represents the central statement of Jesus' mission" (53).

31. For this title's wide range of uses in the ancient world, see Hengel, *Son of God*.

for whom the Son prays.[32] In thanking the Father, Jesus simultaneously rehearses his answered requests, thereby allowing us a brief insight into the substance of his own prayer life. The Son has stepped from heaven onto history's stage and become the praying mediator of divine revelation. For a moment he pulls back the curtain of his own prayer closet and lets us eavesdrop on his plea that the Father "open their eyes" (see Luke 10:23–24). The "things" now revealed to babes and hidden from the arrogant are Jesus's status as the only Son of the Father and Yahweh's role as the only Father of the Son. The prayer's internal logic can be outlined like this:

> A I thank you Father for revealing the nature of the Son to whomever you choose.
>> B Only the Father knows the Son.
>>> C Therefore, only the Father can reveal the Son.
>> B′ Only the Son knows the Father.
> A′ Therefore, only the Son can reveal the nature of the Father to whomever he chooses.

The Father reveals the Son; the Son reveals the Father. To experience God's fatherhood means that the Son has prayed for our eyes to be opened. To reach for God as Father means that he has responded by opening our hearts to the Son. To apprehend God as Father is to be embraced by and adopted into the heavenly family of the Father and the Son.

Praying "Our Father"

Ultimately, the full Christian significance of God's fatherhood is not uncovered by cultural-historical studies into ancient languages and Palestinian family life, as useful as they may be. Study must eventually be transformed into a personal confrontation with the man from Galilee, and in that confrontation analysis must give way to decision. Studying the Lord's Prayer does not in itself enhance anyone's ability to pray; yet, learning to pray is the very reason that the Lord's Prayer was given to us in the first place: "One day Jesus was praying in a certain place. When he finished, one of his disciples said to him, 'Lord, teach us to pray'" (Luke 11:1). The Lord's Prayer should be a reflection of Jesus's prayer life taking up residence in our own lives, sending down its roots and weaving

---

32. Luke particularly highlights this function of Jesus's prayer, while the theme is more rudimentary in Matthew's version; Crump, *Jesus the Intercessor,* 56–59, 66.

invasive tendrils throughout the fabric of our daily existence. Studying the Lord's Prayer while neglecting to participate in the existential reality of God's fatherhood is like a condemned death-row criminal minutely analyzing the governor's signature at the bottom of the pardon while refusing to exit the cell.

Jesus has become the gatekeeper of the divine, not by way of the things he taught about God's fatherhood, but through his own experience of it. He knows himself to be the only Son sent from the Father. Therefore, inviting others to the Father requires that they first come to him. Herein lies the prayer's uniqueness, for it becomes a genuine prayer only among those who have been adopted into heaven's family by first surrendering to the Father's one and only Son. The ancient church's efforts to guard the Lord's Prayer against abuse by teaching it only to catechized believers reflects their appreciation of this fact.[33] These are not words to be memorized and rotely repeated at the correct place in the liturgy. Rather, understanding the conceptual contours of God's fatherhood ought, ideally, to augment an increasingly stark, defining experience of being loved and owned by heaven. May our prayers to "our Father who is in heaven" do the same for us today.

Excursus: Jewish Prayer at the Time of Jesus

Baruch Graubard, late professor of postbiblical Judaism at the University of Marburg, tells how he first encountered the Lord's Prayer while hiding from the Nazis under a false identity in a Franciscan monastery. By sharing in the Catholic services he says that he was able to rediscover "a token" of his Jewish identity by reciting the Lord's Prayer: "[It] was like a Jewish prayer, like an abbreviation of the Prayer of the Eighteen Benedictions" (the central prayer in Jewish piety).[34] This identification is no accident; the Lord's Prayer sounds like a Jewish prayer precisely because it *is* a Jewish prayer, distinctive in its own right but thoroughly Jewish nonetheless.

Unfortunately, Christian scholarship has a long history of misrepresenting the Jewish religion for its own theological purposes. Sadly, validating Christian piety has sometimes depended on denigrating Jewish piety. Thus Christian prayer, tracing its impetus back to Jesus, was a free, spontaneous, intimate expression of heartfelt devotion to a personal God, whereas Jewish prayer, the precedent from which Jesus

---

33. For the prayer's use in the early church, see Chase, *Lord's Prayer in the Early Church* (still the classic treatment of this issue); Manson, "Lord's Prayer"; Bahr, "Use of the Lord's Prayer"; Rordorf, "Lord's Prayer"; and Stuckwisch, "Principles of Christian Prayer."

34. Graubard, "*Kaddish* Prayer," 61.

thankfully shook himself free, was a calculated, rote, impersonal expression of ritual obligation to a distant God. Granted, this caricature describes only the worst examples of misrepresentation, but even more moderate authors frequently lean in the same direction. For example, Gerhard Kittel, the founding editor of the ten-volume *Theological Dictionary of the New Testament*, offers this observation on the father language of the Lord's Prayer in his influential article "Ἀββᾶ": "Jewish usage shows how this Father-child relationship to God far surpasses any possibilities of intimacy assumed in Judaism, introducing indeed something which is wholly new."[35] In other words, Jesus was Jewish but not too Jewish. The significance of Christian prayer is found in its superiority over Jewish prayer. Christian readers want points of connection between the New Testament and the ancient Palestinian heritage that gave birth to Jesus of Nazareth, but we tend to mold the elusive carpenter into someone that James Charlesworth calls a "bewitching oxymoron," a Jew who is not really Jewish after all.[36] This method, however, will never lead us to an honest appreciation of the Lord's Prayer. Jewish piety must be studied on its own terms—not misconstrued for the purposes of a preconceived Christian agenda. Keeping such warnings in mind will prepare us to examine the two ancient prayers most relevant to study of the Lord's Prayer: the Tefillah and the Kaddish.[37] Before looking at those prayers, however, we also need to understand two methodological complications that bear on any study of first-century Jewish prayer.

The first problem involves the question of dating. The primary source materials of Jewish prayer are found in the various Qumran prayer texts uncovered among the Dead Sea Scrolls,[38] the pseudepigraphal literature,[39] and the rabbinic texts known as the Mishnah, Talmud, and Siddur.[40] While each of these collections preserves information from the

35. Kittel, "Ἀββᾶ," 6. Similar examples could be multiplied many times over.

36. Charlesworth, "Caveat on Textual Transmission," 5.

37. If this were simply a study of Jewish prayer, we must of course begin with the Shema, the twice daily recitation of Deut. 6:4–9; 11:13–21; and Num. 15:37–41, which lay at the heart of all Jewish devotion. Strictly speaking, however, the Shema was "not a prayer at all" but "a pledge of allegiance, an oath of loyalty to God the king, followed by a pledge to obey the laws of the king" (Hammer, *Entering Jewish Prayer*, 121, 131; see 121–55 for the complete discussion). The individual first hears (*šāmaʿ*) God's self-revelation and then recites the revelation back to God as an act of submission.

38. The Qumran texts are all pre-Christian; relevant prayers from both Qumran and the Pseudepigrapha will be discussed at the appropriate junctures of our study.

39. For prayer in the Pseudepigrapha, see N. Johnson, *Prayer in the Apocrypha and Pseudepigrapha*; Crump, *Jesus the Intercessor*, 204–31; Charlesworth, "Jewish Prayers"; and Werline, *Penitential Prayer*.

40. The Mishnah is the codification of the oral Torah under the sponsorship of Rabbi Judah ha-Nasi (the Prince) (ca. AD 135–210). The Talmud in turn is the later rabbinic

first century AD (and earlier), disentangling the early traditions from later, post-Christian developments, especially in the rabbinic texts, is not only an arduous task that must be attended to quite closely, but one that many Christian scholars are ill equipped to perform.[41] Assuming that all rabbinic discussions offer an unbiased glimpse into first-century Judaism is a major methodological mistake found in past New Testament scholarship, a mistake that we would do well to avoid today.

The second related issue is that during Jesus's lifetime, and for many centuries thereafter, it was forbidden to write a prayer. Rabbinic tradition voices strong prohibitions against not only writing out a prayer but the recitation of fixed prayers.[42] For example, tractate *Shabbat* 115b in the Babylonian Talmud says, "Those who write down benedictions [i.e., prayers] are as though they burned the Torah." A sharp distinction was made between the written and the oral law; the two ought not to be confused or mixed. Since prayers were a part of the oral tradition, writing them down was an impious assault against the written tradition of Scripture. Similarly, the Mishnah forbids the recitation of memorized prayers: "One who makes his prayer a fixed task—his prayers are not [valid] supplications [of God]" (tractate *Berakhot* 4.4).[43] The motivation behind such prohibitions was the fear that set prayers too easily became rote ceremonies no longer expressing the heartfelt intentions, confessions, requests, and deliberations of the pious individual standing face to face before God. Authentic prayer was spontaneous, personal, expressed in one's own words, and characterized by *kavanah*, that is,

---

exposition (largely third to fifth centuries) of the Mishnah. The Siddur is the Jewish prayer book, which was not written until the ninth century. As one can see by the dates involved, the reader must be very careful not to assume that all rabbinic evidence is automatically pertinent to the New Testament period. A great deal of evolutionary development took place in Judaism between the destruction of Jerusalem, the eventual establishment of rabbinic religion, and the medieval standardization of synagogue prayer. For a good introduction to the creation of the Siddur, see Di Sante, *Jewish Prayer*, 27–31; and Hammer, *Entering Jewish Prayer*, 96–99. More technical discussions may be found in Hoffman, *Canonization of the Synagogue Service*; and Reif, *Judaism and Hebrew Prayer*, 122–52.

41. Now see the important work by David Instone-Brewer, *Traditions of the Rabbis from the Era of the New Testament*, vol. 1, *Prayer and Agriculture* (Grand Rapids: Eerdmans, 2004). Unfortunately, I was unable to consult Instone-Brewer's work before completing this manuscript. However, his results do not require any substantive changes to my argument.

42. Moore, *Judaism*, 2.219–21; Bahr, "Use of the Lord's Prayer," 157; and B. Martin, *Prayer in Judaism*, 10.

43. The word for "fixed task" (*qb'*) appears often in such discussions and is defined as "repeating a set text, not using one's own words, or using the same words day after day"; see Moore, *Judaism*, 2.221. All Mishnah translations are from J. Neusner, *The Mishnah: A New Translation* (New Haven: Yale University Press, 1988).

focused, spiritual concentration.[44] As the Mishnah says, "Be meticulous in the recitation of the Shema and the Prayer [the Tefillah]. When you pray, do not treat your praying as a matter of routine. But let it be a [plea for] mercy and supplication before the Omnipresent, blessed be he" (tractate *Avot* 2.13).

The Tefillah ("Prayer") is the first prayer with which we should be familiar. Also known as the Amidah ("Standing [Prayer]") or the Shemoneh Esreh ("Eighteen [Benedictions]"), the Tefillah was the central prayer of Second Temple Judaism, at least among the adherents of Pharisaism. There is no certainty that the Tefillah (or its ancestor) is representative of non-Pharisaic or nonrabbinic prayer.[45] It is, however, central to the Pharisaic-rabbinic tradition. The Tefillah consists of eighteen (sometimes nineteen) benedictions or blessings that follow a threefold pattern of praise (first three), petition (middle twelve or thirteen), and thanksgiving (final three).[46] These blessings were recited three times each day: morning and evening in conjunction with the Shema, and midday on its own. There is a general consensus that the roots of the Tefillah go back at least several centuries before the destruction of the second temple in AD 70, circulating in a variety of different forms until Rabbi Gamaliel II (ca. AD 90–110) moved toward standardization at the legendary council of Yavneh at the end of the first century.[47] Rabbinic evidence, however, also demonstrates that a significant amount of diversity regarding both the order and the number of benedictions continued well after the formalization of the Mishnah in the late second/early third century. In fact, until that time there was probably no common order to the middle section of the prayer. The Tefillah was not something to be memorized verbatim; it was an outline, a general organizational plan for personal prayer, not a set liturgical pattern.[48] Each of the benedictions focused the individual's attention on a specific feature

44. On *kavanah*, see B. Martin, *Prayer in Judaism*, 20; and Steinsaltz, *Guide to Jewish Prayer*, 34–44.

45. E. Sanders, *Judaism*, 203–5. The Tefillah has not been found among the sectarian texts at Qumran. An abundance of Qumranian and pseudepigraphal prayer texts may provide better evidence of what typical personalized prayer was like within non-Pharisaic circles at the time.

46. For a detailed exposition of the Tefillah, see B. Martin, *Prayer in Judaism*, 113–38; Di Sante, *Jewish Prayer*, 78–112; and Hammer, *Entering Jewish Prayer*, 156–97. Rather than outlining all nineteen benedictions, I simply elaborate on the most relevant portions of the Tefillah while examining each petition of the Lord's Prayer.

47. It is often noted that the Tefillah shares a number of parallels with the Hebrew version of Sir. 38 and 51 (dating to the second century BC); Heinemann, *Prayer in the Talmud*, 218–20; and Hoffman, *Canonization of the Synagogue Service*, 24, 50.

48. Heinemann, *Prayer in the Talmud*, 47, 51; Hoffman, *Canonization of the Synagogue Service*, 4, 50; Zahavy, *Studies in Jewish Prayer*, 12–16, 24; Reif, *Judaism and Hebrew Prayer*, 124; and E. Sanders, *Judaism*, 203. Reif argues that there is no extant evidence of

of the divine-human relationship, but at each juncture the worshiper was to spontaneously compose his or her own prayers with regard to that particular concern. Additional personal matters could either be expressed at the end or inserted into the sixteenth benediction (a prayer for forgiveness asking that God mercifully hear our requests) as one saw fit.[49] If such an approach to congregational prayer sounds potentially chaotic, it would have been what J. Heinemann calls "structural chaos,"[50] for, as E. P. Sanders observes, "first century Jews probably did not do anything in unison. . . . If Jews were in a synagogue at a time for prayer . . . they may all have prayed, but not necessarily precisely the same prayer, and probably not in unison."[51]

Similar flexibility persisted within the second relevant prayer, the Kaddish.[52] This prayer originally served as the benediction recited by both preacher and congregation at the end of every synagogue homily, although it eventually became known as the mourners' prayer due to its later inclusion in the funeral liturgy. The Kaddish is a request for the sanctification of God's name through the imminent establishment of his kingdom on earth, an association (between sanctifying the name and establishing God's kingdom) traceable to the prophet Ezekiel (36:23–31; 38:23). Although no one knows when the Kaddish originated,[53] the majority of scholars date its beginnings prior to the time of Jesus because (1) its theological affinity links it with the exilic prophet Ezekiel;[54] (2) unlike the Shema and Tefillah, it was recited in Aramaic;[55] (3) it appears to be a well-established part of the synagogue service that, many suggest, began its development during the Babylonian exile;[56] and (4) it exhibits several important similarities to the Lord's Prayer.[57] Jeremias postulates that the oldest form of the Kaddish was as follows:

---

the Tefillah's middle section existing prior to AD 70 and no set structure at all prior to the Tannaim in the second and third centuries (60, 84).

49. The appropriate place for prayers unrelated to any of the benedictions was debated; see Moore, *Judaism*, 2.214–19.

50. Heinemann, *Prayer in the Talmud*, 156.

51. E. Sanders, *Judaism*, 207.

52. For good explorations of the Kaddish, see Pool, *Kaddish*; Graubard, "*Kaddish* Prayer"; Di Sante, *Jewish Prayer*, 171–73; and Hammer, *Entering Jewish Prayer*, 281–85.

53. B. Martin, *Prayer in Judaism*, 148, asserts that the Kaddish originated in Palestine during the first century BC. Hoffman, *Canonization of the Synagogue Service*, 56, conjectures a Pharisaic origin.

54. Pool, *Kaddish*, 27.

55. Jeremias, *Prayers of Jesus*, 76. Aramaic was probably the language spoken by Jesus.

56. Pool, *Kaddish*, 1–2, 8–9.

57. Admittedly, this final point is something of a circular argument: the Kaddish is assumed to go back to the first century because of its similarity to a first-century prayer

> May His great name be magnified and sanctified
>   According to His will in the world he created.
> May He establish His kingdom in our lifetime, in our days,
>   and in the lifetime of the house of Israel, speedily and soon—
>   and to this say: Amen.[58]

Similarities to the first half of the Lord's Prayer are not hard to find.

Finally, it would be a mistake to leave the impression that first-century Jewish prayer was permissible at only certain places during certain times of the day. Nothing could be further from the truth. Private prayer throughout the day was strongly encouraged, particularly in the form of frequent blessings or benedictions (*berakhot*). These blessings acknowledged God's goodness and creative power by recognizing our dependence and thanking him for his faithfulness in caring for us. Consequently, not only are we to offer a blessing over every meal, but at the spontaneous events of everyday life; benedictions are prescribed at the sight of meteors, earthquakes, lightning, thunder, wind, mountains, hills, sea, rivers, even desert, as well as when building a new home or buying new clothes (Mishnah, tractate *Berakhot* 9.1–3). Each occasion gives reason to pause, reflect, and thank God for a new experience of divine goodness. Every moment of every day was to be lived in a continuous self-conscious state of thankfulness at the mercy, generosity, and faithfulness of our gracious Savior God.[59] Prayer with *kavanah* sanctified life as a sacred dance, the holy leading the mundane.

---

taught by Jesus; then the prayer taught by Jesus is interpreted in light of the (supposedly) first-century Kaddish. This is a common weakness in biblical studies, but the problem is not insurmountable as long as the tenuous nature of its results are kept in mind; see Jeremias, *Prayers of Jesus*, 76–78, 98–99, for the classic discussion of the relevance of the Kaddish to the study of the Lord's Prayer.

58. Jeremias, *Prayers of Jesus*, 98. For a more expansive and presumably later form, see Hammer, *Entering Jewish Prayer*, 282–83. I follow Jeremias's form but Hammer's more modern wording.

59. For an excellent discussion of the priority of intimacy between the individual and God, see Charlesworth, "Jewish Prayers." The importance of *berakhot* will be explored more thoroughly when we examine Paul's teaching on prayer.

6

God's Will and Our Wishes

The Lord's Prayer, part 2

The phrase 'if it be thy will' is more often than not a cop-out. It means I don't have to come to grips with God. . . . 'If it be thy will' is lazy pseudoreverence."[1]

Hmm.

These were disturbing words when I first read them as a twenty-one-year-old keenly investigating the meaning of prayer and how I might cultivate a deeper devotional life. I was immediately struck by the suspicion that Jesus might have a problem with this statement. Was he displaying pseudoreverence when he wept and prayed in Gethsemane, "Not my will, but yours," or when he taught the disciples to say, "Your will be done"? I suspect that this author did not intend his lesson to be as narrow as his rhetoric. Yet, there is a long-standing tradition within fundamentalist and evangelical circles asserting that true prayer is not only exclusively petitionary but persistently specific. Anything else fails to qualify as genuine prayer.[2]

---

1. J. White, *Daring to Draw Near: People in Prayer and People Open to God* (Downers Grove, IL: InterVarsity, 1977), 19.

2. For another contemporary example, see J. Bisagno, *The Power of Positive Prayer: Provocative Hints for Peace and Power through Confident Prayer* (Grand Rapids: Zondervan,

If you have read the previous chapters of this book, you know already that the concerns of this particular school of piety are, indeed, an important component of New Testament teaching. Jesus is clear that the person who prays in faith not only asks specifically but has the faith to ask specifically for miracles. Virtues, however, can become vices when taken to extremes. Just ask the young lady who unwittingly transforms from a conscientious dieter into an emaciated specter hospitalized for anorexia.

Unfortunately, the most dangerous extremism often arrives in a religious package. I sometimes tell my students that there is no extremist like a religious extremist. It is easy to become so entranced by a good idea, especially when passion is fueled by the fires of religious conviction, that we ignore all else, forgetting that in the complexities of the real world even good ideas are regularly constrained by equally good or even better ideas. This is no less true of Christian theology than it is of political policy; even the best theological concepts must always be integrated within the full spectrum of biblical teaching. We are not free to pick and choose among the more personally appealing pieces of theology while ignoring the unsavory remainder. God's revelation is to be imbibed, not grazed selectively. To do so surrenders the authority of Scripture to the tyranny of personal preference—the very antithesis of true discipleship. When a person is driven by a conviction that his or her beliefs are the best for everybody, regardless of individual circumstances, one had better (at the very least) be thoroughly versed in all the evidence and options and possess a comprehensive explanation for why a particular position is clearly preferable before taking the audacious step of insisting that his or her case trumps all others.[3] An isolated doctrine is a dangerous doctrine. This is why systematic theology must always hold itself responsible to reflect the full spectrum of scriptural evidence.

1972), 9–10: "God can only answer specific prayer. . . . Answered prayer is not a miracle, it is a *law*. It *will* always be, when the laws are kept and certain rules are observed" (emphasis original). Ostrander, *Life of Prayer*, 35–55, offers a fascinating study of the roots of this brand of theology in the late-nineteenth-century "answered prayer movement" and the pivotal role it played in evangelical apologetics responding to scientific empiricism—specific answers to specific prayers offered the best tangible "proof" for the existence of God. Charles Blanchard, an early president of Wheaton College, states it plainly in his book, *Getting Things from God*: "If there is no request, there is no prayer" (cited in Ostrander, 39).

3. I am not saying that this can never be the case. Many people believe that proclaiming Christ as the only Savior of the world is just such an audacious statement. Irreconcilable differences are sometimes unavoidable. Trusting in the Spirit rather than our rhetoric to persuade, however, goes a long way toward separating humble conviction from corrosive zeal. As Paul says in Phil. 3:15b–16: "If you have come to a different opinion, God will make things clear to you. Only behave in a manner consistent with maturity" (my translation).

Somehow we must find a way to act upon two equally vital truths: (1) Jesus invites every believer to confidently bring specific requests to God's throne while (2) simultaneously requiring that we humbly surrender personal interests to the Father's plan. How do these two expectations fit together? Before reaching for one of the several theological solutions available for this conundrum (something saved for chapter 14), we must complete an examination of the Lord's Prayer, one place where this ask/surrender tension is presented most starkly. Understanding these six petitions should enable us to avoid the extremist ditch, whether to the right or to the left, while offering the tools necessary for constructing a proper theology.

May Your Name Be Sanctified

The prayer's first concern is the glory of God. By making this the first petition, Jesus not only reveals his own priorities in life but insists that they become the priorities of every disciple. It is essential, therefore, to understand Jesus's intent clearly.

God's Name

The name is a circumlocution for God's own person. To know the name is to know the individual. When Jesus prays, "Father, glorify your name!" (John 12:28), he asks the Father to exalt himself before the watching world. As Moses conversed with a burning bush, he asked for the name of this unusual flaming God who had called out, "Moses, Moses!" Yahweh answered Moses's request by explaining that his name is "I AM," Yahweh, the faithful covenant-keeping God of Abraham, Isaac, and Jacob (Exod. 3:4, 13–15). When Moses expressed doubts about his ability to complete God's mission, Yahweh offered this assurance: "I will be with you" (3:12). As God gives his name to Moses, he also gives himself and reveals his nature; he is the God of covenant faithfulness who promises always *to be with* his people, never to leave them or forsake them.[4]

Similarly, when Jeremiah castigates the Israelite priesthood for desecrating the Jerusalem temple, his horror springs from the knowledge that Yahweh had made the temple his dwelling place: "Has this house,

4. The Tetragrammaton, YHWH, is lexically related to the Hebrew verb "to be." This promise of God's presence, together with his identification with the patriarchs, establishes the context for understanding Yahweh's claim that "I AM WHO I AM" or, better yet, "I WILL BE WHAT I WILL BE" (Exod. 3:14). God's name is not a metaphysical statement of divine ontology (I am the ground of all being) as much as it is a revelation of divine character and personhood (I am always faithfully in relationship with you, fulfilling my promises).

which bears my Name, become a den of robbers to you?" (Jer. 7:11). The temple bore God's name because it was God's residence. The name and the person are one.[5]

Praying "hallowed be your name" asks that God do something for himself. What might that be? A more modern rendering of the Greek word *hagiazein* ("to hallow, to sanctify") yields, "May your name be sanctified."[6] God's name, or person, is sanctified by his exaltation, not only among his people, although this is where it begins, but ultimately throughout all the people of the earth.[7] It is his global glorification. Ezekiel speaks to the nations, explaining Yahweh's plan for Israel's restoration: "In days to come, O Gog, I will bring you against my land, so that the nations may know me when I show myself to be holy through you before their eyes" (38:16). Thus the first petition of the Lord's Prayer is a request for God the Father, Creator, King, and Redeemer to be publicly recognized as awesome, merciful, majestic, righteous, holy, tender, and terrible throughout every dimension of creation, in heaven and on earth and under the earth as every knee bows and every tongue confesses the glory of the one and only God (Isa. 45:23; cf. Phil. 2:10).

Another important feature of this verb is that it is passive. The subject is not expressed. Who, exactly, is supposed to bring about the Father's sanctification? There are several possibilities, but I am persuaded, along with the majority of commentators, that the verb serves as a divine passive.[8] In other words, God is the implied subject. Eager to avoid even

5. For other texts illustrating the identification of the name and the person, see Gen. 32:28–29; 2 Sam. 6:2; Isa. 29:23; 52:6; Ezek. 36:22–28; 39:7, 25; Amos 9:12; Zech. 14:9; Mal. 1:6; John 17:6; Rom. 9:17.

6. A rare word outside the Greek Bible, *hagiazein* regularly translates some form of the Hebrew *qdš* ("holy") in the Septuagint. "To sanctify the name" became a traditional Hebrew formula for the public display of God's holiness (Lev. 22:32; Isa. 29:23; Ezek. 36:23; *1 Enoch* 61.12; Babylonian Talmud, tractate *Yevamot* 79a); see Davies and Allison, *Matthew*, 1.602. For additional examples of Yahweh sanctifying himself, see Lev. 10:3; Num. 20:13; Isa. 5:16; Ezek. 20:41; 28:22.

7. Schürmann, *Praying with Christ*, 23–25; Lohmeyer, *Lord's Prayer*, 69–70; and Davies and Allison, *Matthew*, 1.602–3.

8. Nolland, *Luke*, 613–14, provides a good overview of the options: (1) God is being asked to glorify himself, a distinctly eschatological expectation (Ezek. 36:23); or (2) we are asking for the ability to bring glory to God, a position that can be further divided into two possibilities: (a) we are asking for the eschatological consummation when all the world will glorify God (Isa. 29:23); or (b) we are making the noneschatological request that God's name be obediently glorified among his people here and now (à la Lev. 19:2: "Be holy because I, the LORD your God, am holy"). Ancient commentators tended toward option 2b; see Origen, *On Prayer* 26.2, 6; Tertullian, *On Prayer* 4; and Gregory of Nyssa, *Lord's Prayer*, sermon 3. Most modern commentators, on the other hand, prioritize eschatology by choosing option 1. Some argue for a combination of options 1 and 2, as I will. Nolland argues for option 2b because "it provides a closer fit with Jewish prayer practice . . . and its wider scope leads on more naturally to the petitions of the rest of the prayer" (614).

inadvertent slights to God's holiness, ancient Judaism devised various circumlocutions that would allow a person to talk about God without actually using the divine name (e.g., "Do not get into the habit of swearing [oaths], / do not make a habit of naming the Holy One"; Sir. 23:9 NJB). For instance, Matthew refers to the kingdom of heaven rather than the kingdom of God. Employing the divine passive was another common technique. For example: "In the same way you judge others, you will be judged [by God], and with the measure you use, it will be measured to you [by God]" (Matt. 7:2); or, "So will it be with the resurrection of the dead. The body that is sown [by God] is perishable, it is raised [by God] imperishable" (1 Cor. 15:42).[9]

What Is Distinctive about This Petition?

Even though this first petition shares the same Old Testament background as other Jewish prayers, we have seen that Jesus's distinctive awareness of God's fatherhood distinguishes this request from similar Jewish prayers such as the Kaddish, another ancient prayer linking the sanctification of God's name with the establishment of his kingdom on earth (see the excursus in chapter 5). Disciples are told to pray for God's final, complete self-revelation. Thus we ask that the Father thoroughly unveil his (currently unacknowledged) majesty for every creature to behold, great and small, temporal and eternal. More specifically, a vital precedent found in the Old Testament prophet Ezekiel indicates that God finally accomplishes just such a revelation by consummating Israel's redemption. Yahweh consoled the exiled nation by promising it the future forgiveness of all its sins, restoration to the promised land, and the renewal of his presence:

> Therefore say to the house of Israel, "This is what the Sovereign LORD says: It is not for your sake, O house of Israel, that I am going to do these things, but for the sake of my holy name, which you have profaned among the nations where you have gone. I will show the holiness of my great name, which has been profaned among the nations, the name you have profaned among them. Then the nations will know that I am the LORD, declares the Sovereign LORD, when I show myself holy through you before their eyes." (Ezek. 36:22–23; see also 38:16, 23; 39:7–8, 21–29)

Must, however, Jesus's prayers always repeat Jewish practice? Also, there is more than one way to find a natural connection between the first set of petitions and the second. Both issues will be explored more thoroughly below.

9. A representative, but far from comprehensive, list of additional examples includes Mark 4:24; Matt. 7:7; Luke 6:38; 12:20; 2 Pet. 3:14; see Blass, Debrunner, and Funk, *Greek Grammar of the New Testament* §130.1–2, §313, §342.1. For a good discussion of the divine passive in Jesus's teaching, see Jeremias, *New Testament Theology*, 9–14.

Immediately following this amazing redemptive declaration, the Lord adds the promise of a new covenant:

> I will take you out of the nations; I will gather you from all the countries and bring you back into your own land. I will sprinkle clean water on you, and you will be clean; I will cleanse you from all your impurities and from all your idols. I will give you a new heart and put a new spirit in you; I will remove from you your heart of stone and give you a heart of flesh. And I will put my Spirit in you and move you to follow my decrees and be careful to keep my laws. You will live in the land I gave your forefathers; you will be my people, and I will be your God. I will save you from all your uncleanness. (Ezek. 36:24–29)

Ultimately, God alone is capable of sanctifying his name. And, quite remarkably, the most profound declaration of the Father's holiness is his gracious redemption of his rebellious Israel.[10] Only he can perform this miracle, and ultimately these promises are not fulfilled until the work of his Messiah, Jesus Christ, is complete. Once again, we see that Jesus—his person, identity, and mission—lay at the heart of the prayer's significance. Jesus, after all, inaugurated the new covenant (Acts 2:14–24; Heb. 8). Consequently, in asking the Father to sanctify his name, we make the fulfillment of God's salvific work through Abraham, Israel, and finally through Christ our deepest, most passionate longing. We yearn for the speedy return of "the Son of Man coming in the clouds with great power and glory" (Mark 13:26), surrounded by legion upon legion of archangels shouting, "Holy, holy, holy is the LORD Almighty; / the whole earth is full of his glory" (Isa. 6:3). We ache for this Father of the one and only Son to be finally, irresistibly acknowledged by all as the All in All, the compassionate Redeemer-King who gladly made the ultimate sacrifice for the humanity—for the universe—he so desperately loves: the offering of his Son.

Asking for the sanctification of God's name was a typical feature of Jewish prayer. The first petition of the Kaddish asks, "May his great name be magnified and sanctified according to his will in the world he created."[11] The third benediction of the Tefillah, called the "Kiddush ha-Shem" ("Sanctifying the Name"), says, "You are holy, and your name is holy. Holy beings praise you every day. Blessed are you, Lord, holy God."[12] Pharisaic-rabbinic Judaism typically understood God's name

10. "Deliver us in accordance with your marvelous works, / and bring glory to your name, O Lord" (*Prayer of Azariah* 20 NRSV). For additional extrabiblical examples of God sanctifying his name through his people, see Sir. 36:4, 17–22; Bar. 2:11; 3:5; 3 Macc. 2:9; 2 Esdras (= 4 Ezra) 1:24; 2:16; 7:60; 9:8.

11. See Jeremias, *Prayers of Jesus*, 98; and Hammer, *Entering Jewish Prayer*, 282.

12. Donin, *To Pray as a Jew*, 81; and Hammer, *Entering Jewish Prayer*, 169. The first three benedictions of the Tefillah are among those with the greatest likelihood of going

to be sanctified in the same way that it was profaned: by the actions of his people. For example, reciting the third benediction of the Tefillah "sanctifies God's name" through the praises of his praying people. The rabbis exposited the previously mentioned texts from Ezekiel with reference to Lev. 19:2, "Be holy because I, the LORD your God, am holy," and 22:31–32, "Keep my commands and follow them. I am the LORD. Do not profane my holy name. I must be acknowledged as holy by the Israelites. I am the LORD, who makes you holy." The belief that hallowing the name occurred when one's actions caused others to recognize God's greatness eventually led to a conviction that martyrdom was the ultimate expression of Kiddush ha-Shem.[13]

Obviously, if Jesus intended the first petition to refer exclusively to human behavior, then it is a mistake to read the verb "to sanctify" as a divine passive. Jesus would be making an ethical statement reminiscent of the teaching found in Matt. 5:16: "Let your light shine before men, that they may see your good deeds and praise your Father in heaven"; and 5:48: "Be perfect, therefore, as your heavenly Father is perfect." If Jesus were simply another rabbi, a purely ethical interpretation becomes the most likely interpretation. Jesus was not a rabbi, however, at least not in the technical sense.[14] His theology was finally determined by his unique self-consciousness and identity, not by the traditions of the elders. Jesus understood his role to be supremely eschatological. He was inaugurating the last days. This fundamental point leads many commentators to reject the possibility of any ethical content to this petition; it is solely eschatological.

---

back to the first century or earlier. A later prayer called Kedusha, a liturgical poem known as a *piyyut* that was sometimes incorporated within the Kiddush ha-Shem, elaborates: "We will hallow your name in this world as they hallow it in the heavens above, As it is written by your prophet: And one would call to the other—'Holy, holy, holy! The Lord of Hosts! His presence fills all the earth'" (cited from Hammer, *Entering Jewish Prayer*, 171).

13. Young, *Jewish Background of the Lord's Prayer*, 8–9; and Hammer, *Entering Jewish Prayer*, 282.

14. Despite the popularity of this misconception, it is unsubstantiated; see the excellent analysis in Hengel, *Charismatic Leader*, 42–57. Though Jesus is called "rabbi" in the Gospel tradition, the word simply means "my master," hardly the technical term it eventually became after the Roman destruction of the temple; see also Chilton, *Pure Kingdom*, 46–47. Jesus obviously exhibits many affinities to his multidimensional religious and cultural environments, but he is not obligated to, or constrained by, any one in particular. Hengel's conclusion that "Jesus stood outside *any discoverable uniform teaching tradition of Judaism*" (emphasis original) is definitive. Far too many New Testament researchers, especially those with a particular interest in Jewish backgrounds, appear to assume that Palestinian Judaism was the *only* influence on Jesus and that all Judaism was Pharisaic-rabbinic Judaism. The logic appears to run something like this: Jewish thought = rabbinic thought = Jesus's thought. Each of these assumptions is completely untrue.

Why, however, cannot the petition be read as *both* eschatological and ethical, simultaneously? Must we choose between only one or the other? Some commentators, in fact, do argue for a twofold understanding of hallowing the name.[15] And I am persuaded of this position *as long as the priority of the Father's work remains central*: we look for Yahweh to bring the denouement. Jesus *first* teaches disciples to yearn for the Father's ultimate, eternal glorification in the return of Christ and the establishment of the new heavens and the new earth. We are emphatically reminded of our total dependence on God to perform his own work in his own timing, something the early church reinforced each time it cried out in worship, "Maranatha—Come, O Lord" (1 Cor. 16:22). Then and only then are we free to consider an important secondary dimension: that Jesus's disciples must meanwhile walk a daily path of preparation for his coming in joyful surrender and the consequent obedience proving our devotion true. As we wait for the Father to act, there are proper and improper ways to pass the time. An authentic disciple never forgets that, finally, she is known by her fruit, and a good tree does not produce bad fruit (Matt. 7:16–20).

May Your Kingdom Come

"The programmatic centre of Jesus's ministry was not the concept of love, but that of God's rule."[16] The second of the Lord's petitions reflects this kingdom priority, not only by illuminating the first petition, but by bringing the proclamation of Jesus to center stage. Chapter 5 has already shown the natural connection within Judaism between God's fatherhood and his kingship. Blessings 2, 8, and 11 of the Tefillah refer to Yahweh as Israel's rightful King, while benedictions 5 and 6 extol him as "our Father, our King." Blessings 10, 11, 14, 15, and 17 all invoke the reestablishment of one aspect or another of God's kingdom on earth, such as the regathering of Israel into the promised land (10), national surrender to the yoke of God's rule (11), the enthronement of a Davidic king on the Jerusalem throne (14–15), and the restoration of the Jerusalem temple (17). The Kaddish understands the sanctification of God's name to occur in the kingdom's arrival on earth:

> May His great name be magnified and sanctified
>   According to His will in the world he created.
> May He establish His kingdom in our lifetime, and in our days.

15. Hagner, *Matthew*, 1.148; and Cullmann, *Prayer in the New Testament*, 44.
16. Chilton and McDonald, *Jesus and the Ethics of the Kingdom*, 3.

The establishment of God's glory in this earthly kingdom is also a significant concern in the pseudepigraphal literature and the Dead Sea Scrolls, especially among those works highlighted with an apocalyptic brush.[17] *Psalms of Solomon* 17 is an extensive praise poem anticipating the final establishment of God's glorious kingship over all nations once the Davidic Messiah is revealed and assumes his Jerusalem throne.[18] In a similar vein, the Qumran community could say:

> You are terrible, O God, in the glory of Your kingdom, and the congregation of Your Holy Ones is among us for everlasting support. We will depose kings, we will mock and scorn the mighty; for our Lord is holy, and the King of Glory is with us together with the Holy Ones. Valiant warriors of the angelic host are among our numbered men. (1QM 12.7–8)[19]

Ultimately, God's name is sanctified when his kingdom definitively arrives on earth, an arrival that means that God judges this wicked world with righteousness and that he completes the salvation of his chosen people.

We see, then, that God's kingdom entails the universal establishment of his sovereignty over the creation, finally demonstrated in both the eradication and the punishment of all rebellion, as well as the total vindication and redemption of his people with righteousness. As with the sanctification of God's name, this too is something that only God can perform. "The Kingdom of God refers to God's dynamic presence as he reveals himself in strength."[20] As God's definitive, future act, this final, divine intervention means the end of the world as we now know it; the

17. Put very simply, apocalyptic literature grew out of the Old Testament prophets and wisdom literature as an expression of Jewish hopes for God's miraculous intervention into world affairs in order to rescue his people from injustice and finally establish his kingdom on earth.

18. The *Psalms of Solomon* appears to have been originally composed in Hebrew not long after Jerusalem's fall to the Romans in 63 BC. These extrabiblical psalms emanated from a community longing for Israel's renewed independence; see Charlesworth, *Old Testament Pseudepigrapha*, 2.639–49, 665–69.

19. 1QM, also known as the *War Scroll*, describes the final great confrontation between the children of light and the children of darkness, a battle that finally inaugurates God's kingdom on earth; see Vermes, *Complete Dead Sea Scrolls*, 175. Additional expressions of Jewish hope for the kingdom among nonrabbinic sources may be found in the numerous texts cited by Beasley-Murray, *Jesus and the Kingdom of God*, 39–62; and Davies and Allison, *Matthew*, 1.604.

20. Chilton, *God in Strength*, 89. The close affinity between Jesus's usage and the Jewish meaning of the kingdom of God is what leads me to agree with those who insist that Jesus's concept of the kingdom of God is fundamentally Jewish; it is how Jesus then relates himself to the kingdom that sets his theology apart.

realization of God's kingdom is *the* eschatological event introducing God's people perfectly into eternity.

Of course, this begs the question of whether this is what *Jesus* meant when *he* announced the coming of God's kingdom.[21] Correctly observing that the coming of God's kingdom lay at the heart of Jesus's ministry is still a far cry from understanding what he intended to communicate by his programmatic declaration: "The time has come. . . . The kingdom of God is near. Repent and believe the good news!" (Mark 1:15).[22] Aside from Jesus's proclamation of "the kingdom's coming" remaining unparalleled in Jewish literature,[23] the attention that Jesus gave to explaining the nature of the kingdom and the consequences of its arrival suggests that his intent was at the very least distinctive, if not unique.[24] We cannot automatically assume a direct line of influence, or even correlation, between Jesus's contemporaries and his personal theology.

Has the Kingdom Come?

It is extremely telling that the central theme of Jesus's preaching is also his most distinctive. Jesus announced that the kingdom has come. Typically, both the Old Testament and Judaism spoke of the kingdom as something to be "revealed." The language of "coming" was reserved exclusively for God, particularly his coming on the day of the Lord.[25] Thus Isaiah proclaimed:

21. Opinions vary widely. Some insist that Jesus's kingdom teaching is unlike anything that preceded him; see, for example, Jeremias, *New Testament Theology*, 96. Others insist that Jesus's conception of the kingdom is similar if not identical to contemporary Jewish hopes; Young, *Jewish Background of the Lord's Prayer*, 11–16; and Davies and Allison, *Matthew*, 1.604.

22. Chilton, *God in Strength*, 29–95, conducts the most exhaustive examination of this text in its programmatic significance for Jesus's ministry. For a shorter look, see Beasley-Murray, *Jesus and the Kingdom of God*, 71–75.

23. "'Kingdom of God' as the subject of 'come' is unattested in the OT, in ancient Jewish texts, and in the NT outside the gospels"; Davies and Allison, *Matthew*, 1.604; similarly, see Nolland, *Luke*, 614.

24. Caird, *New Testament Theology*, 367: "If the Synoptic gospels are right to insist that Jesus spent much of his time explaining what he meant by the Kingdom, would it not follow that he did not mean what everybody else meant by it?" While an affirmative answer is not obvious, the question is evocative.

25. Beasley-Murray, *Jesus and the Kingdom of God*, 3–51; and Chilton, *Pure Kingdom*, 60–62; see also note 21 above. For further examples of the coming of God, see 1 Chron. 16:33; Pss. 96:13; 98:9; Isa. 26:21; 40:9–10; Mic. 1:3; Zech. 14:5; *1 Enoch* 1.3–9; 25.3; *Jubilees* 1.22–28; *Assumption of Moses* 10.1–12; for the future coming of God as King, see Isa. 24:23; 33:22; 52:7; Zeph. 3:15; Zech. 14:9; for the coming of the day of the Lord, see Isa. 13:6; Joel 2:1; Zech. 14:1; Mal. 4:5.

>   Be strong, do not fear;
>   your God will come,
>   he will come with vengeance;
>   with divine retribution
>   he will come to save you. (Isa. 35:4)

Isaiah connects two crucial kingdom themes—judgment and salvation—to the coming of Yahweh. Now we are in a position to grasp Jesus's defining innovation. As the messenger of the kingdom, he proclaimed the long-awaited arrival of God-in-strength come to accomplish the works of the kingdom: to rescue his people, to complete their redemption, to eradicate their enemies, to demonstrate his glory by revealing the perfection of his holiness—all while transforming this fallen universe into the long-awaited new creation. Furthermore, Jesus was emphatic that entering into God's now-present kingdom was synonymous with surrendering to his claims of messiahship. "If I drive out demons by the Spirit of God, then the kingdom of God has come upon you," he boldly warned his opponents (Matt. 12:28). In Luke, Jesus inaugurates his ministry from the hometown synagogue in Nazareth, where he conflates two Isaianic kingdom passages (58:6; 61:1–2), lays claim to the eschatological anointing of the Spirit, and then insists: "Today this scripture is fulfilled in your hearing" (Luke 4:21). The old debate about whether Jesus brought the kingdom or the kingdom brought him is irrelevant. They arrived in history simultaneously like newborn twins, inextricably intertwined, indivisibly bound together. It is impossible to divorce the two or to comprehend the one without the other. As Mark's Gospel unfolds, it becomes increasingly clear that Jesus's opening declaration of the kingdom's appearance (1:15) not only introduces the central plot device of Mark's narrative, but launches an eschatological shot across history's bow. From now on, entrance into the kingdom of God is synonymous with following Jesus, the crucified and resurrected Messiah.[26]

These observations yield several results. First, we are again instructed to ask the Father to perform something for himself. Human beings are neither asked to introduce nor are they capable of introducing God's kingdom into the world.[27] The second petition is not a request that disciples somehow behave in a way sufficient for the establishment of God's reign. Rather, the Father is the only power capable of launching a supernatural invasion into history that not only lands a successful beachhead in space and time, but then proceeds to conquer and control

26. I recommend Caird's lucid synthesis of Jesus's theology of the kingdom in *New Testament Theology*, 129–35, 366–69.

27. See Schürmann, *Praying with Christ*, 34–35; and Fitzmyer, *Luke*, 898.

the high ground of creation by permanently reversing humanity's absurd venture into rebellion.

Second, we should also ask if Jesus's instructions are coherent. If he says that the kingdom comes with him, then why are disciples instructed to pray that God bring his kingdom in the future? Is the kingdom here? This tension, in and of itself, is not unique to Jesus.[28] The roots of a slightly different already/not yet kingdom are found in the Old Testament, for example, when the psalmist sings: "Your kingdom is an everlasting kingdom, / and your dominion endures through all generations" (Ps. 145:13). As sovereign Creator, God rules the universe now and always, yet as long as pagan nations such as Assyria, Babylon, and Rome lord it over the earth, God's people must patiently wait for the completed, historical manifestation of that dominion.

The Qumran covenanters took an innovative step in synthesizing from this background a perspective that allowed the kingdom to become *dynamically present* while remaining *historically future*. In other words, as God's faithful people they (1) experienced the current spiritual reality of the kingdom among themselves while (2) preparing the way for its future realization in the final coming of God.[29]

Jesus similarly insisted that the kingdom of God had (1) arrived with him, bringing all of its benefits for those who believed, while (2) also warning everyone to prepare themselves for the kingdom's future arrival, where the unprepared will be excluded like foolish wedding guests (Matt. 25:1–12).[30] The difference, once again, was Jesus's conviction that God's

28. Surveys of this central tension in the teaching of Jesus, as well as in the rest of the New Testament, may be found in the classic treatments of Manson, *Teaching of Jesus*, 134–41; Kümmel, *Promise and Fulfilment*; Cullmann, *Christ and Time*; and idem, *Salvation in History*.

29. See Beasley-Murray, *Jesus and the Kingdom of God*, 49–51, building on the work of H. Kuhn, *Enderwartung und Gegenwärtiges Heil*. Beasley-Murray concludes that "the juxtaposition of present and future notions of the eschatological kingdom is not so foreign to Jewish eschatology as was once thought" (51). We previously saw a passage from the *War Scroll* (1QM 12.7–8) describing the last battle where God establishes his earthly throne in the last days. A passage from the *Community Rule* (1QS 11.5–8) also describes the present spiritual benefits of God's kingdom within the community: "From the source of His righteousness is my justification, and from His marvelous mysteries is the light in my heart. My eyes have gazed on that which is eternal, on wisdom concealed from men . . . on a spring of glory (hidden) from the assembly of humanity. God has given them to his chosen ones as an everlasting possession."

This passage is reminiscent of Jesus's claims to an exclusive relationship with the Father in Luke 10:21–22 (‖ Matt. 11:25–27). What the Qumran community believed they received in the wilderness, Jesus claimed to offer exclusively to his followers. See Vermes, *Complete Dead Sea Scrolls*, 115, for this translation; I also draw on Beasley-Murray's rendering (50).

30. This already/not yet account of New Testament theology is called "biblical realism." For further discussion, see Lundström, *Kingdom of God*; and Ladd, *Presence of the Future*.

kingdom was a reality limited to him and his disciples. Consequently, only Jesus's followers can possibly be prepared for the Father's final curtain call at the end of time. Before one can pray, "May your kingdom come," one must first ask, "What is my relationship to the crucified, resurrected King?" G. B. Caird puts a characteristically fine point on it: "The question which is here at stake is not the distance of the Kingdom from the present, but the distance of a potential disciple from the Kingdom (Mark 12:34)."[31] Standing far from Jesus is to live far from God's rule.

Living Like Kingdom People

As with the first petition, the second also raises certain ethical questions, and once again, I prefer to avoid an either/or solution by finding the middle ground. In fact, the already/not yet dimension of the kingdom requires just such a hybrid solution. To pray for God's kingdom is to ask for three things.

First, just as God's glorification is eschatological, so too is the coming of his kingdom. We are not asked to pray for a slow evolutionary process unveiling God's kingdom in this world, but the final cosmic intervention by God bringing a new creation where even the stones cry out, "Blessed is the King who comes in the name of the Lord!" (Luke 19:38–40).[32] We hunger to see our Father vindicate his great name and eliminate all resistance to his lordship, wherever it may appear. So, the first challenge is: Do I value my Lord's honor and reputation above all else? Am I captivated by the prospect of soon seeing the entire world bow before my Father's throne?

Entailed within that request, however, is the individual question of personal allegiance. To pray for God's kingdom sincerely is to submit to the lordship of Christ. Secondarily, then, this eschatological petition yields an existential demand. I may not be able to bring the kingdom, but I am required to yield my all to the King. The second challenge becomes: Do I continually renew my submission to Christ's lordship among the ever-changing details of life?

Finally, Jesus makes it clear that life in the kingdom requires a kingdom lifestyle. His extensive ethical teaching is instruction for kingdom living; it is not a prescription for entrance, but the description of authentic

31. Caird, *New Testament Theology*, 132.
32. Brown, "Pater Noster," 189–90. In my opinion, Weiss made this conclusion axiomatic with his 1892 publication (see *Jesus' Proclamation of the Kingdom of God*). Recent attempts in American scholarship to turn back the clock and ignore Weiss's insights, together with the long history of New Testament scholarship that followed, are a curious example of American idiosyncrasy.

inhabitants.[33] "Congratulations when you are persecuted for the sake of righteousness, for yours is the kingdom of heaven," says Jesus (Matt. 5:10, my translation). In this derived sense, the early church fathers were correct; prayer for the kingdom becomes prayer for oneself; we ask that God's transforming power reshape our inner and outer lives, molding us into the new people that the King originally intended. Thus the final kingdom question remains: Am I experiencing the requisite metamorphosis from fleshly sinner to luminous saint required of all the King's subjects?

May Your Will Be Done on Earth

Perhaps it is already apparent that each of these three petitions is orbiting within the same gravitational field around a common set of concerns. The three are nearly synonymous, making the same request in three slightly altered expressions.[34] Just as praying for the kingdom to come is to ask for the sanctification of God's name, so too is it asking for the Father's "will to be done." Consequently, Luke's version of the prayer loses nothing by the absence of the third petition. It may also be more than coincidental that this distinctive line in Matthew's version is identical to a phrase found only in Matthew's account of Jesus's Gethsemane prayer: "My Father, if it is not possible for this cup to be taken away unless I drink it, *may your will be done*" (26:42).[35] Matthew reminds the sensitive reader that Jesus has walked our road before us. He is teaching the disciples to pray as he prays and to do as he does, not requiring anything of them that he has not first fulfilled himself.

Jesus's Gethsemane prayer also demonstrates that God's will involves more than the individual direction we seek in the course of life's trials. Ultimately, God's will is to accomplish all of his goals for salvation-history, including the strategy "to reconcile to himself all things, whether things on earth or things in heaven, by making peace through his blood, shed on the cross" (Col. 1:20). When the exalted Christ revealed himself to Paul on the Damascus road, calling him to take his gospel to the Gentiles, Ananias exclaimed: "The God of our fathers has chosen you *to know his will*" (Acts 22:14). Knowing God's will requires that we lift our eyes (like Jesus and Paul) beyond individual requests for guidance and embrace the Father's universal vision

33. On Jesus's ethics as descriptive of kingdom living, see Ladd, *Presence of the Future*, 278–304; and Chilton and McDonald, *Jesus and the Ethics of the Kingdom*.

34. This is a common observation; see Harner, *Understanding the Lord's Prayer*, 75; Gerhardsson, "Matthean Version of the Lord's Prayer," 209–11; and Hagner, *Matthew*, 1.148.

35. Cullmann, *Prayer in the New Testament*, 47–48.

of redemption and restoration through Christ, a vision encompassing heaven and earth.

Third-century church father Origen may have been the first to recognize the significance of Matthew's reference to heaven and earth for all three of these initial petitions.[36] As Paul says in his letter to the Colossians, the Father's plan of salvation encompasses all of creation, temporal and eternal, physical and spiritual. Thus the disciple prays that the Father will be sanctified, that the kingdom will come, and that God's will is achieved on this earth just as all three are now transacted in heaven. The earth's eventual conformity to the ideal standards of heaven becomes all encompassing:

> Father,
> may your name be sanctified
> may your kingdom come   on earth as it is in heaven
> may your will be done

Some commentators suggest that heaven and earth designate two spheres of rebellion both in need of the Father's restoration. The spiritual realm requires conquest as much as the earthly. Though texts such as Col. 1:20 may reflect such an attitude, it is unlikely that this is what Matthew had in mind, given the positive association of heaven with the Father in Matt. 6:9b and its designation as the place of God's throne in 5:34.[37] Matthew's hope is that heaven comes to earth in our lifetime.

Jewish prayer was typically cosmic prayer that looked to the final coordination of every dimension in God's universe, while insisting that the prayers of God's people had a role to play in the process. Human petition and worship were lifted up to coalesce with the angelic praise and adoration sung by the heavenly community.[38] The eternal paradigm of salvation impatiently awaits the divinely appointed moment to overflow its eternal banks like a wild, swollen river bursting to finally envelop the earth whole. Asking that "God's will be done" is to pray that the plan

36. Origen, *On Prayer* 26.2. This position has been adopted by numerous commentators since; for example, see Pool, *Kaddish*, 112; G. Thompson, "Thy Will Be Done in Earth," 381; and Cullmann, *Prayer in the New Testament*, 50–51.

37. G. Thompson, "Thy Will Be Done in Earth," 379–81, attempts a detailed syntactical defense of the view that both heaven and earth require God's will. His numerous qualifications (the words "maybe" and "sometimes" abound) demonstrate, however, that the tentative grammatical evidence fails to overthrow the greater contextual, historical, and literary clues.

38. Chase, *Lord's Prayer in the Early Church*; Cullmann, *Prayer in the New Testament*, 48–49; E. Sanders, *Judaism*, 371–72; Charlesworth, "Jewish Prayers"; and Newsom, "Songs of the Sabbath Sacrifice," 28–32.

inaugurated in Gen. 12 with the elderly, pagan Abraham, advanced by Israel's deliverance through the Red Sea, established with the conquest of Canaan, enthroned through David's ascension to kingship, and finally actualized in the man from Galilee will finally be consummated sooner rather than later in the new heaven and earth.

This is not to say that praying with an eye on the end of time automatically excludes all immediate personal requests for divine guidance. The ubiquitous twenty-first-century Christian angst over "finding God's will for my life" is, however, a distinctly modern phenomenon, one that we would do well to reconsider. The ancient Israelite did not need to search for the Father's will because it had already been fully revealed in Scripture, in the Torah. God's word offers a plethora of detailed instructions on how to conduct oneself in any of life's circumstances. Our task is to obey what we have already received—*that* is God's will. There is no need to search any further. Consequently, I suspect that we will remain blinded to the individualized guidance we scurry after in life until the Father's heavenly, eschatological frame of reference is first allowed to corral, even to extinguish, our modern obsession with self-centered individualism. Should I pray for divine direction in making wise, God-honoring choices? By all means! But my search for God's answers will prove successful only when I approach my Father as a foot soldier in heaven's army, freely enlisted to do the King's bidding, ready and willing to lay down my life, possessed by the knowledge that, even after giving my all, I remain an unworthy servant who has only performed his duty (Luke 17:10).

Why Pray for God's Will?

The first section of the Lord's Prayer comes to a close by again instructing us (through another divine passive) to pray that the Father might accomplish something for himself. In this instance, we ask that God consummate his will for restoring creation. To the extent that my salvation is included within that plan, my existence becomes most meaningful as I fulfill my God-given responsibilities in submission and obedience, such that my prayers for the fulfillment of God's cosmic will become my surrender as an instrument of that will. In this sense, the prayer provides its own answer.

Of course, this raises a further question. Why pray for God to perform his own will? Is that not exactly what he intends to do anyway, whether we pray for it? Without surveying all the possible answers offered throughout history, let me briefly touch on two of the more common suggestions. A more thorough analysis must wait for the rest of the New

Testament evidence to be examined, but it may prove helpful to begin that discussion here.

First, many writers suggest that the benefits of praying for God's will have primarily to do with the internal transformation effected within us. When genuine, such prayers become acts of submission in which the lordship of Christ is personally strengthened. For example, John Calvin writes: "Even though all these things must nonetheless come to pass in their time, without any thought or desire or petition of ours, still we ought to desire and request them."[39] His rationale was that the praying process functions as a spiritual discipline transforming us from the inside out. Our disobedient desires melt away and are replaced by God's righteous desires as we pray.

Second, many Reformed thinkers develop this suggestion even further, stating that God ordains our prayers as tools in accomplishing his will: "God moves men to pray in order that he may respond to their prayers, and thus carry out his will. God ordains *means* as well as *ends*."[40] Thus God's "response" to prayer is not an innovation; it is a part of his foreordained plan now advanced through the prayer we were ordained to pray. In other words, God moves us to pray for the things he wants to give us and then answers our prayers "as though" he were moved to respond.[41] Since God cannot change, however, neither in purpose nor in knowledge, it would be more accurate to say that his "answer" is not a response to our prayer as much as our prayer is a response to his predetermined answer.

There is a significant difference between these two related solutions to the problem of praying for God's will. The first suggestion wrestles with the issue in a way that respects the contours of the biblical text. Though neither the Lord's Prayer nor any other portion of Scripture explicitly tries to resolve this intellectual dilemma, the argument that prayer facilitates a disciple's sanctification fits comfortably within the eschatological (already) and ethical (not yet) dimensions of Jesus's teaching. The second suggestion, on the other hand, attempts to construct a theological solution that not only reaches well beyond the contours of the biblical passages, but leaves significant textual wreckage behind. It is very difficult to read the Lord's Prayer—not to mention the rest of Jesus's prayer teaching—as anything but misleading, even deceptive, if God's responses to petition are only "apparent." From this perspective,

39. Calvin, *Institutes of the Christian Religion* §3.20.43.
40. Spear, *Theology of Prayer*, 69 (emphasis original).
41. J. Edwards, "Most High a Prayer-Hearing God," 505 (sermon 4): "God is sometimes represented as if he were moved and persuaded by the prayers of his people; yet it is not to be thought that God is properly moved or made willing by our prayers; for it is no more possible that there should be any new inclination or will in God, than new knowledge."

an informed surface reading of the prayer is inexplicably replaced by a dogmatic paradigm that leaves the text no longer meaning what it straightforwardly appears to mean.

Prayer was not understood this way in Jesus's day! When reciting the Tefillah, Kaddish, or related prayers, members of the ancient synagogue were keenly aware that they asked God to perform works he had already begun, works he fully intended to complete when the time was right. Judas Maccabeus, for example, shouted before leading Israel's attack against Antiochus IV Epiphanes: "As God's will is in heaven, so he will perform" (1 Macc. 3:60, my translation). Nevertheless, prayers could influence the outcome of God's plan—that was, after all, the essence of petition! Yahweh regularly collaborated with his people by means of prayer, beginning with Abraham (Gen. 18:16–33) and continuing through Moses (Exod. 32:7–14) and the later prophets.[42] Consequently, various pietistic groups, such as the Pharisees and the members of Qumran, believed that God would send his kingdom only upon Israel's wholehearted repentance and renewal, demonstrated in acts of piety such as almsgiving, study, and prayer. Human behavior was fully capable of influencing God's timing and the particulars of its fulfillment.[43] God not only listened to his people but enlisted them as genuine partners in accomplishing his purposes for the world.

When Jesus invites disciples to pray that the Father's glory, kingdom, and plan will be accomplished on earth as in heaven, they can ask with assurance, knowing that their prayers will be answered positively. They ask according to God's sovereign will, and God's will is always accomplished. To this extent the first theological solution offered above is very useful. Affirming that God's goals are always fulfilled does not, however, necessarily require that every detail of the plan is eternally set in stone, nor does it preclude genuine human participation in shaping its unfolding contours. Thus, from a biblical perspective, the second proposal is inconsistent with the textual evidence and, for that reason alone, extremely unhelpful. Before our study is complete, we must look further for a more satisfactory solution.

For now it is sufficiently overwhelming to know that the first half of the Lord's Prayer creates a world in which God's people live exclusively for the honor, praise, and glory of the Holy One. It is a new spiritual dimension born of a belief that the Father's way is the only way because it was the only way for Jesus. Far from expressing pseudoreverence, honestly praying "your will be done" is the key to authentic petitionary

42. For an introduction to the idea of God acting collaboratively with humans, see Goldingay, "Logic of Intercession." Further discussion will be reserved for chapter 14.

43. E. Sanders, *Judaism*, 286–88, 376.

prayer (see also Acts 21:14). In these three requests, we acknowledge that even as we pray for miracles with a faith that moves mountains, we would gladly exchange the most astounding miracle for the smallest mundane moment, if the mundane will bring greater glory to our Father who is in heaven.

7

Our Wishes and God's Will

The Lord's Prayer, part 3

After an initial focus on the eschatological work that God accomplishes for himself, the three we-petitions in the second half of the Lord's Prayer turn to address the individual needs of the person praying. The exact nature of this shift is a matter of some debate, however. Two schools of thought dominate the discussion.[1]

Many commentators adhere to an exclusively apocalyptic-eschatological interpretation popularized by, though not originating with, J. Jeremias. According to this view, the kingdom dimension of the first three petitions remains the overarching principle defining the following section, such that all six requests become thoroughly future oriented. In other words, the request for daily bread anticipates the bread of life assuring eternal salvation. Asking for the forgiveness of sins looks to God's acquittal at the last judgment, while deliverance from temptation and evil (or the evil one) assures the disciple's preservation from apostasy in the great tribulation. Thus, none of these requests particularly pertain to life today.

1. Davies and Allison, *Matthew*, 1.593–94, provide a succinct survey of the two positions and their principal adherents.

Another significant contingent, on the other hand, argues that while such interpretations provide an ostensible thematic unity to the prayer, they are hardly self-evident. It is more natural, while granting the eschatological orientation of petitions 1–3, to allow for a midpoint shift in the prayer's focus at petitions 4–6. Consequently, the first half of the prayer seeks the Father's future apocalyptic intervention in history, while the following requests for daily bread, forgiveness, and deliverance from temptation address the noneschatological, real-world necessities for temporal, physical, and spiritual well-being.

Although it is difficult to be adamant, I am generally convinced that the second approach is preferable, albeit with one important proviso. Even though I cannot find an exclusively end-time orientation to petitions 4–6, as Jeremias argues, neither can the two halves of the Lord's Prayer be divorced from each other; they function as a greater whole, not as two independent units. If Jeremias's thoroughly eschatological interpretation appears forced and unnatural, it is even less convincing to read the second half of the prayer as a thoroughly noneschatological segment theologically unrelated to the first. The imminence of God's kingdom and all that it entails casts an eschatological shadow over the entire prayer, including this final set of real-time, mundane concerns. After all, these are not the pious prayers of conventional men and women conducting their lives as always. The Lord's Prayer is offered by disciples who self-consciously live within the already realized/but not yet completed kingdom of God. All of existence—including daily provisions, personal relationships, and devotion—are now determined by the present reality of the Father's salvation inaugurated by personal faith in Jesus of Nazareth. Consequently, each request is conditioned by the demands of Christian discipleship. Many others, including Pharisees, Sadducees, and the common people, also waited and prayed for the coming of God's kingdom, but Jesus's followers believed it had already arrived; their waiting was over. For them, the question now became: How does the real presence of the kingdom determine my current, earthly existence? How do I pray for material goods as one who lives under the Father's sovereign power? What are the appropriate kingdom qualifications of personal relationships and spiritual life? While the Lord's Prayer may not be a list of exclusively eschatological concerns, it is dominated from beginning to end by the historical institution of God's mighty reign. Perhaps a good key for unlocking this part of the prayer is found in Luke 12:31 (∥ Matt. 6:33), "Seek his kingdom first, and these other things will be added to you" (my translation).[2] Petitions 1–3 lead us to seek

2. See Beasley-Murray, *Jesus and the Kingdom of God*, 152–57, for a good discussion of the position adopted here.

the kingdom first; now petitions 4–6 outline how the "other things" are added appropriately.

Praying for Life's Essentials

No part of the Lord's Prayer has undergone such intense scrutiny as the petition for bread. The only adjective in the prayer (*epiousios*, "daily") has the distinction of not only failing to appear anywhere else in the Greek Bible but, as far as we know, appears nowhere else in all of Greek literature (apart from Christian writings discussing the Lord's Prayer).[3] This poses an interesting problem for interpretation, to say the least. The request for bread serves as a bridge transitioning from the first to the second part of the prayer. Consequently, our understanding of this request will have a significant bearing on whether we align ourselves with the eschatological or the noneschatological schools of interpretation. Origen, for instance, commented on the difficulty he faced in shifting abruptly from an eschatological/spiritual focus to merely temporal/mundane concerns: "Since some understand that we are commanded to pray for material bread, it will be well to refute their error here. . . . We must ask them how it could be that he who enjoined us to ask for great and heavenly favors, should command us to intercede with the Father for what is small and of the earth" (*On Prayer* 27). To Origen's mind, such a stark transition was unthinkable, thus he sought to find a more "appropriate" meaning for the word, thereby fueling an exegetical controversy that—short of some new archaeological discovery—shows no signs of abating.[4]

In contrast to Origen and his followers, however, Jewish prayers had always afforded an honorable place to the expression of mundane, material concerns. Old Testament wisdom asked: "Give me neither poverty nor riches, / but give me only my daily bread" (Prov. 30:8). The Tefillah combined prayers for God's kingdom with requests for daily needs. The ninth benediction seeks God's physical provision for his people:[5]

3. Greek father Origen suggests that the evangelists invented the word (*On Prayer* 27.7). One extrabiblical occurrence may have been published in 1889; unfortunately, the original papyrus is now lost. For an interesting account of this mystery, see Metzger, "How Many Times Does '*Epiousios*' Occur?"

4. See excursus 1 at the end of this chapter for a survey of the various meanings, some of them spiritualized "supersubstantial" meanings, proposed for the difficult word "daily."

5. Donin, *To Pray as a Jew*, 86; and Di Sante, *Jewish Prayer*, 95.

> Bless this year for us, O Lord our God, and all its varied produce that it
>   be for our welfare;
> Provide dew and rain as a blessing on the face of the earth.
> Satisfy us with your goodness, and bless this year like other good years.
> Blessed, art thou, Lord, who blesses the years.

Ancient inhabitants of an agricultural society were painfully aware of their dependence on the seasonal rains, and since Yahweh was the Creator, it only made sense to turn to him for the moisture necessary to each year's crop. Since human produce is dependent on divine provision, the pious prayed for daily needs.

Jesus certainly recognized this connection between heaven's gifts and the earth's requirements (Matt. 5:45; 6:25–34), although his conviction that he and the Father were coconspirators in birthing the kingdom of heaven produced a distinctive perspective on physical necessity. Jesus was not an antimaterialist (like certain Greek philosophers); the creation and its physical blessings are supremely important, but the kingdom's arrival radically rearranged all previous priorities. For example, Jesus's own mendicant, peripatetic lifestyle, left him "no place to lay his head" (Luke 9:58), dependent on the financial contributions of generous friends (8:3). The disciples followed suit, leaving home, family, and business behind in order to follow their wandering Master throughout the length and breadth of Palestine. The kingdom's arrival demanded just such a reorganization of personal priorities; nothing else could hold a candle to its requirements and opportunities. When Jesus sent the disciples out on their own preaching tours, they were to "take nothing for the journey—no staff, no bag, no bread, no money, no extra tunic" (Luke 9:1–6; 10:4 and parallels)—depending entirely on the Father's faithfulness to provide. The point is not that every disciple must take a vow of poverty; that would be a serious anachronism. The point, rather, is that Jesus and the Twelve responded in a manner appropriate to their own time and tasks to the same reality that impresses identical demands on disciples today: the incontestable supremacy of God's kingdom over everything else in life, including physical and material comfort: "Seek first his kingdom and his righteousness, and all these things will be given to you as well" (Matt. 6:33); "no one who puts his hand to the plow and looks back is fit for service in the kingdom of God" (Luke 9:62).

The first section of the Lord's Prayer demonstrates that disciples are to live and to pray as transformed human beings who fine-tune each moment of their existence to resonate with the cosmic vibrations of God's good will; they yearn for their Father's holiness, sovereignty, and eternal purposes to be comprehensively accomplished within them and throughout the rest of creation. Genuinely believing the substance of the first three petitions will have a profound effect on how one defines personal necessity (once you *finally* get there in petition 4!). Terms such as comfort, safety, accumulation, and excess face radical redefinition. This reminds us of Jesus's parable about the rich fool who filled new barns to overflowing but finally lost everything because he ignored God's kingdom requirements (Luke 12:16–21).

It is worth observing, at this point, that whereas the Tefillah prays for a prosperous year, the Lord's Prayer merely requests one sufficient day—give us what is necessary for our existence right now.[6] The difference is that the former prayer hopes for a kingdom that is still a distant dream, while the latter already inhabits the kingdom as an imminent demand. Rich and poor alike must bend to the yoke of a new "Maslovian hierarchy" of human needs (Matt. 11:29–30). The early church appears to have grasped this kingdom priority quite well. For example, the Jerusalem church voluntarily shared its resources so that no one went hungry (Acts 4:32–35; 6:1). Paul admonished Timothy to remember that "we brought nothing into the world, and we can take nothing out of it. But if we have food and clothing, we will be content" (1 Tim. 6:7–8). He obviously spoke to Timothy from his own hard-won experience: "I have learned the secret of being content in any and every situation, whether well fed or hungry, whether living in plenty or in want. I can do everything through him who gives me strength" (Phil. 4:12–13). Paul's goal was not self-denial for the sake of self-denial, but enthusiastic kingdom service that unhesitantly demoted every other concern to second, third, fourth place, or less. The Lord's Prayer does not require anyone to become a neo-Marxist, a socialist, or even a vegetarian who recycles. The fourth petition does not impose a particular political agenda or economic philosophy; it simply requires that one's material existence be utterly conditioned by the reign of God. Followers of Jesus are to hold on to nothing as tightly as they hold on to their King, and when it comes time to act on their stated values—as it does for all of us every day—they will go anywhere and do anything the Father asks, regardless of the cost, because they know that he will faithfully supply their needs.[7]

6. Beasley-Murray, *Jesus and the Kingdom of God*, 154–56, sees great significance in this comparison; I am hesitant to view the contrast quite as starkly as he does.

7. Gregory of Nyssa offers a refreshingly direct exposition of this petition, avoiding the all-too-common spiritualizing and allegorization of his peers: "We say to God: Give us bread. Not delicacies or riches, nor magnificent purple robes, golden ornaments, precious stones, or silver dishes. Nor do we ask him for landed estates, or military commands, or political leadership. . . . We do not say, give us a prominent position in assemblies or monuments and statues raised to us—but only bread!" (*Lord's Prayer*, sermon 4).

Asking for Forgiveness

Forgiveness from God

Yahweh was known to be a God of abundant mercy who faithfully forgave his people's disobedience (Exod. 33:19; 34:6–7). The Old Testament writers freely turned to him, asking for the forgiveness of individual as well as national sin, confident of God's positive reply (Pss. 19:12; 25:11, 18; 79:9; 103:3, 10–14; Isa. 55:6–7; Jer. 36:3, 7; 50:19–20; Dan. 9:19; Hosea 14:2; Amos 7:2). This confidence in the covenant is preserved in an apocryphal psalm discovered among the Dead Sea Scrolls:

> Near death was I for my sins,
>   and my iniquities had sold me to the grave;
> But thou didst save me, O Lord,
>   according to your great mercy,
>   and according to thy many righteous deeds.
> . . . .
> Forgive my sin, O Lord,
>   and purify me from my iniquity. (11QPs^a 19.9–11, 13–14)[8]

It was also reaffirmed each day as the Tefillah instituted prayers of repentance (benediction 5) and a request for forgiveness (benediction 6):

> Forgive us, our Father, for we have sinned,
> Pardon us, our King, for we have transgressed,
> For You are a pardoner and forgiver.
> Blessed art Thou, Lord, Gracious One who forgives abundantly.[9]

The future assurance of forgiveness contained in Jeremiah's new covenant becomes particularly important for the New Testament. While Israel was carted off into exile by its Babylonian taskmasters, the Lord prophetically declared that a time would come when he "will forgive their wickedness / and will remember their sins no more" (Jer. 31:34; also 33:8; compare Isa. 40:2; Ezek. 36:25–32). Jesus appeared as the solitary messenger of that covenant announcing the arrival of God's long-awaited kingdom, an ever-expanding domain where forgiveness of the penitent and condemnation of the rebellious—the indivisible expressions of any righteous judgment—were being actualized in this world (Matt. 3:1–12 ‖ Luke 3:3–18). On this score, Jesus's teaching was characterized by a nonnegotiable connection between (a) receiving forgiveness from the

---

8. J. A. Sanders, *Psalms Scroll*, 78; and Vermes, *Complete Dead Sea Scrolls*, 305.
9. Donin, *To Pray as a Jew*, 84; and Di Sante, *Jewish Prayer*, 95.

Father and (b) extending forgiveness to others. The one always implies the other.

Centuries before Jesus's birth, Jewish sage ben Sira wrote in a similar vein:[10]

> If you forgive someone who has wronged you,
> your sins will be forgiven when you pray.
> You cannot expect the Lord to pardon you
> while you are holding a grudge against someone else. (Sir. 28:2–3
>   TEV)

Jesus's words in Mark 11:25 are similar: "When you stand to pray, if you forgive whatever you have against another, your Father in heaven will forgive your sins" (my translation). Jesus made similar statements on other occasions, often centering around questions of debt and repayment (Matt. 5:23–26, 43–48; 6:14–15; 18:21–35; Luke 6:35; 17:4). Obviously, sustaining the flow of forgiveness from heaven to earth, among brothers and sisters, ranked high on Jesus's kingdom agenda. Some of his statements, however, read more clearly than others, causing many interpreters to puzzle over the chicken-or-egg question of cause and effect. Whose offer of forgiveness comes first? Must we forgive in order to qualify for God's forgiveness; is it a heavenly quid pro quo? Or is our extension of forgiveness to others an expected response to God's grace?

Forgiving and Being Forgiven

If read in isolation, Matthew's language could be taken to mean that God forgives only those who bear no grudges. In fact, many read the entire Sermon on the Mount as a lengthy explanation of "entrance requirements" to the kingdom of God.[11] Luke's phrasing, "forgive us our sins, as we are forgiving all those indebted to us," offers a subtle distinction from Matthew's "forgive us our debts, as we also have forgiven our

10. Similar, apparently conditional, statements are found in the Tosefta tractate *Zevahim* 5.3; the Babylonian Talmud tractate *Yoma* 23a; and Mishnah tractate *Yoma* 8.9.

11. For example, see the classic articulations of this position by Weiss, *Jesus' Proclamation of the Kingdom*, 105–14 (titled "The Ethics of Preparation"); and Windisch, *Meaning of the Sermon on the Mount*, who says, "All the teaching of the Sermon on the Mount is meant to summon men to exert themselves to the utmost to obtain entrance to the Kingdom of God" (27). In explaining the fifth petition for forgiveness, he writes: "In both instances [praying for forgiveness and loving one's enemies] an act of God is dependent on an act of the devout man. If we at least forgive our enemies, we can petition the Father in full confidence for the forgiveness of our sins" (181).

debtors."[12] Matthew's perfect tense ("we have forgiven") refers to past, completed action, suggesting that the petitioner's prior forgiveness of others qualifies him or her for God's forgiveness now. On the other hand, Luke's present tense ("we are forgiving") connotes continuous action occurring simultaneously with God's forgiveness. The change is slight though not insignificant; some suggest that Luke is distancing himself from any suggestion of forgiveness based on personal merit, although others insist that, in either case, merit is at least implicit. Before accepting that conclusion, however, it is important to place the fifth petition within the broader context of Jesus's teaching on forgiveness. Two parables are particularly relevant: the unmerciful servant (Matt. 18:21–35) and the story of two debtors embedded in Jesus's encounter with a so-called sinful woman (Luke 7:36–50). Both explicitly address what is only implied in the Lord's Prayer: the proper relationship between receiving and extending forgiveness.

In the first passage, an astronomical debt is forgiven and then reinstated for a heartless servant who refuses to pass on his master's forgiveness to a fellow worker owing him money. The master's evaluation of the servant's behavior demonstrates a crucial assumption: experiencing forgiveness is transformative, and it will be replicated when genuine. The master marvels, "I canceled all that debt of yours because you begged me to. Shouldn't you have had mercy on your fellow servant just as I had on you?" (Matt. 18:32–33). The master's forgiveness was an undeserved gift of mercy; the servant could do nothing that would entitle him to the cancellation of his debt. Consequently, forgiving someone else is not the condition but the evidence of being forgiven yourself.

An identical point is made during Jesus's dinner with a Lukan Pharisee. A disreputable woman invades a Pharisee's home to anoint Jesus's feet and becomes exemplary of the personal transformation effected by divine forgiveness. Jesus's story of two debtors illustrates that the greater our experience of forgiveness, the greater our expressions of love and gratitude (Luke 7:41–43). He explains, therefore, that the woman with an alabaster jar of perfume is responding to a previous encounter with God's grace; she has already been forgiven and comes now to express her deep appreciation: "Because of this I can say to you, her many sins

12. The different vocabulary (Matthew's "debts" versus Luke's "sins") is one piece of evidence that leads many, following Jeremias, to suggest that Matthew preserves the more original vocabulary, while Luke preserves the more original outline of the Lord's Prayer. The Aramaic word *ḥôbā'* refers to "sin, guilt" but properly means "debt, money owed." Thus Matthew's translation is more literal; Luke's is adapted to his Gentile audience; see Dalman, *Die Worte Jesu*, 335–38 (unfortunately, the lengthy discussion of the Lord's Prayer is omitted from the English version: *Words of Jesus*). Jeremias, *Prayers of Jesus*, 92, is following Dalman's lead.

have been forgiven, for she loves a great deal" (7:47, my translation).[13] Jesus's confirmation of forgiveness (7:48) underscores the woman's earlier experience; she is assured that her new relationship with God exists by virtue of her faith alone, not by her demonstrations of love (7:50).

Apparently, since forgiveness and reconciliation are interpersonal transactions, God anticipates an inevitable reciprocity as testimony to their authenticity; such gifts cannot be experienced without their mutual interaction. Expecting the forgiven to forgive does not make forgiveness conditional. As C. F. D. Moule writes, "The key lies in distinguishing between, on the one hand, earning or meriting forgiveness, and, on the other hand, adopting an attitude which makes forgiveness possible."[14] The repentance, confession, and faith receptive to God's grace will invariably share that gift with others. Therefore, whether Matthew asks for forgiveness "as we also have forgiven" or Luke requests forgiveness "as we are forgiving," the reality described entails an inextricable connection between divine initiative and human response. The capacity to receive the Father's forgiveness does not constitute merit, but it does guarantee mercy. You cannot receive grace without sharing it.

One question remains: How often must the disciple request forgiveness before finding the freedom to rest confidently in God's guarantee?[15] Since Jesus's arrival, God's eschatological judgment has cast a long shadow over all of world history, national and individual. The king's final verdict has invaded life here and now, even as we continue to struggle and fail in a fallen world. Just as we pray for necessary bread "day by day," we must also regularly examine ourselves and confess our need for a daily cleansing of the multiple cuts and bruises acquired in

---

13. The language alone is not decisive in interpretation. The context makes plain, however, that the first "because/for this reason" is linked with "I say to you" and logically refers to the preceding discussion of forgiveness. The second "because/for" is not causal but logical, expressing the basis of (not the actual reason for) the previous statement. The connection also depends on the verb "I tell you (because)" rather than "she is forgiven (because)." In other words, her love is the evidence of her forgiveness, not its antecedent. For a survey of the grammatical options and various arguments, see Nolland, *Luke*, 357–58; and Moule, "As We Forgive," 72–74. Moule translates: "The reason why I am able to tell you that her many sins are forgiven is the fact that she is showing so much love" (74).

14. Moule, "As We Forgive," 71.

15. The eschatological interpretation of the Lord's Prayer argues that this petition is a single request covering "the summation of a lifetime, treated as one action before God's judgment seat" (Brown, "Pater Noster," 199). In other words, disciples prayerfully anticipate the Father's judgment rendering them free of guilt and accusation. While this is no doubt the final disposition in view, we have already rejected rigid distinctions between present and future realities in the coming of God's kingdom. Furthermore, the transition to mundane concerns in the second half of the Lord's Prayer means that there is no justification for limiting this petition solely to the last judgment.

our fallenness.[16] As Peter learns in John's Gospel, being cleansed by Christ does not prevent a disciple from becoming temporarily soiled, although we can take heart that dirty hands and feet are far removed from our original filthiness. "A person who has had a bath needs only to wash his feet; his whole body is clean," says Jesus (John 13:10). Therefore, fully confident of a complete cleansing, the motley disciple gladly submits to the Father's daily scrubbings, no matter how rough. And if the failure to forgive others obstructs our communion with the Father, it is only because that failure constitutes one more sin requiring our confession.

Deliver Us from Evil

The sixth petition contains the prayer's only negative request asking God *not* to do something. Luke shares the first line with Matthew, "Do not lead us into *peirasmos* [temptation, testing]," whereas Matthew has an additional, parallel line elaborating the concern, "But rescue us from evil [*or* the evil one]." Several thorny problems of interpretation lie hidden in this seemingly simple sentence because of the ambiguous word commonly translated "temptation." Rather than burrowing through all those complications here, let me simply say, in my opinion, that both the vocabulary and the context of the petition are best respected by understanding this word to mean periodic trials/tests by God intended for the strengthening of his people (for details on this interpretation of *peirasmos*, see excursus 2 at the end of this chapter). The intended outcome of divine testing is that God's people will grow and mature through the periodic stresses and strains of day-to-day life as they seek to make the decisions and lead the lives required of men and women now inhabiting the kingdom of God.

Testing from God or Satan?

This particular rendering of temptation, however, raises at least two pressing questions. First, why should anyone ask to be "delivered from" (or "not led into") God's tests if they are beneficial? Does not this turn the petition into a request to avoid spiritual growth, especially when we are assured elsewhere that "God will not let you be tested beyond what you can bear; but when you are tested, he will also provide a way out so that you can stand up under it" (1 Cor. 10:13, my translation)? Second,

16. This is also the first petition associated with its predecessor by the conjunction "and," forging a clear connection to daily earthly necessities, whether bread or forgiveness.

what is the relationship between the Father's beneficial tests and the request to be delivered from evil?[17] How can God's tests be equated with wickedness? In what sense could evil ever be considered beneficial?

Neither the New Testament nor Second Temple Judaism gave much attention to precisely defining who is immediately responsible for life's testings, and the ambiguity of the Greek word *peirasmos* made it a perfect tool for conveying the ambivalent, real-world struggles of faith. It is no accident that James uses the same word to describe both divine testing (1:2) and evil temptation (1:12–14); deciding how to distinguish the two is finally determined more by our response than it is by the circumstances themselves. Whether a difficult situation is sent directly from God or originates in some wily, demonic stratagem is irrelevant to its final outcome and evaluation. God's tests are not always easy, and demonic temptations need not be successful. If we pass the challenge faithfully, then we thank our Father for a renewed faith, tested and strengthened. On the other hand, if we fail and yield to temptation, we confess, repent, and consider the cause of our failure so as to improve the chances of endurance next time around. The New Testament is content to leave us with a thoroughly experiential delineation of temptation from testing. Rather than discerning the ostensibly demonic versus divine origins of every trauma in advance, we are simply called to focus our energies on the final goal of steadfastness, regardless of the circumstances. Granted, this seemingly murky approach to the practical questions of theodicy may not sit well with modern, post-Enlightenment minds, but Jewish (and biblical) theology has never been as driven by the quest for logical clarity as have the traditions of Western, European theology.[18]

The wisdom of ben Sira warned the ancient saint: "My child, when you come to serve the Lord, / prepare yourself for testing [*peirasmos*]" (Sir. 2:1 NRSV). But with that warning also came a promise: "No evil will befall the one who fears the Lord, / but in trials [*peirasmos*] such a one will be rescued again and again" (33:1 NRSV). These dual promises of earthly struggle accompanied by heavenly strength gave birth, not surprisingly, to prayers for deliverance, prayers offered without any fear

17. See point I.B in excursus 2 for the relationship between divine testing and the promise in James 1:13: "God cannot be tempted by evil, nor does he tempt anyone."

18. Rabbinic scholar G. Scholem writes, "Not system but *commentary* is the legitimate form through which truth is approached"; *Messianic Idea in Judaism*, 289 (emphasis original). Also consult the discussion regarding this issue and related questions addressing the comparative absence of Jewish voices from the study of Old Testament (biblical) theology in Levenson, "Why Jews Are Not Interested in Biblical Theology"; Goshen-Gottstein, "Tanakh Theology"; Rendtorff, "Future of Biblical Theology"; Brettler, "Biblical History"; and Kalimi, "History of Israelite Religion."

that such requests might contradict God's plan. For example, Ps. 155 from Qumran asks:

> Remember me and do not forget me,
>> and do not lead me into situations too hard for me. (11QPs[a] 24.11)[19]

Keenly aware of human frailty, the speaker specifically asks Yahweh not to lead the petitioner into predicaments that could produce overwhelming temptation, which is precisely what the disciple requests in the Lord's Prayer. The imminent possibility of moral failure reminds every saint that circumstantial domination by Satan is an ever-present danger requiring regular prayers for protection. Several texts from Qumran (11QPs[a] 19.15 and 4QTLevi 21.17) plead, "Do not let Satan[20] rule over me,"[21] language highly reminiscent of Matthew's parallel phrase "deliver us from the evil one."[22]

Father, Take This Cup from Me

Jesus's own life of ministry and prayer aptly illustrates the ambiguity inherent to the human experience of testing and temptation. His life was a spiritual obstacle course (Luke 22:28; Heb. 2:18; 4:15), successfully navigated only because he relied on the wisdom and strength made available by the spiritual compass found in prayer. Although he was tested as we in every way, Jesus's prayers were answered because of his unconditional submission to the Father's will; this was the key to his success (Heb. 5:7–9). Three Gospel passages are particularly illuminating in this respect:

19. J. A. Sanders, *Dead Sea Psalms Scroll*, 110–11. The verb "to lead" is from the Hebrew word *bô'*, a causative verb that almost always translates *eispherein*, the Greek verb used in the Lord's Prayer. Jeremias, *Lord's Prayer*, 105, also points to a talmudic prayer in the Babylonian Talmud, tractate *Berakhot* 60b: "Lead my foot not into the power of sin, / And bring me not into the power of iniquity, / And not into the power of temptation, / And not into the power of anything shameful."

20. In both texts the Hebrew word is *śṭn*, the adversary/accuser.

21. The apocryphal psalm may be found in J. A. Sanders, *Psalms Scroll*, 77–78; and idem, *Dead Sea Psalms Scroll*, 70–71. The *Testament of Levi* text may be found in Fitzmyer and Harrington, *Manual of Palestinian Aramaic Texts*, 90–91.

22. The debate whether *tou ponērou* (Matt. 6:13) should be translated "evil" (neuter) or "the evil one" (masculine) strikes me as a classic distinction without a difference. As long as we remember that satanic temptation is not restricted to the final eschaton, there is no substantial difference between the two renderings; see Gerhardsson, "Matthean Version of the Lord's Prayer," 217.

1. "Watch and pray so that you will not fall into temptation [*peirasmos*]. The spirit is willing, but the body is weak" (Mark 14:38). As Jesus began his late-night vigil in Gethsemane, he warned the disciples about a looming cosmic storm that would inevitably lead to their downfall. Human frailty cannot withstand the dark forces about to be unleashed by the prince of evil. The only conceivable shelter was to be discovered in prayers for God's deliverance.[23] This impending trial is an essential feature of the Father's plan, yet if the disciples are wise, they will earnestly ask to be spared the test.

2. "Simon, Simon, Satan has asked to sift you as wheat. But I have prayed for you. . . . When you have turned back, strengthen your brothers" (Luke 22:31–32). Once again, we see the themes of satanic assault and preservation through prayer, but this time the prayers offered are intercessory.[24] Apparently, Peter's ultimate survival was due only to the powerful efficacy of the Son of Man's requests on his behalf. Even so, Peter was doomed to a temporary apostasy that stopped short of permanence only because Jesus asked the Father to protect him. Satan's activity is described as "sifting," which is not necessarily a destructive process as much as it is a "proving" or a purifying that separates the usable wheat from the unusable husk (compare this image with point II.B.2.a in excursus 2). Even so, the implication is that without Jesus's intercessory protection Simon Peter would fail even his sifting, yielding nothing but chaff, going the way of Judas Iscariot.

3. "Abba, Father, . . . everything is possible for you. Take this cup from me. Yet not what I will, but what you will" (Mark 14:36; Matt. 26:39, 42; Luke 22:40, 46). The quintessential paradigm of testing survived through prayer is Jesus's own turmoil in Gethsemane. The stark contrast between the disciples who fail to pray and so fail their test, on the one hand, compared to the agonizing Jesus who passes his test through prayer and hard-won obedience, on the other hand, clearly portrays Jesus as the preeminent man of effective petition. Not even the Son of God can survive trials and temptations solely

---

23. The verb "come into" (*eiserchomesthai*) is very similar to the "lead into" (*eispherein*) of the Lord's Prayer. Some interpreters argue for the importance of the pronouns and pronominal prefixes involved in the sixth petition. For instance, Powell, "Lead Us Not into Temptation," emphasizes the distinction between "lead to" versus "lead into (the hands of)" temptation, while Chase, *Lord's Prayer in the Early Church*, 72, 84, 103, points out the distinction between "from" (*apo*), the word used in Matt. 6:13, and "out of" (*ek*): "When *apo* is used with a verb meaning deliverance, it properly implies nothing more than that the threatened danger has been averted" (72).

24. For a thorough exegetical and theological examination of this passage, see Crump, *Jesus the Intercessor*, 154–62.

through individual willpower, whatever his personal resources, whether human or divine. The man Jesus of Nazareth lives a life of thoroughgoing dependence; he is dependent on the heavenly strength made available to him through prayer—just like any other human being who endures hunger, sorrow, and exhaustion.[25] When Jesus tells his followers to pray, "Do not lead us into temptation, but deliver us from evil," he is sharing the content of his own private petitions, the prayers that removed the obstacles and paved the way for his successful journey to Calvary and beyond.

These observations also provide the key to resolving the nagging question about an apparent contradiction between the Father's will to test his people and our prayers to be spared such tests. An identical tension lay at the heart of Jesus's Gethsemane prayer. On the one hand, Jesus well knew that Calvary was his divine destiny; he had been teaching his disciples about the inevitability of death in Jerusalem for some time (Mark 8:31–32; 9:12–13; 10:32–34; 12:1–12; 14:17–25 and parallels). In fact, Jesus renounced Peter's insistence that he avoid this fate as one more instance of satanic temptation (8:33). Yet, he enters Gethsemane specifically praying to be spared; he groaned, "Take this cup from me." Seemingly, Jesus has succumbed to temptation! The tension is blatant, and it is relieved only by the proviso, "If it is possible." What are we to make of all this?

Biblical thought often prefers to hold alternative truths in tension, rather than explore the finer logical relationships holding them together.[26] In this instance, Jesus is balancing four theological truths simultaneously: (1) nothing is impossible for the Father; (2) it is God's will to test his people; (3) God urges his people to avoid all avoidable testing; and (4) we are welcome to bring any request to the Father, as long as we finally surrender our wishes to his will. How these four assertions cohere with one another in specific situations is not explained logically or didactically, but is vividly demonstrated through Jesus's behavior. We observe a living answer in the Gospel narrative rather than study abstractions divorced from the particularities of life. In this instance, the one perfect man, Jesus of Nazareth, desperately but obedi-

25. I establish the exegetical foundations for these observations and their theological implications in *Jesus the Intercessor*, 109–53, 166–75.

26. The classic example is the paradoxical relationship between divine sovereignty and the freedom of the human will. Are we predestined to have faith, or do we choose to believe? Various theological and philosophical constructs have been advanced throughout church history to answer these questions, but none of them are explicitly articulated anywhere in the New Testament. Scripture is content to leave the raw data of (paradoxical?) theological assertions embedded within the texts.

ently asked to be spared the final test that would forever determine his acceptability (or unacceptability) before God and the heavenly court. Yet, in the very same breath he simultaneously abandoned his own will to the Father's eternal salvific purposes: "Spare me this fate, but above all else, do your own will." He leaves it for the Father to determine how the proper balance is struck.

From this vantage point, we can see that the last petition of the Lord's Prayer is intimately connected with the third: "Father, may your will be done." As we repeat these two requests, we do more than embrace a theological tension; we echo the Savior's Gethsemane prayer: "Father, spare me from this test, but execute your plan first and foremost." Similarly, the praying disciple first surrenders to the sovereignty of God's reign and his kingdom plan for creation; then and only then do we ask for deliverance from testing while trusting the Father to know when, where, and how to best consent or refuse. In any event, repeated prayers for the sanctification of God's name, the establishment of his reign, the simple supply of daily sustenance, the forgiveness of sin, and reconciliation with our neighbor will have already gone a long way toward not only answering specific questions about what the Father expects of us in each new test, but shaping a godly character that will intuit the best course for faithfulness under duress.

The Lord's Prayer Now and Then

"To three sins man is daily susceptible—thoughts of evil, reliance on prayer, and slander."[27] This surprising adage appears in several different portions of the Babylonian Talmud (tractates *Berakhot* 32b, 55a and *Bava Batra* 164b), but why would any of the rabbis think to lump prayer together with such blatant sins as slander and perverse fantasies? Their observations reveal a depth of insight gained only by the experienced, for they grasped, in ways that modern Westerners have mostly forgotten, that human approach to God is both an awesome and a precarious encounter. Communication with the Holy One is the most important conversation that any human being will ever have, which also makes it liable to the most egregious abuse by even the most well-intentioned petitioner. The individual bowing before God in prayer is the same person guilty of perverse fantasies and neighborly backstabbing. In how many different ways will we bring similar perversions (consciously or unconsciously) to our communication with our heavenly Father? The rabbis merely recognized a fact of life: the same sin that all too easily

27. See B. Martin, *Prayer in Judaism*, 17.

causes us to malign our innocent neighbors also leads us to abuse the gift of prayer.

Aware of prayer's privilege, and awakened to Jesus's bringing of something new, the disciples asked to be taught to pray as Jesus prayed (Luke 11:1). The Lord's Prayer is given as a paradigm that facilitates genuine prayer while combating the perverse prayer that naturally arises whenever we are left to our own spiritual devices. Jesus first points us away from ourselves. There is a complete reorientation of natural human priorities. My tendency to view petition as an opportunity to permanently inscribe my felt needs at the top of God's agenda is abolished. Anyone who genuinely encounters the king bringing in his kingdom becomes immediately entranced by his majesty and impassioned by the vision of every knee bowing and every tongue confessing the lordship of God the Father. Consequently, Christian prayer "seeks first the kingdom of God," articulating the disciple's passion to see the Father-King honored and obeyed throughout every nook and cranny of creation. Then, as subjects of the King and children of the Father, disciples implement kingdom priorities to honor and obey in their daily lives. Material goods are held responsibly but very loosely; we are satisfied with just enough of life's necessities to facilitate continued service. The remainder of our priorities similarly inhabit a spiritual dimension embracing the forgiveness of sin, reconciliation with our neighbor, and faithfulness in the face of testing. An initial reading might easily conclude that this is a terribly constricted set of concerns; certainly, it is only a drop in the bucket of an overwhelming deluge of challenges and apparent necessities that arise every day in families, jobs, neighborhoods, and society. But further consideration reveals that this brief, simple prayer indicates the essentials, and by underscoring these essential components of a Christian prayer life, it provides guidance far more comprehensive than any casuistic listing could ever convey. Of course, Jesus is not saying that we dare not pray for anything else—additional personal petitions could always be added even to synagogue prayers. Rather, the question becomes, Do we pray for these things first? Are these our top priorities in life? And whenever additional concerns arise, are they filtered through this "kingdom grid" given to us by Jesus? Do we pray as American citizens, mothers of preschool children, bankers, lawyers, and Girl Scout leaders who happen to be members of the kingdom of God? Or do we pray as the Father's kingdom people who momentarily happen to be American citizens, parents, bankers, and neighbors to all those desperately in need of the kingdom?

All people adopt, or are adopted by, a fundamental passion that serves (knowingly or unwittingly) to organize their view of the world and then determines where, when, and how they invest their time and energy.

For many years of my young life that basic organizational commitment was falconry—the training of and hunting with hawks. The rigors of this ancient sport are such that every decision in a falconer's life must accommodate the hawk's needs. Its requirements—special diet, housing, training, equipment, exercise, and attention—must rule over every dimension of a falconer's existence. I chose this lifestyle for many years and was quite happy to coordinate work, vacations, weekends, meals, social activities—virtually every component of every day—around my bird's requirements. The only way to let a bird of prey into your life is to let it fly to the top of your priority list (which is precisely where it immediately insists on going). Any successful falconer will agree that falconry is never just a part of your life; falconry becomes your life.

Whether we acknowledge it, all people are controlled by their own peculiar bird of prey. It circles upward through the imagination, hovers over major decisions, and clings tightly to every personal passion. Jesus came into the world and announced that his bird of prey was the Father's plan to usher the kingdom into our world. The Lord's Prayer now insists that it must become our top priority as well.

Excursus 1: Our *Epiousios* Bread

The various possible meanings of the fourth petition can be grouped into four basic categories:[28]

1. The difficult word (*epiousios*) is created from the preposition *epi* plus the noun *ousia* ("being, existence"). This yields two possible senses. First, it could straightforwardly refer to "the bread necessary for our existence," the food essential to human survival. On the other hand, Origen advocates the same etymology but draws on Platonic philosophy and John 6 to construct another, highly spiritualized interpretation yielding the sense "supersubstantial bread," the heavenly bread of life that comes through the gift of the Spirit.[29] This second proposal was particularly popular among Roman Catholic commentators throughout the ages.

28. See Donn, "Our Daily Bread"; Brown, "Pater Noster"; Orchard, "Meaning of *ton Epiousion*"; I. Marshall, *Luke*, 459–60; M. John, "Give Us This Day"; Hemer, "Ἐπιούσιος"; Hultgren, "Bread Petition of the Lord's Prayer"; Hagner, *Matthew*, 1.149–50; and Nolland, *Luke*, 615–16.

29. Hemer, "Ἐπιούσιος," 88–89, provides a good critique of Origen. Critics of views 1 and 2 often contend that the *iota* of the prefixed *epi* would have elided, yielding either *epousia* (#1) or *epousa* (#2). While this would have been the case in Classical Greek, the rules may not have been enforced in a later Koine Greek derivation; see Nolland, *Luke*, 615.

2. *Epiousios* may be a contraction of the temporal phrase *epi tēn ousan* [*hēmeran*] ("for the present [day]"). Advocates of this view often refer to God's daily provision of heavenly manna in Exod. 16:4 and the faith required to collect only one day's portion at a time: "I will rain down bread from heaven for you. The people are to go out each day and gather enough for that day."[30]

3. The third etymological option, increasingly popular among scholars, derives *epiousios* from the feminine participle of the verb *epeimi* ("to come upon, arrive").[31] In this case, the petition is translated "give us today our bread for the coming day," with an emphasis on immediacy rather than chronology. In other words, when offered as a morning prayer it becomes a petition for today's necessities; when prayed in the evening it looks to tomorrow's requirements.[32] Although critics of this view claim that it contravenes Jesus's injunction about not worrying for tomorrow (Matt. 6:34), adherents respond that prayer for tomorrow is not the same thing as worry over tomorrow. Indeed, prayer may provide the perfect prophylactic to anxiety.[33]

4. The final school of thought is related to the third option but builds its argument independently of any particular etymology. The early church fathers recognized that, regardless of the linguistic details, the implicit contrast between bread for "today" and "tomorrow" was quite clear. Consequently, they believed themselves justified in extrapolating that comparison between now and then into a spiritual contrast between two different epochs, the present age and the future age.[34] The "bread for tomorrow" became the messianic banquet, the inauguration of the end time brought by God's Messiah. A principal modern advocate of this view is Jeremias, who writes, "in ancient Judaism 'tomorrow' meant not only the next day but also the great Tomorrow, the final consummation," although he fails to

30. Critics of this suggestion point out that it makes both Matthew's "today" and Luke's "day by day" redundant tautologies.

31. The articular participle *hē epiousa* is used in the New Testament for "the next day, tomorrow" (Acts 7:26; 16:11; 20:15; 21:18; 23:11). Origen acknowledged this possibility but rejected it (*On Prayer* 27.13). Chase, *Lord's Prayer in the Early Church*, 44–53, argues strongly for this view; the argument was strengthened significantly by Hemer, "Ἐπιούσιος."

32. In this case, *epiousios* would indicate that the Lord's Prayer was being repeated by the Christian community in lieu of (in addition to?) the Shema. *Didache* 8 makes this practice explicit, but Matthew and Luke may offer earlier evidence of the practice within the Gospel tradition.

33. Both Tertullian (*On Prayer* 6) and Gregory of Nyssa (*Lord's Prayer*, sermon 5) make similar observations.

34. See Hultgren, "Bread Petition of the Lord's Prayer," 46nn27–28, for references to ancient and modern adherents of this perspective.

provide any textual evidence for this assertion.[35] According to these interpreters, the petition for bread becomes another iteration of the previous requests that God's kingdom come and will be done.[36]

What are we to make of these different interpretations? First, the variations between the four schools of thought disperse themselves along two different axes. One line of reasoning attempts to determine the original, root meaning of the word *epiousios* and then build its interpretation accordingly, although it is interesting that the final results produce little in the way of significant differences. Whether the petition is read as a request for "bread for subsistence," "bread for today," or "bread for the coming day" hardly matters; the upshot is much the same. Jesus is instructing his disciples to turn to the Father for their earthly necessities, with an emphasis on *necessity*.

The second interpretive axis not only functions independently of the diverse theories about word derivation, but also produces a sizable difference in how the petition is finally understood. Regardless of the origin of *epiousios*, various interpreters find different ways to spiritualize its significance, reading it either as the "supersubstantial bread" of eternal life and all that this entails or finding here a request that God immediately consummate all the eschatological promises of the coming kingdom. Whatever the particular permutation, the word "bread" ends up carrying a very heavy theological load in this reading, a load that many, including myself, believe it is hardly fit to bear. When Jesus elsewhere makes a metaphorical reference to bread, the context indicates its significance: "Watch out for the yeast of the Pharisees" (Mark 8:15); "blessed is the man who will eat at the feast in the kingdom of God" (Luke 14:15); "I confer on you a kingdom, . . . so that you may eat and drink at my table in my kingdom" (22:29–30). Judaism often described the kingdom of God in terms of an opulent banquet where no one would ever again go hungry or thirsty, but the literary context indicated that the food was symbolic. Such symbolism, however, is hardly self-evident, much less compelling, when reading the simple words "give us today our necessary bread." As for Origen's introduction of Platonic categories to his exegesis and the propensity of certain commentators to follow his lead—as if "patristic"

---

35. Jeremias, *Prayers of Jesus*, 100.

36. Critics rightly assert that (a) this view cannot cohere with Luke's "day by day"; (b) the plural personal pronoun "our" most easily fits with the human need for basic sustenance (Ps. 102:4; Lam. 5:9; Isa. 4:1; Ezek. 4:15; 5:16; 12:19; Sir. 12:5; Hosea 2:5); (c) "tomorrow" never appears in Jesus's teaching as a reference to the consummation; and (d) Luke 14:15, with its reference to "eating bread in the kingdom of God," is the closest approximation to this view found in the Gospels; it is, however, a long way from this phraseology to praying for "the bread of tomorrow."

were synonymous with "inspired"—I hardly need to comment on how inappropriate it is to overwhelm the biblical text with such personal prejudice, no matter how well intended.[37]

Excursus 2: *Peirasmos* in the Lord's Prayer

In New Testament Greek the word *peirasmos* is open to two different, albeit related, translations: temptation to sin, and testing for the purposes of proving. The proper sense is generally determined by the context in which the word appears. Unfortunately, context alone is not always decisive. Beginning with this fundamental division, interpreters explore a wide variety of extrapolated nuances, depending on who is viewed as the agent of *peirasmos*, its intended outcome, and the precise meaning of that agent's "leading us into" such difficult circumstances. The logical relationships among the numerous interpretations of *peirasmos* in Matt. 6:13 are depicted in the following chart.

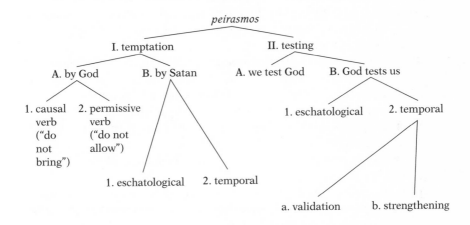

37. "Ousia, properly understood, is regarded as incorporeal by the philosophers who insist that the preeminent reality is incorporeal. It has, then, for them an unchanging existence which admits neither increase nor decrease. . . . The supersubstantial bread, then, is that which is most adapted to the rational nature and is akin to its very substance" (Origen, *On Prayer* 27.8–9). Is any more required to show that the venerable Origen has more to do with Plotinus than Jesus at this point in his thinking? Chase's observations are apropos: "The statement of this [mystical/spiritual] view is, it seems to me, its best refutation. If so many layers of meaning . . . could be wrapped up in one single word, human language could not bear the strain" (*Lord's Prayer in the Early Church*, 44n1).

I.A.1. When *peirasmos* is translated "temptation" the agent can be either God or Satan. As far back as Tertullian (*On Prayer* 8), the majority of commentators pointed out that James 1:13 assures disciples that "God cannot be tempted with evil, neither does he tempt anyone." Therefore, since God will not cause anyone to be tempted by sin or actively lead anyone into sin, this option is immediately excluded.

I.A.2. There is another sense, however, in which God might still be associated with temptation. Those who explore Aramaic reconstructions of the original prayer claim that the Aramaic verb underlying Greek *peirasmos* could convey, instead of a causative "do not bring/lead me into temptation" (#I.A.1), a permissive "do not allow/permit me to come into temptation."[38] In other words, Satan is the tempter while God remains the sovereign protector able to deliver his children from satanic attack. This yields a sense that was commonly offered by the church fathers (although they were not relying on Aramaic suggestions), wherein the prayer was interpreted to say, "Do not allow us to succumb/yield to temptation." Temptations will come, but we pray that God strengthens us enough to stand firm.[39] The problem here is that, aside from the dubious nature of basing an interpretation on hypothetical Aramaic originals, this is not the obvious meaning of the Greek words preserved in the Gospel tradition.

I.B. Satan is typically the agent of temptation in the New Testament (1 Cor. 7:5; James 1:13; Rev. 2:10); hence his occasional epithet as "the tempter" (Matt. 4:3; 1 Thess. 3:5). Demonic assaults may appear in either earthly attempts to lead God's people into daily faithlessness (#I.B.2) or (as Jeremias prefers) one final eschatological assault (#I.B.1), the last desperate satanic testing, which includes the rise of the antichrist, the abomination of desolation, and the final persecution of God's people before the last judgment.[40]

The principal objection to Jeremias's popular eschatological perspective on satanic temptation is that there is no precedent for the word *peirasmos* (particularly when lacking the definite article) being used as a technical term for the final apocalyptic crisis.[41] To complicate matters further, this entire category of interpretation (both #I.B.1 and

38. Jeremias, *Prayers of Jesus*, 104–5; and Willis, "Lead Us Not into Temptation," 282–83.

39. Cameron, "Lead Us Not into Temptation," 299–300. For examples in some early commentators, see Tertullian, *On Prayer* 8; Origen, *On Prayer* 30; and Calvin, *Institutes of the Christian Religion* §3.20.46. This is a popular interpretation, although its rationale can vary widely from person to person.

40. Jeremias, *Prayers of Jesus*, 105–6.

41. Moule, "Unsolved Problem," 66–67; and Gerhardsson, "Matthean Version of the Lord's Prayer," 216.

#I.B.2) overlaps the earlier possibility of God's permissive allowance of satanic temptations among his people (#I.A.2). While James may have abhorred the suggestion that God might be the direct agent of temptation (#I.A.1), elsewhere in the New Testament the Father is freely described as the indirect agent of his people's testing by allowing satanic temptation to occur.[42] Consequently, Satan tempted Jesus in the wilderness, but the Gospel writers make it clear that Jesus was led into the desert by the Holy Spirit for that very purpose (Mark 1:12 || Matt. 4:1 || Luke 4:1–2). God's indirect agency is also seen in the Old Testament story of Job (1:6–2:10). Satanic temptation thus serves as God's tool for divine trial and approval, which leads us to *peirasmos* as testing (#II).

II.A. Scripture regularly affirms the value of divine testing and the many personal benefits that accrue to those who are stretched by their heavenly Father. Old Testament prophet Zechariah praises the Lord's plan to "refine [his people] like silver and test them like gold" (13:9), while New Testament writer James assures his readers that they can "consider it pure joy . . . whenever [they] face trials of many kinds" (1:2). In light of passages such as these, some commentators draw attention to the logical inconsistency of disciples now being instructed to ask that they be delivered from any and all testing. Why should we pray to escape God's program for personal growth and maturation? In order to eliminate this apparent contradiction, some suggest that the testing being referred to is not God's testing of us, but our testing of God.[43] The principal example offered on behalf of this interpretation is Israel's testing of God at Massah (Exod. 17:1–7; the Hebrew word means testing); by failing God's test, faithless Israel tested and provoked the Lord through their disobedience (Ps. 95:8–9; Heb. 3:7–11; compare Acts 5:9; 15:10).[44]

According to this perspective, the sixth petition asks, "Father, do not allow us to put you to the test." In effect, it becomes another version of the view that we ask God not to allow us to "succumb" or "yield" to sin and fail the test (#I.A.2). But there are several problems with this suggestion. First, it is hardly a straightforward translation of the sentence, owing more to reading this petition through the lens of Exod. 17 than

42. K. Kuhn's important study of testing in the Qumran literature fails at this point. He assumes that the New Testament must strictly adhere to Qumran categories and that, since *peirasmos* at Qumran was the exclusive domain of Satan, God could never be its agent in the New Testament; see "New Light on Temptation," 108.

43. This is also the rationale for K. Kuhn's agreement with the church fathers in wanting the petition to mean "let us not come into the danger of falling"; "New Light on Temptation," 109.

44. Houk, "*Peirasmos*"; and Grayston, "Decline of Temptation."

to anything else. Second, it does not cohere with Matthew's additional line, where the focus is clearly on God's efforts on our behalf ("deliver us from evil"), not on our actions toward God ("do not let us test you"). Finally, this argument is rooted in a false premise; there is no need to alleviate any apparent contradiction between God's desire to test his people and our prayers for deliverance. Those two statements can live together very nicely, as they did for Jesus in Gethsemane.

II.B.1. Many others are quite happy to embrace the notion of divine testing without hesitation. Some still sidestep the apparent tension involved by suggesting that Jesus is referring, not to ongoing, mundane trials, but to the final, divine test at the end of history referred to in Rev. 3:10: "I will also keep you from the hour of trial that is going to come upon the whole world to test those who live on the earth." The earlier criticisms leveled against an eschatological temptation by Satan (#I.B.1) continue to apply here as well. Revelation 3 is indeed describing cosmic trials at the end of time, but we know this not because the word *peirasmos* is used, but because of the context in which it appears, an apocalyptic context that is nowhere to be seen in the Lord's Prayer. If one insists that the overall kingdom perspective of the prayer implies just such an eschatological testing, then I remind the reader that we have now entered the second half of the Lord's Prayer, where the daily quest for mundane direction in kingdom living takes over the agenda.

II.B.2.a. Finally, once God is seen to be the one testing his people, there are still two possible renderings of the test. A few commentators argue that God's tests are not simply to stretch or strengthen us, but to provide visible validation of our faithfulness.[45] Yahweh tested the Israelites in the wilderness in order "to know what was in [their] heart" (Deut. 8:2). He provided an opportunity for them to reveal their reliability and commitment. Similarly, Paul urges the Corinthians "to test themselves to see whether they are holding on to the faith" (2 Cor. 13:5, my translation). Such divine testing is intended to expose the true inner character, to vindicate the faithful. Hence, the psalmist prays, "Test me, O LORD, and try me, / examine my heart" (Ps. 26:2). He wants to prove his faithfulness to God. Unfortunately for this argument, C. F. D. Moule conducted a thorough investigation of *peirasmos* in the Greek Bible and concluded that the sense "validation" is proper to the *dokimasia/dokimazein* word group but not to *peirasmos*.[46] Furthermore, it once again neglects to take account of Matthew's "deliver us from evil." The first evangelist

45. Cameron, "Lead Us Not Into Temptation," 300.
46. Moule, "Unsolved Problem," 67–69.

does not seem to have validation in mind, but a potentially dangerous assault requiring deliverance.

II.B.2.b. I prefer the sense of *peirasmos* as referring to God's temporal interests in strengthening the faith of his people. The interpretive significance of this rendering has already been explored in the chapter.

Theological Reflections
on the Lord's Prayer

We pause again to step back and survey the results of our look at the Lord's Prayer in order to expand the more generalized theological understanding of prayer already uncovered in the Synoptic Gospels. Conclusions from the earlier chapters probing the Gospel constraints on petition have been confirmed, while several new factors have been added to the theological mix.

First and foremost, we discovered that specifically Christian prayer arises from the centrality of Jesus Christ in all genuine relationship with God. The Lord's Prayer is decidedly Christocentric in the sense that it can be prayed authentically only by those who surrender themselves in discipleship to Jesus the Messiah, the inaugurator of God's kingdom on earth. The Lord's Prayer is not a liturgical blessing invoked over the daily itineraries of religious people. The Lord's Prayer can be grasped only by people who first find themselves grasped by the Spirit of Jesus; wrenched from their old way of living; transplanted into the new, invasively eschatological dimension of kingdom living; and now consistently seeking the glory and honor of God their Father. To pray the Lord's Prayer is to pray as Jesus prayed while having "no place to lay his head," sacrificing his life to the consequences, both wonderful and wanton, of proclaiming that "you must repent, for the kingdom of God is near."

Such surrender to the personal coming of Christ (historically and existentially) introduces a complex multidimensional relationship with God as Father. He is simultaneously Creator, King, and Redeemer, both the Holy One whose name demands universal sanctification and the provider who answers our requests for daily bread just as he clothes the lilies of the field in colorful splendor. We are called to abandon all simplistic, one-dimensional portraits of God, whether as daddy, love personified, or impersonal grumpy autocrat. The cosmic Father of Jesus Christ comes to us as both awful and intimate, commanding and tender, exalted and humiliated all at the same time; and we are drawn to him as sinners, beloved, guilty, forgiven, liberated, and subservient in precisely the same instant. He becomes our Father in his capacity as Jesus's Father. The Lord's Prayer requires that we explore the full range of this multifaceted relationship with the one who is now incorporating each of us, individually by faith, into his plan for restoring the universe to its proper place before his throne through the work of Jesus Christ his Son.

The prayer's preoccupation with God's kingdom reorients a disciple's attitudes toward this world in ways that easily cohere with the lessons of chapters 1–4. The Lord's Prayer reiterates Jesus's requirement that every disciple abandon his or her own will to the will of the Father—"your kingdom come, your will be done" is every believer's supreme concern. Realizing that God intends to overturn the worldly status quo, faithful disciples believe in the possibility of miracles and pray in faith that the Father intervene supernaturally wherever, whenever necessary. Faith that looks for miracles, however, should also produce enough spiritual sensitivity to realize that what we sometimes assume is beneficial can, in fact, be as destructive as the pit viper requested by a naïve eight-year-old who just saw a National Geographic special about tropical snakes. When judged by the wisdom of our heavenly Father, we are no less impressionable and naïve than that child. Therefore, while disciples pray for miracles with faith, they also admit that the truly necessary miracles are whatever acts of power—sometimes public and overt, at other times privately erupting in quiet recesses—advance the Father's kingdom on earth.

Finally, as the Messiah's new temple, disciples pray for the elimination of every sin and impurity, whether it occurs privately within ourselves or collectively among our relationships. The King's arrival has made us a holy people who confess, repent, and forgive as we ourselves have been forgiven. In this way, the purity of the Spirit's new, earthly sanctuary is maintained, and the efficacy of prayer offered from the new temple is assured. Prayer is not only private and personal, offered secretly from our hidden closets (Matt. 6:5–6); it is also the collective voice of Christ's church, the worldwide people of God adoring, surrendering, asking, and confessing in unison.

8

Asking in Jesus's Name

Johannine Prayer

L ike many college students, I was something of a church shopper in my younger days; my ecclesiastical selections were often influenced by which young ladies currently attended which local churches. For a brief period I fired up my blue 1962 Volkswagen Beetle each Sunday morning and drove several miles to a small rural fellowship because it was the church home of my most recent infatuation. I can still recall the tiny Sunday school class meeting in a closet-sized corner of an unfinished basement where an older gentleman with a black pencil mustache taught a course on prayer. While highlighting the Christian's privilege in being invited to approach the God of all holiness, he declared that acceptable reverence required us to use both King James English and the exact benediction, "In Jesus's name, Amen."

My eyes widened, and I asked for clarification. He meant exactly what he said. God hears only prayers offered in Elizabethan diction and then precisely concluded in Jesus's name. I decided then and there it was fortunate for both my spiritual and my dating life that my latest infatuation remained thoroughly unrequited. I quickly moved on without regrets.

Prayer is difficult enough without fanciful legalisms demanding that antiquated language be added to the mix. There is something vaguely pagan about such thinking, as it transforms prayer into magical incantation dependent on the proper recitation of stock phrases memorized from the dead, or at least anachronistic, language of a bygone era. It is not hard for us to move beyond the dangerous misconception that God answers to only "thee" and "thou." What, however, about the other claim? Does not the New Testament clearly instruct us to pray "in Jesus's name"? In fact, the Johannine Jesus says, "You may ask me for anything in my name, and I will do it" (John 14:14). The gates of faith are once again opened wide, seemingly without limit. Here is a mandate, not just for praying in the name of Jesus, but for knowing that any and every request will be granted when it is so blessed. Yet, the thoughtful person cannot help but revisit the questions raised in an earlier chapter. What about the many heartfelt prayers of sincere believing men and women of faith who anguished in the name of Jesus with enough faith to move the entire Himalayan range, yet whose prayers remain stubbornly unanswered? Is there a special secret way to repeat Jesus's name before success is eventually squeezed out of heaven, before my particular "anything" is finally granted?

What, exactly, does it mean to ask in Jesus's name?

What's in a Name?

The basic spadework for answering this question was already performed when we examined the first petition of the Lord's Prayer: "Father, sanctify your name." John employs the same idiom as Matthew and Luke when he enjoins his readers to find eternal life by "believing in his [Jesus's] name" (John 1:12; 2:23; 3:18; 20:31). To believe in Jesus's name is to confess his true identity as the Son sent from the Father now offering us eternal life. Confessing Jesus's name is equivalent to surrendering to his lordship as the Savior. Just as sanctifying the divine name (in the Lord's Prayer) entails recognizing the holiness of God's character, so asking in Jesus's name (in John's Gospel) involves praying according to the character of this one and only Son.[1] It is not the simple repetition of a stock phrase, but the (re)direction of an entire life. To clarify this point further, let us look more closely at the

1. Some scholars suggest that this is only one of a number of instances where John reveals his affinity for the Lord's Prayer; see George, *Communion with God*, 203; Dodd, *Historical Tradition in the Fourth Gospel*, 333–34; Walker, "Lord's Prayer"; and Cullmann, *Prayer in the New Testament*, 107.

Johannine passages where this language appears, all in the so-called
Farewell Discourse:[2]

> And whatever you ask in my name, I will do it, so that the Father may be
> glorified in the Son. Whatever you ask in my name, I will do. (14:13–14)

> If you remain in me and my word remains in you, ask for whatever you
> wish and it will be given to you. . . . You did not choose me, but I chose
> you and appointed you to go and bear fruit that will last so that whatever
> you ask the Father in my name will be given to you. (15:7, 16)

> Truly, truly I say to you, whatever you ask the Father in my name, he will
> give to you. Until now you have not asked for anything in my name. Ask
> and you will receive and your joy will be complete. . . . In that day you will
> ask in my name. (16:23, 26)

Johannine discipleship emulates the Father's sending of the Son. Just
as the Father sent Jesus into the world, so Jesus sends his disciples to
continue his work (20:21). Jesus announced that he had "come in the
name of the Father" (5:43) and "performed miracles in the Father's
name" (10:25) because he was obediently fulfilling God's plan for the
world's salvation.[3] Acting as the Father's agent—in his name—did not
grant Jesus the power to autonomously perform anything he wished,
willy-nilly. He was constrained as any agent is constrained by the character and the purposes of the authority being represented.[4] This was
no less true for the Son of God than for his followers. Jesus unabash-
edly explained that "the Son can do nothing by himself; he can only
do what he sees his Father doing, because whatever the Father does
the Son also does" (5:19 NIV; see the entire discourse in 5:19–30).
This is a remarkable christological statement of the Son's absolute
subordination to the Father's will. For Jesus to act in the name of the

2. All translations from the Gospel of John in this chapter are my own, unless otherwise stated.

3. There is tremendous variety in the significance of the idiom "in the name of,"
depending on its context. For instance, "sanctifying a name," "coming in a name," and
"asking in a name" all have different, though related, nuances; for a good discussion of this
flexibility and its Hebrew-Aramaic background, see Hartman, "Into the Name of Jesus."

4. Schnackenburg, *John*, 3.73; Cullmann, *Prayer in the New Testament*, 100–101; and
Lincoln, "God's Name," 173–76. This was every prophet's responsibility: "If anyone does
not listen to my words that the prophet speaks in my name, I myself will call him to account. But a prophet who presumes to speak in my name anything I have not commanded
him to say . . . must be put to death" (Deut. 18:19–20; compare James 5:10, 14). Speaking
and acting in the name of another was synonymous with executing the other's will, taking
the other's place as if he or she were actually present. For an illuminating exploration of
personal agency in the ancient world, see S. Elliott, "John 15:15."

Father was for him to speak and to perform only those things that the Father wanted him to say and to do. There is no independent activity whatsoever in the Son's life—only obedience, subservience, yielding, surrender, a total acquiescence to another's eternal plan. The Son's motives are never his own, but always the Father's, and only for the Father's greater glory (1:18; 8:49–50; 11:4; 13:31; 14:13; 15:8; 17:4). Jesus echoes the same prioritizing of divine honor found in the Lord's Prayer when he prays, reaffirming his own subordination, "Father, glorify your name" (12:28).

John 14:13–14

In response to Philip's question about the Father's identity (14:8), Jesus answered by explaining his union, or "abiding," with the Father (14:10a: "I am in the Father and the Father is in me"), and the complete obedience that this union created in Jesus's life (14:10b: "The words I say are not just my own. Rather, it is the Father, living in me, who is doing his work"). Thus to know Jesus was to know the Father. Within that framework, Jesus made several promises to his followers. First, he promised to hear their prayers and to serve as the mediator who makes the Father's answers a reality (14:13–14: "I will do whatever you ask in my name").[5] Second, Jesus specified the precise content of the prayers about which he offered that guarantee. He did not promise a positive response to any and every personal request but only to those that aimed at following his ministry of bringing glory to God. The "greater works" (14:12) are answers to the prayers of obedient men and women abiding in Jesus just as Jesus was abiding in the Father, disciples who, like Jesus, sought God's glory first and foremost (14:13).[6]

Finally, the result of these two promises will be that a disciple's prayers will enjoy the same significance with the Father as Jesus's own. Previously, as Jesus faced the stench of Lazarus's tomb, he expressed the assurance of knowing that the Father always heard whatever he asked in prayer (11:41–42), a confidence shared by Martha, who exclaimed, "Lord, . . . I know that even now God will give you whatever you ask" (11:21–22 NIV). These earlier statements establish the proper context for Jesus's later promises concerning prayer. The Farewell Discourse elaborates how the impregnable efficacy of Jesus's prayer life will eventually be transferred

5. Although some witnesses omit the pronoun "me" or replace it with "the Father," the superior reading retains "ask *me* in *my* name"; see Metzger, *Textual Commentary*, 208.

6. See the uniform expositions of Westcott, *John*, 204–5; Brown, *John*, 636; Bultmann, *John*, 611–12; Schnackenburg, *John*, 3.72; Fee, "John 14:8–17," 170–74; and Beasley-Murray, *John*, 255.

to his followers.[7] The Father will receive our prayers in the same fashion as he received the Son's, promising to advance his mission through those who learn to live as Jesus lived and to pray as Jesus prayed. Such men and women will experience miracles because they renounce self-interest and participate in the Son's motivating vision: *sola gloria Deo*.

John 15:7, 16

Jesus employs the metaphor of a vine and its branches in order to call disciples to "remain" in him as he has "remained" in the Father (14:10–11; 15:1–8). Apart from Jesus the disciple can do nothing (15:5), just as apart from the Father Jesus could do nothing (14:10). Yet, just as Jesus's union with the Father produced miraculous fruit (14:11), so our union with Jesus will also produce abundant fruit (15:5). The key, therefore, to answered prayer resides here in this promise of spiritual fruit. Once again, Jesus is not referring to any request whatsoever but to prayers conceived in the union of God's will and our own, wherein personal desires are recreated by the eschatological promises of eternal life.[8] In John 15 "abiding" becomes the functional equivalent of "in Jesus's name," requiring conformity to the revelation of Jesus in every respect.[9]

It is particularly important that the promise of guaranteed prayer is couched in a conditional clause: "*If* you remain in me and my words remain in you, ask whatever you wish, and it will be given to you" (15:7 NIV). Once again, prayer is not a blank check but an extended vision of the spiritual possibilities available to those who continually abide in obedience. The promise of "bearing abundant fruit" (15:8, 16) is a restatement of Jesus's prediction that disciples will eventually do "greater works" than he (14:12). Both the fruit and answered prayer are the products of union with Christ, and their outcome is always glory to the Father (15:8). This is Jesus's recipe for efficacious prayer: it always arises from perfect union with the will of God; it aims to realize his plans for ministry; it begins and ends with a passion for the Father's exaltation, not as pious window dressing, but as the catalytic, erupting passion.

Jesus's second promise comes at the end of the vineyard metaphor where he elaborates the demands of Christian obedience (15:9–17). Jesus reiterates his earlier instructions that disciples arrive at the desired destination of fruitfulness only by walking the course of complete

7. M. Thompson, "Intercession in the Johannine Community"; and Dowd, "Toward a Johannine Theology of Prayer."

8. Westcott, *John*, 218; Bultmann, *John*, 538–39, 546; Schnackenburg, *John*, 3.102, 112–13; and Beasley-Murray, *John*, 273.

9. Lincoln, "God's Name," 174.

submission (15:15–16). All those who genuinely abide in the Father and the Son demonstrate authentic devotion by obeying Christ's commandments; we will love and obey Jesus just as he has loved and obeyed the Father (15:10, 12, 14). He warns that "apart from me you can do nothing" (15:4–5 NIV), a warning that includes our ability to pray meaningfully at all, for the Father grants a hearing only to those who appear before him immersed in the life of Christ. These are the people who may hope that the "Father will give them whatever they ask in Jesus's name," a promise solidly couched in the unequivocal demands of unconditional love. We are assured that the Father responds to the prayers of Jesus's true friends (15:15) as they identify themselves by requests rooted in the ground of self-sacrificial devotion.

John 16:23, 26

The disciples are thoroughly confused by Jesus's instruction on the impending gift of the Spirit (waiting to be sent from the Father "in Jesus's name"; 14:26; 15:26) and Jesus's own imminent return to the Father (15:26–27; 16:5–18). As one might expect, the Twelve had posed numerous questions throughout the Farewell Discourse, reflecting how little they understood and how much was yet to be resolved (13:24–25, 37; 14:5, 8, 22; 16:17–18). In partial response to this confusion, Jesus delineated two eras separated by his approaching glorification on the cross (12:23–28; 17:1, 5, 24); now is the time of questions and confusion, but soon Jesus will leave the disciples and open heaven's gate so that his Spirit may resolve all their remaining uncertainties (16:4–7, 16; 17:13). John connects his final promise of answered prayer to the Spirit's future work "in that day" after Jesus's resurrection and ascension (16:23, 26).[10] Consequently, "in that day they will no longer ask Jesus any more questions" because they will finally be taught by the Spirit who brings enlightenment.[11]

With this gift of the Spirit, the Son's return to heaven simultaneously creates the possibility of immediate communication with the Father.

10. "That day" or "those days" is often a technical term in the New Testament for the eschaton, the end of the age; see Mark 13:17, 19, 24, 32; 14:25; Acts 2:18; 2 Tim. 1:12, 18; 4:8; Heb. 8:10; 10:16; Rev. 9:6.

11. John uses two different words for "ask." Erōtan (16:23a) and aitein (16:23b, 24, 26a) were partial synonyms distinguished in classical usage as "to ask a question" (erōtan) and "to ask for something/petition" (aitein). The distinction weakened in Koine Greek but remains present, though not absolute, in John's Gospel. Consequently, the sense of 16:23 is, "In that day you will not ask me any more questions. I assure you that whatever you petition the Father in my name will be given to you." For a thorough analysis of the options, see Barrett, John, 412; and Bultmann, John, 583–84.

Previously, there had been no option of direct address to the Father, only prayers directed to or through Jesus (14:14) made effective when offered in his name (14:13; 15:16). Now a radical new dimension is added to the spiritual landscape. Petitionary power continues to be determined by conformity to the will of God as expressed through union with Christ—"the Father will give you whatever you ask in my name" (16:23). Spiritual union with the resurrected, ascended Jesus, however, now ushers the disciple immediately into the Father's presence! Jesus explains that there is no longer any need for him to speak on our behalf (16:26b); he neither persuades the Father to listen nor averts divine wrath. Disciples are free to address the Father themselves, speaking with God face to face as the heavenly Father inclined to embrace us (compare 1:18!).[12] Union with the Son who lives in eternal union with the Father creates the disciple's own divine union such that the Father now receives our prayers from our own lips: "Until now you have not asked for anything in my name. Ask and you will receive. . . . I am not saying that I will ask the Father on your behalf. No, the Father himself loves you" (16:24, 26–27 NIV).

Summary

These three passages are united by at least two recurring themes. First, Jesus's work as mediator is central to Christian prayer. Even when we are finally enabled to approach God's throne directly through the Spirit, our entrance occurs only in the name of Jesus. Prayer becomes possible when we are members of the Son's entourage, granted access to the King's inner sanctum by faithful union to the obedient life of the ascended Son of Man. There is no such thing as Christian prayer apart from the living presence of Christ, both with the believer in this world and at the right hand of the Father in heaven. The so-called high priestly prayer in John 17 provides the exemplar of Christ's intercession on our behalf, an intercession that we know has already been answered because the Father "always hears whatever Jesus asks" (11:22, 42). At this point John's Gospel provides a very important link to the biblical perspective on heavenly mediation found elsewhere in the New Testament (Rom. 8:26, 34; Heb. 7:25; 1 John 2:1; see chapter 10).[13]

12. See Bultmann, *John*, 588–89; Schnackenburg, *John*, 3.163; Boyle, "Last Discourse," 218–19; and Beasley-Murray, *John*, 287.

13. On the surface, Jesus's claim that "in that day" there will no longer be a need for him to ask on our behalf (John 16:26) appears to contradict the promises of heavenly intercession found in Paul, 1 John, and Hebrews. Perhaps this is to demand too much of John's narrative; the emphasis in John 16 is the freedom of immediate access to the Father enjoyed by every believer.

Second, it may initially appear that John confronts us with such utterly unrealistic expectations that Christian prayer becomes at best an intimidating burden and at worst an absolute impossibility. Authentic prayer "in Jesus's name" looks like a pipe dream for spiritual egomaniacs. If, indeed, heaven responds positively only to requests made in complete conformity to the Father's plans, why bother?

The seemingly negative implications of John's theology at this point are the result of his emphasis on the "already" dimension of eschatology, what New Testament scholar C. H. Dodd dubs "realized eschatology." Eternity is now, in John's mind. No need to wait for future developments; eternal life is fully present today (3:36; 5:24); resurrection life is already available (5:21, 24, 26); the final judgment occurs here (3:18; 9:39). Consequently, John seems to assume that complete union, submission, and devotion to the Father also define discipleship in this present age (14:13–14; 15:7–16). "It is as though the union with Christ in Johannine prayer was experienced so intensely that there was no problem in leaving all individual wishes out of account."[14]

Yet, this is not the complete picture. John's Gospel does preserve the futuristic, "not yet" dimension typical of New Testament eschatology; eternal life looks forward to a future expansion (12:25); humanity awaits a final resurrection (6:39–40, 54) and judgment (12:48), while the Son of Man promises to return for his own (14:3, 18, 28). The link uniting these two sides of the eschatological tension is the perfect life of Jesus of Nazareth. Even in John, Jesus does not experience his own union with the Father by virtue of a divine nature or a special trinitarian status. Rather, Jesus was able to live in the Father, as the Father lived in him, because he self-consciously chose, each moment of every day, to deliberately surrender his will to the Father's. As the only human being ever to actualize heaven's perfect possibilities on this earth, he opened the eternal floodgates allowing God's coming age to inundate the here and now. On the one hand, the Father's expectations of perfect submission from his people remain binding because they have already been fulfilled in Christ. However far short we may fall of this ideal, our union with the Father will endure through faith in the perfectly obedient Son. On the other hand, as long as we live in this world we are tarnished by the spiritual rebellion from which Christ came to set us free. Consequently, even the most well-intentioned prayers "in Jesus's name" are always muddled and conflicted requests distorted by contradictory, competing aspirations: "In the name of Jesus, Gordon, Susan, social expectations, and personal selfishness I pray, Amen." Our contemporary hope in this dilemma is found in Jesus's promise of the Spirit. Whereas the salvation-

14. Cullmann, *Prayer in the New Testament*, 106.

historical dimension of the tension is resolved in the person of Jesus, the existential dimension is resolved by the Spirit sent from Jesus, the Spirit now working within us to create an ever-expanding and willing psychic space where the name of Jesus, and only the name of Jesus, has truly staked its claim. That particular Spirit-inspired dimension of prayer is guaranteed to perform even greater works than Jesus himself (14:12).[15]

A Final Johannine Clarification

Although the common authorship of John's Gospel and the three letters bearing his name remains subject to debate, there is a general consensus today that, at the very least, all four documents emanated from a common circle of shared influences and ideas. It is not surprising, then, to find that two further assurances of answered prayer appear in the Letter of 1 John, albeit with a bit of a twist:

> If our hearts do not condemn us, we have confidence before God and receive from him anything we ask, because we obey his commands and do what pleases him. And this is his command: to believe in the name of his Son, Jesus Christ, and to love one another as he commanded us. (3:21–23)

> This is the confidence we have in approaching God: that if we ask anything according to his will, he hears us. And if we know that he hears us—whatever we ask—we know that we have what we asked of him. (5:14–15)

Can there be any doubt that the author is reflecting on the same concerns raised in John's Gospel? Some commentators, such as R. Schnackenburg, suggest that these two passages offer explicit commentary on John 14–16 in an effort to correct a dangerous misunderstanding:

> The addition of the phrase "according to his will" suggests that the author has reflected on the promises of the Johannine Jesus. . . . People are not always conscious of being the people of God. They often lapse back into purely private prayer (cf. James 5:16–17). They came to expect that the dominical promise would be fulfilled not only in the missionary activity of the church (cf. John 14:12; 15:16), not only in the supernatural fruits of

15. It is a mystery to me how Cullmann can say that the struggle of unanswered prayer has no place in Johannine teaching; he mistakenly says, "It is unconditionally promised that prayer will be heard" (*Prayer in the New Testament*, 106). This is precisely what the Johannine Jesus does not say.

those united with Christ (cf. John 15:7), but also in the private or purely earthly realm.[16]

Granted, Schnackenburg's theory is just that, but theories are partly judged by their usefulness, and this theory offers a compelling account of how the complete body of Johannine prayer teaching can coexist within the same body of literature.[17]

1 John 3:21–23

John's first letter revisits the central Johannine theme of abiding/indwelling and obedience to God's commands. Answered prayer is not assured unconditionally to anyone and everyone; it is limited to those living "a life pleasing to God" (3:22), a life demonstrated by obedience to the commands of faith and love (3:23). Such a lifestyle reveals true spiritual union wherein "we abide in him and he abides in us" (3:24); these are the men and women assured of a clear conscience and confidence before God in prayer (3:21). Again, the promise of answered prayer is conditioned by the same obedience required by Jesus's Gospel teaching: abiding in the one who abides in us by surrendering our will to the Father.[18] Those who, even secretly, remain unwilling to obey and to serve should not be surprised when their requests go unanswered, an outcome that should drive us all (for who has not experienced frustration in prayer?) to reexamine the darkened corners of our own convoluted hearts.

1 John 5:14–15

The final explanation is short and to the point. The Father answers requests made according to his will. Period. That is the Christian's assurance. R. Bultmann limits the relevance of 1 John 5:14–15 to the cir-

16. Schnackenburg, *Johannine Epistles*, 247. See also I. Marshall, *Epistles of John*, 199.

17. For those who remain skeptical, I add that finding the interpretive coherence here does not depend on any particular theory of community development.

18. The *hoti* clause in 3:22b, explaining why prayer is heard (because we keep his commandments), does not establish a conditional quid pro quo but depicts the loving, reciprocal relationship of mutual "abiding" that exists between the children who pray and the Father who answers (3:1); see Bultmann, *Johannine Epistles*, 58; I. Marshall, *Epistles of John*, 200; Smalley, *1, 2, 3 John*, 205–6; and Schnackenburg, *Johannine Epistles*, 187. In stating that John holds out "the certainty that these prayers, the content of which is not restricted and which therefore can address the fulfillment of every possible kind of concrete wish, will find a hearing," Strecker, *Johannine Letters*, 124–25, fails to situate 3:22 adequately within the surrounding context.

cumstances described in 5:6–17.[19] In other words, God wills us to pray for community members guilty of venial (forgivable) sins but not mortal sins; do not bother to pray for what God refuses to do. Although John does use this scenario as a specific application of his teaching, it hardly limits the original horizon of effective prayer as described in 5:14–15.[20] Assured of the Father's undivided attention (5:15), Christians may rest in the confidence of knowing that our prayers are an important tool in the accomplishment of God's will (5:14).[21]

Of course, we find ourselves returning to the age-old question: Why bother praying if every prayer must conform to God's predetermined plan? Will not God accomplish his will anyway, whether we prayed for it? This question was examined briefly in our earlier discussion of the Lord's Prayer. Johannine theology now constructs the chief cornerstone for the traditional Reformed solution mentioned in chapter 6: the principal outcome of Christian prayer is not receiving answers to particular requests but experiencing increased conformity to the will of God. Though I previously argued that this perspective fails as an adequate explanation of the Lord's Prayer, we are now in a position to understand why it is required nonetheless as one piece of a complete biblical theology. John's teaching requires it.

At the same time, John's material principally concerns the relationship between requests and answers, not requests and possibilities. In other words, when I ask the question, "Why are some of my prayers answered affirmatively, while others seem to be ignored?" John replies, "Because some are in accord with God's will, while others are not." Of course, patience always factors into the equation too. Perhaps my disappointment will eventually be relieved when I learn that I had asked according to God's will after all, but I had not waited long enough to see his timing.

In any event, neither of these answers, true as they may be, accounts for all eventualities, particularly if we assume that God may not predetermine all future possibilities. The biblical emphasis on the dynamic personal interaction existing between God and his people compellingly suggests that God, in fact, has not predetermined all future possibilities.

19. Bultmann, *Johannine Epistles*, 85. Though she does not express any obvious sympathy with Bultmann on this point, M. Thompson supplies the exegetical evidence for this interpretation lacking in Bultmann's commentary; see "Intercession in the Johannine Community," 237–45.

20. Schnackenburg, *Johannine Epistles*, 247–48; and Smalley, *1, 2, 3 John*, 295–96.

21. This time Strecker is more helpful: "The present verse, with its observation that prayer must be spoken 'according to God's will,' calls attention to the fact that proper prayer should not place human will and desire in the foreground, but should open itself without reservation to God's demand. . . . It was a matter of general conviction in primitive Christianity that one who does not meet God's ethical demands is also incapable of praying properly"; *Johannine Letters*, 200–201.

A more thorough discussion of this theological position will be offered in chapter 14; for now suffice it to say that John's theology does not preclude the possibility that we are free to pray for a good many things that have not been divinely predetermined. Perhaps God has determined many things but not all things. On the one hand, prayer remains the principal avenue by which the Father's will subsumes our own, teaching us simultaneously to yield thoroughly and to ask boldly, while receiving thankfully whatever God has decided to grant. On the other hand, prayer remains an open-ended exploration of new horizons waiting to be outlined by the cooperative initiatives shared between a Father who waits to hear and the children who venture to ask.

Abracadabra, in Jesus's Name

John's emphasis on praying in God's name was not unique to early Christianity; it was, in fact, a widespread religious practice that found particular expression in what is traditionally labeled magic. For example, here is an ancient magic spell offered in the name of Jesus:

> I adjure you by your name and your power and your figure and your amulet of salvation. . . .
>> Yea, yea, now, now, at once, at once! . . .
>> Jesus Jesus Jesus Jesus Jesus Jesus Jesus Jesus
>> † † † † † † † †
>> Sara = Mar = Bi = Sara =
>> Mar = Thar = Thathrar =
>> D D AAAAAAA OOOOOOO
>> D D
>> D D AAAAAAA OOOOOOO
>> D D
>> D D AAAAAAA OOOOOOO
>> D D Christ Christ Christ Christ Christ Christ Christ
>> D D AAAAAAA † † † † † † †
>> D D[22]

This particular prayer in Jesus's name was written on a 15″ x 9″ piece of parchment, folded repeatedly into a tight leather ball and then worn

22. Excerpt from a Coptic prayer for protection during pregnancy and childbirth; see Meyer, Smith, and Kelsey, *Ancient Christian Magic*, 120, 122. No date is offered for this particular text, although the collection ranges from the first to eleventh centuries, with the majority dating to late antiquity (ibid., 1). Magic was highly eclectic, and the presence of Christian (or Jewish) names alone does not necessarily indicate adherence to any particular form of the religion; see Roberts, *Manuscript, Society, and Belief*, 82–83.

or carried by a pregnant woman hoping for her infant's safe delivery into the world of ancient Egypt. The anonymous mother was a Christian trusting her Lord to ward off the evil spirits that would look for every opportunity to harm her newborn child. In an effort to bolster the prayer's potency, she called not only on Jesus's name but on a wide variety of hidden divine names that could maximize her access to heavenly power; so she also appealed to Yao, Sabbaoth, Adonai, Eloei, Elemas, Miksanther, Abrasakks, the seven sacred vowels, and many others.[23] All of them are invocations of the power of her God.

To suggest that this woman was confusing prayer and piety with magic and superstition would have made as much sense to her as insisting that she stop up the Nile or move the pyramids. Her Christian devotion was framed within the context of a long-standing cultural and religious tradition that well knew the value of invoking God's name(s). Compare her Christian prayer to the following prayer composed in Demotic (ancient Egyptian) and offered centuries earlier to the Egyptian moon god Khonsu:

> [Hail] to you, Khonsu in Thebes . . . whose name cannot be known. . . . I know your name. . . . "Great" is your name; "Heir" is your name; "Beneficial" is your name; "Hidden" is your name; . . . "AMAKHR of heaven" is your name; . . . "EI IO NE EI O" is your name.[24]

Effective prayer was always offered according to the proper—often secret, usually cryptic—divine name(s); in this regard, practitioners of magic were simply reflecting standard religious convention. Invoking God's secret names demonstrated the magician's credentials, imbuing the prayer with legitimacy; it was obviously offered by someone with the right to be there.[25] Consequently, it was not difficult for ancient Christians to find themselves approaching God in a manner reminiscent of non-Christian prayer or magical incantation, even composing written prayers as healing amulets to be carried for protection.

Why has a discussion of Johannine petition suddenly transformed itself into a peek at the shadowy world of ancient magic? Because it is

23. Yao is a form of "Yahweh" (Exod. 3:15); Sabbaoth, a form of "LORD Almighty/of Hosts" (1 Sam. 17:45); Adonai, "my Lord" (Gen. 18:3); Eloei, a form of Aramaic "Eloi" (Mark 15:34); Elemas, probably from "Elymas the magician" (Acts 13:8); Miksanther, the source of which is uncertain; Abrasakks, a variant of Abrasax, a common magical name where the numerical value of the letters add up to 365; and the seven Greek vowels (*aeēiouō*), which had astrological associations with the seven known planets of the solar system.

24. Betz, *Greek Magical Papyri*, 209–10 (*PDM* xiv.239–95). All translations and citations of *PDM* (*Papyri demoticae magicae*) texts are from Betz's volume; this collection of texts dates from the second century BC to the fifth century AD (ibid., xli).

25. Graf, *Magic in the Ancient World*, 192.

precisely at this point—petition in the name of Jesus—that New Testament prayer is most easily confused with magic, in both the ancient and the modern worlds. For example, Acts 19:13–16 tells the story of seven Jewish exorcists who tried adding Jesus's name to the litany of incantations they employed against unclean spirits, only to discover, much to their painful dismay, that their use of "the name" was substantially different from the apostle Paul's. On a more contemporary note, at least one modern commentator on John's Gospel suggests that John's peculiar insistence on "asking in Jesus's name" was an invention of the early church, born of a need to offer something "superior to the magical names that would otherwise be employed" by the apostles' religious competitors.[26]

Before comforting ourselves with the thought that such archaic notions are irrelevant to modern-day prayers recited among the enlightened citizens of a scientific age, let me recount a conversation I had with a friend not too many years ago. The middle-aged mother of three was excitedly explaining a recent breakthrough she had experienced in her prayer life. For many years she had agonized over the apparent powerlessness of her intercessory requests for family and friends. She pleaded for hearts open to the gospel and met nothing but hostility and resistance. Why were her prayers not being answered? An answer to that question finally appeared once she began attending a new church where the leaders taught her how to pray correctly. Not only must she ensure that every prayer was precisely concluded in Jesus's name, but prayers for "open doors" demanded physical proximity to the doors waiting to be opened. The leaders explained that answers would appear once she began stationing herself, physically, on the pavement in front of her loved ones' homes. By literally directing the name of Jesus at the front door of each house, she could focus God's power laser-like into the lives inside. Now she knew that she had to pray for family and friends while facing their front door, pausing to "anoint" each house with intercession. A proper method guaranteed that answers were just a matter of time.

What might the author of John's Gospel say in response to this advice? Was my friend receiving wise biblical insight on intercessory prayer?

Prayer or Magic?

I tend to agree with those who insist that there is no clear-cut line of conceptual demarcation between magic and religion, for magic is

26. Haenchen, *John*, 126.

itself a particular expression of religious conviction.[27] Ancient magicians understood their spells and incantations to be acts of prayer; prayer vocabulary, even statements of personal devotion, occurs quite often in the magical texts, whether Christian or pagan.[28] Although this is not the place to explore the fascinating debate over Jesus's relationship to magic, careful research shows that even "Jesus was a man of his time in at least using recognizable formulae or incantations" in his capacity as exorcist.[29] In other words, Jesus sometimes behaved like a magician. Nevertheless, when the horizon is expanded beyond a quest for the historical Jesus to include a quest for prayer in the New Testament church, I remain convinced that at least seven substantive distinctions separate New Testament petitionary prayer from magical prayer, and even though the distinctions may not be absolute, the exceptions are of the sort that prove the rule.[30]

First and foremost, New Testament prayer is governed by eschatology; magic is governed by immediacy. Eschatology is definitive to the New Testament theology of prayer and finds its origins in the ministry of the historical Jesus. G. Twelftree's careful research demonstrates that Jesus was unique among ancient exorcists in that he gave "his exorcisms a dimension of significance beyond the mere healing of demented individuals. . . . *Jesus was the first one to link the relatively common phenomenon*

27. See Hammond, "Magic"; Geertz, "Anthropology of Religion"; Betz, "Magic and Mystery"; Graf, "Prayer in Magic"; idem, *Magic in the Ancient World*, 1–19; Phillips, "*Nullum crimen sine lege*"; Versnel, "Some Reflections"; Cunningham, *Religion and Magic*; Dickie, *Magic and Magicians*, 18–46; and Janowitz, *Magic in the Roman World*, 1–26.

28. For example, *PGM* II.28–30; III.107–8, 175, 499, 585–91; IV.273. All translations and citations of *PGM* (*Papyri graecae magicae*) texts are from Betz, *Greek Magical Papyri*.

29. Twelftree, *Jesus the Exorcist*, 153. The chief advocate for Jesus-as-magician remains M. Smith, *Jesus the Magician*; his arguments are embraced by scholars such as E. Sanders, *Jesus and Judaism*, 165–73; and Crossan, *Historical Jesus*, 304–10. Twelftree clearly shows, however, why Smith's arguments finally fail to convince; see *Jesus the Exorcist*, 190–207. For additional bibliography on this debate, see Crump, *Jesus the Intercessor*, 136.

30. I have no interest in devising generalized, definitive distinctions between religion and magic per se. My only concern is to describe how the New Testament theology of petition is categorically distinct from the worldview typically associated with magic. With this in mind, Versnel, "Some Reflections," offers a helpful discussion of the value of *proximate definitions* that maintain the frequently confused distinction between functional and substantive evaluations. The seven traits I outline here are substantive observations of major tendencies, not functional comparisons of exceptional phenomena. For those who still think this illegitimate, Meier makes a valuable observation: "Perhaps part of the problem is that the total identification of miracle and magic sometimes championed today may reflect a reaction against the older, acritical assumption that miracle and magic (or religion and magic) are clearly different and even opposite phenomena. . . . Complete dichotomy may have begotten the opposite view of complete identification" (*Marginal Jew*, 2.540). Meier adopts constraints and arrives at conclusions similar to my own (ibid., 541–52).

of exorcism with eschatology."[31] Jesus's innovation became the church's bread and butter. The new reality governing Jesus's approach to exorcism and miracle—the inbreaking of God's kingdom here and now—set the trajectory for the New Testament community's growing understanding of all prayer. Believers pray as inhabitants of the already/not yet kingdom.

The objective of a magician's prayer was the immediate transformation of some life circumstance: physical healing, abundant crops, business success, sexual conquest, athletic victory.[32] Failure indicated the need for a new spell, an alternative approach that would prove more satisfying to the requisite deities. Thus the refrain, "Yea, yea, now, now, at once, at once!" appears frequently in one form or another throughout the magical papyri. Magical textbooks often list a series of multiple incantations to be tried successively until the magician strikes the proper chord; as a last resort, the petitioner may even threaten any deity recalcitrant enough to ignore his entreaties: "ABRI and ABRO EXANTIABIL, God of gods, king of kings, now force a friendly daimon of prophecy to come to me, lest I apply worse tortures to you, the things written on the strips of papyrus."[33] The magician was willing to use any means necessary to achieve his or her client's immediate goals. Magical faith was enervated by temporal success, not eschatological hope.[34]

New Testament prayer, on the other hand, arises from hopeful expectation and is always informed by the already/not yet reality of salvation-history. True Christian petition can also emanate from an immediate desire for miracles, food, forgiveness, or other personal needs, but these requests are offered by the subjects of God's kingdom, who not only experience salvation's present reality, but knowingly await its fulfillment. Prayer is a bridge stretched between the two horizons of New Testament expectation. All things may be requested, but nothing can be demanded. Only the coming kingdom (and all that it entails) is ever guaranteed.

31. Twelftree, *Jesus the Exorcist*, 173 (emphasis added); see also 217–24.

32. Not to ignore the occasional references to union with god (*PGM* IV.710; VII.503; VIII.50; XIII.795); deification (*PGM* III.600); heavenly ascent and encounter with god (*PGM* III.695; IV.220, 484, 542, 1015–36; XIII.345); worship (*PGM* IV.649); praise (*PGM* III.191, 253; IV.1115–65, 1170, 1204; VII.503; XXXVI.166); and thanksgiving (*PGM* III.591, 598; IV.1061). But even these remain embedded within the larger context of requests for immediate, tangible results.

33. *PGM* II.53–54 (Betz, *Greek Magical Papyri*, 14). Threats were particularly common in Egyptian magic; they are less frequent in the Greco-Roman texts (lvii). "Daimon" is the transliteration of a Greek word referring to spiritual beings in general. Its transformation into the evil "demon" was a later Christian development; see V. Flint, "Demonization of Magic."

34. See similar observations with respect to Jesus's miracles in Meier, *Marginal Jew*, 2.549.

Negative replies do not call for new and greater prayers but a renewed and enlarged faith.

Second, New Testament prayer is consequently offered exclusively to the King who has inaugurated his kingdom. Unlike magic, which typically invokes the powers of lesser spirits, ghosts, angels, and demigods, the disciple turns only to the Father by calling on the Son. The New Testament emphatically asserts that the church has only one intercessor, one mediator between heaven and earth (Rom. 8:34; 1 Tim. 2:5; Heb. 7:25; 8:6; 9:15; 12:24; 1 John 2:1). Christians need not concern themselves with lesser spiritual beings, intermediaries, ghostly messengers, or spirit guides. When the nascent church in Colossae entertained contrary notions, Paul was quick to correct their error (Col. 1:15–20; 2:18–3:4). Luke's account of Simon Magus, the converted magician who mistakenly aspired to purchase the Spirit's power, served as a powerful warning for anyone who believed that Christian faith could be mingled with a belief in magic (Acts 8:9–25).[35]

Third, New Testament prayer is always an expression of trusting relationship, whereas magic is principally utilitarian.[36] Granted, all petition, whether devotional or magical, entails a quest for some *thing*; magic, however, typically attains its goals by expertise attained through practice. Praying in Jesus's name is much more than the skillful repetition of a proper noun appropriately embedded in a nuanced benediction, as the seven sons of Sceva rudely discovered (Acts 19:15–16). In fact, it is entirely possible to pray in the name of Jesus without ever uttering those particular words at all, for it is a matter of willing with one will, desiring with one heart, not rotely repeating a stock phrase.

Magic, on the other hand, was a professional skill acquired through apprenticeship, training, and practice.[37] Because magicians typically charged for their services, accuracy and effectiveness were more important than understanding. Whether a magician understood or appreciated the original religious significance of the names being used was irrelevant. "Divine names most importantly have reference (to the divine being) and not sense. All divine names, therefore, and especially international divine names, do not have to have any clear meaning" for the one using them.[38] The magician was a cosmic harpist who, through

---

35. Klauck, *Magic and Paganism*, 23.

36. Even the spells aimed at deification and union with the divine strictly depend on technique and the manipulation of esoteric knowledge. For example, "MOKRIMO PHERIMO PHERERI, life of me, [supply name]: Stay! Dwell in my soul! Do not abandon me, for ENTHO PHENEN THROPIŌTH commands you" (*PGM* IV.710–11 [Betz, *Greek Magical Papyri*, 52]).

37. Graf, *Magic in the Ancient World*, 89–117; Dickie, *Magic and Magicians*, 221; and Janowitz, *Magic in the Roman World*, 51.

38. Janowitz, *Magic in the Roman World*, 52.

years of study and practice, knew where and how to pluck the elemental forces strung across the universe to produce whatever spiritual harmony (or disharmony) the client wished to enjoy.[39] One did not have to be a student of music theory to know how to play the instrument.

Fourth, New Testament prayer is always rooted in community, whereas magic is fundamentally individualistic. Every disciple offering personal petition enjoys access to the Father only by virtue of incorporation into the body of Christ and consequent membership in the kingdom of God. We have repeatedly seen how this corporate identity shapes and defines the content of even the most personalized Christian petition. Magical efficacy, on the other hand, is "natural" in the sense that it employs the predictable cause-and-effect relationships uniting the visible and invisible realms of life. Magic ritual does not presume any new community formation, spiritual or otherwise; it simply takes advantage of the natural processes available to anyone who understands how to exploit them. This was not only the taxonomic basis for the ancient connection between magic and science, but it was also the standard accusation brought against Greco-Roman magicians as antisocial individuals bent on undermining community standards and civic religion.[40]

Fifth, this naturalistic perspective on magical operations also distinguishes the function of magical ritual as compared with Christian. The spells, incantations, esoteric recipes of exotic ingredients, wax dolls, and lead tablets employed by magicians all had specific roles to play in the manipulation of natural, cosmic forces. New Testament ritual, on the other hand, is not rooted in nature but in human history.[41] The sacraments and the prayers associated with them are acts of historical reminiscence in which the believer supranaturally participates in God's work of salvation-historical intervention. New Testament ritual does not strum the cosmic harp but commemorates and reenacts unique events in time and space.[42]

Sixth, the New Testament lacks any instruction about associating specific prayers with particular ritual/sacramental actions or vice versa. The

39. "He knew the code words needed to communicate with the gods, the demons, and the dead. He could tap, regulate, and manipulate the invisible energies"; Betz, *Greek Magical Papyri*, xlvii.

40. Kolenkow, "Problem of Power," 105–10; Graf, "Prayer in Magic," 195–96; Phillips, "*Nullum crimen sine lege*"; and Pulleyn, *Prayer in Greek Religion*, 93–94.

41. See Sharot, *Messianism, Mysticism, and Magic*, 30–31. Although Sharot's analysis is applied to the Old Testament and Judaism, his observations are equally pertinent to New Testament religion and Christianity.

42. Christian magic, in particular, will sometimes include a *historiola*, that is, a narrative fragment, usually from one of the Gospels, retelling part of a miracle story similar to what the magician hopes to replicate. The reminiscences are, however, variable; there is no one paradigmatic event to be recalled. Also, they are exceptional, not typical elements of a spell.

spoken word is consistently assumed to be perfectly effective in and of itself, unlike magic, which demands that word and ritual coincide before either can be efficacious.[43] Charms, amulets, and so-called voodoo dolls become potent only in concert with the written and oral spells engraved on them and/or recited over them; likewise, magical prayers become powerful via their connection with the physical objects manipulated during their recitation.[44] The clearest testimony to this mutual dependency is seen in the requirement either to wear amulets (when the spell is for oneself) or to secretly place them in physical proximity (usually by burying) near the intended "beneficiary" to assure their effectiveness. The prayer/spell then conveys its potency through bodily contact while the inscribed letters serve as a continual recitation of one's prayer.[45]

This mindset stands in sharp contrast to the New Testament assurances that the heavenly Father hears his children the first time they ask, irrespective of the brevity or simplicity of their requests, simply because he loves them. Here is another instance of a distinguishing (though not entirely unique or consistent) behavior traceable to the earthly Jesus. "Jesus does not seem to have used mechanical aids" in performing his exorcisms, but depended primarily on simple words of command.[46] The Lord's model of miracle working continued within the church's practice of prayer; there is no need for code words, repetitious formulas, physical manipulations, or secret rituals to gain or to sustain God's attention, much less to lend extra efficacy to a request (Matt. 6:5–8; 7:7–11; Luke 11:9–13).[47] Neither is there any need to concern oneself with the effects—

43. Betz, "Magic and Mystery," 248, disputes this by referring to *PGM* IV.2081–87 (Betz, *Greek Magical Papyri*, 74) as distinguishing "a superior magic, employing magical words only." This text, however, offers no evaluation of what is "superior," merely noting the possibility of a magician setting aside his instruments in order to rely solely on his daimonic assistant (a daimon previously conjured by ritual!).

44. Kotansky, "Incantations and Prayers," 108–10. Meyer, Smith, and Kelsey, *Ancient Christian Magic*, 16, quote J. Bourghouts that in Egyptian magic "no spell can be detached from an accompanying magical action."

45. Meyer, Smith, and Kelsey, *Ancient Christian Magic*, 81, 147–48; for example, a typical spell for sexual conquest instructs, "Write these signs on a sheet of tin. Off[ering]: wild herb, froth from the mouth of a completely black horse, and a bat. Bury it at the woman's door. You will see its potency quickly" (159) (the words would be recited as they were written). Additional examples highlighting the importance of physical proximity appear on pp. 161, 169, 174–77, 221, 268, 272.

46. See Twelftree, *Jesus the Exorcist*, 159. Twelftree reaches this conclusion after examining the few exceptions where Jesus also used mud, spittle, and physical contact.

47. When reading instructions such as "say the designated seven formulas [seven] times, requesting an encounter with [the] god" (*PGM* III.695 [Betz, *Greek Magical Papyri*, 35]) or "[say] Amen, 17 (times). Jesus, 21 (times). Holy one, 21 (times). Holy paraclete, 21 (times). Holy invisible one, 21 (times). Holy bridegroom, 21 (times). Holy almighty one, 21 (times). Kalampsoel Thoel Thumiael Thoroloel Akxukunur" (Meyer, Smith, and Kelsey, *Ancient Christian Magic*, 131), it is difficult not to think of Jesus's injunction: "Do

or lack thereof—of physical proximity. Questions of geographical distance and spatial relationship are irrelevant when praying to the Creator "in [whom] all things hold together" (Col. 1:17). Perhaps the radical (even unbelievable) nature of these truths underlies the pastoral preaching of the early church fathers, who regularly contended against the apparently widespread use of magic among their congregations. John Chrysostom (fourth century), for example, applauds the faith of a mother who, relying on simple prayer alone, would rather see her sick child die than resort to the amulets commonly used by others: "Only one incantation (if I may call it that) is left to the faithful: to praise the will of God; and one effective action or ritual: to make the sign of the cross."[48]

Finally, despite the tendency among modern anthropologists to deny the observation that magic employs coercion while religion supplicates and surrenders, I am convinced that this typology remains an accurate description of the difference between New Testament petition and magical prayer. Jesus emphatically invites, in fact requires, personal petition that will stretch even the heartiest saint's faith. These requests, however, must always be subordinate to serving the Father's good pleasure. Suppressing the supplicant's own will in this way is *extraordinarily atypical of magic*, regardless of its provenance, whether pagan or Christian.[49]

Identifying Magic Today

I once read the promotional flier of a large-scale evangelistic campaign in a major American city where hot-air balloons were used to literally

---

not keep on babbling like pagans, for they think they will be heard because of their many words" (Matt. 6:7).

48. Cited by Barb, "Survival of Magic Arts," 106; see also the extensive discussion of the ancient confrontation between magic and Christianity in Dickie, *Magic and Magicians*, 251–321 (especially 281–84 and n. 24 for John Chrysostom).

49. The language of coercion is typically directed at lesser spiritual powers, seldom (if ever) at the supreme deity. Christian magic typically reflects a much greater appreciation of the divine will, but the language of demand and coercion is common nonetheless, irrespective of its direct object; for example, "Yasabaoth Adonai, the one who rules over the four corners of the world, in whatever I want—I, [petitioner supplies his/her name]—now, now, at once, at once!" (Meyer, Smith, and Kelsey, *Ancient Christian Magic*, 88); or "If you do not carry out my wishes, O Gabriel, and fulfill my command, I shall always despise you, cut you off from me, anathematize you, revile you, and loathe you. The father must assign you no place in heaven" (157). Two exceptions in the Greek magical papyri are noteworthy because they stand entirely alone: "Now if it be your will, METERTA / PHŌTH IEREZATH, give me over to immortal birth" (*PGM* IV.500 [Betz, *Greek Magical Papyri*, 48]); and "Increase my life . . . for I am your slave and petitioner and have hymned your valid and holy name" (*PGM* XIII.636 [Betz, *Greek Magical Papyri*, 187]). Once again, these two texts appear to be the exceptions that prove the rule.

cover the downtown area with prayer. Volunteers floated through the sky suspended in baskets while praying against "the spiritual powers of the air" (Eph. 6:12). Presumably, this facilitated a face-to-face confrontation between their invocations and the demonic forces impeding God's work.

I cannot deny the psychological value that some people find in such rituals, as does my friend who now makes it a point to pray in front of her neighbors' homes. Whether these prayer rituals involve the recitation of memorized formulas, using specific vocabulary, the laying on of hands, raising arms, anointing with oil, sprinkling holy water, even flying over a target area in airplanes and balloons, many people discover that such acts can infuse new energy into a moribund faith and bolster failing spiritual commitments. Tests of faith are daunting enough—and who has not experienced prayer as a test of faith?—that I am hesitant to criticize anything (short of outright heresy) that genuinely energizes authentic Christian prayer (and life is complicated enough that even the odd heresy may, on occasion, stir genuine faith). But a serious danger arises any time we confuse a spiritually, psychologically encouraging action with a divinely proscribed essential action. This is a confusion of categories that creates a fertile seedbed for spiritual imperialism, where personal preferences are translated into universal requirements and where the elusive measure of faith is quantified into formulas and ritual. Equally misleading is the suggestion, implicit or explicit, that God's ability or willingness to answer prayer is somehow tied to certain ritual actions.

John Chrysostom's congregation was not the first or the last body of believers to fumble along the boundaries separating legitimate petition from magical incantation. The book of Acts recounts several confrontations between the apostles and magicians (13:6–12; 16:16–21; 19:13–20), suggesting that from Luke's perspective a significant "obstacle to the spread of the Christian message is an all-devouring syncretism which at its worst even usurps Christian substance such as the name of Jesus, and hence threatens the church from within."[50] We would do well to regularly scrutinize our own evolving prayer habits, feeling free to change, experiment, learn, and grow, but always with an eye to the intrusive peculiarities of magic, for, ultimately, magic is irreconcilable with the freedom promised to those invited to simply pray in the name of Jesus. Whether there is a difference between magic and religion, Jesus and the New Testament insist that there is a great difference between magical prayer and Christian prayer.

---

50. Klauck, *Magic and Paganism*, 54; see also 65–69, 100–102, 120–21.

9

The Early Church at Prayer

The Acts of the Apostles

I f we could only get back to the early church in the book of Acts, then we would experience God's real power." It is an old refrain that we have all heard, and perhaps even said, at some time or another. In many people's eyes, the Acts of the Apostles portrays a pristine, idealized, bygone era where the Spirit flowed, the church performed miracles, and revival erupted as the rule of the day. Furthermore, many suspect that this description not only captures the past experience of the apostolic church, but could just as easily describe the contemporary church *if* we only understood where and how God's people departed from the original plan and returned ourselves to the proper paradigm. Entire denominations have sprung up under the banner of restoring God's church to its apostolic roots. One of the more frequent suggestions along this line highlights the many references to prayer throughout the book of Acts, concluding that the perceived lack of power in the modern church is traceable to a commensurate lack of prayer, "an acute crisis of piety" to use one scholar's phrase.[1] I will let others decide whether the church, in fact, labors under such a crisis. Personally, I suspect that the

---

1. Wiles, *Paul's Intercessory Prayers*, ix. For similar perceptions, see Bloesch, *Struggle of Prayer*, 11; and Hunter, *God Who Hears*, 10–13.

consistencies of human nature spanning the generations leave very little that is new under the sun; our struggles were our forebearers' struggles, and vice versa. I suggest, however, that while we certainly need to learn from Luke's depiction of the church in Acts, we dare not idealize the past or naïvely assume that we can solve all our problems by seizing upon any one particular remedy.

I was once gruffly accused of "gross primitivism" for arguing that Christian vocabulary ought to be self-consciously rooted in biblical usage (in this instance, I was presenting a paper on the New Testament use of the word "worship"). Apparently, my questioner thought that by arguing for some normative value to the biblical use of language I also sought conformity to my particular interpretation of biblical practice. Not so (even if there was one uniform praxis, which is unlikely). There is a significant difference between (a) understanding biblical origins and (b) idealistically absolutizing biblical practices. I am in favor of a not b. What this means for our study of prayer in Acts is this: we need to give close attention to the prayer habits of the apostolic church, learning all we can about both its behavior and its beliefs. Gleaning such insights is the purpose of this book and will, I am convinced, go a long way toward informing and stimulating healthy Christian prayer today. We will fall into serious error, however, if we think that Acts describes a golden age in church history that can be recreated by digging up this or that lost key. The Acts of the Apostles is not a treasure map leading to long-ago buried spiritual treasure. By all means, the book of Acts has a tremendous amount to teach us about the place of prayer in the Christian life, but I want to begin this chapter by offering a warning: beware of jumping to one-dimensional applications that simplistically associate Acts with power and the modern church with impotence. This will not do. The early church was just as fractured and fractious, weak and haughty, as well as Spirit-filled and remarkable, as any corner of the worldwide church today. No cluster of issues, no matter how theologically significant—whether prayer, baptism, speaking in tongues, or preaching—will single-handedly bear the burden of miraculously supplying ready-made solutions to whatever problems contemporary analysts think they find in the modern church.[2]

2. Perhaps this introduction sounds like a bit of a digression, but I do not think it is. Over the years, I have spoken with many young men and women preparing for ministry in the local church. The book of Acts naturally stirs their enthusiasm and expectations, but it can also produce a deep sense of disjointedness when compared with their own church experience. Far too often, I hear confident analyses that go something like this: "I've discovered the secret! We need to get back to prayer (or baptism in the Spirit, or biblical preaching, or expecting miracles, etc.)." I am afraid that this is a recipe for disillusionment, in part, because it is an unhealthy way to read Scripture.

Granted, Acts does not provide the earliest record of church life in the New Testament. That prize goes to Paul's letters. When we begin studying Paul's writings in the next chapter, we will significantly expand our understanding of how the earliest Christian communities experienced petitionary prayer. (Our analysis of the four Gospels not only revealed the teaching of Jesus but also reflected something of the early communities' concerns about proper and improper ways to pray.) Consequently, even though the Acts of the Apostles was in all likelihood completed after Paul's letters (excepting, perhaps, the Pastorals), it preserves equally early traditions testifying to the pre-Pauline life of the church. That, combined with its connections to the Gospel of Luke, accounts for my decision to investigate prayer in the Acts of the Apostles before delving into Paul's letters.

The Prayers of Acts

It is a truism to observe that the author of Luke-Acts shows a particular interest in prayer. Several writers observe a distinct parallelism between the prayers of Jesus in the Gospels and the church's prayers in Acts. Luke seems to arrange his materials such that Jesus's model "comes to life" in the experience of his earliest followers.[3] Jesus is both the model and the enabler of Christian prayer, not only for his disciples but also for the ever-expanding church throughout salvation-history. By my reckoning, Luke's second volume contains twenty instances of prayer that need to be examined. I arrange them in three categories: (1) prayers with explicit content where the prayer is recorded or the context makes it clear (Acts 4:23–31; 7:59–60; 8:15, 22, 24; 14:23; 26:29); (2) prayers with contextually implied content (6:6; 9:40; 12:5, 12; 13:3; 16:25; 20:36; 21:5; 28:8); and (3) uncertain prayer notices where the context fails to supply any clear content (1:14; 2:42; 6:4; 9:11; 10:2, 4, 9, 30; 22:17).[4] By beginning with the explicit petitionary prayers, then moving from the known to the unknown, I believe that we can reach fairly certain conclusions about the place of prayer in the earliest Christian communities.

3. Green, "Persevering Together in Prayer," 183; see also O'Brien, "Prayer in Luke-Acts"; Turner, "Prayer in the Gospels," 72–73; and Karris, *Prayer and the New Testament*, 75–76. The most thorough literary analysis of these parallels is Feldkämper, *Der betende Jesus*. For the christological significance of the Lukan Jesus as praying mediator/intercessor, see Crump, *Jesus the Intercessor*.

4. This final category will be the most controversial of the three. Numerous commentators would argue with my selection, insisting that context does supply the content of some if not all of these prayers. It is important, however, to err on the side of caution in this regard. Otherwise, it is far too easy to read our own theological biases into such questionable texts.

A Threatened Church Prays for Boldness

Acts 4:23–31

The first healing miracle in Acts precipitates significant opposition from the Sanhedrin (3:1–4:21). Peter and John are arrested and ordered to halt all healing and preaching in the name of Jesus. Intimidated by a populace sympathetic to this new movement, the Jewish leadership reluctantly releases the apostles after threatening them to keep silent—threats that the apostles promptly ignore. Peter and John immediately recount their experience "to their own people,"[5] igniting a corporate outburst of praise, thanksgiving, and petition:

> "Sovereign Lord," they said, "you made the heaven and the earth and the sea, and everything in them. You spoke by the Holy Spirit through the mouth of your servant, our father David:
>
>> 'Why do the nations rage
>>   and the peoples plot in vain?
>> The kings of the earth take their stand
>>   and the rulers gather together
>> against the Lord
>>   and against his Anointed One.'
>
> Indeed Herod and Pontius Pilate met together with the Gentiles and the people of Israel in this city to conspire against your holy servant Jesus, whom you anointed. They did what your power and will had decided beforehand should happen. Now, Lord, consider their threats and enable your servants to speak your word with great boldness. Stretch out your hand to heal and perform miraculous signs and wonders through the name of your holy servant Jesus."

The church's prayer was answered immediately as the Holy Spirit appears with both physical and spiritual tremors, empowering God's people to do exactly what they requested: to speak God's word boldly (4:31).

It is especially noteworthy that the threatened church does not ask for protection from its enemies. The church begins with praise extolling the power of God, acknowledging his universal lordship and sovereignty as Creator (4:24). Rather than trade off this confidence by pleading for deliverance, the community finds reassurance in the personal implications of their adoration—the same sovereign Creator who anointed Jesus at his baptism continues to lead the nascent church (4:27–29). Theirs

---

5. The debate over whether this phrase in 4:23 refers to the entire church, a subgroup within the church, or the apostolic circle alone will not be addressed since it has no significant effect on the outcome of the present argument.

is not wishful thinking but an exegetical conclusion derived from the Psalter (4:25–26); Ps. 2 is a royal psalm in which the threatened Davidic king (the Anointed One) asserts the impotence of all pagan plots against God's covenant people. Yahweh's protection of Judah's kings is ultimately fulfilled in the Father's vindication of the crucified Son of David.[6] How ironic that the Gentile nations and their pagan rulers now find historical counterparts in the full array of Roman soldiers (the nations), disbelieving Israel (the peoples),[7] Herod (the kings), and Pilate (the rulers), just as the victorious King now reigns triumphant from a cross. The church fully understands that its current situation emerges in complete continuity with God's salvation-historical plan for its Lord.[8] The disciples' persecution is Jesus's persecution; God's enemies have always assaulted God's people.[9] Such opponents supply bleak testimony to human intransigence, not divine powerlessness, as some cynics might suggest; theirs is a wicked stubbornness that will continually confront the faithful community with as much vehemence as it attacked the Son of God himself.

This, then, becomes the source of the community's confidence; the sovereign Lord-Creator can be trusted to maintain control over his salvation-history. Christ's opponents only "did what [God's] power and will had decided beforehand should happen" (4:28; compare 2:23; 3:18). The same promise is, therefore, assumed to be true for every disciple who lives in conformity to Christ. At least that assumption proved true for those rejoicing over Peter's and John's deliverance in Acts 4. Luke's narrative is not supplying an abstract basis for a generalized doctrine of historical determinism, nor is it asserting divine intention behind every event in a believer's life. The point is not that everything that ever happens anywhere at any time always occurs exactly as "God's power and will decided beforehand"; it is, rather, that *those particular events necessarily entailed within God's plan of salvation always unfold as he intends.*[10] These are two very different positions, and the context clearly establishes Luke's

6. There is no clear evidence that the second psalm was ever interpreted messianically by pre-Christian Judaism; see Fitzmyer, *Acts*, 309; contrary to the suggestion of Bruce, *Acts*, 98. The salvation-historical perspective embedded in Acts is clearly a theological development of the early church as it reinterpreted its Scriptures in light of the life, death, and resurrection of Christ.

7. Tannehill, "Israel in Luke-Acts."

8. Moessner, "Christ Must Suffer."

9. Stephen draws precisely the same salvation-historical analogies in correlating (a) Israel's persecution of the prophets with (b) unbelieving Israel's rejection of Jesus and with (c) the synagogue's rejection of Stephen's own preaching (Acts 7:51–53); see Gaventa, "To Speak Thy Word," 79.

10. Barrett, *Acts*, 1.248. Less-precise assessments are misleading and must be guarded against; for example, Wahlde, "Theological Assessment," 528, concludes, "The God of cre-

focus on particularity. It is this specific assurance that fuels the initial confidence of the one praying and the prayer's final efficacy.

This analysis yields at least four points crucial, not just to this particular prayer, but to the entire theology of prayer introduced by the first paradigmatic prayer in Acts. First, the prayer's content is determined by the church's commitment to participate fully in God's plan for salvation-history. In this sense, Acts 4 demonstrates the disciples' appropriation of Jesus's instruction to pray: "Father, may your kingdom come and your will be done." Personal, idiosyncratic concerns never appear on Luke's radar screen; the community's sole interest lies in faithfully obeying God's intentions for the mission of the gospel. The united community requests boldness, courage, and divine confirmation that they are, in fact, walking their appointed path; there is no interest in personal benefits or in being rescued from persecution.[11] Quite the contrary. Prayer is not a means to seek relief, but an avenue for enlarging the horizons of kingdom service.

Second, it is clear that the church in Acts is learning the lessons conveyed by Jesus's own prayer life. His centrality to their corporate identity has been thoroughly assimilated. Just as the Lord's Prayer presumes a life reoriented by faith in Jesus's messiahship, just as John's Gospel predicates genuine prayer on personal union with the true vine, so too the church's preoccupation with living, preaching, healing, and praying "in the name of Jesus" confirms Christ's place, not only as model, but as mediator of the Christian's relationship with God (Acts 3:16; 4:7, 10, 12, 17, 18, 30). When the Twelve first confronted suffering in the Garden of Gethsemane, they failed the test because they failed to pray (Matt. 26:36–46 ‖ Mark 14:32–43 ‖ Luke 22:39–46).[12] They do not repeat that mistake here. The church is a thoroughly transformed assembly; like Jesus, they now triumph over persecution through prayer.

Third, Acts 3–4 illustrates the points made in chapter 8 that invoking the name of Jesus is not a magical formula but the indication of personal surrender.[13] The community's unreserved submission to the Father's will is not only suggested by its repeated appeal to Jesus's name, but is thoroughly vindicated by the immediate positive response to their petition. All those praying are promptly filled with the Holy Spirit (for the second

ation is now shown also to be the God of history. *Nothing* happens without his allowance" (emphasis added). Such global conclusions significantly overshoot the biblical data.

11. At this point, the frequently observed parallelism with Hezekiah's prayer in Isa. 37:15–20 breaks down; Hezekiah's petition focuses on the nation's deliverance.

12. Crump, *Jesus the Intercessor*, 167–75; and Green, "Persevering Together in Prayer," 198.

13. Could this provide another evocative correlation between the authors of Luke-Acts and the Gospel of John? See J. Bailey, *Traditions Common to the Gospels*.

time, no less; compare 1:4; 4:31)[14] and are enabled to do precisely what they ask: proclaim the gospel boldly in the face of violent opposition (4:29, 31). Obedient requests made by men and women who genuinely abide in union with Christ and are living to serve their master in the mission of God's kingdom will be answered positively.

Finally, both the community's perspective on salvation-history and the nature of the petition itself indicate that kingdom service is a joint venture.[15] God's servants are responsible to proclaim the name of Jesus, but the church is dependent on its Creator-Lord to vindicate his message by "stretch[ing] out [his] hand to heal and perform miraculous signs and wonders" (4:30). Either part without the other is only half an equation yielding nothing. The church commits itself to risking obedience by stepping out; God commits himself to maintaining faithfulness by showing up.[16] Negotiating that interface between responsibility and faithfulness—two qualities incumbent on both God and his people—lies at the heart of the existential dilemma, the human struggle, in learning to pray. Luke's introductory lesson on authentic, effective prayer is paradigmatic for how the dramatic tension between a creature's call and the Creator's response can result in an ideal rather than a disappointing conclusion.

The five remaining prayers with explicit content are brief by any measure, but they are noticeably terse when read in light of 4:23–31, bolstering my suggestion that Luke intends Acts 4 to be read paradigmatically. In other words, the commitments and theological explanation introduced there continue to inform the following accounts. Brief as these prayers may be, however, a noticeable common thread solidly anchored to the opening prayer in Acts 4 continues to unwind.

Acts 7:59–60

Stephen's prayer dramatically displays the full measure of a disciple's conformity to the Savior. In this way, Steven too becomes a paradigm:

14. Not that the Spirit comes and goes. The Holy Spirit in Luke-Acts is the Spirit of prophecy, the power for effective proclamation and mission; see Menzies, *Development of Early Christian Pneumatology*, 224–29, 278–79. "Spirit-filled" is Luke's way of describing the Christian's empowerment for witnessing to God's work of salvation in a particular situation; thus from Luke's perspective every believer, who according to Paul never loses the Spirit, may be filled many times.

15. Witherington, *Acts*, 203–4.

16. A similar sense of theological synergism is also evident in Acts 4:25: "You spoke by the Holy Spirit through the mouth of your servant . . . David." Although the text-critical problems are thorny, the sense of this verse is clear: Ps. 2 is the product of a cooperative effort involving both the Spirit of God and the human author (compare Acts 1:16 for an identical thought). Luke seems to understand the operations of petitionary prayer in a manner similar to his understanding of the inspiration of Scripture.

"While they were stoning him, Stephen prayed, 'Lord Jesus, receive my spirit.' Then he fell on his knees and cried out, 'Lord, do not hold this sin against them.'" For the first time, prayer is directly addressed to Jesus instead of the Father. That Stephen utters a traditional evening prayer based on Ps. 31:6, originally addressed to Yahweh,[17] indicates how rapidly the early church developed a high Christology exalting Jesus to the same level as God.[18] Luke's first martyr follows the model of Jesus:[19]

Luke	Acts
From now on, the Son of Man will be seated at the right hand of the mighty God. (22:69)	I see heaven opened and the Son of Man standing at the right hand of God. (7:56)
Jesus called out with a loud voice, "Father, into your hands I commit my spirit." (23:46)	Stephen prayed, "Lord Jesus, receive my spirit." (7:59)
Jesus said, "Father, forgive them, for they do not know what they are doing." (23:34)	He fell on his knees and cried out, "Lord, do not hold this sin against them." (7:60)

Such conformity requires not only Stephen's obedience to death but his plea for the extension of God's forgiveness to his executioners (Matt. 6:12 || Luke 11:4). There is still no appeal for deliverance from the suffering; in Acts 4 the church was (momentarily) delivered, but this time Stephen pays the ultimate price. Effective prayer arises from and bolsters obedience.

Acts 8:15

Philip's successful mission to Samaria confronts the Jerusalem church with a profound challenge (8:4–17). Can the Jewish community receive the previously despised Samaritans as equal partners in their emerging assembly? The separation of the Spirit's reception from the Samaritans' baptism in the name of Jesus "is perhaps the most extraordinary statement in Acts."[20] A modern consensus explains this strange situation by way of the historic antipathy between the two ethnic groups.[21] Philip has taken a bold step; undoubtedly, for many it was an unthinkable step.

17. Haenchen, *Acts*, 293; and Fitzmyer, *Acts*, 394.

18. I. Marshall, *Acts*, 150.

19. Haenchen, *Acts*, 293n9; Conzelmann, *Acts*, 60; and Moessner, "Christ Must Suffer," 233–35, 255–56.

20. I. Marshall, *Acts*, 157.

21. So Bruce, *Acts*, 170, contrary to the position of Fitzmyer (*Acts*, 400) and others (of a Roman Catholic persuasion) that the church is becoming institutionalized such that the Spirit is available only from the apostles.

As apostolic emissaries from the Jewish mother church, Peter and John visit Samaria to investigate the results of Philip's efforts. By allowing these two apostles to become agents of the Spirit's arrival (8:17), God addresses Jewish hesitations in no uncertain terms. Samaritan faith in Jesus as their Taheb is every bit as legitimate as Jewish faith in Jesus's messiahship.[22] Both groups receive the Holy Spirit on the same terms.

Prayer is a central feature of the Spirit's bestowal, for his arrival is an immediate response to a specific request: "They prayed for them that [*hopōs*] they might receive the Holy Spirit" (8:15).[23] Luke has already assured his readers that the Spirit is the best of all possible gifts and that the Father looks for every opportunity to answer prayer in the best possible way. Once again, the petition is immediately answered positively, not only because it publicly legitimates Samaritan inclusion, but because it perfectly conforms to God's will: "How much more will your Father in heaven give the Holy Spirit to those who ask him!" (Luke 11:13).

Acts 8:22, 24

The principal character in the Samaritan material is Simon the magician (8:9, 11). In chapter 8 we touched on the polemical role that this portion of Luke's narrative plays in his condemnation of Christian magic. Extrabiblical literature extensively develops the role of Simon Magus (as he comes to be called) as the first Christian heretic,[24] a background that leads commentators to suspiciously read this story as an account of Simon's subterfuge. In other words, Simon only masquerades as a believer in order to add the Holy Spirit to his list of spiritual assistants.

22. Taheb was the Samaritan title for Messiah.

23. Bauer, Arndt, Gingrich, and Danker, *Greek-English Lexicon of the New Testament*, 718 §2b, cite Acts 8:15 as an example of the tendency for *hopōs* to replace "the inf[initive] after verbs of asking."

24. Eusebius, *Ecclesiastical History* 2.1.10–11: "So greatly did the divine grace cooperate with [Philip], that even Simon Magus, with a great number of other men, were attracted by his discourses. . . . This same Simon, also, astonished at the extraordinary miracles performed by Philip through the power of God, artfully assumed and even pretended faith in Christ so far as to be baptized; and what is surprising, the same thing is done even to this day by those who adopt his most foul heresy" (see also 2.13). Simon Magus and his sect, the Simonians, are discussed by Justin Martyr (*Apology* 1.26.1–6; 1.56.2; *Dialogue with Trypho* 120.6), Irenaeus (*Adversus haereses* 1.23.1–4; 1.16; 1.20), Tertullian (*De anima* 34; *Adversus omnes haereses* 1), Clement of Alexandria (*Stromata* 2.52.2), and Epiphanius (*Panarion* 21.1–4). The chief difficulty is reconciling the absence of corroborating historical evidence with the accusations made by these writers. It seems more likely that some of the earliest second-century Gnostics falsely claimed Simon as their progenitor, and these early Christian apologists believed their claims; see Klauck, *Magic and Paganism*, 16–17. For more extensive discussion, see Drane, "Simon the Samaritan"; Meeks, "Simon Magus"; Wilson, "Simon and Gnostic Origins"; and Lüdemann, "Acts of the Apostles."

Such interpretations, however, fail to take 8:13 seriously: "Simon himself believed and was baptized." There is no suggestion that Simon's conversion was anything but genuine.[25] True enough, he is still thinking like a magician when he tries to purchase whatever secrets have given Peter and John authority over this new Spirit (8:18–19).[26] But the past dies hard, and Luke offers no reason to doubt the sincerity of Simon's implicit repentance when Simon begs Peter to intercede on his behalf. The context is clear: repentant prayers for forgiveness are always answered positively by the Father (8:22, 24). Peter's provisional "perhaps" (*ei ara*) reflects uncertainty not about God's desires but about Simon's. Like the gift of the Holy Spirit, the offer of forgiveness is extended unreservedly, with no strings attached, to all those with faith in Jesus. Luke's narrative closes on the presumption that Peter did, in fact, intercede for a repentant Simon, who was forgiven and restored a wiser disciple.[27] Luke, however, is a clever narrator; by leaving the conclusion evocatively open-ended, he also invites his audience to examine their own hearts and to confront the latent magician lurking within us all.

Acts 14:23

Petitionary prayer often takes the form of intercession for fellow believers. We will eventually see this writ large in Paul's letters. Here, at the close of Paul's first missionary journey, Paul and Barnabas follow the model of commissioning set for them at Antioch (13:3); the newly appointed elders in every community are "committed . . . to the Lord" (compare 20:32) with prayer and fasting (14:23a). This is the only text in Acts recording an explicit prayer of dedication, but the contexts of at least three additional passages imply similar dedicatory prayers (6:6; 13:3; 20:36), while half of the uncertain prayer notices (1:14; 2:42; 6:4) are at least amenable to a similar reading.

As the summary statement describing the status of the recently launched Gentile mission, 14:22–23 offers considerable insight into the content of these prayers by explicitly linking the apostolic exhortation (14:22) with the associated prayers of dedication (14:23). The admonition in 14:22 aims at three things: (1) strengthening the spirits of the disciples by solidifying their inner resolve, (2) encouraging endurance

25. I. Marshall, *Acts*, 159; and Fitzmyer, *Acts*, 401, 405; contrary to the representative arguments of Witherington, *Acts*, 288–89.

26. This request makes perfect sense given his not-so-distant past. Simon was persuaded by Philip's preaching and miracles (Acts 8:12–13), but Philip was apparently unable to share the spiritual power effecting those miracles; access to that Spirit was provided by the apostles. Consequently, Simon approaches Peter requesting that ability for himself.

27. Barrett, "Light on the Holy Spirit," 294.

in the faith, and (3) warning of the inevitable hardships to come. The following prayer flows directly out of this instruction, providing considerable insight into the prayer's content. In fact, it details what is meant by "committing them to the Lord." Paul and Barnabas pray that these three lessons will become actualized in the lives of the newly appointed elders by employing a twofold use of commitment language; disciples are committed to God both actively and passively. First, leaders are called to commit themselves (active sense) to the Lord (14:22), while the apostles then simultaneously commit them (passive sense) to the Lord in prayer (14:23). Committing someone else to God's care in this way obviously assumes that such intercessory prayers can effect a genuine transaction between God and a third party.

Paul and Barnabas, then, are praying for the Spirit of God to accomplish the personal transformation among their listeners demanded by their teaching. Once again, growth in discipleship is described as a joint venture involving the coordination of human effort and divine power. The church's leaders must self-consciously integrate the apostles' message into their lives, but this effort alone is insufficient. It must be accompanied, even enabled, by the supernatural work of the Spirit, something best accessed by prayer, whether their own or someone else's. Paul and Barnabas extend one of the lessons learned earlier from 4:23–31—the word unaccompanied by prayer is only a half measure. How transformational is eloquence devoid of God's healing hand (4:30)? Not very. But thankfully, God's hand is moved by prayer.

Acts 26:29

The final example of a prayer with explicit content is as tantalizing as it is uncertain. After two years of imprisonment, Paul has an opportunity to defend himself against the false charges brought by Jerusalem's leaders before the newly appointed provincial governor, Porcius Festus (25:1–12). Unlike his predecessor, Festus gives every indication of being a competent ruler; for instance, he readily admits his limited understanding of local religious customs when he invites the Jewish ruler Herod Agrippa II to help adjudicate Paul's case (25:13–27). Thus for the second time in the book of Acts, Paul rehearses his life-changing confrontation with the exalted Jesus on the Damascus road (26:1–23; see 22:1–21). The apostle adeptly (and quite predictably) transforms his own story into a paradigm of the personal encounter with Jesus now confronting Festus and Agrippa. When they both protest Paul's apparent presumption (26:24–28), he replies, "I pray God that not only you but all who are listening to me today may become what I am, except for these chains" (26:29). Paul's passionate desire is that everyone within earshot would respond to his message in repentance and faith.

These words provide the sole indication in the Acts of the Apostles that early Christians may have prayed for the audiences of their missionary proclamation.[28] Given the overwhelming importance assigned to prayers for the unconverted throughout Christian history (at least among evangelicals and fundamentalists), this observation is more than noteworthy; for some it may be downright shocking. The book of Acts provides numerous opportunities for Luke to describe how Christians prayed for those beyond their community; after all, their chief responsibility was to be "witnesses in Jerusalem, and in all Judea and Samaria, and to the ends of the earth" (1:8). Yet, apart from 26:29, there is a noticeable absence of anything that might be called evangelistic intercession in the early church. The community readily prays for itself to speak boldly; Paul intercedes for leaders to grow in commitment; but where does anyone pray for outsiders to hear and to respond?[29]

Luke's choice of words merits particular attention, for Paul uses a construction rare in the New Testament.[30] In effect, he declares, "I wish to God that everyone who hears me would become a Christian."[31] What does Paul mean? Is this a petition or an exclamatory remark? In other words, is 26:29 a summary of Paul's previous intercession for Festus, Herod, and the rest of his audience? Is Luke granting us a peek at Paul's preparation for preaching, indicating that he regularly prays for all the members of his audience before speaking? Or is Paul merely expressing a heartfelt desire that everyone would eventually come to share his faith? As evocative as these questions may be, especially for Western Christians raised in a revivalist ethos geared to "praying people into the kingdom," the answer must remain uncertain. The most we can positively affirm is that Paul passionately desired all those who ever heard him proclaim the gospel to repent and believe, making it all the more noteworthy that none of Paul's audience in Acts 26 responded positively to his message—at least, if they did, we do not hear about it. So, does Paul's prayer go unanswered? Or did he pray, "Lord, convert all those who are your own"? Luke consistently affirms that conversion is the result of divine

28. See the discussion in Crump, *Jesus the Intercessor*, 127–28.

29. A similar situation arises in the Q tradition about the need for workers in the harvest (Matt. 9:37–38 ‖ Luke 10:2). The disciples are not told to pray for their listeners but to pray for additional workers; the limiting factor to be overcome by prayer is not a lack of receptivity to the kingdom but more emissaries to proclaim the kingdom.

30. Luke employs a potential optative of the verb *euchesthai*. The more common New Testament word for prayer is *proseuchesthai*. The truncated form of the verb in 26:29 not only means "to pray," but more typically means "to wish." After all, petitioning God expresses what a person wishes might happen.

31. Haenchen, *Acts*, 689; I. Marshall, *Acts*, 400; and Witherington, *Acts*, 751.

appointment (Acts 2:39; 13:48; 18:10). Maybe Paul prayed, "Lord, open people's hearts so that at least some will respond." Perhaps the church felt no need to pray for outsiders at all, believing that if their prayers for boldness were effective, the appropriate results would appear in God's timing. Acts 26:29 offers no clear answers to any of these questions. All we can say for sure is that Paul firmly believes that the gospel of Jesus Christ is the truth for everyone, and he prays that his proclamation will be used as widely as possible to usher as many as possible into the kingdom of God. But there is no indication, here or anywhere else in the book of Acts, that effective proclamation is tied to, or dependent on, specific intercessory prayers for particular groups or individuals. If the early church did pray like this, there is no evidence of it here.

Listening for Prayer between the Lines

Only a few passages remain to complete our study of petitionary prayer in Acts. Three prayers with implied content (6:6; 13:3; 20:36) and three notices of uncertain content (1:14; 2:42; 6:4) have already been related to the apostles' prayers for a strengthened community in 14:23. The remaining seven passages can be dealt with more briefly.

Acts 9:40; 16:25; 28:8

Three texts connect prayer to a miracle. In Acts 9:40 Peter prays before raising Tabitha from the dead in a manner reminiscent of Jesus's miracle in Mark 5:40–42. Publius's father is healed of a fever and dysentery after Paul prays and lays his hands on him in Acts 28:8. In 16:25 Paul and Silas are miraculously released from prison while "praying and singing hymns to God." In at least the first two instances, commentators often suggest that the proximity of prayer to the miracle indicates that the healings occurred as God's response to specific requests.[32] This may, indeed, be the case, although it is only an inference; it is not explicit. Luke certainly locates the effectiveness of divine healing power within the context of prayer, but as with so many of Luke's prayer notices, there is no specific content mentioned (in addition to Acts, see Luke 1:10–13; 2:37; 3:21–22; 5:16; 6:12; 9:18, 28–29; 11:1).[33] The context of Acts 16:25 suggests that Paul's and Silas's prayers accompanied their hymns, indi-

32. See, for example, Haenchen, *Acts*, 714; Bruce, *Acts*, 499; and Barrett, *Acts*, 1.485; 2.1225.
33. See the discussion of this Lukan tendency in Crump, *Jesus the Intercessor*, 113–16.

cating that they were prayers of praise. Might the other two situations have given opportunity for similar prayers of praise to God's power? Or could Peter and Paul have prayed along the lines of Jesus's Gethsemane request: "Please heal, but your will be done"? Luke does not say.

Acts 12:5, 12

The community's intercessions for Peter during his second imprisonment are central to a curious incident providing comic relief to a tragic story. Herod Agrippa I has executed the apostle James and set his sights on Peter, who is quickly put in chains (12:1–4). The church immediately begins praying "earnestly" on Peter's behalf (12:5), implying that they are pleading for his safe release.[34] Initially, that does indeed seem to be Luke's implicit intent, until the reader comes to 12:12–17. After describing the angelic intervention that sets the apostle free, Luke turns to the community continuing their prayers in the middle of the night. The praying church is flabbergasted by the news of Peter's release! A startled servant girl slams the door in Peter's face and runs, leaving him to knock in the dark while the church insists that she must have seen a ghost.

Could they really have been asking for a miracle? Perhaps they were praying for Peter's comfort and continued faithfulness as he contemplated martyrdom. (Were they remembering his less than exemplary behavior the night of Jesus's arrest?) If they were praying for a miraculous intervention, their stunned incredulity seems to indict them of praying with a noticeable lack of faith. I cannot help but agree with C. K. Barrett, who says that the church's astonishment "must mean that they had no hope of his release,"[35] leaving us again with a close association between prayer and miracle, but no straightforward cause-and-effect connection between a specific request and a particular response.

Acts 21:5

The disciples in Tyre greet Paul at the completion of his third missionary journey and prophetically warn him "through the Spirit" not to return to Jerusalem (21:4), apparently because they had foreseen the fierce opposition that awaits him there.[36] As Paul departs, the entire community stops for corporate prayer, leaving the impression that the prayers are

---

34. So I. Marshall, *Acts*, 208; and Fitzmyer, *Acts*, 486. For a more extensive discussion of the role that this material plays in Acts, see Garrett, "Exodus from Bondage"; Wall, "Successors to 'the Twelve'"; and Parry, "Release of the Captives."

35. Barrett, *Acts*, 1.585; see also Crump, *Jesus the Intercessor*, 135.

36. How the Spirit could offer such contradictory advice is a curious question. Perhaps the Tyrian prophets had correctly foreseen Paul's arrest but then mistakenly took it upon

mutual. Paul intercedes again for the church and its leaders as in 14:23, while the church prays for Paul and his impending fate. Though the exact content is left uncertain, Luke's context suggests possible requests for mutual guidance, endurance, faithfulness, and protection.

Acts 9:11; 10:2, 4, 9, 30; 22:17

Several prayer notices are associated with a visionary experience, although the prayer's content appears to be irrelevant to the content of the vision. First, Ananias receives visionary instructions to search for the now-blind Saul of Tarsus; Saul can be recognized because he will be praying (9:11). Perhaps Ananias's vision comes in response to Paul's prayers for direction, or is he asking to be healed of his blindness? Is Paul searching for answers to the multitude of questions now racing through his head? Is Paul confessing and repenting of his prior hostility to the plan of God? Or is he extolling the grandeur of the exalted Lord so recently revealed to him? Maybe Paul is interceding for his fellow Pharisees, equally hostile to the new church. All we can say with certainty is that Paul and Ananias's encounter fits within Luke's overall pattern of coordinating prayer with divine revelation. Throughout the book of Acts, God regularly unfolds the next step in his plan for salvation-history in connection with the prayers of his people.

Similarly, Cornelius and Peter are brought together as two devout men who pray (10:2, 4, 9, 30). The several references to personal piety portray them as men faithful to the daily prayers expected of Jews and proselytes, although Peter is particularly devout since the noon hour was not an hour designated for statutory prayer (10:9). Undoubtedly, their prayers encompassed the full range of religious expression; Luke's point is not that God sends visions in response to specific requests, but that God reveals his plans to men and women devout in prayer.

Finally, while explaining himself to the hostile mob in Jerusalem, Paul recounts a divine revelation he once received while praying inside the temple precincts (22:17), a vision that forecast his mission to the Gentiles. Once again, divine revelation takes place within the context of prayer regardless of the prayer's specific content or requests.[37]

---

themselves to prevent Paul from going. In any event, the answer to this question does not affect our understanding of Acts 21:5.

37. It is standard fare in the literature on Luke-Acts to conclude that the Jerusalem church retained its traditional Jewish prayer habits by faithfully attending the temple at the designated hours of prayer and sacrifice (Acts 2:46; 3:1; 5:20–21; 10:2–3; 22:17); see I. Marshall, *Acts*, 357; Turner, "Prayer in the Gospels," 72; Thurston, *Spiritual Life in the Early Church*, 27; Barrett, *Acts*, 1.176; Fitzmyer, *Acts*, 277; and Green, "Persevering Together in Prayer," 186–87. The evidence does not, however, support this conclusion; with the sole

Lessons from the Church in Acts

The ancient church depicted by Luke is anything but perfect; the oft-repeated notion that Luke idealized the first Christian community can be perpetuated only by ignoring significant portions of his story. The Jerusalem community wrestled with dishonesty and greed (5:1–11), discrimination (6:1), an unwillingness to embrace outsiders (9:26), as well as serious theological disagreements (15:1–5) that eventually divided the church and issued in Paul's abandonment to a religious lynch mob (21:20–31).[38] Luke's portrait, complete with warts and blemishes, reveals a church like any other, ancient or modern; it is a collection of fallible, redeemed people living with both strengths and weaknesses. Their actions delineate prominent pitfalls to avoid, but also model exemplary behaviors indicating the true value and the proper practice of prayer for the corporate life of God's people.

I conclude this chapter by summarizing three of these results. First, the early church somehow manages to sustain a significant degree of unity through corporate prayer. Regardless of various errors, struggles, and disagreements, the church sustains a crucial ability to pray together through thick and thin. Luke's favorite word to describe this commonality (*homothymadon*) is used six times of the church in Acts (1:14; 2:46; 4:24; 5:12; 8:6; 15:25) and only once elsewhere in the New Testament (Rom. 15:6). I suspect that this devotion to common prayer accounts for Luke's general lack of interest in supplying the actual substance of those prayers. Collective prayer is significant in and of itself, quite apart from any particular content or specific request. The community that openly and frequently prays together places itself in a perfect position to witness the Holy Spirit's activity unfurled around them. The well-rounded collection of diverse minds, emotions, concerns, interests, passions,

---

exception of 22:17, Luke never actually depicts believers praying in the temple! The early Christians attend the temple, not to pray, but to take advantage of a public venue with a ready-made audience for their proclamation. Whenever Luke describes Christian activity in the temple, it involves preaching and miracles, not prayer (2:42–47; 3:1–12; 5:12–28, 42). This practice by the Jerusalem church serves as the model for Paul's later strategy of always attending the local synagogue before "turning to the Gentiles" (13:14, 46; 14:1–2; 17:1–4, 10–13, 17; 18:4–7, 19, 26; 19:8–10; 22:19; 26:11). Paul's visit to Philippi is paradigmatic in this regard; he searches for "a place of prayer" (16:13), not to pray but to preach. The sole exception in 22:17 serves an apologetic purpose as Paul defends himself against accusations of desecrating the temple. Temple (and synagogue) attendance was a part of the apostolic missionary strategy; expressions of Christian devotion were quickly relocated to their own community gatherings (2:42–47; 4:32–35; 5:41–42).

38. Paul's Jerusalem opponents grossly misrepresented his message (Acts 21:21). How can James and the other elders report this without also describing their efforts to put a stop to it?

and insights assembled by an entire community at prayer creates an open tinderbox receptive to whatever sparks are struck by the collision between devout petition and divine intent. There is no better place to pray than with the assembled body of Christ.

Second, the emerging church rapidly adopts both Christ's model and his teaching about personal prayer. The Christians assimilate their Lord's habits and allow his instruction to shape their execution. For example, the priorities of the Lord's Prayer serve as guiding principles (if not explicit directions) that shape the way the church framed its requests and behaved in the face of hostility. The Christian community is a family of servants passionate for sustained boldness as its members obey their Lord by announcing his kingdom in the name of Jesus as broadly and as frequently as possible. The complete absence of personal, idiosyncratic prayers, whether for individual needs or the salvation of specific friends and neighbors, looms like a large black hole in the middle of this Lukan constellation. Given the modern church's propensity to view petitionary prayer as the chief instrument of Christian wish fulfillment, the book of Acts provides a clarion call to a serious reorientation of priorities within (at least) the Western church. Is petitionary prayer a means of service or a way to be served? Luke's answer to that question is unambiguous and biting. We dare not forget that the church in Acts urgently prays for faithful endurance throughout, but never expects relief from, the pain that inevitably accompanies a faithful Christian life.

Third, prayer is the way for believers to find their lives realigned with God's redemptive plans. Luke-Acts describes no particular correlation between specific petitions (whether they are offered persistently, faithfully, or forcefully) and divine response. What is consistently portrayed is the Father's willingness to act on behalf of and to reveal himself among those men and women who regularly pray. In the past, certain scholars argued that Luke's evidence portrays prayer as the chief means by which God directs the progress of salvation-history.[39] In other words, God is able to accomplish his plans when and where the church prays. Careful examination of Luke-Acts demonstrates, however, that this scenario puts the cart before the horse. Actually, Luke's consistent concern for the integrity of divine sovereignty means that human beings are the beneficiaries of God's desires, not vice versa. Prayer, regardless of its specific content, creates an open channel of two-way communication between heaven and earth. Not only is the Father the recipient of our messages, but prayer opens us simultaneously to his. However unexpected, coun-

39. A thesis first articulated by Harris, "Prayer in Luke-Acts," and then popularized by others; see O'Brien, "Prayer in Luke-Acts"; Smalley, "Spirit, Kingdom, and Prayer"; and Trites, "Prayer Motif in Luke-Acts." For my critique of this position, see Crump, *Jesus the Intercessor*, 5–7, 113–15, 121–26, 134–36.

terintuitive, or shocking God's word to us may seem, the act of prayer transforms praying people into spiritually accessible recipients of divine communication, whether that message arrives through a vision or miraculous act, through life's humble circumstances, or through a subtle godly inclination. As I have written elsewhere, "Prayer opens up a doorway between earth and heaven, but once that door is opened only God himself knows what may pass back through it from heaven to earth."[40] This simple conclusion may sound pedestrian, but it is worth repeating: people who pray receive the guidance they need from God.

Luke's theological tendencies in this regard make his perspective on prayer more congenial to John than to Matthew or Mark, both of whom leave greater room for the influences of personal petition. We must somehow find a way to hold these various perspectives together as complementary pieces of the same picture. While Luke largely agrees with John's account of the power of prayer deriving from the disciple's submission to God's plan, we have also seen that prayer, regardless of its purpose or type, cultivates the necessary spirit of cooperation essential to any effective divine-human endeavor. The Father enlists his people as real (not silent) partners in his work, and even though the final outcome of the plan was decided ages ago, disciples have a genuine role to play in shaping the finishing touches of that outcome through the nature of their requests. Luke's understanding of divine sovereignty does not extend universally to encompass complete historical determinism. There is no evidence to suggest that salvation-history, over which God exercises providential control, is exactly coterminous with the history of the world, a history where the foibles and the genius, the folly and the beauty, of human endeavor are free to paint a canvas permitted, but not necessarily determined, by the Creator. God commissions and directs history's portrait, but it is not all paint-by-numbers. A good deal of room yet remains for individual decision, cooperation, searching, and experimentation, all of which unfold existentially through our own individual habits of personal prayer. Some details are filled in by God's own hand with a very fine brush, while others are left to his trusted community of faithful apprentices to color with broader, even faltering, strokes.

40. Crump, *Jesus the Intercessor*, 115.

10

The Impossibility of Petition and Prayers of the Spirit

Pauline Prayer, part 1

Years ago I had a conversation with a heartbroken young woman devastated by the recent breakup of her engagement to the man she believed to be the love of her life. Her depth of anguish was measured only partly by her profound sense of loss; the greater portion of her brokenness arose from an all-consuming guilt she felt over destroying so many lives. After all, her relationship began as a delightful answer to the passionately insistent prayers that God give her this one man. Now the man was gone, the relationship over. In retrospect, she believed that her prayers had been seriously misguided; she begged God for the wrong relationship with the wrong guy at the wrong time. Now she was forced to consider the fallout of her mistake, and she feared that the time wasted on her preoccupation with Mr. Wrong had caused them both to miss out on Mr. and Mrs. Right. I found her weeping, convinced that her misdirected prayers had set in motion an unstoppable chain reaction of missed opportunities. How many lives had her prayers ruined? How many lonely men and women would never meet their ideal spouses, all because of her ill-informed petitions?

According to my friend's (unarticulated) theology, prayer was a dangerous weapon, not unlike a loaded pistol. When used frivolously by the inexperienced it can do more harm than good. Wise prayer, when aimed properly, brings comfort and safety, but the inherent dangers of misguided prayer make it more life threatening than no prayer at all.

I admit that this young woman offers an extreme example of a particularly distorted view of God and prayer. Yet, her fears reflect an important concern. What is the relationship between God's will and human ignorance, especially when they clash, as at times they must, in petitionary prayer? Not even the holiest saint can claim perfect insight into God's intentions for every situation. Not knowing how to pray is a common quandary for anyone truly sensitive to the priority of the Father's will over one's own. Unless we are fully satisfied with the oblique surrender yielded by a generalized "your will be done," spiritually inquisitive minds cannot help but wonder how to shift the balance of personal petition from uncertain guesswork to confidence in heaven's agreement.

As the next few chapters turn to the Pauline treatment of petitionary prayer, the existential dilemma created by not knowing how best to pray occupies center stage, not only because it lies at the heart of Rom. 8:26–27 (our subject for this chapter), but more important because, in my judgment, this passage comprises the heart and soul, the sine qua non, of Paul's theology of Christian prayer. In starting with Rom. 8, we begin at the center and work our way to the periphery where even the outer edges of Pauline prayer receive their final shape from the spiritual transactions at the core.

Living in Tension

It has become a truism to say that Rom. 8:26–27 is unparalleled in the New Testament, both in its view of prayer and the role given to the Holy Spirit:[1] "In the same way, the Spirit helps us in our weakness. We do not know what we ought to pray for, but the Spirit himself intercedes for us with groans that words cannot express. And he who searches our hearts knows the mind of the Spirit, because the Spirit intercedes for the saints in accordance with God's will." Romans 8 is more densely populated with references to the Holy Spirit than any other segment of Pauline literature, and these two verses explaining the Spirit's work as intercessor provide the chapter's dramatic conclusion. Paul's opening comparative phrase,

1. This evaluation is largely due to the work of Käsemann, *Perspectives on Paul*, 127; and idem, *Romans*, 239; see the responses of MacRae, "Note on Romans 8:26–27"; and Obeng, "Reconciliation of Rom. 8.26f."

"in the same way," indicates that 8:26–27 is logically dependent on his preceding argument.[2] Thus, before we can unpack these two verses, we first need to uncover the line of argument that eventually leads Paul to his confident repose in the Spirit's intercession.

The majority of commentators agree that 8:26–27 coheres with the preceding unit of thought beginning at 8:18. The logic of Paul's argument unfolds like this:

Thesis: Our present suffering will be overshadowed by our future glory (8:18).
    A. All creation, subject to futility, groans in expectation of our glory (8:19–22).
        1. We too groan, having the Spirit and awaiting our adoption/resurrection (8:23).
            [a. Digression on the nature of hope (8:24–25).]
            b. The Holy Spirit helps us in our weakness (8:26a).
                i. We do not know what to pray for (8:26b).
                    (a) But the Spirit intercedes with groans (8:26c).
                ii. God knows the Spirit's mind (8:27a).
                    (a) Because the Spirit intercedes in accordance with God's will (8:27b).

The unifying theme of the entire chapter, including 8:18–30, is the ever-present tension created by Christian eschatology: Christ has inaugurated the last days, but he introduced only the beginning of the end. The finality of the final era has yet to appear. Consequently, believers inhabit an overlapping existence of two equally imposing realities: the already and the not yet. Nowhere is the Christian's dual citizenship demonstrated more blatantly than in the Spirit's implementation of our adoption as God's children. On the one hand, the Father's gift of the Spirit demonstrates that we have *already* been adopted into God's family. This Spirit enables every believer to honestly call God Father (8:15). On the other hand, the same Spirit is simultaneously a down payment guaranteeing that our current yearning and suffering are not in vain; we will *eventually* be adopted at the resurrection (8:23). We have been adopted; we have yet to be adopted. Not only are both statements equally true, but the truth of each is demonstrated by the same work of the one Spirit. In fact, the

2. Identifying the precise antecedent to the comparative adverb *hōsautōs* is notoriously difficult. Suggested interpretations include the hope of 8:25, the groanings of 8:22–23, the Spirit in 8:23, and the Spirit's testimony in 8:16. Personally, I am most sympathetic to this final suggestion; see G. Smith, "Function of 'Likewise.'" Fortunately for our purposes, settling on a precise answer to this question does not affect the overall argument made here.

Holy Spirit becomes the divine prism through which both realities first converge and then diverge in the experience of God's people.[3]

These paradoxical expressions of the Spirit's testimony in the believer's life are revealed step by step as Paul explains the eschatological consequences of creation's redemption through a three-stage reference to "groaning." Paul describes successive levels of increasingly localized anguish: first creation groans (8:18–22), then God's children groan within creation (8:23–25), and finally the Holy Spirit groans within God's children (8:26–27). Clarifying the various ways in which this groaning arises from the current eschatological tension sheds light on both the Christian's place in this world and the Spirit's role in prayer.

All Creation Groans

"We know that the whole creation has been groaning as in the pains of childbirth right up to the present time" (Rom. 8:22). Paul reminds us that the curse of Gen. 3:17 saw the entire cosmos engulfed by the ravaging consequences of Adam's sin (Rom. 8:20).[4] As humanity goes, so goes the universe, for better or for worse. Not only did the first Adam's fall cause serious bruising to the rest of the world, but the second Adam's triumph brings complete healing for that world, animate and inanimate alike (5:12–21). The cosmos now eagerly anticipates its own deliverance, its restoration to the Father's original design, to be consummated at the final unveiling of God's adopted children (8:21). In the meantime, caught between the collision of two opposing spiritual forces, the cosmos groans under the combined weight of both. First, this world suffers the anguish of its own futility (8:20); for millennia it has remained a cosmos alienated from its Cause, unable to function as intended. From this vantage point, creation's groaning first arose from the ash heap of human rebellion, but those groans were soon augmented by a second factor. Just as childbirth is accompanied by labor pains, so the Father determined that severe cosmic distress will precede creation's rebirth (8:22), demanding that faith in God's promises must outweigh any temptation to lose hope in the process (8:18).[5] Whatever Paul intended by his vivid personifica-

3. Dunn offers an insightful exploration of the Spirit and Pauline eschatology in Rom. 8; see *Romans*, 433–46, 457–95.

4. I agree with Cranfield in understanding creation to entail "the sum-total of sub-human nature both animate and inanimate" excluding humanity; for a survey and critique of the various options, see *Romans*, 411–12.

5. This childbirth metaphor appears in the Old Testament (Isa. 66:7–9; Mic. 4:10) and is applied to the parousia in the New Testament (Mark 13:8; John 16:21; 1 Thess. 5:3). Some commentators suggest that Paul's usage is derived from the rabbinic notion of the

tion of the nonhuman realm, it is clear that salvation and its paradoxes encompass the whole of creation, both seen and unseen, both explored and unexplored.[6] Whatever believers experience in their fallen and redeemed humanity is somehow commensurate with creation's own experience of fallenness and redemption.

The creation does not suffer alone. As the universe agonizes, so do God's people (8:23), although in our case there is at least one significant difference. Creation first groaned under a newly imposed oppression because it was subjected unwillingly to Adam's sin (8:20).[7] No member of humanity—with the exception of Jesus of Nazareth—could ever make this claim. Paul's preceding argument asserts that human sinfulness was not an unwanted foreign power imposed from without; it is a happily embraced corrupter resident within (1:18–3:20). Consequently, not only does fallen humanity fail to groan with creation over its own fallenness, but it remains blind and deaf to the ubiquitous travail of a fallen universe. Whatever sensitivity believers may have to the destructive outworkings of sin is solely a gift of the Spirit: "We ourselves, who have the firstfruits of the Spirit, groan inwardly as we wait eagerly for our adoption" (8:23).

The importance of this point cannot be overstated. A Christian's groaning is the fruit of salvation. We must be very clear about this, no matter how counterintuitive it might first appear. For the remainder of creation, anguish precedes rebirth, but for the believer, rebirth gives rise to anguish (compare Rom. 7:24; 2 Cor. 5:2). God's Spirit lifts the veil of sin that blinded us to the consequences of our rebellion. We may not have groaned previously over creation's futility, but now we can see the devastation left in the wake of Adam's flight into disobedience. The Father's light illuminates the danker recesses of our shoddy hovel called "the flesh," and we finally begin to understand how depraved our circumstances have been, just how far we have fallen. Yet, rather than immediately delivering us from our weakness, the Spirit endows us with

---

"woes of the Messiah" (a time of cosmic turmoil preceding the coming of the messianic kingdom). Fitzmyer is correct, however, to point out that the relevant rabbinic literature is later than the New Testament; whether the idea of the messianic woes "was current in the first century or known to Paul is hard to say"; see *Romans*, 509.

6. For a good discussion of the theological significance of Paul's thought here, see Bolt, "Relation between Creation and Redemption."

7. This interpretation remains valid regardless of the subject of the participle "the one who subjected it." Whether the direct agent was God or Adam (Christ and Satan are also suggested), the consequences for creation (subjection to frustration) are due to Adam's sin; see the discussions in Cranfield, *Romans*, 413–14; Dunn, *Romans*, 471; and Fitzmyer, *Romans*, 507–8. I am inclined to understand God as the subject, but I cannot help wondering if Paul intended his ambiguity to evoke the dual responsibilities of God and Adam as the efficient and formal causes, respectively.

a divine perspective, eternal promises, faith to persevere, and the gift of prayer to a heavenly Father. Perhaps we can say that our groans are not the melody but the harmony that accompanies Christ's song of redemption, for while we struggle we also remember that our present suffering is nothing compared with the coming glory (Rom. 8:18). Nevertheless, the groans are real, and anyone who has seriously pursued personal conformity to the mind of God knows how intimacy with Christ can easily engender a coincidental sense of unworthiness. The closer we come, the farther we know we have to go; yet this growing sense of distance occurs for only those whose rooms in heaven have already had the beds turned down. Ironically, our groans are God's gift, for genuine praise is always watered by tears of repentance, while adoration reminds the worshiper of how much we withhold and refuse to surrender. Authentic prayer always springs from the soil of discontent.

Once again, we have encountered the existential dimension of New Testament eschatology. Alarm bells should sound in the absence of such turmoil in a person's life, for anyone "content to live only in and for this world, as Paul would say, at the level of the flesh, stands in greater peril."[8] To feel perfectly at home in sin's squalor indicates that no true adoption has occurred; such a person is not a child of God after all, for God's children eagerly anticipate their resurrection and the end of this mortal existence (8:23). The reality of this personal eschatological turmoil has significant implications for the Christian experience of prayer, as we shall see shortly.

Groaning in Prayer

Finally, we encounter the amazing claim that the Holy Spirit groans on our behalf. Not uncommonly, commentators fudge this statement by finding various ways to shift the activity away from God's Spirit onto the person praying, for certainly the Spirit of God cannot groan![9] Perhaps Paul is referring to glossalalia, "speaking in tongues"?[10] Or, better yet, he must be describing a cooperative activity in which our groans are either elicited by or become the medium of the Spirit's interces-

8. Dunn, *Romans*, 490.
9. "We are not to suppose that the Spirit itself prays, or utters the inarticulate groans. . . . He is said to do what he causes us to do" (Hodge, *Romans*, 279).
10. Käsemann is the best-known commentator who interprets "inarticulate groans" as expressions of glossalalia in corporate worship (*Perspectives on Paul*, 129; *Romans*, 240–41). Few, however, follow this untenable position (which is at least as old as Origen); for a thorough critique, see Cranfield, *Romans*, 422–24; Wedderburn, "Romans 8.26"; Obeng, "Spirit Intercession Motif," 362; and Fitzmyer, *Romans*, 519.

sion.[11] Thus the Spirit offers his own prayers through our groaning. If any such suggestions were, however, a part of Paul's intent, there are certainly much clearer ways to have said it. Rather, the plain sense of 8:26 is that *the Spirit* is groaning within us.[12] It is important to notice, too, that the Spirit's groans are not restricted to the believer's moments of prayer; Paul does not say that the Spirit begins groaning as we wrestle with our petitions. Rather, whatever we understand these groans to be, they are an ongoing activity of the Spirit within God's children. Just as the believer's travail emerges through a new awareness of our inextricable entanglement within creation's futility, so the groaning of God's Spirit arises because he now inhabits the stymied, struggling existence of children who still anxiously await the "not yet" of their promised adoption (8:21, 23). The Spirit groans as he indwells and identifies with our fallenness; although our incapacity for proper prayer provides the occasion for Paul's reflection on this aspect of the Spirit's work, it is not the cause or the explanation of the work itself. That fountainhead flows from the heart of the Father, and it explains why this text becomes the climax of Paul's treatment of the Holy Spirit's place in Christian eschatology. We are given a fully trinitarian account of God's identification with fallen human circumstance: the Father loves this fallen world enough to send his only Son; the Son obediently assumes our fallen humanity; and the Spirit shares in the full measure of our interim groaning.[13]

If the primary cause of the Spirit's groaning is the grace of God, the secondary cause is human frailty: "The Spirit helps us in our weakness" (8:26). This is a general evaluation of the human condition, something from which the redeemed have yet to be delivered, and it lays the basis for the following assertion that no believer properly understands the contours of correct petition.[14] As long as we inhabit a fallen world with all

11. Sanday and Headlam, *Romans*, 213; R. Boyd, "Work of the Holy Spirit in Prayer," 40; Dodd, *Romans*, 150; Murray, *Romans*, 1.312; Wedderburn, "Romans 8.26," 375; C. C. Mitchell, "The Holy Spirit's Intercessory Ministry," *Bibliotheca Sacra* 139 (1982): 239–40; Obeng, "Spirit Intercession Motif," 362–63; and Wright, *Romans*, 599.

12. Nygren, *Romans*, 336; Cranfield, *Romans*, 423; and Fitzmyer, *Romans*, 518–19.

13. MacRae, "Note on Romans 8:26–27," objects to such latent trinitarianism, claiming that 8:27 "supposes a form of communication between the divine persons which is much more at home in later Trinitarian theology than in Paul" (228). Consequently, he argues that "he who searches our hearts" (8:27a) is not God but the Holy Spirit, while "the mind of the Spirit" (8:27b) refers to the human spirit rather than the divine. Aside from the presumption of knowing better than Paul what is "more at home" in his theology, this reading hardly comports well with the plain meaning of 8:26. It is exceedingly awkward to shift from *pneuma* = the Holy Spirit in 8:26 to *pneuma* = the human spirit in 8:27.

14. The broader context of Rom. 8 indicates that our "weakness" encompasses both the external/fleshly as well as the internal/spiritual struggles of existence; see Nygren, *Romans*, 336. Attempts to limit this weakness in some way, whether to external tempta-

of its temptations, illusions, and perverse obstructions to perfect divine communion—in other words, as long as we inhabit this temporal realm of weakness—every believer ranks among those who are incapable of expressing appropriate petition.[15] "We do not know what to pray for," Paul says. We remain finite creatures subject to the constraints of fallen finitude. This is Paul's universal description of the Christian predicament, independent of any particular situation, sin, or personal failure. He is not distinguishing between the spiritual versus the carnal, mature versus immature, disciple versus backslider. All those who still hope for the resurrection continue to slog through the mire of this sinful, terrestrial bog and find themselves so thoroughly hampered by their fallenness that formulating prayers fully submitted to the mind of God—prayers that always conform to his plans and desires, that reliably elicit the Father's "amen"—remains far beyond their mortal grasp no matter how long or how hard they may try. Petitionary prayer is always a responsibility in which we will flounder, a continual invitation to confront our failure, a divine enabling of human inability.

The obvious question becomes, Why bother? We must tackle one more issue before grappling with that problem.

Crying Out to Abba

What Jesus charges us to do generally, Paul warns us, is specifically impossible. The heart of the Lord's Prayer is the cultivation of complete surrender to the will of God. "Father, may your will be done" was the substance of both Jesus's theology as well as his own personal practice in prayer. Yet, there is no need to compare Romans with the Synoptic tradition to establish this tension; it is resident within Rom. 8 itself. Romans 8:15 has already announced that the gift of the Spirit not only guarantees our adoption but frees us from slavery, allowing every believer to cry out, "Abba, Father!" (see Mark 14:36; Gal. 4:6). Whether this phrase is a specific allusion to the use of the Lord's Prayer in the worship of Paul's

tions (Käsemann, *Romans*, 240) or to an internal inability to pray (Sanday and Headlam, *Romans*, 213; Murray, *Romans*, 1.311), fall short. Paul's logic shows that the Christian's inability to petition correctly is one particular expression of the generalized problem of human weakness.

15. Commentators generally agree that the article *to* makes the entire following clause (*ti proseuxōmetha katho dei*) the object of "we do not know." The sense is, "we do not know what is right for us to pray (for)"; see Cranfield, *Romans*, 421; Dunn, *Romans*, 477; and Fitzmyer, *Romans*, 518. The issue is not that we fail to understand the proper method or form of prayer—contrary to Barrett's translation: "we do not even know what prayer to offer" (*Romans*, 168)—but that we do not understand the appropriate content of correct petition.

communities, as some suggest,[16] it certainly testifies to the longevity and continuing influence of Jesus's own exemplary prayer life within the thought, teaching, and practice of the earliest Christian gatherings. The church self-consciously sought to pray as Jesus had prayed. Thus to call God "Abba" not only confirms our status as children, but ideally should reinforce our commitment to behave, to think, and to pray only in ways fully pleasing to our Lord and to his heavenly Father.

Paul begins his explanation of the Spirit's indwelling by declaring the Spirit's accomplishments: he empowers all Christian prayer, the principal expression of our confidence in being adopted into God's family. But before Paul's discussion draws to a close, these very same cries of the Spirit also betray our anxiety as children, not to mention our failure to pray correctly. The eschatological tension strikes again. The Spirit frees us while our flesh imprisons us. The Spirit evokes perfect prayer while our sin gags us and keeps us mute. No more profound description of spiritual turmoil appears anywhere in the New Testament. The Spirit's gift of prayer becomes a lightning rod for whatever doubts and fears cripple believers in their journey toward faithful, emotional, psychological, intellectual, spiritual dependence on God as Abba. In our humanity no believer ever knows precisely what to pray; in fact, the more thoroughly the Spirit of adoption cleanses us of fear, the more powerfully our conscience grasps that prayer, the Spirit's great gift, becomes the field of our greatest struggles. Prayer is the focal point of brilliant illumination as well as bleakest darkness, the schoolroom where we finally comprehend that we have never known anything at all.

Only the Holy Spirit makes prayer a possible impossibility. In the logical structure of 8:26–27 outlined above, Paul offers two sets of comparisons: (1) what we do not know (8:26b) is compared with what God does know (8:27a); and (2) the Spirit's unspoken groanings (8:26c) are actually prayers made according to the will of God (8:27b). The Father and the Spirit have a perfect, mutual understanding. In an earlier letter, at 1 Cor. 2:11, Paul explains how the Spirit possesses full knowledge of God's mind. Now the roles are reversed as the Father "who searches our hearts" also possesses perfect apprehension of the Spirit's mind.[17] And

16. For example, Barrett, *Romans*, 164; and Wright, *Romans*, 593; for the arguments against this possibility, see Dunn, *Romans*, 453–54.

17. "The one who searches hearts" is a characteristic Old Testament description of Yahweh (1 Sam. 16:7; 1 Kings 8:39; Pss. 17:3; 26:2; 44:21; 139:1–2, 23; Prov. 15:11; Jer. 11:20; 12:3; 17:10). Paul makes an a fortiori argument: If God knows everything in the human heart, how much more will he know the mind of his own Spirit? MacRae ("Note on Romans 8:26–27") appeals to 1 Cor. 2:11 to buttress his claim that Paul's phrase denotes the Spirit; he would do better, however, to reevaluate his claim that Paul's writings contain nothing so overtly trinitarian.

what the mind of the Spirit offers to the Father are not simply groans of commiseration but groans of unspoken intercession in perfect conformity to God's purposes for his struggling children.[18] Consequently, although the believer never knows what to pray for, the Spirit of adoption, constantly sharing in our weakness, is perpetually praying to the Father on our behalf, always offering prayers that are in absolute agreement with the Father's will and are therefore always receiving affirmative responses from our Abba. Just as the incarnate Son became the perfect Savior by being "made like his brothers in every way," including "suffer[ing] when he was tempted" (Heb. 2:17–18), so the indwelling Spirit becomes the perfect intercessor by inhabiting the brokenness that keeps us "groan[ing] inwardly as we wait eagerly for . . . the redemption of our bodies" (Rom. 8:23). Although Paul never uses the word, his theology comes remarkably close to the Johannine notion of the Spirit as Paraclete, our Advocate with the Father (John 14:16, 26; 15:26; 16:7). In fact, both the Pauline and the Johannine literature link the Spirit with the Son in joint advocacy, for while the Spirit intercedes from within our current human experience, the Son intercedes from the throne of God, continually applying the benefits of his salvation while defeating satanic accusation (Rom. 8:34; 1 John 2:1; also Heb. 7:25).[19]

Paul's assurances of a successful cooperation between the Father, Son, and Spirit on our behalf lay an immovable theological foundation for the concluding guarantee of Rom. 8:28–30. We are ultimately assured that "in all things God works for the good of those who love him" because the Spirit ceaselessly requests that each of life's new adventures and disappointments, successes and tragedies, be woven throughout the tenuous threads of our mortal existence in precisely that pattern best designed to create an eternal fabric of wholeness and peace for sons and daughters resting in their Father's love. The Christian has become fully engulfed by the inner life of the triune God. The Son's heavenly intercessions for us, the life of the Spirit offering up our prayers, and the Father's embrace as our Abba all give potent testimony that "our knowledge of God and His ways is, so to speak, God within us recognizing Himself."[20] And

18. It is difficult to decide whether *alalētois*, which occurs only here in biblical Greek, should be translated "unspoken" or "unspeakable." Are the groans unarticulated or ineffable? I tend toward the former view, since the Father's knowledge of the Spirit's mind makes the spoken word unnecessary. In any case, one cannot help but wonder what the Spirit's voice would sound like to the Father! In the final analysis, either translation is feasible and makes little difference to interpretation as long as we avoid the mistake of relating the groans to human prayer. The unspoken groans are not ours. We may pray fluently and at length, but all the while the Spirit groans silently on our behalf.

19. See Crump, *Jesus the Intercessor*, 14–20, for a more detailed examination of these three important passages.

20. Dodd, *Romans*, 151. For a similar exposition, see Wright, *Romans*, 600.

whatever else we may not fathom, we can always rest assured that this God of grace "cannot disown himself" (2 Tim. 2:13).

Learning to Pray with the Spirit

We are now in a position to revisit the vexing question raised earlier. Why pray? If proper petition is impossible for us and if the Spirit is continually interceding quite effectively on our behalf, then why bother to petition God at all? Would we not do ourselves a favor by forswearing the inevitable selfishness of personal requests and entrusting ourselves instead to the sovereign benevolence of the God who has devoted himself to our best interests? Would this not prove a more agreeable route to true peace of mind? Though some may undoubtedly answer yes to this question, a more extensive reading of Paul reveals that he himself did not come to this conclusion. Paul's letters are replete with specific petitions and intercessory requests for particular individuals with special needs. Obviously, his theology of the Spirit's intercession did not prevent Paul from asking God to work specifically in his own life and the lives of others. While chapters 11–12 will shed further light on the parameters and motivations of Pauline petition, Romans 8 suggests at least four reasons to continue in petitionary prayer while confronting our inadequacies.

First, the Spirit compels God's people to pray, leading them into the Father's presence to deeply enjoy all the benefits of their adoption. Prayer is not a function of our intelligence or understanding but of the Spirit's internal renewal. Being reconciled with God entails the opportunity of "crying out" to our Father, knowing that we will be heard. This language of emotional outcry is regularly used in the Old Testament to describe insistent, urgent prayer (irrespective of whether it is verbal or silent, public or private, formal or informal) offered by those who know themselves to be utterly dependent on heaven's reply.[21] Although we may never foresee exactly how the Father will answer, the Spirit reveals that God is calling us to throw ourselves into his care, nonetheless. Certainly, human resistance to this lesson supplies a partial explanation for at least some of our periodic struggles in life. In any case, the Spirit insists that our Father's reach is broad enough and his arms strong enough to catch, comfort, and redirect all of his children whatever their circumstances. Our specific petitions may be thoroughly misdirected, but turning to the Father for help and implicitly acknowledging our inability to solve every problem are the very lessons that the Spirit works to inculcate in

21. Cranfield, *Romans*, 399; for example, see Pss. 3:4; 4:3; 18:6.

God's children. Prayer of any sort, whether confident or uncertain, is the station at which "the Spirit himself testifies with our spirit that we are children of God" (Rom. 8:16).

The second lesson follows from the first. Obedient children learn to appreciate the Father's superior wisdom and to place their faith in the unwavering reliability of his love. Authentic faith never insists on a divine yes but gratefully recognizes God's no or not now as equally gracious and acceptable replies. Part of the Spirit's lesson plan is to teach us that we do not know what is best, neither for ourselves nor for anybody else, friend and foe alike. I am the child; God is the Father. I am the servant; God is the King. I am the creature, God is the Creator. I am ignorant; only he is truly wise. I am selfish; he alone is thoroughly selfless. I am the tool; my Father is the master craftsman carving perfection from the flawed blocks left to him in this darkened quarry we call life. The goal of our adoption is the eventual restitution of a divine-human relationship wherein the confession that "I do not know what to pray" is not a reluctant admission of weakness or defeat but a joyful eruption of surrender and release. To admit that "I do not know what to pray" means that prayer is never a loaded gun threatening the future prospects of life's innocent bystanders. My young, recently engaged friend had no reason to fear that her prayers had demolished the love-lives of strangers. To say "I do not know what to pray" means that I can rest confidently in the Spirit's faithfulness and attune my ear to the echoes of his unspoken groans indicating how to do what I cannot yet do for myself: pray effectively.

Third, in teaching us to genuinely pray "your will be done," the Spirit conforms us to the life of Jesus. But this becomes true only for those who underscore the word "genuinely." To conclude "if it be your will" is not an endorsement of laissez-faire spirituality; it is not a free pass excusing us from the rigors of conformity to the mind of God (rather, our conformity is not a passive process; we must be engaged); nor are we relieved of the need for life-stretching faith when we submit our requests to heaven. Jesus exemplified each of these qualities himself—active engagement, conformity, and faith—yet, at the end of the day, his final wish was "not my will but the Father's be done." Engagement and surrender must coexist.

Romans 8 assumes this connection between the disciple and the Savior's model. Paul squarely locates the Spirit's work within the context of suffering; in fact, all of God's children are promised periodic turmoil until the end of the age. Within this context, we might reasonably assume the Spirit's intercessions to focus on the Christian's need for strength, comfort, endurance, or renewed hope—or, better yet, relief from pain, deliverance from tragedy, or sustained good health. But if this is what the reader expects, reading Paul will prove sorely disappointing. Instead of tangible signs of earthly relief, our primary assurance for the here and now is the Spirit's prayer "according to God" (*kata theon*). Why? Paul's answer is revealed in the preceding Spirit-induced cries to "Abba, Father."[22] The Spirit moves God's children to pray as Jesus prayed, to inhabit their own Gethsemane as Jesus had passed through his. "Abba, Father," he said, "everything is possible for you. Take this cup from me. Yet not what I will, but what you will" (Mark 14:36). These words are not a detached deferment of responsibility mumbled by the spiritually disengaged. They are the Spirit-inspired cry of someone who seriously sought to discern the Father's plan, groaned a prayer requiring mountain-moving faith, and was then led by that same faith to rest in the assurance of "according to God" (*kata theon*). Learning to pray is learning to be like Jesus; they are the same work of the one Spirit.

Finally, as I have argued throughout this study, we should beware of assuming more than any particular text requires. For example, to say that the Spirit always intercedes according to the Father's will does not tell us anything about the extent of God's will. The context certainly demonstrates that, at the very least, God's will includes our final "conform[ity] to the likeness of his Son" (8:29) and our eternal glorification (8:18, 21, 30). But this is a far cry from affirming that every decision ever faced by God's child has a divinely preferred or predetermined outcome for which the Spirit is silently groaning. I suspect that such notions of divine providence and universal sovereignty are regularly read into Rom. 8, sometimes overtly, sometimes not, but we would do well to recognize that Paul explicitly says nothing of the sort. To assert that we do not know what to pray for is not synonymous with saying that all personal petition is nullified or overridden by the Spirit's voice or that none of our petitions are ever germane to God's purposes. There may still be room for efficacious personal requests. Neither does Paul's claim that the Spirit continually intercedes in accordance with the plan of God necessarily require that every moment of personal decision be subject to the Spirit's predetermined intercession. The Spirit may well intercede continually for junctures that have been decided providentially—moments that we neither perceive correctly nor pray for properly—but then just as freely allow our intercessions about other moments to have a significant bearing on what the Father actually performs. We must beware of loading the biblical text with more theological freight than it is prepared to bear. This, too, is a part of what it means to submit ourselves to God's word.

22. Wu, "Spirit's Intercession," 13.

Many discussions of prayer fall prey to a serious error in assuming that every statement about prayer in any given situation is necessarily a universal statement about prayer in every situation. This is a logical error. True, I do not understand the Father's plan for my life, and I fail to understand how always to pray according to his will, but this does not preclude the possibility that in many situations my feeble attempts at ill-informed prayer may have a direct bearing on how our Father unfolds the latest wrinkle in life's path. Our ignorance of the big picture does not necessarily exclude the possibility that we may help to shape the details. True, the Spirit is continually and efficaciously interceding to implement God's plan, but that does not mean we never have any freedom of choice whatsoever.[23] Perhaps the Spirit sometimes prays that we will faithfully glorify the Father whichever option we prefer. Perhaps his intercession pleads for strength and wisdom that we faithfully bear up under the pressures inevitably accompanying every impending scenario. Is it safe to assume that the Spirit prays for our obedience? If so, we may have occasion to wonder why it is so remarkably easy for us to stumble and fall, as if intercessions for our failure were the Spirit's preferred daily entrée. Obviously, Paul would never countenance such a suggestion, yet are not the Spirit's requests always assured an affirmative response?

Once again, we must acknowledge that a text can answer only what it was written to address, and very few texts ever address all the questions we would like to raise. Romans 8 is not intended to provide a Christian theodicy or an explanation of human free will. It serves to partially explain the Spirit's work in assuring the believer's perseverance to the end. Paul's explanation leaves several mysteries but also offers significant assurances, particularly the promises of prayer. When our petitions agree with the Father's plans, they are also in agreement with the Spirit's intercessions; our prayers become the Spirit's just as the Spirit's become ours. When our requests are antagonistic to the Father's intentions, the Spirit sees that they dissipate, vanishing harmlessly in their heavenly ascent to be replaced by obedient longings guaranteed God's fatherly affirmation. When we have no words to offer at all because our feeble hope has been eclipsed and ground to dust by the incessant groaning of this worldly travail, even then the Holy Spirit continues to plead for us "according to God," securing holy guarantees that will one day usher us into "the glorious freedom of

---

23. The debates concerning determinism and libertarian versus compatibilist notions of free will are philosophically interesting but exegetically tendentious. However the philosopher's scalpel theoretically dissects human volition, the Scriptures are clear in presenting the divine-human relationship as one in which personal decision makes a real difference with respect to divine action.

the children of God." And finally, it is always possible that, at times, our petitions arise from concerns that God has left for us to decide, in which case we unwittingly, but nonetheless genuinely and deliberately, help to shape the particular route by which the Father is fulfilling his foreordained purposes for our lives.

11

Petitionary Prayer in the Life of Paul

Pauline Prayer, part 2

It should come as no surprise to learn that the New Testament's most prolific letter writer deposited a sizable collection of prayers within his personal correspondence. Paul's letters are a treasure trove of highly diverse prayer materials, including prayer requests, liturgical expressions, doxologies, benedictions, blessings, curses, introductory thanksgivings, reports of specific petitions, exhortations to pray, and, of course, explicit teaching about the nature of prayer. The preceding chapter explored the most extensive theological discussion of prayer in Paul's letters, found in Rom. 8. Having established Paul's theological foundation for the peculiar status of Christian prayer as a work of the Holy Spirit amid the present eschatological tension (and all that it entails), we are ready to examine the evidence of prayer in Paul's own life. In order to keep the task manageable and focused on our present purposes, the study will be restricted to those texts with an explicit bearing on Paul's view of petitionary prayer. I divide the wealth of material into four major categories: general exhortations to pray, Paul's petitionary prayers for himself, Paul's requests for intercessory prayer from others, and Paul's intercessory prayers for others.[1] The first

1. Detailed analysis of Paul's prayers may be found in Schubert, *Form and Function*; Wiles, *Paul's Intercessory Prayers*; and O'Brien, *Introductory Thanksgivings*. See especially Wiles's extensive categorizations of Pauline prayer (297–302). More accessible treatments

three categories are examined in this chapter, and the fourth category is the focus of chapter 12. In these two chapters we will discover that even the smallest junctures of Paul's life and ministry were thoroughly cross-sectioned by prayer, prayer, and more prayer, although it may not be the specific type of prayer many would expect.

Paul's Exhortations to Pray

General exhortations to faithfulness in prayer are found in seven Pauline passages:[2]

Be joyful in hope, patient in affliction, faithful in prayer. . . . Bless those who persecute you; bless and do not curse. (Rom. 12:12, 14)

Pray in the Spirit on all occasions with all kinds of prayers and requests. With this in mind, be alert and always keep on praying for all the saints. (Eph. 6:18)

Do not be anxious about anything, but in everything, by prayer and petition, with thanksgiving, present your requests to God. And the peace of God, which transcends all understanding, will guard your hearts and your minds in Christ Jesus. (Phil. 4:6–7)

Devote yourselves to prayer, being watchful and thankful. (Col. 4:2)

---

of Paul's prayers may be found in Stanley, *Boasting in the Lord*; Carson, *Call to Spiritual Reformation*; and Longenecker, "Prayer in the Pauline Letters."

2. All thirteen letters traditionally associated with Paul will be examined without concern for the common distinction between Pauline (Romans, 1–2 Corinthians, Galatians, Philippians, Colossians[?], 1 Thessalonians, 2 Thessalonians[?], Philemon) and deutero-Pauline (Ephesians, Colossians[?], 2 Thessalonians[?], 1–2 Timothy, Titus) authorship. First, this is a study of New Testament theology, and I am not convinced that such distinctions make any difference to the final outline of a canonical theology. Second, while some write as if the existence of a post-Pauline school composing pseudonymous epistles in the name of Paul was an assured result of New Testament criticism, it remains a contentious topic; for example, see Reicke, *Re-examining Paul's Letters*. Reicke was hardly a fundamentalist, yet he argues that all thirteen of the letters are genuinely Pauline. Regardless, whether every letter is Pauline in the traditional sense, I will refer to their author as Paul for the sake of convenience. For a small sampling of others who similarly argue in favor of Pauline authorship for some or all of the deutero-Paulines, see Kelly, *Pastoral Epistles* (1–2 Timothy, Titus); Van Roon, *Authenticity of Ephesians* (Ephesians); Schweizer, *Colossians* (Colossians); O'Brien, *Introductory Thanksgivings* (Ephesians); Bruce, *1–2 Thessalonians* (2 Thessalonians); O'Brien, *Colossians, Philemon* (Colossians); I. Marshall, *1 and 2 Thessalonians* (2 Thessalonians); Knight, *Pastoral Epistles* (1–2 Timothy, Titus); Murphy-O'Connor, *Paul* (2 Thessalonians, Colossians, 2 Timothy); and W. Mounce, *Pastoral Epistles* (1–2 Timothy, Titus).

Be joyful always; pray continually; give thanks in all circumstances, for this is God's will for you in Christ Jesus. (1 Thess. 5:16–18)

I urge, then, first of all, that requests, prayers, intercession and thanksgiving be made for everyone—for kings and all those in authority, that we may live peaceful and quiet lives. (1 Tim. 2:1–2)

The widow who is really in need and left all alone puts her hope in God and continues night and day to pray and to ask God for help. (1 Tim. 5:5)[3]

Three of these passages are general enough that it is uncertain whether they are concerned specifically with petition or with prayer more broadly conceived (Rom. 12:12; Col. 4:2; 1 Thess. 5:16–18). The repeated exhortations to faithfulness, watchfulness, and constancy are such common themes in all the texts, however, that it seems most likely that Paul's advice concerning petitionary prayer (in the four remaining texts) is simply a particular expression of his general attitude toward all types of prayer (as seen in Rom. 12:12; Col. 4:2; 1 Thess. 5:16–18). When taken as a whole, all of these passages demonstrate a remarkable continuity of concern revealing at least six traits characteristic of the Pauline perspective on petitionary prayer. These overarching theological commitments consistently reappear in the particulars of the specific pastoral prayers examined in the rest of this chapter and the next.

First, all prayer, but especially petition and intercession, is invariably linked with thanksgiving and/or joy (Rom. 12:12; Phil. 4:6; Col. 4:2; 1 Thess. 5:16–18; 1 Tim. 2:1). Study of the introductory thanksgiving prayers (see chapter 12) that open most of Paul's letters will clarify the connection between thanksgiving and petition in Paul's own pastoral relationships. However, these seven texts are sufficient to show that gratitude is an essential ingredient of appropriate petition. In fact, from Paul's perspective, thanksgiving becomes the quintessential activity of the entire Christian life par excellence; he elevates the word group to a status previously unknown in Greek literature, "using these terms more frequently per page than any other Hellenistic author, pagan or Christian."[4] Any Christian who approaches the throne of God with any degree of self-awareness is supremely sensitized to the incarnate gift of grace that swept away all former alienation and now makes current intimacy with the Father possible. Bringing our requests to the King of heaven

3. Although this sentence is declarative rather than hortatory, I include it here because it serves an exemplary, and therefore a hortatory, function in its context. Paul is describing the ideal widow, and thereby exhorting all widows to behave this way.

4. Schubert, *Form and Function*, 42. For a more extensive discussion, see O'Brien, "Thanksgiving within the Structure of Pauline Theology."

and knowing that we are guaranteed a hearing—more than this, that we are shown empathetic, passionate concern—is an unspeakable gift that inevitably prompts awe and gratitude from anyone who asks. It is characteristic of Paul that his bleak assessment of godless humanity, as outlined in his letter to the Romans, reaches its nadir in these words: "They neither glorified him as God nor gave thanks to him" (1:21).[5] The essence of godlessness is thanklessness. The coexistence of thanksgiving and petition continually testifies to our existence in eschatological tension: on the one hand, we genuinely rejoice in our present redemption; on the other hand, we are frequently reminded of all that we lack and are driven to petitionary prayer again and again.[6]

Second, prayer is a chief indicator of Christian perseverance, so persistent prayer characterizes the faithful. Paul seems incapable of encouraging his readers to pray without emphasizing the need for "constancy," suggesting that he is intimately familiar with the ever-present dangers of diminished enthusiasm and the eventual abandonment of prayer altogether, whether from weariness, apathy, cynicism, or creeping unbelief. Paul's vocabulary is varied but consistent: he urges his readers "to hold fast, continue, persevere" in prayer (*proskarterein*; Rom. 12:12; Eph. 6:18; Col. 4:2); to pray "constantly, unceasingly" (*adialeiptōs*; 1 Thess. 5:17); "to remain true, stay with, continue in" prayer (*prosmenein*; 1 Tim. 5:5); and he never asks others to do anything he does not first practice himself—that is, "pray constantly" (Rom. 1:9; 1 Cor. 1:4; Eph. 1:16; Phil. 1:4; Col. 1:3; 1 Thess. 1:2; 3:10; 2 Thess. 1:11; 2 Tim. 1:3; Philem. 4).[7]

Paul's point is not that we must repetitiously reiterate rote requests, although there is nothing wrong with repetition per se, but rather that we steadfastly maintain a belief in the Father's commitment to hear his children's requests no matter how militantly our circumstances suggest otherwise. The atmosphere of persecution surrounding his exhortations in the Prison Letters (Ephesians, Philippians, Colossians, Philemon) makes this dimension of Paul's insistence particularly clear. In Paul's view, to give up on petition, regardless of the circumstances, is to give up on God. Granted, none of these passages explicitly articulates the nature of the relationship between constant prayer and its "results." There are

5. See especially Pao's discussion of ingratitude in *Thanksgiving*, 145–64.

6. For related observations, see Wiles, *Paul's Intercessory Prayers*, 168–70.

7. While it is true that such pledges of continual prayer were characteristic of the epistolary form used in private correspondence (Schubert, *Form and Function*, 52, 172; Wiles, *Paul's Intercessory Prayers*, 158–59), there is no need to doubt Paul's sincerity, especially when he repeats the exhortations in nonformulaic didactic material. As Wiles notes, "We must weigh the conventional nature of such an assurance, and the ambiguity of the language, against the wider evidence for his constant practice of intercessory prayer" (189).

no promises that faithful prayer is more likely to receive a positive reply than is sporadic prayer. Nor does Paul explain exactly how a person's faith is bolstered by ceaseless prayer. (In fact, some claim that it was an attempt at such ceaseless prayer that finally led them to hopelessness. Paul is not, however, now addressing our questions about why some persevere while others give up.) Perhaps the idea is simply that frequent petition allows increased opportunity for God to display his faithfulness. In any case, Paul's urgent insistence on praying without ceasing paints a vivid spiritual backdrop against which we are compelled to infer that constant prayer is essential to Christian longevity—a connection made all the more emphatic by prayer's frequent association with hope and watchfulness (Rom. 12:12; Eph. 6:18; Phil. 4:6; Col. 4:2; 1 Tim. 5:5). At this point, Paul's exhortations are reminiscent of Luke's parable of the persistent widow (Luke 18:1–8), for once again enduring prayer fortifies the faithful as they await the imminent, though long-delayed, return of Christ (see chapter 4). New Testament eschatology remains the fabric through which constant prayer is interwoven with hopeful expectation. We can persist, not because we anticipate every intervening word along life's way, but because we already know the Father's final answer.

The third observation follows from the second. Paul's emphasis on watchfulness (*grēgorein*; Col. 4:2) and remaining alert (*agrypnein*; Eph. 6:18) pertains both to consistent prayer and to persistence in godliness. All those who faithfully await the end persist in prayer and, by means of that prayer, also persist in personal holiness. This connection between prayer and sanctity is particularly explicit in Eph. 6:10–18 where the injunction to petitionary prayer concludes a poignant description of how to "put on the full armor of God so that you can take your stand against the devil's schemes" (6:11).[8] Prayer is one of the means by which God effects our sanctification, sensitizing us to temptation, strengthening our resolve to obey, and broadening our avenues of escape. The Spirit not only intercedes on our behalf (Rom. 8:26–27), he makes himself the answer to his own prayers, supplying us with the resources he knows we need to endure. Paul anticipates a genuine cause-and-effect relationship between our prayers and the final measure of our sanctity. He emphatically believes that the ultimate blamelessness for which every saint hopes is facilitated by petition and intercession to stand firm (Phil. 1:10; 1 Thess. 3:13; 5:23).

---

8. Commentators debate whether prayer is intended to be the final piece of spiritual armor. Does the military metaphor conclude with 6:17 or 6:18? In either case, the participles and connecting *dia* ("through") in 6:18 make it clear that "prayer for strengthening from God can be seen as a major way in which believers appropriate the divine armor and are enabled to stand" (Lincoln, *Ephesians*, 452). For a thorough discussion of the question, see M. Barth, *Ephesians*, 777–86.

Fourth, the Spirit's influence is to become all pervasive in the Christian life; we are to "pray at all times in the Spirit" (Eph. 6:18, my translation). The occasional suggestion that Paul refers here to glossalalia is even less convincing than it is for Rom. 8:26–27 (see chapter 10).[9] Jude 20–21 offers similar advice: "Build yourselves up in your most holy faith and pray in the Holy Spirit. Keep yourselves in God's love as you wait for the mercy of our Lord Jesus Christ." In both contexts, prayer in the Spirit is part and parcel of the spiritual development that facilitates faithful endurance until the Lord returns. Although neither reference provides an explicit definition of how we are to pray in the Spirit, certainly A. T. Lincoln is not far off the mark when he suggests, "The writer is calling for prayer inspired, guided, and made effective through the Spirit."[10] Elsewhere Paul describes the Spirit-directed life as the *summa bonum* of Christian existence (Rom. 8:1–17; Gal. 5:16–26); the Holy Spirit is the one who works the internal transformation by which we become God's new creation (1 Cor. 2:6–15); the Spirit enables us to pray in the first place, inducting us into the family of God, making it possible for us to call God Father (Rom. 8:14–17). The idea of seeking guidance from the Spirit in prayer is not far removed from the broader Pauline concept of following the Spirit's direction throughout all of life. Thus, the admonition to pray in the Spirit is a corollary of Paul's overarching instructions to walk in the Spirit, to "keep in step with the Spirit" (Gal. 5:25). Just as the Spirit-directed life is a multistep process that begins with a fundamental adherence to clear moral directives (repent and believe, put off the old nature, put on the new, etc.) and then expands toward a sensitive application of godly character (pursuing love, joy, peace, patience, etc.), so too must Spirit-led prayer arise from the discipline of divinely ordained petition (pray for those who persecute you, give thanks in all circumstances, etc.) that then evolves throughout years of persistent submission into Spirit-nuanced prayers for the specific grace required in each new circumstance. Apparently, even though we do not know what to pray for in all of life's situations (Rom. 8:26), spiritual maturation entails a deepening sensitivity to the Spirit's guidance, cultivating wisdom enough to learn how we ought to pray in some, if not all, situations. We should thank the Spirit not only for praying on our behalf but also for teaching us how to pray more meaningfully ourselves.

Fifth, the priority of prayer is specifically associated with the memory of Jesus's life and teaching; Christ's model continues to inform Christian practice. Paul's maxim, "bless those who persecute you; bless and do not

9. Glossalalia is linked with corporate worship (1 Cor. 14:1–28), whereas Eph. 6:18 offers instruction on petitionary prayer "at all times." The gift of tongues is defined as praying with "my [human] spirit" (1 Cor. 14:14), not the divine Spirit as in Ephesians.

10. Lincoln, *Ephesians*, 452.

curse" (Rom. 12:14), is another form of the Jesus tradition found in Matt. 5:44 ‖ Luke 6:28, where he instructs the disciples to "pray for/bless those who persecute/curse you" (a conflation of the variant vocabularies).[11] Whereas the Synoptic (Q?) tradition diverges between related injunctions to bless and to pray, Paul embeds the exhortation to bless within his parenesis on prayer, firmly uniting the thematic import of each variant. Christian prayer is directed by the love of one's enemy while remaining "patient in affliction" (Rom. 12:12) as modeled by the Savior.

Finally, Paul was convinced that petitionary prayer can change the world around us. While his principal word for prayer (*proseuchē, proseuchesthai*) is not always specific as to the type of devotion intended (whether praise, thanksgiving, confession, etc.), the various synonyms used, "request" (*deēsis*; Eph. 6:18; Phil. 4:6; 1 Tim. 2:1; 5:5), "petition" (*aitēma*; Phil. 4:6), and "intercession" (*enteuxis*; 1 Tim. 2:1), specifically denote prayers that ask things of God.[12] While the goal of interpretation is always to allow the text to speak for itself, it is impossible (and not always commendable) to isolate interpretation from any and all theological conviction. And so we again face an important theological question: in what sense did Paul believe that petitionary prayer can influence God?

Of course, some readers will want to argue that all seven passages fit a different theological model in which petition influences only the one who prays. Philippians 4:6–7 is most amenable to this sort of self-referential interpretation, for persistent prayer is linked to "the peace of God, which transcends all understanding,"[13] implying that petition changes one's own frame of mind. Romans 12 is rather ambiguous in this regard, although the context does focus on the needs of others—community members (12:10, 13, 15–16) and enemies (12:14, 17)—rather than on the one who prays. Still, one might argue that the benefit of petition remains largely self-referential; praying for others, first and foremost, turns us into more loving neighbors. The remaining passages are less pliable, but perhaps this type of rendering is not beyond the realm of possibility. Thus in Col. 4:2 devotion to prayer encourages watchfulness

11. I am not assuming that Paul reflects firsthand knowledge of the Gospel tradition, but he is clearly familiar with some form of the oral Jesus tradition; see Neirynck, "Paul and the Sayings of Jesus"; Dunn, *Romans*, 745; Holtz, "Paul and the Oral Gospel Tradition," 391–93; Wenham, "Paul's Use of the Jesus Tradition," 15–17; and idem, *Paul*, 250–51. O'Brien suggests that Jesus's teaching in Matt. 6:25–34 similarly echoes in the admonition of Phil. 4:6: "Do not be anxious about anything"; see "Divine Provision for Our Needs," 23.

12. For a complete accounting of the Pauline prayer vocabulary, see Longenecker, "Prayer in the Pauline Letters," 204–6.

13. Wiles, *Paul's Intercessory Prayers*, 288: "Prayer is urged as the antidote for anxiety."

and thankfulness; in 1 Thess. 5:16 continual prayer facilitates joyfulness; in 1 Tim. 2:1–2 readers are advised to pray in order to lead "peaceful and quiet personal lives"; and in 1 Tim. 5:5 the prayerful widow is the one most amenable to accepting the church's assistance.

Ephesians 6:18 is not, however, so cooperative. Undoubtedly, personal prayer is essential to anyone's ability to "put on the full armor of God" (6:11), but Paul's insistence that we simultaneously "make requests [*deēseōs*] for all the saints" indicates that one person's prayer for another has a bearing on that other person's ability to stand firm. This is a crucial observation: *intercessory prayer genuinely assists in the spiritual success of fellow believers*. Once we admit this unavoidable dimension of Eph. 6, it is a small step to recognize the very same dynamic in the other Pauline exhortations. For instance, only exegetical slight of hand can avoid the conclusion that 1 Tim. 2:1–2 encourages prayer for secular authorities because Christian petitions result in better governance, not just better citizenship.[14] Similarly, the poor widow in 1 Tim. 5:5 prays about her imminent physical needs not because she believes that prayer will improve her attitude but because she knows it may improve her situation. The God in whom she "puts her hope" will vindicate that hope by providing the help required.

When petitionary prayer is explained in this way, it is sometimes called "impetratory prayer." Impetratory prayer is petitionary prayer that actually influences God and makes a difference in the way things happen, moving God to do something he otherwise may not have done. Certain long-standing philosophical-theological theories want to deny that prayer could ever be genuinely impetratory, insisting instead that God predestined our petitions in connection with his predetermined actions. In other words, there is a foreordained association between our divinely ordained requests and the Father's predetermined responses such that he is not "reacting" to prayer, at least not in the sense that he is doing something he would not have done otherwise. God is simply doing what he predetermined he would do in response to the prayers he predetermined we would pray. According to this type of theology, petitionary prayer is "asking God to make happen what *will* happen" not "asking that he *will* make something happen."[15] Whether this particular solution proves intellectually or spiritually satisfying will depend largely on the reader's religious predispositions, and we will return to this discussion at greater length in chapter 14. It is worth considering, however, whether such theories can cohere with the exegetical evidence now being accumulated. I suggest

14. Wainwright, "Praying for Kings"; and Reumann, "How Do We Interpret 1 Timothy 2:1–5?"

15. Tiessen, *Providence and Prayer*, 174.

not. In fact, it appears to be a classic example of eisegesis (reading what you want to find into the text rather than allowing the text to speak for itself), the bane of all honest encounter with Scripture.

Paul Prays for Himself

Paul as Model

Paul's extensive pastoral correspondence offered numerous opportunities for the apostle to hold up his own prayers as models to be emulated or as words of encouragement to be remembered. Yet, when we consider his readiness to write yet another letter, it is curious that he rarely says anything resembling, "This is how I pray myself." Although some bemoan Paul's apparent reticence to divulge anything beyond the barest details of his own interior life, what he does reveal is both instructive and more substantive than is often recognized.[16] The New Testament records five instances where Paul pulls back the curtain of his personal prayer closet; at least one of these texts illuminates a profoundly existential component in the evolution of Paul's thinking, demonstrating the commingling of theological heart and mind throughout the apostle's life:

I pray that now at last by God's will the way may be opened for me to come to you. (Rom. 1:10)

I could wish that I myself were cursed and cut off from Christ for the sake of my brothers, those of my own race, the people of Israel. (Rom. 9:3)

Brothers, my heart's desire and prayer to God for the Israelites is that they may be saved. (Rom. 10:1)[17]

Three times I pleaded with the Lord to take it away from me. But he said to me, "My grace is sufficient for you, for my power is made perfect in weakness." (2 Cor. 12:8–9)

Night and day we pray most earnestly that we may see you again and supply what is lacking in your faith. Now may our God and Father himself and our Lord Jesus clear the way for us to come to you. (1 Thess. 3:10–11)

16. See Stanley, *Boasting in the Lord*, 4, 44. Stanley overlooks the gold mine of information later explored by O'Brien's study (*Introductory Thanksgivings*) of Paul's introductory thanksgivings and the abundance of personal information about Paul's prayer life embedded in those passages.
17. Even though Rom. 10:1 is an intercessory prayer, I include it here because of its connection to the startling petition in 9:3.

The first impression left by these passages is the passionate intensity of Paul's concern for the spiritual welfare of his congregations, of anyone and everyone he encounters through his apostolic mission. Each prayer reflects a different facet of one central concern: the successful completion of his work as an apostle of Jesus Christ. Twice Paul describes how he prays over his travel plans, describing an urgent desire to (re)visit Christian communities in order to bolster their spiritual growth (Rom. 1:10; 1 Thess. 3:10–11). In the heart of his letter to the Romans, Paul strikes a note of near-spiritual profligacy when he admits a willingness to surrender his own salvation in the cause of Israel's inclusion within the church (Rom. 9:3; 10:1). These words are more than rhetorical flourish; Paul vents a genuine desire expressed in real petitions to God.[18] Though he never suggests that his suffering adds anything to the work of Christ, Paul is captivated by an authentic willingness to sacrifice himself on behalf of Israel, just as Moses once proffered his own life in exchange for an idolatrous nation (Exod. 32:32). Even when Paul prays for himself, he is praying for others. Granted, the sample size is small, and the accidents of history make it difficult to draw hard and fast conclusions as to the representative value of these fragmentary images of Pauline petition. Certainly, the formulary constraints of a personal letter help to explain Paul's laser-like focus on the needs of his readers, even when touching on the content of his own petitionary prayers; yet this hardly diminishes the significance of the observation: even when Paul prays for himself he is praying for others, asking the Father to use his life as an instrument for maximizing the spiritual prosperity of those around him.

The one passage we have yet to consider illustrates these same observations and the one major point remaining—learning to pray while surrendering to God's will. Both Rom. 1:10 and 1 Thess. 3:10–11 demonstrate Paul's sensitivity to this issue; while he does not hesitate to bring specific requests to God, he also knows that God answers in his own timing, according to his own designs. Paul was not previously free to visit Rome or to revisit Thessalonica, because it was not yet God's will for "the way to be open." Nevertheless, he continued to ask, believing that his requests may yet prevail. Paul petitions God with passion, understanding that passion alone, even passion emphatically reiterated, is not sufficient in and of itself to move God's hand. Certainly, the most dramatic example of this interplay between personal desire and divine guidance appears in 2 Cor. 12:7–10.

18. Wiles, *Paul's Intercessory Prayers*, 255–56; and Dunn, *Romans*, 524–25.

Praying to Remove a Thorn

Early in his career Paul became convinced that some new impediment, something he describes only as "a thorn in my flesh," was significantly hindering his effectiveness as an apostle (2 Cor. 12:7). Sometime during his so-called silent years, the decade in which he seems to have lived in the province of Syria-Cilicia (Gal. 1:21; 2:1; Acts 9:30; 11:25), Paul received an ecstatic vision of Christ; he calls it a vision of "paradise" in which he was "caught up to the third heaven" (2 Cor. 12:1–4).[19] As a spiritual prophylactic against the hubris that would inevitably tempt even Paul, he was afflicted with a mysterious malady characterized by four distinct traits:

1. It was seriously debilitating; Paul described it as a "thorn" or "stake" that "beat/abused" him, probably physically.[20]
2. It was intended to keep Paul humble, to serve as a constant reminder of his dependency on the Savior; he highlights this by twice repeating its value for "preventing his conceit."[21]
3. It was inherently evil, "a messenger of Satan," because (at least, in Paul's mind) it hindered his ability to preach the gospel, and anything that worked to stymie the message of Christ was demonic by definition.
4. It was given to him by God. Paul's use of a passive verb (*edothē*) strongly suggests divine agency.[22] God gave Paul both the ecstatic revelation and his debilitating thorn. What's more, he deliberately chose to use something that, in and of itself, was simply evil in order to accomplish his work.

19. The vision is usually thought to have occurred sometime between AD 40 and AD 44; for further analysis, see Bowker, "'Merkabah' Visions"; Spittler, "Limits of Ecstasy"; Lincoln, "Paul the Visionary"; idem, *Paradise Now and Not Yet*, 71–86; Price, "Punished in Paradise"; and Rowland, *Open Heaven*, 380–86.

20. For a survey of the numerous suggestions made throughout the history of interpretation, see D. Black, *Paul, Apostle of Weakness*, 152–54; R. Martin, *2 Corinthians*, 411–17; Mullins, "Paul's Thorn in the Flesh"; N. Smith, "Thorn That Stayed"; Nisbet, "Thorn in the Flesh," 126; and Park, "Paul's Σκόλοψ τῇ Σαρκί." It is impossible to know the specific nature of Paul's thorn. Fortunately, it is not essential to a sufficient understanding of Paul's meaning.

21. Unfortunately, the NIV translation of 12:7 renders the phrase only once.

22. Some suggest satanic agency, but this is doubtful. Paul uses this particular verb regularly to denote gifts of God's favor; there are several other verbs Paul would have been more likely to employ had he intended to describe a demonic affliction; see R. Martin, *2 Corinthians*, 412.

Paul's straightforward description of his repeated prayers for release suggest that initially he fully anticipated a positive response.[23] Surely, anything so self-evidently crippling to God's mission must be an evil that the Father will eagerly eradicate! Furthermore, Paul's admission that he repeatedly "pleaded"[24] with the Lord for the satanic thorn's removal also intimates his initial presumption of a positive reply. How long did it take Paul to reconcile himself to God's shockingly resounding no? Who can say? Yet, reconcile himself he did. Paul's language clearly indicates that he describes a past struggle, not a continuing request. He stopped offering this petition long ago, for he eventually made peace with the Lord's unexpected reply.

At this point, three further conclusions about Pauline petition need to be highlighted from the autobiographical scene in 2 Cor. 12. First, while God hears prayer, he is never bound by prayer; he always remains free to answer yes or no to any request, depending on his designs. Neither repetition (Paul asked three times) nor earnestness (Paul pleaded) conjures up the power to contravene the Father's intentions. Paul's persistence in other requests—visiting Rome and Thessalonica—illustrates a living conviction that God's hand can be moved by petitionary prayer, but living with Satan's messenger also taught him that all circumstances are not equal. No particular moment is paradigmatic for any other. Prayer's outcome in one situation is never the inevitable exemplar for appropriate petition in any other. Each circumstance must be lived in its own moment on its own terms, terms that are excavated within the give and take of a divine-human interaction experienced while praying. We ask, sometimes again and again, and God responds, eventually, when the time is right. What the outcome of each conversation will be is discovered only in the process of conversing. Paul does not explain the Lord's mode of communication. What does he mean by the phrase "he said to me" (12:9)? Did Paul receive another vision? Did he hear a voice? Or was it a transforming inner conviction? Whatever the answer, the point is that Paul somehow found himself in the grip of a new—and, at least initially, unwanted—apprehension that his impairment was actually God's work in his life.

Second, prayer became an avenue for Paul's confrontation with the inscrutable wisdom of God. Perhaps this series of events provided the personal prick that eventually gave birth to his mature admission that "we do not know what we ought to pray for" (Rom. 8:26). Not even the devout, self-sacrificial inclinations of the great apostle could safely cor-

23. Stanley, *Boasting in the Lord*, 55. Stanley offers a thorough examination of the light shed by 2 Cor. 12:1–10 on Paul's prayer life (44–60).
24. This is the only instance where Paul uses "beseech" (*parakaleō*) for prayer.

relate the calculations of human sensibility to the divine wisdom veiled within the contortions of salvation-history. Like any other Christian, Paul required correction by the interceding Spirit, learning that even good requests are not necessarily the best requests and that the Father intends the best for his children even when it requires the use of an apparent evil. Once again, we must beware of careless generalizations. Paul is not providing a theodicy; he is not commenting on the source of any and all evil in life. Apparently, not only is it possible for God to make use of evil, to transform a sinful situation of our own making in order to bring something good out of something bad, but it is also possible for the Father to allow—even to send—evil, to manufacture an apparent evil all his own in order to bring about the very best for his children. The paradox is palpable. Yet, this is not a proof-text for an all-pervasive theological determinism. Paul may be portrayed as a New Testament example of Job-like suffering, but neither Job nor Paul compels us to conclude that God is the efficient cause behind every one of life's situations, the evil as well as the good. To admit that God sent Paul a thorny satanic affliction does not demand similar conclusions about the Holocaust, hurricane Katrina, or my cousin's terminal cancer. Every situation is as unique as the individual tears shed by those who suffer through it. What God may do and what he has actually done are two very different things. Untangling the meandering threads of possibility and actuality is a lengthy process accessible only to those who pray persistently, earnestly, patiently, and submissively. And in the end, final answers may still elude us.

Third, through the struggle of petitionary prayer, Paul learned a new lesson about the sufficiency of God's grace. The best answer to every prayer is an expanded awareness of how the Father's unconditional love, experienced here and now as well as anticipated in his eternal promises, is all we require to sustain us through life. For many, this claim will sound utterly absurd, but Paul insists that embracing such apparent absurdity is the measure of authentic Christian faith. Only after Paul had surrendered to the Father's response—that having once received the grace of Jesus Christ he did not require deliverance from his satanic thorn—only then did he go on to experience the paradox of divine power magnified in human weakness.[25] Such surrender was not the means to a greater end. Surrender was the end itself, just as it had been for Jesus in the Garden of Gethsemane. Three times the plea, three times the denial, until it became a thrice-born acquiescence to the divine mystery, containing no certain vision of anything beyond the pain but

25. Some describe 2 Cor. 12:9 as the climax of the entire letter; see D. Black, *Paul, Apostle of Weakness*, 151.

only a finely tempered confidence that "as the heavens are higher than the earth, / so are [God's] ways higher than [our] ways / and [God's] thoughts higher than [our] thoughts" (Isa. 55:9).

Paul tells us that the goal of life is the glory of God, the exhibition of his grace and his greatness. The highest goal of petitionary prayer is the maximizing of divinely glorious circumstances. Paul discovered that the best answer to his request was the very condition he sought to escape, because that was where God's own power could best be displayed. If this initially sounds suspiciously like heavenly egomania, join the club of human confusion. If we want to move beyond confusion to experience personal peace, join Paul's club of prayerful surrender. Perhaps Paul's experience of wrestling at prayer paved an existential pathway for the evolution of his theology of the cross, for it certainly coheres with his conviction that God's ultimate display of wisdom and power appeared at Calvary in the battered, abandoned carpenter who despaired, "My God, my God, why have you forsaken me?" (Mark 15:34; 1 Cor. 1:20–31). No disciple can ever suggest that sharing in the Savior's suffering is somehow inappropriate or unfair, especially when the Father has promised that conformity to the image of his Son is the pathway to our perfection. In God's economy, less is often more, and loss frequently becomes gain. Unhindered advancement does not necessarily produce the greatest results, not in Paul's life, not in our own.

Paul's Requests for Prayer

On eight occasions Paul explicitly asks the church to pray for him and his ministry:[26]

> I urge you, brothers, by our Lord Jesus Christ and by the love of the Spirit, to join me in my struggle by praying to God for me. Pray that I may be rescued from the unbelievers in Judea and that my service in Jerusalem may be acceptable to the saints there, so that by God's will I may come to you. (Rom. 15:30–32)

> On him we have set our hope that he will continue to deliver us, as you help us by your prayers. Then many will give thanks on our behalf for the gracious favor granted us in answer to the prayers of many. (2 Cor. 1:10–11)

26. We have already examined the two occasions where Paul urges his readers to pray for others, both embedded in broader exhortations to prayer (Eph. 6:18; 1 Tim. 2:1–2); in one additional instance, he simply states that the Macedonians are praying for the church in Corinth (2 Cor. 9:14).

Pray also for me, that whenever I open my mouth, words may be given me so that I will fearlessly make known the mystery of the gospel, for which I am an ambassador in chains. Pray that I may declare it fearlessly, as I should. (Eph. 6:19–20)

I know that through your prayers and the help given by the Spirit of Jesus Christ, what has happened to me will turn out for my deliverance. (Phil. 1:19)

And pray for us, too, that God may open a door for our message, so that we may proclaim the mystery of Christ, for which I am in chains. Pray that I may proclaim it clearly, as I should. (Col. 4:3–4)

Brothers, pray for us. (1 Thess. 5:25)

Finally, brothers, pray for us that the message of the Lord may spread rapidly and be honored, just as it was with you. And pray that we may be delivered from wicked and evil men. (2 Thess. 3:1–2)

Prepare a guest room for me, because I hope to be restored to you in answer to your prayers. (Philem. 22)

Overcoming serious obstacles appears to have been a common feature of the apostolic lifestyle. All eight passages refer to an experience of persecution or suffering and then enlist the church's prayers for Paul's deliverance. Apparently, that God denied his request to be relieved of a fleshly thorn never stopped Paul from asking for future heavenly rescue. Each new struggle was another opportunity to make his requests known to God (Phil. 4:6) and to wait for the Father's timely response; it was also another occasion to remind the community how dependent are all believers on mutual prayer. Three observations are worth further attention before closing this chapter and moving on to the next stage of our investigation.

First, intercessory prayer is not a quaint religious activity for those, such as the weak and enfeebled, who are unable to contribute "actively" to God's work. The emphatic nature of Paul's prayer requests hints at a far deeper, efficacious connection between those who pray and those for whom prayer is offered. As Paul and his various communities continually pray over their common labor in the work of the gospel, they forge a shared engagement in the apostolic mission. In fact, the effectiveness of every ministerial effort is somehow connected to the church's petition. Paul describes himself as an intercessor for the people of Israel (Rom. 9:3; 10:1) and then asks the new Israel, the church, to intercede for him. The intercessor needs his brothers and sisters to intercede, while remembering that the heavenly intercessor prays for all (8:34). The apostle does not accomplish his work alone, but as the representative of a prayerful confederation of mutually concerned men and women who pray. Such petition weaves a complex spiritual web of reciprocity that effects a tangible, substantive difference in the arenas for which God's people pray.[27] Accordingly, in Rom. 15:30 Paul invites his readers "to join . . . in my struggle" by praying for his impending travels. Both 2 Cor. 1:10–11 and Phil. 1:19 allude to the tangible assistance that Paul anticipates via his readers' prayers; in 2 Cor. 1:10–11 Paul describes his good fortune in escaping Asia as a "gracious favor granted . . . in answer to the prayers of many," while in Phil. 1:19 he explains his own experience of the Spirit's power as a direct result of the Philippians' intercessions.[28] In fact, Paul implies that he counts on the continued prayers from Philippi "as a necessary condition of his deliverance."[29] The church's petitions are an essential ingredient to Paul's future success.

Second, Paul's prayer requests invariably concern the progress of his apostolic ministry, never focusing on the personal wants of a man in need, although this contrast may assume too much, since by all accounts Paul made no distinction between his existence as an individual and his responsibilities as an apostle: in his mind "to live is Christ and to die is gain" (Phil. 1:21). Four of his letters were composed from a prison cell (Ephesians, Philippians, Colossians, Philemon). The two Thessalonian letters were written in the wake of riots that forced him out of town under cover of darkness (Acts 17:1–10). Second Corinthians recounts the recent life-threatening events narrowly escaped during his work in the province of Asia (Acts 19:28–40), while the letter to Rome was drafted by a man who knew full well that an impending trip to Jerusalem would put his life in grave danger (Rom. 15:31; Acts 21:27–36; 22:22–29; 23:12–15). Yet, not once does Paul express any interest in self-preservation for its own sake. If he asks the church to pray for his protection or rescue, it is only that he might remain free to preach the gospel. While imprisoned, he never requests better treatment, more comfortable circumstances, or clean linen—only the strength to remain faithful in proclaiming Christ "fearlessly, as [he] should" (Eph. 6:20; Col. 4:3–4).[30] As previously noted, though we are not free to assume that these eight passages exhaustively portray Paul's habits of personal petition, the

27. Elsewhere Paul writes about his own spiritual presence among the community, presumably as he prays for them (1 Cor. 5:3–5); see Wiles, *Paul's Intercessory Prayers*, 145.

28. Hawthorne, *Philippians*, 40–41.

29. Wiles, *Paul's Intercessory Prayers*, 277.

30. For a helpful analysis of Ephesians and its parallels in Colossians, see Smillie, "Ephesians 6:19–20."

evidence is quite striking and completely in keeping with everything else that we have learned about him thus far. As a man convinced that to live is Christ and to die is gain, Paul prays with the conviction that petition's proper subjects are not comfort or convenience, improved health or less stress, increased income or financial independence, or any of the other numerous concerns that so easily reflect a preoccupation with material existence; rather, prayer's proper preoccupation is the swelling of daily faithfulness until it finally penetrates every nook and cranny of life's unfolding, undulating irregularities, transforming each moment into an experience of Christlikeness.

Third, Paul continually lived within the flexible exchange of prayer and providence. Once again, the communities' intercessions illustrate both the importance of our petitions and the unpredictability of God's replies. We have already seen that, in Paul's view, prayer can and does move God; it makes a difference. Some things in life occur, at least in part, because God's people asked him to act accordingly (2 Cor. 1:11; Phil. 1:19; Philem. 22). Furthermore, some things should always be sought without hesitation, such as increased effectiveness in one's service to Christ, with a general expectation that a positive reply is at hand (Rom. 15:30–32; Eph. 6:19–20; Phil. 1:19; Col. 4:3–4; 2 Thess. 3:1–2). Paul's experience also suggests, however, that we may want to prepare ourselves for our own tailor-made bouquet of thorns. Not only did the Father say no to Paul's pleading for his thorn's removal, but the Father also replied negatively to the Romans' prayers that Paul be kept safe during his final visit to Jerusalem (Rom. 15:30–32). Paul solicited intercession for three serious concerns, knowing that his future depended on God's response: (1) he hoped to be rescued from the hostility of the Jewish community; (2) obviously fearful that his Gentile collection would be refused, he asks that it prove "acceptable to the saints"; and (3) he hoped that after passing safely through Jerusalem, he might extend his missionary enterprise to Rome and beyond, eventually traveling as far as Spain (Rom. 1:10–13; 15:21–24, 28).

Luke's account of Paul's arrival in Jerusalem describes a visit that could not have diverged further from the Romans' prayerful expectations. First, Paul is quickly attacked by a Jewish mob bent on seeing him dead (Acts 21:27–36; 22:22–23:24). Far from being rescued from the synagogue's hostility, he is beaten and imprisoned.[31] Second, Luke never mentions Paul's collection, an oversight that causes some commentators to suggest that this overture from the Gentile mission proved unacceptable to

31. Conceivably, the warning by Paul's nephew (Acts 23:12–24) and his overall preservation might be interpreted as a "rescue" in answer to prayer, but such a reading strikes me as special pleading when placed within the overall context of Jewish persecution.

the Jerusalem church.[32] And, finally, though he does eventually journey to Rome, Paul arrives as a prisoner awaiting trial, not as a missionary heading off to Spain (Acts 28:11–31). Once again, individual petitions and divine planning intersected and then reverberated in curious trajectories. God's response to this particular threefold petition from Rome seems to have been, "No. No. Yes—but not in the way you wish." Paul remains steadfastly amenable to whatever the Father offers, whether the answer is yes, no, or maybe, for he knows by faith that the God of grace hears, cares, and responds, sometimes according to our requests, at other times according to his own predetermined design, occasionally creating some unique hybrid between the two, but always in a fashion that serves our best interests and his own greater glory. Convictions such as these form the substance of Paul's faith in the value of petitionary prayer.

32. Admittedly, this is a tenuous argument from silence. We cannot avoid lingering suspicions about the church's duplicity when we observe that after Paul's arrest the Jerusalem church vanishes almost completely from Luke's narrative. Given the persistent antagonism of the so-called Judaizing party throughout Paul's life (Galatians; 2 Cor. 10–13; Phil. 3), Luke's silence (with the possible exception of Acts 24:17) is entirely in keeping with the evidence of Paul's letters; for similar observations, see Dunn, *Romans*, 879–80. Even Bruce, hardly a scholar prone to flights of fancy, observes that Luke's reticence to mention the collection "may have been because the enterprise ended in disaster"; *Acts*, 445.

12

Paul the Intercessor

Pauline Prayer, part 3

Talking about prayer and being about the business of praying are two very different things. Despite the apparent confusion in the occasional contemporary prayer meeting, the apostle Paul clearly understood the distinction. Unlike many of us who sometimes substitute talk among ourselves for conversation with God, Paul was in a unique position to combine these two modes of discourse into a single communicative moment. As an apostle who regularly corresponded with parishioners, he freely modeled pastoral advice after the manner of his intercessory prayers, killing both proverbial birds with one stone. Paul's letters frequently intersperse teaching, advice, and encouragement with reports, direct and indirect, about his petitions to God. In fact, Paul's aspirations for his churches are often expressed, not by way of deliberate exhortation, but as the heartfelt desires of personal prayers now publicized in his writing. The wealth of intercessory prayer requests embedded within these letters sheds considerable light on how Paul prayed for others, what he considered important priorities for intercession, and the proper relationship between such petition and a healthy Christian life. Chapter 11 examined (1) Paul's admonitions to pray, (2) Paul's prayers for himself, and (3) Paul's requests that the churches pray for him. Now we turn to (4) the apostle's intercessory prayers for his readers, a large body of material that can be further subdivided into three categories: (a) wish prayers, (b) prayer reports lodged in the body of a letter, and (c) prayers unveiled within a letter's introductory thanksgiving.

Wish Prayers

Paul's wish prayers merit particular attention because, apart from such exclamations as Abba and Maranatha, they are "the closest approximation to direct praying" found anywhere in Paul's letters.[1] These junctures emerge like literary icebergs revealing only the tip of a vast, invisible spiritual connection between apostolic instruction and private prayer, an interpenetration characteristic of Paul's self-understanding as the apostle to the Gentiles:

> May the God who gives endurance and encouragement give you a spirit of unity among yourselves as you follow Christ Jesus, so that with one heart and mouth you may glorify the God and Father of our Lord Jesus Christ. (Rom. 15:5–6)

> May the God of hope fill you with all joy and peace as you trust in him, so that you may overflow with hope by the power of the Holy Spirit. (Rom. 15:13)

> May the Lord make your love increase and overflow for each other and for everyone else, just as ours does for you. May he strengthen your hearts so that you will be blameless and holy in the presence of our God and Father when our Lord Jesus comes with all his holy ones. (1 Thess. 3:12–13)

> May God himself, the God of peace, sanctify you through and through. May your whole spirit, soul and body be kept blameless at the coming of our Lord Jesus Christ. (1 Thess. 5:23)

1. Wiles, *Paul's Intercessory Prayers*, 22. I limit this study to those prayers with the aorist optative verb. Several questionable examples of wish prayers in the future indicative (Rom. 16:20; 1 Cor. 1:8; Phil. 4:19), as well as one where the verb is omitted (Rom. 15:33), together with the standard epistolary salutations ("grace and peace to you"), benedictions ("the God of peace be with you all"), and occasional curses (Gal. 1:8–9; 1 Cor. 16:22) are all omitted from consideration. First, the curses seem to function as emotive declarations, not prayers. Second, the salutations and benedictions primarily serve epistolary form. Third, space limitations demand some principle of selection, and nothing substantive is lost by a narrower focus. For similar considerations, see Longenecker, "Prayer in the Pauline Letters," 205.

May our Lord Jesus Christ himself and God our Father, who loved us and by his grace gave us eternal encouragement and good hope, encourage your hearts and strengthen you in every good deed and word. (2 Thess. 2:16–17)

May the Lord direct your hearts into God's love and Christ's perseverance. (2 Thess. 3:5)

Now may the Lord of peace himself give you peace at all times and in every way. The Lord be with all of you. (2 Thess. 3:16)

May the Lord show mercy to the household of Onesiphorus, because he often refreshed me and was not ashamed of my chains. . . . May the Lord grant that he will find mercy from the Lord on that day. (2 Tim. 1:16, 18)

At my first defense, no one came to my support, but everyone deserted me. May it not be held against them. (2 Tim. 4:16)

It is impossible to read these wish prayers without sensing the intercessory foundation that undergirds every Pauline letter. The introductory thanksgivings will eventually offer a perfect occasion for exploring the intercessory nature of Paul's epistolary advice more thoroughly, but now is a good moment to begin observing how Paul consistently prays for the church in conjunction with his correspondence. Paul understands his apostolic pastoral responsibilities to comprise a "priestly duty," an act of "worship" (*latreuein* in Rom. 1:9; *leitourgos* and *hierourgein* in 15:16), in which he offers up his congregations as an "acceptable sacrifice" to the Father (15:15–17).[2] Intercessory prayer occupies the heart of this apostolic activity, where he brings the word of God to the people and the needs of the people before the Father. It is no accident that his letter to the Romans, Paul's most expansive treatise on the theological justification of his Gentile mission, both opens (1:9–10) and concludes (15:16) with a clear explanation of his prayers' mediatorial function. Paul's proclamation of the gospel, his urgent appeals for personal sanctification, and his heartfelt intercessions on behalf of all his communities intertwine in a single braided effort toward the final presentation of these disparate churches before the throne of God. It is not the least bit surprising that purported distinctions between exhortation and prayer regularly blur and disappear as Paul answers questions and dictates pastoral advice for those to whom he is spiritually responsible. Paul's instructions and

2. Cooper, "Leitourgos Christou Iesou," rightly argues that Rom. 15:16 illuminates intercessory prayer "as a presenting in sacrifice before God those for whom we pray" (271).

prayers are one. He tells them what he prays for, and he prays for what he tells them. Consequently, a number of scholars observe that Paul's wish prayers typically summarize central themes and mark crucial transitions in the progress of a letter's argumentation,[3] giving them an aura of passionate pastoral eruptions in the middle of fundamental theological spadework. One example, Paul's wish prayer in 1 Thess. 3:12–13, must suffice to illustrate the various ways in which the wish prayers can gather together and recapitulate a letter's principal themes.[4] Although O'Brien rightly warns that "too much ought not to be read" into isolated verbal correspondences,[5] since the repetition of characteristically Christian vocabulary is to be expected over the course of an entire letter, it is still worth noting the frequency and contextual significance of the themes created by such verbal repetitions:

theme in the wish prayer of 1 Thess. 3:12–13	elsewhere in 1 Thessalonians
Paul's wish to see the Thessalonians (3:11)	2:17–18; 3:1, 5
love (3:12)	1:3; 2:8; 3:6–8; 4:9–12; 5:8, 13–15
standing firm/holiness (3:13)	1:3; 3:2, 8; 4:1–8
Christ's coming (3:13)	1:10; 2:4, 16, 19; 3:9; 4:13–5:11

The same pastoral heart also accounts for the blatant extravagance of every Pauline request.[6] Paul asks for nothing in moderation when praying for his converts; in fact, superlatives become the lingua franca of intercession. He asks that they "be filled to overflowing," "abound in love," "be sanctified through and through," "remain thoroughly blameless," "be strengthened in every good work," and "filled with peace at all times in every way." God is the only source of answers to prayer, and the lavishly generous Father begrudges his children no good thing. Thus when Paul wishes that the Romans would "overflow with hope," he turns to "the God of hope" (Rom. 15:13); when the Thessalonians require encouragement, he prays to the "God [of] . . . encouragement" (2 Thess. 2:16–17); when he wishes them peace, he asks "the Lord of peace" to intervene (3:16). This confluence of Paul's passion for his churches together with

3. Wiles, *Paul's Intercessory Prayers*, 41–42 (on Rom. 15:5–6, 13; 1 Thess. 3:11–13; 5:23), 53–54 (on 1 Thess. 3:11–13), 63–64 (on 1 Thess. 5:23), 81 (on Rom. 15:5–6), 87 (on Rom. 15:13); also Stanley, *Boasting in the Lord*, 81–82.

4. For a detailed discussion, see Wiles, *Paul's Intercessory Prayers*, 52–63; and O'Brien, *Introductory Thanksgivings*, 160–61.

5. O'Brien, *Introductory Thanksgivings*, 69.

6. Wiles, *Paul's Intercessory Prayers*, 60n4, 85. Carson offers a helpful exploration of this pastoral dimension to Paul's prayers, particularly as expressed in 1 Thess. 3:9–13; see *Call to Spiritual Reformation*, 79–94.

his understanding of the Father's character generates a series of remarkably confident requests that the author of every conceivable blessing open heaven's floodgates and inundate his children with an excess of spiritual treasure. Paul anticipates nothing less than unhindered generosity from the Father who happily supplies any and all requirements for ideal spiritual health.

Though some scholars insist that this generous heavenly Father makes an exclusive claim on the church's petitions,[7] Paul's wish prayers are sometimes offered to both the Father and the Son (1 Thess. 3:11; 2 Thess. 2:16), occasionally even to the exalted Lord Jesus alone (2 Thess. 3:5; 3:16; 2 Tim. 1:16, 18).[8] Though we did not make a point of it while examining 2 Cor. 12, the observant reader may have already noticed that Paul's battle with his thorn in the flesh spurred anguished petitions directly to the resurrected Jesus. Paul finally surrendered to the Lord's "power . . . [being] perfect[ed] in weakness" as the manifestation of "Christ's power . . . rest[ing] on me" (12:8–9). Paul had not prayed *to* the Father *through* the Son but directly *to the Son* himself. Thus Christ is not only the intercessor and mediator of our prayers but also the recipient who hears and answers personally, an exalted status exemplifying the New Testament habit of ascribing divine attributes and functions to Christ. His work is increasingly equated with the work of God. Just as Israel could turn to Yahweh, the church can now turn to the Father *and* the Son, both of whom hear and respond to prayer with the same urgency, grace, and power.

This increasingly narrow focus—or should we say expanding horizon?—on the centrality of Christ for every aspect of the Christian life, including the life of prayer, converges with our final observation on Paul's wish prayers: they are regularly framed in light of Christ's return (1 Thess. 3:13; 5:23; 2 Thess. 1:5–10; 2:16–17; 2 Tim. 1:18). Once again, the shape of prayer is comprehensively determined by eschatology.[9] Not only does Christ hear our prayers and answer them cooperatively with the Father, but his impending return as judge is determinative in distinguishing necessary from unnecessary requests. It is no accident that Paul's petitions are overwhelmingly moral and spiritual, not because he harbors a dualistic antimaterialism denigrating to the flesh, but because he is thoroughly animated by a living conviction that all world history must soon surrender to the judgment of the crucified, resurrected, exalted Lord returning to claim his own. For the obedient,

7. Stendahl, "Paul at Prayer," 246–47; and Osiek, "Paul's Prayer," 149–50.

8. Stanley, *Boasting in the Lord*, 53, 83–84; Wiles, *Paul's Intercessory Prayers*, 55n3; Bruce, *1–2 Thessalonians*, 202, 213; and W. Mounce, *Pastoral Epistles*, 495–96.

9. The classic treatment of this issue remains Greeven, *Gebet und Eschatologie*; see also Wiles, *Paul's Intercessory Prayers*, 41, 49.

the parousia is a beacon of hope illuminating their journey by actively directing personal decisions and priorities for worldly engagement to the very end, but for the disobedient that final day casts a long, ominous shadow. Consequently, Paul intercedes so that his brothers and sisters will walk unswervingly in the light. Once again, I suspect that this accounts for the complete absence of any intercession regarding material concerns, for earthly circumstances are immaterial to one's heavenly standing. Paul does not pray for lower unemployment rates, improved social standing, physical well-being, or financial security, because none of these things has any real bearing on whether we "will be blameless and holy in the presence of our God and Father when our Lord Jesus comes with all his holy ones" (1 Thess. 3:13). Despite some undoubtedly rationalizing their abandonment of Christ's light and their final return to darkness by pointing an accusatory finger at some unrelieved physical suffering, New Testament teaching insists that authentic faith always perseveres, regardless of worldly adversity (e.g., 1 John 2:19). Such suffering facilitates God's sifting of the wheat from the chaff. Paul refuses to pray that the sifting cease, or even that it be eased, but he readily pleads that the genuine fruit of redemption will blossom and grow, sustaining us until the moment of Christ's appearing.

Prayers in the Body of Paul's Letters

We are left with two instances where intercessory prayers are lodged in the bodies of Paul's letters.[10] Since the substance of these prayers closely resembles the content of both Paul's wish prayers (above) and his introductory thanksgivings (below), here we will consider only their functional role in each letter's composition. When we examine Paul's introductory thanksgivings, as much light will be shed on the material content of these two intercessory prayers as on the thanksgiving passages themselves:

> Now we pray to God that you will not do anything wrong. Not that people will see that we have stood the test but that you will do what is right even though we may seem to have failed. . . . We are glad whenever we are weak but you are strong; and our prayer is for your perfection. (2 Cor. 13:7, 9)

> For this reason I kneel before the Father, from whom his whole family in heaven and on earth derives its name. I pray that out of his glorious riches he may strengthen you with power through his Spirit in your inner being,

10. Technically, Rom. 9:3 and 10:1 also fall into this category. As mentioned in chapter 11, however, they were both studied as examples of the way that Paul prays for himself.

so that Christ may dwell in your hearts through faith. And I pray that you, being rooted and established in love, may have power, together with all the saints, to grasp how wide and long and high and deep is the love of Christ, and to know this love that surpasses knowledge—that you may be filled to the measure of all the fullness of God. (Eph. 3:14–19)

Each of these intercessions serves an important role in the course of Paul's argument, demonstrating once again that instruction and prayer evolve hand in hand in the apostle's mind. The prayer in 2 Corinthians concludes the strident defense of Paul's apostleship elaborated in 2 Cor. 10–13, a piece of emotional rhetoric sometimes identified with the "painful letter" mentioned in 2 Cor. 7:8. Whether these four chapters ever circulated independently, the intercessory prayer recorded in 13:7–9 forms a fitting conclusion to Paul's loving rebuke of Corinthian foolishness.[11] Paul prays that they pass their "test" of self-examination (13:5–6), thereby reaffirming that they are, indeed, genuine participants in the true life of Christ. His objective is not vindication before his opponents, the false apostles (10:7–11:33), but restoration of the repentant Corinthians (13:9) to a harmonious relationship with God, one another, and their true apostle.[12] Paul reiterates his commitment to service among the churches, including the obstreperous Corinthians, by revisiting the theology of weakness unveiled in 12:5–10. He would gladly be as "weak" as the false apostles accuse him of being if it would somehow assure the Corinthians' strength and stability in passing the test of authentic faith (13:3–4, 9).[13] That Paul twice describes these intercessions for Corinth in the present tense ("we are praying") confirms that both his instructions and exhortations publicly articulate the insights acquired through private prayer, perhaps, even as he writes; the written words are themselves a prayer, a prayer to be rearticulated with each fresh reading of the letter in Corinthian worship. Paul prays what he writes and writes what he prays. In this way, intercessory prayer serves as a fitting pastoral conclusion to a confrontational piece of correspondence.

The second prayer, found in the letter to the Ephesians, is not only located at a crucial turning point in the letter's argument, but articulates one of the most profound expressions of Christian devotion found anywhere in the New Testament. C. L. Mitton refers to Eph. 3:14–19 as one

11. Wiles, *Paul's Intercessory Prayers*, 239.
12. Second Corinthians 13:9 is the only New Testament occurrence of the noun *katartisis* ("restoration"); for the relationship between Paul's prayer for restoration and the circumstances addressed in 2 Cor. 10–13, see R. Martin, *2 Corinthians*, 480–87; and Thrall, *Second Epistle to the Corinthians*, 2.898–99.
13. Thrall, *Second Epistle to the Corinthians*, 2.897.

of "the gems" of the letter,[14] while M. Barth's magisterial commentary compares Paul's prayer to the so-called high priestly prayer of Jesus in John 17, demonstrating "that praying stands above all reasoning, even theological."[15] The single complex sentence that first unfolds and finally sprawls throughout these six verses conveys the uncontainable mystery of the gospel. That mystery, the unfathomable love of Christ for all humanity, Jew and Gentile alike, energizes the intercession's twofold request that God (1) strengthen the readers through his Spirit that they may experience the depth and stability of Christ's love (3:16–17) and (2) enable them collectively to grasp the vastness of God's power as well as the incomprehensibility of the love of Christ (3:18–19a).[16] Christ's love is at the center of both requests, which together serve as the pivot-point in the letter's development, transitioning from the gospel instruction in Eph. 1–3 to the practical exhortation of Eph. 4–6. This structural function of the prayer is often observed,[17] but its theological significance is generally overlooked. The letter's first half highlights the unveiling of Christ's love through God's eternal plan of salvation (1:4, 6; 2:4); the second half elaborates the practical expressions of this love within Christ's body (4:2, 15, 16; 5:1, 2, 25, 28, 33; 6:21, 23, 24). Yet, since this divine love is incomprehensible as well as unattainable apart from the Spirit of God, the intervening intercession (3:14–19) supplies the essential spiritual bridge connecting these two realms, not just rhetorically but existentially. Except for the immediate efficacy of this prayer, the message of Eph. 1–3 remains incomprehensible, while the exhortations of Eph. 4–6 urge the impossible.

So central is this prayer's location that its thematic connection to the introductory thanksgiving in 1:15–19 causes the entire first half of the letter (1:15–3:21) to be animated by intercessory prayer in much the same way that the first half of other Pauline letters are characterized by doctrinal instruction.[18] A thematic comparison of the two prayers reveals that both are focused on the same set of central concerns:[19] that

14. Mitton, *Ephesians*, 236.

15. M. Barth, *Ephesians*, 377.

16. Paul concocts a deliberate paradox. He prays that they will "know th[e] love that surpasses knowledge." In other words, catching even a glimpse of Christ's love is a miraculous gift of the Holy Spirit (compare 2:8). Rather than interpreting 2:19b as a third petition, Arnold (*Ephesians*, 86) argues that it is a summary statement conveying the consequences of the prior two petitions' fulfillment. Paul offers the first two requests so that his readers would be "filled . . . [with] all the fullness of God."

17. Lincoln, *Ephesians*, 200–201; and Best, *Ephesians*, 335–36.

18. "Intercession is such an essential element of the apostolic ministry that it initiates, concludes, and thus dominates all doctrinal and narrative elements of 1:15–3:21"; M. Barth, *Ephesians*, 327.

19. See Arnold, *Ephesians*, 93–94; and Lincoln, *Ephesians*, 200–201.

the power of the Father's indwelling Spirit would expand the believers' apprehension of Christ's universal love now equally available to Jew and Gentile alike. Ephesians 3:14 reintroduces the prayer that Paul was on the verge of offering at 3:1 before he was sidetracked into the digression on apostleship in 3:2–13. Consequently, the logical connector "for this reason" (3:14) refers back to the explanation of Jewish-Gentile equality found in 2:11–22. But since Paul's apostleship is itself defined by mission to the Gentiles, his digression evolves into a restatement of the mystery of Jewish-Gentile inclusion (3:2–13), thus providing a second, equally opportune moment for the prayer.

The prayer's content, like the letter itself, is determined by the focus on universality. For instance, this is the only Pauline example of the decidedly non-Jewish practice of kneeling in prayer (3:14).[20] Though variety was possible, the Hebrew habit was to stand in prayer. Since, however, Paul was interceding for formerly pagan Gentiles, he deliberately adopted (at least, rhetorically) a typically pagan, Gentile posture for this particular prayer.[21] Similarly, the reference to divine fatherhood (3:15) does not refer to God as the Father of the Son but to God as the Father-Creator of all humanity.[22] In fact, God's cosmic fatherhood (3:14–15) becomes the bedrock for both the cosmic Christology (1:4–23) and the cosmic ecclesiology (1:22–23; 2:7–10; 3:10) so distinctive of this letter.[23] These observations on the form, manner, and introductory address of Paul's prayer demonstrate that the apostle who sought to "become all things to all men so that by all possible means [he] might save some" (1 Cor. 9:22) employed the same urgent flexibility when nurturing his spiritual children as he did when first introducing them to "this mystery . . . that through the gospel the Gentiles are heirs together with Israel" (Eph. 3:6).

Introductory Thanksgivings

Of the thirteen Pauline letters, ten begin with extended expressions of thanksgiving that are broadly recognized as accomplishing several

20. M. Barth, *Ephesians*, 378, 383. New Testament references to other postures appear only in Old Testament quotations (Rom. 11:4; 14:11; Phil. 2:10); see Best, *Ephesians*, 337.

21. For example, see Van Straten, "Gifts for the Gods," 83: "Greeks, and, more frequently still, Greek women, did indeed throw themselves on their knees before the deities from whom they expected assistance and salvation, in particular circumstances and in fervent prayers of supplication."

22. Actually, the reference to "his whole family in heaven and on earth" (3:15) indicates that spiritual beings such as angels and demons are included; see Best, *Ephesians*, 337; and especially the excellent discussion in M. Barth, *Ephesians*, 379–84.

23. M. Barth, *Ephesians*, 380.

vital functions:[24] first, they survey the main themes of each letter and introduce the general didactic approach by which those issues will be addressed; second, they demonstrate Paul's deep-seated love for his audience and his gratitude over the visible displays of grace operative in their lives.[25] Furthermore, among those ten introductory thanksgivings, eight also contain intercessory prayers that make their own contribution to the purposes of thanksgiving and the goals of each letter:

> First, I thank my God through Jesus Christ for all of you, because your faith is being reported all over the world. God, whom I serve with my whole heart in preaching the gospel of his Son, is my witness how constantly I remember you in my prayers at all times; and I pray that now at last by God's will the way may be opened for me to come to you. (Rom. 1:8–10)

> I have not stopped giving thanks for you, remembering you in my prayers. I keep asking that the God of our Lord Jesus Christ, the glorious Father, may give you the Spirit of wisdom and revelation, so that you may know him better. I pray also that the eyes of your heart may be enlightened in order that you may know the hope to which he has called you, the riches of his glorious inheritance in the saints, and his incomparably great power for us who believe. (Eph. 1:16–19)

> I thank my God every time I remember you. In all my prayers for all of you, I always pray with joy because of your partnership in the gospel from the first day until now, being confident of this, that he who began a good work in you will carry it on to completion until the day of Christ Jesus. . . . And this is my prayer: that your love may abound more and more in knowledge and depth of insight, so that you may be able to discern what is best and may be pure and blameless until the day of Christ, filled with the fruit of righteousness that comes through Jesus Christ—to the glory and praise of God. (Phil. 1:3–6, 9–11)

> We always thank God, the Father of our Lord Jesus Christ, when we pray for you, because we have heard of your faith in Christ Jesus and of the love you have for all the saints—the faith and love that spring from the hope that is stored up for you in heaven. . . . For this reason, since the day we heard about you, we have not stopped praying for you and asking God to fill you with the knowledge of his will through all spiritual wisdom and understanding. And we pray this in order that you may live a life worthy of the Lord and may please him in every way: bearing fruit in every good

24. Romans, 1–2 Corinthians, Ephesians, Philippians, Colossians, 1–2 Thessalonians, 2 Timothy, and Philemon. See chapter 11n2 for discussion of Pauline authorship and the so-called deutero-Pauline epistles.

25. O'Brien, *Introductory Thanksgivings*, 13–14, 257–63; and Wiles, *Paul's Intercessory Prayers*, 229.

work, growing in the knowledge of God, being strengthened with all power according to his glorious might so that you may have great endurance and patience, and joyfully giving thanks to the Father, who has qualified you to share in the inheritance of the saints in the kingdom of light. (Col. 1:3–5, 9–12)

We always thank God for all of you, mentioning you in our prayers. We continually remember before our God and Father your work produced by faith, your labor prompted by love, and your endurance inspired by hope in our Lord Jesus Christ. (1 Thess. 1:2–3)

We ought always to thank God for you, brothers, and rightly so, because your faith is growing more and more, and the love every one of you has for each other is increasing. . . . With this in mind, we constantly pray for you, that our God may count you worthy of his calling, and that by his power he may fulfill every good purpose of yours and every act prompted by your faith. We pray this so that the name of our Lord Jesus may be glorified in you, and you in him, according to the grace of our God and the Lord Jesus Christ. . . . But we ought always to thank God for you, brothers loved by the Lord, because from the beginning God chose you to be saved through the sanctifying work of the Spirit and through belief in the truth. He called you to this through our gospel, that you might share in the glory of our Lord Jesus Christ. (2 Thess. 1:3, 11–12; 2:13–14)

I thank God, whom I serve, as my forefathers did, with a clear conscience, as night and day I constantly remember you in my prayers. Recalling your tears, I long to see you, so that I may be filled with joy. (2 Tim. 1:3–4)

I always thank my God as I remember you in my prayers, because I hear about your faith in the Lord Jesus and your love for all the saints. I pray that you may be active in sharing your faith, so that you will have a full understanding of every good thing we have in Christ. (Philem. 4–6)

P. Schubert identifies Paul's blending of introductory thanksgiving with petitionary prayer as a predictably formal convention of ancient letter writing.[26] Every convention, however, serves some purpose, no matter how predictable, and the particular purposes that motivated Paul's weaving of introductory thanksgiving with personal petition remain to be uncovered, whether the association itself is finally judged to be innovative or formulaic. Questions of form and function are closely related,

26. Schubert, *Form and Function*, 167–72. He offers several exemplary texts found among the papyri. Schubert's conclusions, however, which were widely accepted within New Testament scholarship, are now challenged by Artz, "Epistolary Introductory Thanksgiving."

but answers to the one do not predetermine all answers to the other, especially when dealing with an author as creative as the apostle Paul. At the very least, this combination of thanksgiving and intercession provides one more example of how an all-pervasive New Testament eschatology conjures the mysterious interim dialectic between the already and the not yet in which the church now finds itself.[27] Thanking the Father for grace already received does not preclude the urgency of requests for grace still lacking, nor do the momentary failings that demand prayer for assistance detract from the all-sufficiency of the saving work that elicits eternal adoration. All Christian prayer stands equally under both horizons until they finally merge and become one perfect reality in the new heaven and the new earth.

In addition to this characteristically eschatological dimension, other familiar features of Pauline petition are found in these introductory thanksgiving prayers:

- the emotional depth of Paul's pastoral concerns for his churches
- the near identity between the content of a letter's introductory prayer and the substance of the teaching that follows
- the overwhelming focus on spiritual growth and maturity in light of the parousia and final judgment
- the apparent fusion between private prayer and public ministry
- the extravagant expectations of God's inevitably positive response
- the conviction that intercession unites the worldwide body of Christ in a transformational network of efficacious prayer transcending every conceivable boundary, whether geographical, political, cultural, or doctrinal

Each of these characteristics of Pauline prayer was adequately examined in previous sections of this study; there is no need to repeat that work here. Now we simply need to observe how these intercessions function within the introductory thanksgivings of these eight letters.

Though not all of Paul's letters begin with thanksgiving to God wedded with intercession for his readers, that most of them do tells us something fairly important about Paul's understanding of the relationship between his Father, himself, and his audience. Apostleship makes Paul an earthly intercessor whose values and priorities have been commandeered and redirected by the gospel; he is first directed outwardly to God and then outwardly toward others.

27. See Wiles, *Paul's Intercessory Prayers*, 296.

Paul is preoccupied with thanking God for the multitude of ways that divine grace has invaded, captured, and transformed his readers' lives: their faith is growing toward maturity and is known throughout the world (Rom. 1:8; Eph. 1:15; Col. 1:4; 1 Thess. 1:3; 2 Thess. 1:3; 2 Tim. 1:3–4; Philem. 5); they love all of God's children (Eph. 1:15; Col. 1:4; 2 Thess. 1:3; Philem. 5); they are partners in the work of the gospel (Phil. 1:5; 2 Tim. 1:3–4; Philem. 6); their faith in the good news visibly demonstrates that they are loved, chosen, and sanctified by the Lord (2 Thess. 2:13–14). Pauline thanksgiving is, first and foremost, focused on the outworking of the gospel in the lives of others, especially as that grace appears in a discreet set of ways. Paul looks for a particular cadre of developments that reappear throughout most of the introductory thanksgivings: (1) the gospel has firmly taken root; (2) God's grace is producing spiritual maturity to sustain them till the parousia; (3) the community remains bound together by love; and (4) they share Paul's commitment to advance the apostolic mission. These four characteristics, visibly demonstrated in the lives of the Pauline churches, are the specific foci of Paul's thanksgiving prayers because together they are indicative of healthy Christian community. This cluster of traits offers visible proof that the church's external confession is, indeed, evidence of a genuine internal transformation. Once again the root and the branch, the beginning and the end, of Pauline thanksgiving is the visible demonstration of God's mercy in Jesus Christ running its own miraculous course throughout the life of the church. These four signs of grace demonstrate that the Son is alive, the Father is faithful, the Spirit is working, and our God deserves all our thanks.

The second half of the apostle's outward orientation is focused on the continuing spiritual requirements of the very communities that provide Paul with occasion for gratitude. Paul's thanksgiving gives birth to his intercession, and his intercession reflects the contours of his thanksgiving. He, quite naturally, wants the distinguishing features of Christian maturity to become more and more pervasive in every believing community; thus the peculiarities of any particular intercession are dictated by the specific community needs eliciting each letter.[28] One example, taken from Phil. 1:3–6, 9–11, will suffice:

28. O'Brien, *Introductory Thanksgivings*, 269–70; and Wiles, *Paul's Intercessory Prayers*, 293–95. For detailed observations on Rom. 1:8–10 see O'Brien 225–29 and Wiles 187–94; on Eph. 1:16–19 see Wiles 514–16; on Phil. 1:3–6, 9–11 see O'Brien 37–41 and Wiles 204–6, 213–14; on Col. 1:3–5, 9–12 see O'Brien 69–70, 100–103; on 1 Thess. 1:2–3 see O'Brien 164–66 and Wiles 179–81; on 2 Thess. 1:3, 11–12 see O'Brien 172–77, who highlights that the thanksgiving in 2 Thessalonians reflects Paul's conviction that the prayers offered in 1 Thess. 3:10–12 had been answered; on 2 Thess. 2:13–14, see O'Brien 184–93; and on Philem. 4–6, see O'Brien 47–61 and Wiles 219–25.

theme in the thanksgiving prayer of Phil. 1:3–6, 9–11	elsewhere in Philippians
joy (1:4)	1:18, 25–26; 2:2, 17–18, 28–29; 3:1; 4:1, 4, 10
partnership in the gospel (1:5)	1:7–8, 12–30; 2:16, 25–30; 4:10–20
completion of God's work/obedience (1:6, 9–11)	1:27–30; 2:1–5, 12–18; 3:2, 15–17; 4:1–9
Christ's coming (1:6, 10)	2:16; 3:8, 20; 4:5
glory of God (1:11)	1:20; 4:20

However the details may vary from letter to letter, Paul's thanksgiving intercessions overwhelmingly focus on the universal importance of continued spiritual development. In this regard, Philippians is typical of both the recurrent themes appearing in all of Paul's introductory intercessions and their circumstantial applications.

A noteworthy feature of the introductory thanksgiving prayers in each of the four captivity letters is the recurring request for "wisdom and knowledge."[29] Paul asks that the churches be given "the Spirit of wisdom and revelation, so that you may know him better" to facilitate "the enlightenment of their hearts" (Eph. 1:17–18); "love . . . abound[ing] . . . in knowledge and depth of insight," leading to discernment (Phil. 1:9–10); "the knowledge of [God's] will through all spiritual wisdom and understanding" (Col. 1:9); and "a full understanding of every good thing we have in Christ" (Philem. 6). This particular intercessory emphasis on wisdom and insight is quite distinct. Apparently, imprisonment (or at least this particular imprisonment) led Paul to reflect on the inevitability of his own mortality and the moment when his churches would need to stand on their own, to combat error, and to make sure-footed ethical decisions without recourse to his guidance. Consequently, he intercedes, not only for immediate spiritual requirements, but also for the personal resources essential to their future maturity. It is noteworthy that the resulting focus is not on adherence to any specific code of conduct or spiritual apparatus, but on an intimate familiarity with the mind of God described elsewhere as the particular domain of the Holy Spirit (1 Cor. 2:10–12; Rom. 8:27). In fact, a specific request for "the Spirit of wisdom and revelation" in Eph. 1:17 makes explicit what is implicit in the other three prayers: Paul's apostolic work as earthly teacher and intercessor is a specific instantiation of the Holy Spirit's ongoing work of leading, instructing, convicting, and illuminating God's people. Therefore, Paul prays for the fruition of the Spirit's work long after his prayers have ended.

29. O'Brien, *Introductory Thanksgivings*, 32, 85–86. The word *epignōsis* ("knowledge") "does not appear in prayer requests outside these four letters" (32). See Eph. 1:17; Phil. 1:9; Col. 1:9; Philem. 6.

Can Paul Be Our Model?

To what extent is the study of Paul's prayer life relevant to the average Christian? K. Stendahl once insisted, "We are not Paul, nor are we apostles as he was an apostle."[30] Consequently, under this view it is a mistake for modern believers to view Paul as a spiritual model to be emulated. Paul's approach to prayer was as distinctive as his apostolic calling. "It would be stifling and wrong to say that Paul taught us what is proper for a Christian to pray about. It could perhaps even be argued that Paul was 'too caught up in his work' and his prayers were also," suggests Stendahl. In other words, Paul demonstrates a single-minded (even excessive) approach to devotion that may have been required of a pioneer church planter in the Roman Empire, but his focus and priorities are certainly not exemplary for anyone interested in a well-balanced, healthy spirituality today. After three chapters devoted to an examination of Pauline prayer, such objections require some response before any assured theological conclusions can safely be drawn. Should the preceding observations on Pauline prayer tickle anything beyond mere historical curiosity? Did Paul's apostleship so condition his practice and understanding of prayer that the two became inseparably fused in his experience, making it impossible for his readers to derive broader lessons for the church at large, whether ancient or modern?

Undoubtedly, the key to understanding Paul at prayer is to come to terms with Paul as apostle to the Gentiles. It would be naïve to read his exhortations, instructions, and recitations about prayer in any other way. Stendahl asks, however, that we not only clean Paul's proverbial tub but throw out his baby with the bathwater. Granted, we may not be apostles, but at least three features of Paul's writings nevertheless require that we strive to reflect his exemplary prayer life: (1) his exhortations to pray, (2) his requests for prayer, and (3) his injunctions to "be like me."

Paul's admonitions to "be faithful in prayer" were examined in chapter 11. What many would label zealous hyperbole—"pray in all occasions," "never be anxious," "devote yourselves to prayer," "pray constantly," "always give thanks"—is typical of these exhortations. The blatant single-mindedness demonstrated in Paul's own prayer life is precisely the mindset he hopes to cultivate in his readers. This symmetry between Paul's descriptions of his own prayer habits and his pastoral urgings to others confirms that he did in fact assume that his enthusiasm and determination should be normative for the church.

Second, Paul's frequent requests that others pray for him, also examined in chapter 11, offer a glimpse into the zealous apostle's own sense of per-

---

30. Stendahl, "Paul at Prayer," 249.

sonal need and frailty. Paul's faithfulness to his calling (both to preach and to pray) was, in part, a consequence of the devoted intercessions offered by brothers and sisters in Christ. He was held up, buoyed toward heaven, by the supportive petitions of numerous communities dotted throughout the Mediterranean. To this degree, Paul's urgency was a partial fruit of the communal intensity shared among his many disciples and prayer partners, wedded undoubtedly with a deep sense of mutual responsibility.

Finally, Paul explicitly offers his life as a model for others to follow in several calls to "be like me" (1 Cor. 4:16; 11:1; Eph. 5:1; Phil. 3:17; 1 Thess. 1:6; 2:14; 2 Thess. 3:7).[31] He clearly believed that he was a paradigm for others in their own Christian journey, and there is no reason to exclude prayer from the list of activities he confidently held out for others to emulate. Paul's devotion to prayer had been forged in the same furnace of suffering that had purified the Son of God's own obedience to the cross, and now his repeated calls to "imitate me as I imitate Christ" establish the same process as normative for us all. While Paul's apostleship certainly placed unique constraints and expectations on his particular expression of discipleship, and thus on his own approach to prayer, the attitudes and passions entailed within those prayers were reflective of the life of Christ radiating through the experience of one particular man, Paul of Tarsus. In this regard, Paul was anything but unique. The same convergence of Christ's passion with individual experience should be typical of any and every follower of Jesus, making Paul's prayers for the church a Spirit-directed extension of Jesus's prayers for his own mission, all of which are in turn a corollary to our Spirit-led intercessions for the body of Christ today.

With all of this in mind, I suspect that I once met the spirit of Paul on a gloomy Tuesday afternoon in the northeast corner of Scotland, not too far from Aberdeen. During my years as a doctoral student I served for a time as a parish assistant in my local church. Each Tuesday afternoon I made pastoral visits to the elderly, shut-ins, and various infrequent attendees belonging to the Church of Scotland. This particular Tuesday brought me to the red door of a smallish council flat (i.e., public housing) that was home to an elderly, gray-haired widow. She invited me in for tea and began to tell me about the losses life had dealt her: a husband's death, deteriorating health, long distances that made visits with children and grandchildren a rarity. She spent most of her time alone tending the small coal-burning fireplace that Scots dub "central heating." I asked how she occupied her time, expecting to see her draw a chest of knitted shawls or crocheted afghans from beneath a living-room chair. Instead, she pointed to the morning paper spread out across her kitchen table.

31. See Stanley, "Become Imitators of Me"; and De Boer, *Imitation of Paul.*

"I pray," she said.

Her eyes sparkled as she described an average day.

"First I read the headlines, the world and local news," she said. "Then I pray that the Lord will give his grace, wisdom, and guidance to all the leaders responsible for making wise and just decisions. I pray for peace wherever there is conflict and relief for all the suffering.

"Then I read the obituaries, and I ask that Christ bring comfort and solace to those who grieve; may he answer their questions and show each family how much he loves them in their time of sadness.

"Then I read the wedding announcements, and I pray that God will fill each couple with his patience and compassion, that every husband and wife will love each other as Christ loves his church, giving them endurance for the tough times ahead.

"Then I read the birth announcements, and I pray that the Holy Spirit will fill the life of every child, transforming each one into the mature holy man or woman of God they all may become in Christ.

"Then I pray for my own family, friends, and neighbors; my community and parish; for acquaintances who are in need. And, finally, I thank God for all his blessings in my life, for my salvation, and my eternal home in heaven. And right about then, I usually find it's time for tea."

I wondered how much of the world this elderly saint had helped to transform. I originally approached her door thinking that I had something to offer her, a modicum of Christian comfort or encouragement, perhaps. When I left several hours later, she was the one who had encouraged me. Not only had she added my name to her prayer list(!), but she had displayed a living, breathing example of passionate, dynamic Pauline prayer in the dim twilight of a Scottish winter. I doubt if she had ever read a learned exegetical treatise on the prayers of Paul, but she was intimately acquainted with the man himself; she had soaked herself in his letters, and from him she had learned how to pray.

Theological Reflections
on Pauline Prayer

For a man who lamented his inability to know what to pray for, Paul certainly spent a lot of time praying for a great many specific things, both for himself and others. Furthermore, once the substance of those prayers is catalogued, one could easily question the need for all that Pauline passion. After all, is it not safe to assume that such qualities as spiritual maturity, wisdom, and the fullness of the Spirit were Christian traits that God would be more than happy to supply, no matter how faint the request? Why, then, the urgent intercessions for personal items that Paul could safely assume the Father already wanted to provide? Perhaps the answer, in part, arises from our first observation: Paul knew that there was no natural affinity between the human heart and divine desire; whatever convergence occurred between these two was a result of the Spirit, the Spirit who also taught Paul that spiritual growth was always an approved item on God's agenda. In this sense, Paul does indeed know exactly how he ought to pray. Specific requests for situational concerns are acceptable, even encouraged, but they yield spotty results if consistent affirmation is the criterion for effective prayer. For Paul, however, all prayer is effective prayer, whether the Father answers yes or no; in either case, communion with God has transpired, and the believer has experienced something new about divine guidance and the Spirit's work within. Since that process of personal transformation comprises the heartland of Christian prayer, according to Paul, prioritizing petitions for spiritual prosperity is an obvious decision.

But this still leaves a question about the need to pray for such self-evident spiritual benefits. Paul tells the Philippians that he is "confident . . . that the one who began a good work in you will carry it on to completion until the day of Christ Jesus" (Phil. 1:6). In other words, the Father promises to finish what he starts in all his children. Would God save us but then shortchange us in the area of personal sanctification because we neglected to petition sufficiently for the requisite spiritual development? Obviously not. Yet, Paul petitions vigorously nonetheless. This apparent conundrum is especially stark in Phil. 1:6, where Paul's assertion of confidence in divine faithfulness appears within another introductory thanksgiving prayer interceding for the church's wisdom and maturity. Obviously, Paul's belief in God's faithfulness to complete our spiritual maturation coexists with an equally firm conviction that prayer makes a genuine difference in what God does. Is the final product a result of the Father's commitment, or is it the fruit of faithful petition? Whatever the final answer, it must encompass both aspects of the conundrum equally. Certainly, there is no starker illustration of this tension than Paul's own periodic requests that others pray for his continued faithfulness in his apostolic mission (Eph. 6:19–20; Phil. 1:19; Col. 4:3–4; 1 Thess. 5:25; 2 Thess. 3:1–2; Philem. 22). On the one hand, the eternal call that made Paul an apostle to the Gentiles was the predestined raison d'être of his existence (Rom. 1:1; 1 Cor. 1:1; 9:16–17; Gal. 1:1, 12; Eph. 1:1; 3:1; Col. 1:1; 1 Thess. 2:4; 1 Tim. 1:1; 2 Tim. 1:1; Titus 1:1–3). On the other hand, not even divine foreordination could wipe away the human frailty that kept him attuned to the continual possibility of failure (1 Cor. 9:26–27; Gal. 2:2; Phil. 2:16) and consistently invited intercessory prayers that he not give up before his race was complete.

There is plenty of evidence elsewhere in Paul to indicate that spiritual maturity can vary widely from person to person and that, even though God's desire is for all of his people to mature to the fullest extent possible, achieving that goal is not automatic. A wide variety of personal choices can affect the sanctification process for good or ill, as seen in Paul's concern that his churches "stand firm until the end." God's final separation of the wheat from the chaff, and the measure of each believer's individual reward, has yet to be determined (1 Cor. 3:12–15). In keeping with this eschatological uncertainty, Paul was convinced that petitionary prayer for ourselves and others is a crucial ingredient in the final outcome of every believer's audience before the throne of God. There is a synergistic component to the Christian life by which each individual is opened to the larger community of faith through intercessory prayer. Praying for the spiritual prosperity of our brothers and sisters in Christ is no substitute for personal accountability and individual responsiveness to the Holy Spirit's prompting; in Paul's mind, however, such intercession is an essential component of all successful Christian living. Healthy discipleship that perseveres to the parousia is the fruit of diverse, essential nutrients intertwining through a variety of spiritual streams, converging in a cooperative work of divine grace, the Holy Spirit, individual obedience, petitions for oneself, and the intercessions of others. No believer can hope to appreciate the fullness of all that God has in store for his people without drinking deeply from the full complement of these ingredients as they commingle throughout the course of life. Intercession, Paul shows us, is integral to the full maturity of the body of Christ. While the Father would never withhold the fruit of the Spirit from any of his children—for to be a child of God is to be inhabited by the Spirit of holiness, who cannot help but cultivate new fruit wherever he takes up residence—the measure of our final harvest is partly determined by the degree to which we have prayed, petitioned, and interceded. Paul knew that there was nothing so divinely determined that its final outcome could not be enhanced or hindered by prayer or its absence. After all, the Father's blanket promise to his children is that we will all be judged righteous at the parousia, not that we will have chosen the fullest measure of righteousness available here and now. It is entirely possible to win eternity while shortchanging our temporal obedience and diminishing our eternal reward.

There is little if any evidence that Paul knew the Lord's Prayer, at least as it is preserved in the Synoptic Gospels. If he did, its traces lie so far in the background of the formative influences on Paul's life that it has fused with any number of other unidentified currents in Jewish-Christian piety. As noted earlier, some suggest that the references to Abba in Gal. 4:6 and Rom. 8:15 are shorthand allusions to the collective use of the Lord's Prayer in the Pauline communities, but this is pure speculation. Regardless of Paul's familiarity (or lack thereof) with this specific prayer, there is, however, ample evidence that his own personal prayers were nonetheless suffused with the distinctive theological convictions that animated Jesus's teaching. Three features are particularly noteworthy.

First, Paul not only prays to God as Father (Eph. 1:17; 3:14; Col. 1:12; 1 Thess. 1:2; 2 Thess. 2:16), an epithet readily familiar to Jewish prayer in his day (see chapter 5), but more important, he prays to God as "the Father of our Lord Jesus Christ" (Rom. 15:6; Col. 1:3; compare 1 Thess. 3:11–13; 2 Thess. 2:16), a uniquely Christian identification that finds a distinctly common bond, if not an explicit articulation, within the Lord's Prayer itself. Whether Paul knew how to recite anything even vaguely reminiscent of our Lord's Prayer, he was thoroughly versed in the theological implications of Christ's self-identification as the only Son of the Father, a claim that provides the key to properly understanding the substance of that Gospel prayer.

Second, we have repeatedly seen how easily Paul focused his prayers on the spiritual requirements of the Christian life, apparently to the near neglect of mundane, material concerns. In this regard, he also appears remarkably in step with the tenor of Jesus's own priorities for discipleship as expressed in the Lord's Prayer. The single petition for daily bread, aside from being a surprisingly simple request, is the fourth of seven petitions following the emphatic prioritizing of the Father's glorification, the establishment of his kingdom, and the accomplishment of his will on earth. Again, whether Paul knew the details of Jesus's prayer, his laser-like focus on spiritual development, the cultivation of holiness while awaiting the parousia, and perseverance to the glory of God all reflect surprisingly similar concerns. Suggesting that Paul's priorities in petitionary prayer were somehow uniquely his, or even inapplicable to the average believer, requires that we first ignore Jesus's own teaching about prayer, for there is a direct line traceable from the substance of Paul's prayers to the priorities of Jesus's instruction. Furthermore, Paul's preoccupation with corporate spiritual development is in keeping with Jesus's repeated use of the plural personal pronouns "we," "our," and "us" (Matt. 6:9–13). What Jesus first instructed, Paul then modeled.

Third, the apocalyptic framework so essential to Jesus's teaching and the eschatological urgency infusing Paul's instruction to his churches make these men two peas in a pod. Jesus taught his disciples how to pray for the victorious establishment of a kingdom that has yet to vanquish all opposition; the battle still rages, and the praying disciple waits for the Father's promised outcome. To use O. Cullmann's well-worn World War II analogy once more, the church celebrates a victorious D-Day in the passion but still anticipates the ultimate V-Day at the parousia.[1] Christ's decisive victory is won and guarantees the final victory of God, but that celebration is still future, and God's people are left to wait patiently, often in no small measure of anguish, for the day of the Lord to dawn.

In the meantime, all of creation, including the inhabitants of God's kingdom, groan with both expectation and frustration in equal measure (Rom. 8:18–27). Christian petition is always prayer arising from within the swells of eschatological turmoil and struggle, groaning and anxiety. Not that prayer itself is ever said to be a struggle, at least not in the sense of our wrestling to gain something from God, as if petitionary prayer transformed the believer into a modern-day Jacob contesting God for some blessing (Gen. 32:22–32). Rather, prayer, for both Jesus and Paul, engages the disciple's holy aspirations in the Father's plan for heavenly victory over cosmic chaos. Thus Paul invites the Roman church "to join me in my struggle by praying to God for me" (Rom. 15:30). He similarly

---

1. Cullmann, *Christ and Time*, 84.

encourages the church in Colossae by assuring the believers "how much I am struggling for you" (Col. 2:1), a struggle that almost certainly included intercessory prayer, while also reminding them that their founder and compatriot, Epaphras, "is always wrestling in prayer for you, that you may stand firm in the will of God, mature and fully assured" (4:12).

Paul struggled as every obedient Christian struggles, exerting himself to obey Christ's call in a hostile world where faithfulness to the gospel often means pain and suffering (Col. 1:29). Prayer itself is not the field of combat but one of the weapons we carry against the enemy (Eph. 6:18). Paul's numerous encouragements to pray constantly, in every situation, presenting every request before God with thanksgiving, serve as regular reminders that, while he may not have always known *what* to request (Rom. 8:26), Paul certainly knew *that* every request was always welcome. Prayer itself is not arduous, constraining, or laborious (at least not to Paul's mind); these are qualities of life itself. In any case, it is the Spirit—not the believer—who groans in intercession. Our groaning is an inescapable quality of eschatological existence; we live stretched between the already and the not yet, and sometimes that tension pulls more tautly than we can bear. So the Father gives us the gift of prayer to bridge the gap.

The struggle is not met in prayer; rather, prayer becomes an answer to the struggle met in life. Petition and intercession provide a way for groaning to be transformed into worship, for despair to give birth to hope, for frustration to melt into peace, and for earthly failure to metamorphose into spiritual victory.

13

Asking Ethically

Petitionary Prayer in the
General Letters and Revelation

A s we approach the end of our study, ten passages remain to
be examined before this survey of New Testament petitionary prayer is complete. Obviously, Paul was not the only New
Testament writer concerned about the place of prayer in the
Christian life. Whether his perspectives and priorities were shared by
others, however, is a separate question that can be answered only after
examining the remaining texts. Unfortunately, the General Letters and
Revelation offer considerably less information about the authors' life
situations and, thus, the circumstances of their prayers; Paul's literary
corpus is downright confessional by comparison. Nevertheless, even
though instances of prayer and reflections upon its significance are
relatively sparse in these works (Hebrews, James, 1–2 Peter, 1–3 John,
Jude, and Revelation), especially when compared with the embarrassment of riches found in Paul's writings, they still make a significant
contribution to our topic.

We will study the ten passages topically, according to the substantive
issues they each raise. They may be organized under four main head-
ings: epistolary prayers (3 John 2; Heb. 13:18–19); revisiting the model
of Jesus (Heb. 5:7–8); prayer and community relationships (James 4:2–3;

5:13–18; 1 Pet. 3:7, 12); and prayer in light of the final judgment (1 Pet. 4:7; Rev. 5:8; 6:9–11; 8:3–5).

Epistolary Prayers

Ancient literary convention frequently included prayers within a letter's introduction. Paul did not invent this practice, although he certainly stretched and exploited it to his pastoral advantage. It is not surprising, then, to find a comparable introductory prayer in one of the Johannine letters: "Dear friend, I pray that you may enjoy good health and that all may go well with you, even as your soul is getting along well" (3 John 2).

Third John opens with a conventional "health wish" typical of ancient personal letters that undoubtedly refers to the author's actual intercessions for his friend Gaius.[1] By interceding for both Gaius's spiritual prosperity ("even as your soul is getting along well") and his physical health and well-being ("I pray that you may enjoy good health"), 3 John sets itself apart from the Pauline introductory prayers with their exclusive focus on spiritual concerns. Unlike Paul, John does not hesitate to pray that his friend will remain physically healthy and enjoy God's blessings in every arena of life. Gaius is one of John's few remaining allies in a divisive struggle over church leadership. Naturally, a healthy spiritual ally is better able to confront false teachers than a faithful brother lying on his deathbed. It is to the community's spiritual advantage that Gaius remain physically well. Thus John does not hesitate to pray for both.

Evidence of a similar situation in Paul's ministry may appear in his letter to the Philippians, when he returns the recently recovered Epaphroditus to his home church after enduring a life-threatening illness (Phil. 2:25–30). Although Paul typically says nothing about prayers for Epaphroditus's recovery, he credits the healing nonetheless to a display of God's mercy (2:27). Did Paul interpret this mercy as God's response to his prayers for a co-worker? Who knows, but I suspect that Paul, no less than John, would have felt free to intercede for another's physical health when the illness threatened the work of the gospel. Advancement of the good news remained primary for both John and Paul.

Finally, a request for intercession in Hebrews is similar to a number of passages in Paul's letters where he solicits prayer (Rom. 15:30–32; Eph. 6:19–20; Col. 4:3–4; 1 Thess. 5:25; 2 Thess. 3:1; see discussion in chapter 11): "Pray for us. We are sure that we have a clear conscience and desire to live honorably in every way. I particularly urge you to pray so that I may be restored to you soon" (Heb. 13:18–19). A strategic request

1. Smalley, *1, 2, 3 John*, 345.

for prayer is used to highlight the author's closing pastoral concerns.[2] This request serves at least three functions as the letter approaches its conclusion.

First, the author uses this prayer request to strategically unite himself and his cause with his fellow leaders in the church. The immediately preceding verses urge obedience to church leaders (13:7–10, 17), leaders who have apparently been combating the same problems now addressed by this letter. The context leaves the opening clause of 13:18, "pray for us," somewhat ambiguous. Does the plural pronoun refer to the author and his traveling companions?[3] Or is the writer including himself within the circle of resident leaders now feeling somewhat alienated from the local community?[4] I suspect that the ambiguity is deliberate. In urging the church to "pray for us," the author reminds his readers that they are responsible to all their leaders, both present and absent. It is difficult to ignore, undermine, or bad-mouth men and women for whom you are intently praying. The author knows this and is not above using a tactical phrasing to advance a spiritual lesson. He also knows that such intercession would be the initial sign of their repentance, indicating that his readers had accepted both his diagnosis of their plight and his remedy for their healing.

Second, the author reaffirms his place as one member among many in the body of Christ. On the one hand, he boldly asserts that he speaks as an "honorable" man who has written to them boldly from the strength of a "clear conscience" (13:18). These are the spiritual credentials that validate his authority to call his readers to account for their recent flir-

---

2. In observing how each of these prayer requests appears near the letter's conclusion, it is tempting to ask if a closing request for intercessory prayer was also a convention of ancient letter writing. Closer examination, however, shows that only 1 Thess. 5:25 is actually a part of an epistolary conclusion (see Weima, *Neglected Endings*, 145–46, 175–76, 187, 220). The other requests for prayer, including Heb. 13:18–19, all occur at the end of the letter body, very near the closings, but they are not actually part of a formal conclusion. They are simply an element of collected exhortations gathered together as the letter writer prepares to finish. Prayer could be an ancient feature of letter closings, as they were of introductions, in that a health wish ("I pray you are well") is not uncommon at either point in Hellenistic letters (White, *Form and Function*, 8–9, 43; Weima, *Neglected Endings*, 34–35). There are, however, no known instances of requests for intercession in Hellenistic letter closings. From this perspective, the New Testament evidence is quite conventional. Yet, White also notes that letter closings often requested a favor from the recipient, "do such-and-such for me, for by doing this you grant me a favor" (*Form and Function*, 47–49). Could this Hellenistic closing convention have migrated to the collected exhortations gathered near the end of these New Testament letters? If this were the case, it might indicate that intercessory prayer was understood as the chief favor that one believer could perform for another.

3. Ellingworth, *Hebrews*, 724.

4. Lane, *Hebrews*, 2.556.

tations with apostasy (2:1–4; 3:7–4:13; 5:11–6:12; 10:19–39; 12:4–28). On the other hand, the author also admits that he stands in need of their prayers. The intercessions of potential apostates will assist him in remaining honorable and blameless! At the heart of this remarkable request is a twofold recognition that (1) even the weakest can pray effectively and (2) even the strongest require such support. There is a double-edged sword encountered in every experience of God's grace, which cuts away equally at the timidity of the feeble and the hubris of the strong. No child is ever so distant that the Father can no longer hear her prayers. Neither is any child so close that he can afford to release the Father's hand. The author of Hebrews graciously reminds his audience that he stands in need of their prayers just as much as they require his instruction. Once again, intercessory prayer transcends every personal, spiritual, and geographical boundary to unite the Christian community in mutual interdependence.

Third, the author believes that prayer can influence the course of future events: "I particularly urge you to pray so that I may be restored to you soon" (13:19). The verb "be restored" is another example of the divine passive indicating God's action, particularly when connected to a request for prayer.[5] More specifically, it is God's action in response to a particular petition. The writer is convinced that he may be returned to the community more quickly if they pray for his return than he would be if they failed to pray.[6] As we have seen elsewhere, the intercessions of fellow Christians can make a substantial difference, not just to one's own life, but also to the lives of others.

Revisiting the Model of Jesus

With the possible exception of Mark 14:32–42 (Jesus in Gethsemane), no New Testament passage confronts its reader with as dense a constellation of christological conundrums as this description of the earthly Jesus: "During the days of Jesus' life on earth, he offered up prayers and petitions with loud cries and tears to the one who could save him from death, and he was heard because of his reverent submission. Although he was a son, he learned obedience from what he suffered" (Heb. 5:7–8). We recognize ourselves in this man of painful prayer, even while real-

5. Ellingworth, *Hebrews*, 727.
6. Lane, *Hebrews*, 2.558. Commentators lean toward reading the *hina* clause in 13:19 as introducing the content rather than the purpose of the prayer. In either case, however, the meaning of 13:19 is not greatly affected; see Bauer, Arndt, Gingrich, and Danker, *Greek-English Lexicon of the New Testament*, 476 §2.a.γ; Attridge, *Hebrews*, 403; and Ellingworth, *Hebrews*, 727.

izing that we are actually not much like him at all. He is simultaneously familiar and utterly strange, accessible yet impenetrable, like us while remaining completely foreign. Little wonder, then, that "commentators have exhausted their ingenuity"[7] attempting to unravel the several Gordian knots that tie these sentences together. Fortunately, for the purposes of our study, it is not necessary to solve every puzzle in this passage. Simply bringing some measure of clarity to three issues will be sufficient: (1) Can we determine the content of Jesus's prayers? (2) What was the substance of the Father's response? (3) What role did Jesus's urgency, reverence, and sonship play in this exchange?

Jesus's Prayers

To begin with, the reference to "prayers and petitions" in Heb. 5:7—more accurately, "petitions" (*deēseis*) and "entreaties" (*hiketērias*)—makes it clear that the writer is concerned with Jesus's petitionary prayers, not prayers of confession, thanksgiving, or praise. Though the references to loud cries, tears, and deliverance from death lead many commentators to explain Heb. 5:7 as a detailed description of Jesus's nocturnal prayer vigil in Gethsemane, I agree with those who hesitate to limit this description to Gethsemane alone. No doubt, the Gethsemane tradition colored the author's choice of words, but there is nothing in the passage that requires its restriction to that single event. In fact, the opening clause, "during his earthly life" (lit., "during the days of his flesh"), points to a lifetime of prayer that periodically entailed loud cries and tears.

But herein also lies the apparent problem with this interpretation: are we to conclude that Jesus's entire prayer life consisted of nothing but suffering and turmoil? The answer to this question reveals itself in the context of Heb. 5; the author is describing our great high priest's identification with all humanity, including human suffering. In 5:7–8 he chooses to focus on the specific way in which human suffering found particular expression in Jesus's prayer life. In choosing to emphasize suffering through prayer, Heb. 5 is not, however, saying that the entirety of Jesus's prayer life was preoccupied with suffering, any more than a passage like Mark 14 is suggesting that the necessity of suffering never entered Jesus's thoughts before Gethsemane. It is dangerous to extrapolate too broadly from any one text. Surely Jesus understood the necessity of suffering and death long before he embarked on that fateful journey to Jerusalem (Mark 8:31–32). Who knows what transpired between the Father and his Son during the solitary moments of prayer that marked his path of unfolding ministry (1:35)? At the very least, Jesus's prayers

7. Purdy, "Hebrews," 644.

from the cross can safely be included in any accounting of petitions offered with loud cries and tears (Mark 15:34; Luke 23:46).[8]

Realizing that Jesus addressed his petitions, throughout a significant period of life wherein he grappled with impending mortality, "to the one who could save him from death" offers the greatest insight into their content. Some commentators insist that this turn of phrase is simply a circumlocution for God (as the one with power over life and death) with no bearing on the content of Jesus's prayers.[9] I find this difficult to accept. Could any author be so blind to the latent implication waiting to emerge from the juxtaposition of this phrase and its surrounding context, pregnant as that context is with the angst of human mortality? I seriously doubt it. Granted, this conclusion is only implicit; the broad contours of Jesus's prayers are implied, but the specific details of those petitions are nowhere described. Consequently, we may not be told exactly what Jesus was asking, but it is safe to conclude that throughout some period of his life Jesus strenuously engaged the Father in prayer concerning the necessity of his death.[10] Although this conclusion returns us to Gethsemane's neighborhood, the journey back reveals that Gethsemane was only one of several lonely corners where Jesus wrestled his way through the valley of the shadow of death.

How Did the Father Answer?

Knowing the end of Jesus's story raises a second important question. Since Jesus did eventually die, in what sense did the Father hear his prayers about deliverance from death? Perhaps an answer lies in the crucial line of the Gethsemane prayer—"not my will, but yours, be done"—being absent from the Hebrews passage. Or is it? The answer to this question lies in knowing that Heb. 5:7–8 does not offer explicit evidence of Jesus's specific petition.

Some commentators insist that the clause "the one who could save him from death" not only describes God but does, indeed, convey the exact content of Jesus's petitions. But, even if this were the case, it still does not necessarily answer our question, for several ambiguities remain. First, what exactly does it mean to be saved from death? Does "salvation" denote physical rescue or spiritual deliverance? The word

8. Though I am not persuaded by his argument, Swetnam argues that Heb. 5:7–8 is dependent on Ps. 22:24, giving it a closer association with Jesus's prayer from the cross (Mark 15:34 quoting Ps. 22:1) than the prayer of Gethsemane; see "Crux at Hebrews 5,7–8."

9. Lane, *Hebrews*, 1.120.

10. Westcott, *Hebrews*, 126; Omark, "Saving of the Savior," 41–43; Attridge, *Hebrews*, 150; and Ellingworth, *Hebrews*, 288.

sōzein is perfectly capable of meaning either. Furthermore, does salvation from death entail physical protection from dying ("prevent me from being killed"), or does it ask to be brought out of death into life again ("rescue me by resurrection")? All of these possibilities have their advocates.[11] If Jesus asked to be spared physical death, then we must presume additional prayers similar to the one in Gethsemane involving the Father's redirection of the Son's anxieties and the Son's eventual admission, "Nevertheless, not my will, but yours." On the other hand, if Jesus asked to be delivered out of death into new life, then we are offered a glimpse of his hope for vindication beyond the cross when the Father responds affirmatively in the resurrection, ascension, and exaltation to his right hand.[12] Frankly, I do not believe that Heb. 5:7–8 provides enough evidence to settle this dispute one way or the other. The author supplies evocative implications of Jesus's general concerns—the necessity of his death and its outcome—but nothing more specific. In any event, it is apparent that whatever the particular private interaction between Jesus and the Father, Jesus derived encouragement to persevere through his prayers. The mere process of communing with God, in and of itself, filled the Son with sufficient strength to live each day by faith.

The Significance of Turmoil, Reverence, and Sonship

Jesus prayed with loud cries and tears, not because the Father is more sympathetic to urgency, fervor, repetition, or volume, but because he was praying about something that caused him pain. The man from Nazareth found himself inhabiting the same eschatological tension that stretches the entire human race to the point of tears (Rom. 8:22–25). Jesus's perfect identification with humanity is at the heart of the distinctive Christology of Hebrews. It was necessary that Christ, our high priest, become like us in every way (2:14, 17–18), because every priest must come from among those he represents (4:14–5:3). According to Hebrews, this was the central purpose behind Jesus's death; it was his final step of conformation. All human beings die; therefore, to truly be one of us Jesus also had to die (9:27–28). His complete conformation to humanity, a humanity that suffers, bleeds, weeps, and expires, required Jesus's "perfection through suffering" (2:10; 5:8; 7:28; 12:2), a suffering

11. Consult the discussions in any of the major commentaries; see Westcott, *Hebrews*, 126–27; Omark, "Saving of the Savior," 41–43; Attridge, *Hebrews*, 150; Lane, *Hebrews*, 1.120; and Ellingworth, *Hebrews*, 288.

12. If this interpretation were correct, it would connect nicely with Heb. 12:2: "Let us fix our eyes on Jesus, the author and perfecter of our faith, who for the joy set before him endured the cross, scorning its shame, and sat down at the right hand of the throne of God."

that could only be experienced by his complete, obedient surrender to the plan of God; in this way "he learned obedience from what he suffered and . . . [became] perfect" (5:8–9).

Why did Jesus pray with loud cries and tears? Because he was just like us. Who among us has never turned to God in a last-ditch, desperate attempt to salvage some semblance of hope from the bitter wreckage looming on life's horizon? We throw ourselves before the Father as our final refuge, and we plead for rescue, not because we really believe that he measures each tear and waits for our grief to tip his scales of mercy, but because life's disasters leave us nowhere else to turn. Weeping before God is the only thing left to do. To not cry out is to be not human. The depth of Jesus's prayerful agonizing was the final measure of his perfect humanity.

Now we are in a better position to understand what it means for Jesus's prayers to be heard because of his "reverence." First, there is no need to assume that "being heard" means that Jesus's requests immediately received an affirmative response.[13] While the psalmists regularly implored the Lord to "hear my prayers," that such pleas predominantly occur in the lament psalms demonstrates that the connection between God's hearing and God's responding is often lengthy and convoluted (Pss. 4:1–3; 5:3; 10:1, 17; 17:1, 6, to list only a few). Jesus is assured, however, of genuine communication with the Father because of his piety and devotion, a reverence that consisted in making the Father's will first and foremost in his life. Elsewhere in Hebrews the word *eulabeia* (or its cognate) denotes an attitude akin to the Old Testament "fear of the Lord" (11:7; 12:28)—true reverence consists in authentic acts of willing obedience. Thus, Jesus could confidently approach the Father in prayer because complete obedience to his Father's plan was his only goal in life (10:5–10).

Even this Son had to experience for himself the ways in which petitionary prayer always remains subject to the will of God. This is the significance of the curious turn of phrase introducing 5:8: "*Although* he was a son, he learned obedience from what he suffered." The author has just finished saying (5:7) that Jesus came to the Father as one who was *already* obedient (also 10:5–10). If he was already obedient when he began to pray, in what sense did he learn obedience afterward? And what was the significance of Jesus's learning obedience "although" he was a Son, especially since every Son can anticipate his Father's discipline (12:4–11)?

Once again, answers emerge from the context. Jesus was not just any Son. He is the Son who serves as final prophet (1:2), the "radiance of God's glory and the exact representation of his being, sustaining all things by his powerful word," who is now enthroned at God's right hand (1:3). He is the

---

13. Attridge, *Hebrews*, 150.

Son who serves from heaven as our one and only Priest-King (1:5, 8; 3:6; 4:14; 5:5; 7:3, 28; 11:17). Hebrews 5:8 must be read against this background; the conjunction "although" highlights that *not even this Son* could avoid the necessary rigors of human existence. Being the eternal Son of God did not exempt Jesus from enduring life's lesson plan for suffering. But what did he have left to learn, since he had already entered the world in perfect obedience?—the full measure of sustained obedience to the bitter end.

Even the best of intentions frequently run aground on the shoals of execution. Commitment fades. Resolve melts away, leaving only the frail skeleton of human vacillation. It was incumbent upon Jesus to ensure that his obedience to God's plan achieved its complete fruition by his obedience to death. He had to persevere through the actual experience of torment on the cross before his submission was complete.[14] Thus 5:8 is saying that "although he was God's own Son, he still had to accomplish absolute obedience by experiencing the full measure of suffering."

The significance of Jesus's turmoil, reverence, and sonship is revealed at these two junctures. First, Jesus's prayer life became the proving ground for both the success of his mission and (consequently) the origin of the Christology of Hebrews. In "being made like us in every way" Jesus entered this world dependent on the same means and criteria of meaningful conversation with the Father as any other human being. He had to learn how to pray, which meant learning to listen, to ask appropriately, to stand corrected, to hear the Father's no as well as his yes. He had to learn how to experience the simple sustaining power of God's loving presence quite apart from any adjudication of answered versus unanswered prayer.

Second, Jesus's prayer life becomes the perfect model for our own communion with God. Prayer is where we too eventually confront our deepest fears, sometimes with loud cries and tears all our own. Prayer is where we learn reverence, for we will quickly discover that self-assertion turns prayer into a monologue with oneself, whereas genuine conversation with the Father presupposes reverent submission. Ultimately, prayer becomes the private preserve of intimacy with our heavenly Father, where we too find ourselves sustained by God's presence regardless of the rocks and chuckholes in the road ahead.

Prayer and Community Relationships

Thus far the only major qualification to the potency of petitionary prayer is conformity to the will of God. The importance of prayers of-

14. For helpful insights along this line, see Attridge, *Hebrews*, 153; Lane, *Hebrews*, 1.121; and Swetnam, "Crux at Hebrews 5,7–8," 352.

fered in obedience appears at every level of the New Testament material, often held in tension with a simultaneous challenge to risk asking for miracles. Jesus elaborates a particularly crucial dimension of God's will for every disciple by highlighting the centrality of forgiveness, indicating that vengefulness and grudge-bearing will always stymie prayer's effectiveness. Both 1 Peter and James make pointed contributions to these warnings. Since it is always the Father's will for his people to live in harmony, broken relationships, whether at home or in the broader community of faith, undermine petition's effectiveness.

First Peter applies this lesson specifically to the nuclear family, focusing on the importance of loving, servant relationships between husbands and wives:

> Husbands, in the same way be considerate as you live with your wives, and treat them with respect as the weaker partner and as heirs with you of the gracious gift of life, so that nothing will hinder your prayers. . . .
>
> > For the eyes of the Lord are on the righteous
> >   and his ears are attentive to their prayer,
> > but the face of the Lord is against those who do evil. (1 Pet. 3:7, 12)

The lesson is clear: men who mistreat their wives lose the ability to communicate freely with God.[15] The purpose clause concluding 3:7 specifies that prayers are specifically "cut off" or "blocked" by God (compare Rom. 15:22; Gal. 5:7; 1 Thess. 2:18) when a husband does not treat his wife honorably as a fellow heir in Christ.[16] Such respect is one characteristic of "the righteous," whose prayers always catch the Lord's attention (1 Pet. 3:12). To be righteous is to do God's will (2:24; 3:14), but mistreating a spouse is the type of disobedience that places a person among "those who do evil" against whom the Lord sets his face. And even though the text, written as it was within a patriarchal society, places the burden of this responsibility on the husband, the believing wife must surely share in these expectations if her prayers are also to ascend freely before God (Eph. 5:21–28).[17]

The New Testament insists on the interconnection of all personal relationships, whether between ourselves and God or between one another: "If anyone says, 'I love God,' yet hates his brother, he is a liar. For anyone who does not love his brother, whom he has seen, cannot love God, whom he has not seen" (1 John 4:20). If prayer is the touchstone of

15. Achtemeier, *1 Peter*, 218.

16. The verb *enkoptesthai* is a divine passive indicating that God himself makes it a point not to receive the petitions of such men.

17. Bigg, *St. Peter and St. Jude*, 155–56; Reicke, *James, Peter, and Jude*, 103; and Michaels, *1 Peter*, 170.

intimacy with God, and God views our attitude toward others as a measure of our true disposition toward him, then prayer becomes supremely sensitive to the disintegration of personal relationships (see, e.g., Mark 11:25; Matt. 5:21–26; 6:12, 14–15; 18:21–35; 1 Tim. 2:8).[18] How much more sensitive must prayer be to the integrity of a godly marriage, where a man and a woman pledge themselves to mutual devotion modeled on the sacrificial love of Christ?

Several passages in the letter of James express similar convictions about the efficacy of prayer and the centrality of loving relationships within the broader family of God. James 4:2–3 is especially blunt about the role of motivation. Wrongly motivated prayers go astray every time: "You do not have, because you do not ask God. When you ask, you do not receive, because you ask with wrong motives, that you may spend what you get on your pleasures."

James begins his letter with a clear affirmation of the type of petition always granted by God: "If any of you lacks wisdom, he should ask God, who gives generously to all without finding fault, and it will be given to him" (1:5). Prayers for wisdom rooted in the desire to navigate life's challenges in ways that honor God and produce righteous results will always elicit heaven's positive response. Little wonder, then, that the antithetical attitudes described in James 4 leave God mute. Initially, the readers are assured that some gifts are never received simply because we never ask (4:2). Apparently, God does certain things only on request; prayer is a necessary condition for the reception of these gifts. Even though James never indicates what these particular gifts may be, it is clearly possible to miss out—perhaps even on wisdom itself (3:13–18)—by refusing to exercise enough faith to ask.

The larger context of James 4:2–3 reaffirms the dissolution of community relationships as another major hindrance to prayer. Praying for the satisfaction of personal pleasures (4:3) is set within the larger context of covetousness and intramural competition motivated by selfish one-upmanship (4:1–2).[19] Far from arousing God's sympathies, such self-centered prayers are actually evidence of apostasy—the final status of "adulterous people" who demonstrate their "hatred toward God" by preferring "friend[ship with] . . . the world" (4:4). James pronounces a harsh verdict on such prayer, but it is also fair warning for those who find their petitions dictated more by furtive glances at others than by concentrated meditation on God. Appropriate requests are never a means of keeping up with the Joneses, much less beating out the Smiths. Regardless of how effective we are in deceiving ourselves, the Father is

18. J. Elliott, *1 Peter*, 582.
19. Laws, *James*, 173.

never tricked by pretense or feigned devotion. Sometimes we miss out on God's gifts because we do not have the faith to ask, but at other times our prayer life remains barren because we lack the wisdom to discriminate between selfish and godly motivations. Any petition rooted in the urgency of personal advancement or outperforming another will never be affirmed by the Father.

The final passage dealing with prayer and community relationships is James 5:13–18, another thorny text that can raise more questions than it answers. But, once again, we need to focus on only a discreet set of issues to answer the questions most important to this study:

> Is any one of you in trouble? He should pray. Is anyone happy? Let him sing songs of praise. Is any one of you sick? He should call the elders of the church to pray over him and anoint him with oil in the name of the Lord. And the prayer offered in faith will make the sick person well; the Lord will raise him up. If he has sinned, he will be forgiven. Therefore confess your sins to each other and pray for each other so that you may be healed. The prayer of a righteous man is powerful and effective.
>
> Elijah was a man just like us. He prayed earnestly that it would not rain, and it did not rain on the land for three and a half years. Again he prayed, and the heavens gave rain, and the earth produced its crops.

James approaches the conclusion of his letter with a final exhortation to community prayer. The corporate dimension of his instruction is a crucial, but sometimes overlooked, aspect of the passage, significantly influencing how we understand both the elders' role as intercessors and the sick person's responsibility to confess. James describes a corporate event where the leaders of a newly evolved spiritual family gather together for the restoration of an ailing family member.[20] He has already alluded to numerous instances of competitiveness, disruption, hostility, and alienation among God's people, all requiring repentance and confession for the healing of their broken relationships (1:9–11, 26–27; 2:1–7, 14–17; 3:1–2, 9–18; 4:1–3, 11, 16; 5:1–6). For the leaders now to be called upon to pray for another's restoration, while hearing his or her confession of sin, indicates that the problem was not a private transgression against personal conscience but a public infraction of community cohesion. James was not referring to sickness in general but to the illness that may result from the mistreatment of a brother or sister; neither was he imagining an anonymous confession in a private sick room, but a face-to-face gathering of key

---

20. Karris, "Some New Angles," 211.

members from the worshiping body.[21] This context helps to clarify several important issues.

First, even though James does not assert that sickness is necessarily the result of sin, he does allow for the possibility (compare Deut. 28:21–22, 27–28; Job 33:19–28; Ps. 38:1–8; John 5:14; 9:2; 1 Cor. 11:30).[22] The preponderance of warnings against community offenses throughout the book, combined with the injunction to collective confession and prayer (James 5:16), strongly suggests that James is affording another insight into the reciprocity between broken relationships and (in)effective prayer. Consequently, efficacious petition presupposes the elimination of sin through public confession and reconciliation, should that prove necessary.

Second, the nature of both the illness and its healing are as ambivalent as is the relationship between sin and sickness. A great deal of honest debate surrounds the correct definition of virtually every key term in this passage: "sick" (*asthenein*; 5:14), "make whole/cure" (*sōzein*; 5:15), "weary/ill" (*kamnein*; 5:15), "raise up" (*egeirein*; 5:15), and "heal" (*iaosthai*; 5:16). Is James describing a literal bodily illness requiring physical healing? Or is he dealing metaphorically with spiritual impairment (weakness, exhaustion, discouragement, depression) necessitating a spiritual solution? Modern consensus suggests that the debate continues because James was deliberately ambiguous. With the possible exception of *iaosthai*, every pivotal word is comfortably bivalent, meaning that it may just as easily refer to one situation as to the other.[23] As J. John notes, "There is a quite remarkable and thoroughgoing ambiguity" in James's promise of healing; "the vocabulary is so strikingly and systematically ambiguous" that one is hard-pressed to explain it in any other way than as the author's deliberate intention.[24] God is able to supply whatever he decides is most essential. He can raise up the sick person, either

21. Omanson, "Certainty of Judgement," 434; R. Martin, *James*, 211; and L. Johnson, *James*, 332–33.

22. The crucial phrase in James 5:15b, *kan* plus the subjunctive, is a future conditional clause that leaves open the final verdict on the sin-sickness relationship; compare Reicke, *James, Peter, and Jude*, 60; Mitton, *James*, 201; Laws, *James*, 229; Omanson, "Certainty of Judgement," 433; R. Martin, *James*, 210–12; and Johnston, "Does James Give Believers?" 174.

23. So Mitton, *James*, 200; R. Martin, *James*, 201, 209–10; Johnston, "Does James Give Believers?" 172–74; L. Johnson, *James*, 333; and Karris, "Some New Angles," 216–17. For continued protests in favor of literalness, see Omanson, "Certainty of Judgement," 433–34; and Thomas, "Devil, Disease, and Deliverance," 30–31, 46. The verb *sōzein* regularly denotes the eschatological salvation of believers, suggesting that James may be referring to deliverance from spiritual death. *Asthenein* can also refer to spiritual weakness (Rom. 14:2; 1 Cor. 8:11–12), as may *kamnein* (Heb. 12:3). Hayden, "Calling the Elders to Pray," is the most thoroughgoing advocate of a completely metaphorical interpretation.

24. J. John, "Anointing in the New Testament," 58–59.

physically now by healing, spiritually now by an infusion of the Spirit's resources, or supernaturally in the future by resurrection. The choice is his, and not only are all options equally feasible as equally faithful answers to the same prayer, but all are equally acceptable to a faithful community—which brings us to the next series of observations.

Third, James describes a very specific type of community prayer in this passage; it is a prayer offered in "faith" (5:15) by "the righteous" (5:16) who ask "in the name of the Lord" (5:14). Each of these three qualifications points the reader in the same direction. James has already defined "asking in faith" as the antithesis of doubt or double-mindedness (1:6–8; 4:8). Doubt is not a weakness in faith but the attempt to maintain faith in two different things at once—hence, to be double-minded. The person who prays for God's wisdom doubtfully is holding on to a backup plan antithetical to the wisdom of the one true God. So, if the Christian God does not seem ready to answer, the person praying may secretly anticipate, for instance, consulting with one of the local Greek oracles, the nearest mendicant or Jewish healer, or offering sacrifice at a local shrine. James is not suggesting that faith can be quantified; it is not that some have strong faith (and see their prayers answered) while others have weak faith (and see their prayers ignored). Rather, the alternative is faith versus double-mindedness, not great faith versus little faith. Doubt undermines prayer because it is unwilling to place *all* of life's eggs in Christ's basket. Praying with faith (5:15), on the other hand, accepts God's answers whatever they may be, without recourse to contrary spiritual alternatives.[25] God concentrates on the behavior under our control, not on the emotions frequently beyond our control. Great faith can easily coexist with fearfulness, second thoughts, anxiety, and apprehension, because what matters at the end of the day is how we actually respond to life's circumstances. The faithful stand or fall, are physically healed or spiritually renewed, whether now or later, as anticipated or in completely unexpected ways, through sustained trust in Christ alone.

---

25. Karris, "Some New Angles," 209–10, constructs the fascinating argument that James is arguing against the use of physicians. In this case, double-mindedness consists in asking God for healing while also calling a doctor (see Sir. 38:9–12). He provides an interesting parallel from Philo (*On the Sacrifices of Abel and Cain* 69–70): "This is the case with almost all the Facing-both-ways. . . . When anything befalls them which they would not, since they have never had any firm faith in God their Saviour, they first flee to the help which things created give, to physicians, herbs, drug-mixtures, strict rules of diet, and all the other aids that mortals use" (translation by F. H. Colson and G. H. Whitaker in Loeb Classical Library). Before concluding that James would frown on the use of modern medicine, however, we must recall the close association between medicine and magic in the ancient world.

James also consistently defines righteousness as a quality of genuine faith (1:20; 2:21, 23–25; 3:18; 5:6). Righteousness is the obedience that always attends true belief. It is not a matter of moral perfection but of willing surrender to the ways of God. The double-minded can never be righteous because they are unwilling to entrust themselves completely to the Father's direction. This is what makes the prayers of the righteous powerful and effective (James 5:16; compare 1 Pet. 3:12; also Pss. 1:5–6; 7:9; 32:1; 34:15–16; 37:39; 146:8)—they are solely concerned with being woven properly into the unfolding tapestry of God's design. The righteous pray for miracles, but they do not begrudge God the mundane. Their submission is always unconditional.

Finally, it is not the least bit surprising to read that such prayers are coordinated with anointing "in the name of the Lord" (James 5:14). Since healing is the result of prayer, not anointing, there is no need for us to settle the debate surrounding this use of olive oil.[26] Rather, prayerful action in the name of the Lord serves as a signpost to the pivotal role of submission in prayer. The meaning of the phrase "in the name of" was examined in chapter 8, and there is no reason to suppose that its meaning in James differs from its use in the Gospel of John. To do anything "in the name of the Lord" is to act as the Lord's appointed representative, employing his power to effect his purposes in complete conformity to his direction.[27] In effect, to pray in the Lord's name is to ask that his will is accomplished, precisely the disposition adopted by the righteous praying with faith.

Now we are set to grapple with the unusual way that James employs Elijah as a model of ideal prayer (5:17–18). Several questions present themselves in these verses. First, James curiously refers to a nature miracle rather than a healing story to illustrate his message about the power of healing prayer. Why did James not build his case around the story of Elijah's healing the widow's son at Zarephath (1 Kings 17:17–23), a story more serviceable to the lessons of James 5:13–16?

Second, even though Elijah eventually became a legendary man of prayer in Jewish tradition (Sir. 48:1–11; 2 Esdras [= 4 Ezra] 7:109; *Lives of the Prophets* 21.4–5), prayer has no role to play in the story of Israel's drought during the reign of King Ahab (1 Kings 17–18). Elijah did not pray for the drought, neither was it terminated in answer to anyone's petitions. God simply confided to the prophet what he intended to do: withhold rain from disobedient Israel. Any praying that

26. For extensive discussions of the numerous possibilities, see Omanson, "Certainty of Judgement," 433; R. Martin, *James*, 207–9; Shogren, "Will God Heal Us?"; J. John, "Anointing in the New Testament"; and Karris, "Some New Angles," 211–14.

27. Davids, *James*, 193; and R. Martin, *James*, 208.

Elijah might have done occurred after God's plans had already been revealed.[28] The one place where Elijah's petitionary prayer is crucial to the story is most notable by its absence: his raising of the widow's son. Why is this?

Once again, the background of this Old Testament material provides help. God had consistently stipulated that his blessings to Israel were conditioned on the people's obedience to the Sinai covenant (Exod. 19:5; Deut. 28:15–68). If the nation rebelled and broke the covenant, then the Lord's just punishment included withholding the seasonal rains and afflicting his people with disease (Deut. 11:13–17; 1 Kings 8:35–36; Jer. 14:1–15:4). Israel suffered through drought in 1 Kings 17–18 as punishment for its apostasy under King Ahab. The ostensible community of faith had become a community rife with sin and plagued by civil war, idolatry, and injustice—the very issues also confronting James's audience. He repeatedly warned them against the inevitable community breakdown that issues from entrenched social barriers, competitiveness, jealousy, and disobedience—all of which characterize apostasy, whether in Israel or the church. The letter's final sentence distills both the danger and the remedy to such communal disintegration, serving as a fitting conclusion to this section: "Brothers, if one of you should wander from the truth and someone should bring him back, remember this: Whoever turns a sinner from the error of his way will save him from death and cover over a multitude of sins" (5:19–20).

By introducing the extrabiblical ingredient of Elijah's prayers in connection with Israel's punishment for apostasy, James provides a final warning to his readers not to follow Israel's example. They, too, are in danger of becoming a fractured, sinful community, suffering with illness, no longer able to pray. James's point is not that fervent petition will heal disease, for if that had been his intent, he surely dropped the ball by ignoring the one time that Elijah's prayers actually healed someone. What James accomplished, however, is more subtle and universally applicable. The willful destruction of community life removes God's blessing from his people, opens the door to various forms of suffering, and impedes the church's ability to pray. Elijah, "a man just like us" (5:17), once confronted a similarly dire situation. Yet, by obeying the Father's directions, he prayed as he was instructed and labored for the community's healing and restoration. By reminding his own community about Elijah's story,

28. Later tradition focused on Elijah's "stand[ing]" before the Lord (1 Kings 17:1 AV) and "ben[ding] down to the ground and put[ting] his face between his knees" (18:42) as intimations of petitionary prayer moving God. Perhaps, but there are more self-evident ways for James to make this point if, indeed, that was his purpose in referring to Elijah.

James underscored God's unchanging call to obedience, repentance, confession, and prayerful reconciliation in the body of Christ.[29]

Prayer in Light of the Final Judgment

Chapter 12 surveyed the numerous places where Paul prays for his churches to remain blameless until the final judgment. First Peter 4:7 affords a variation on that concern by describing the personal disposition necessary to sustain effective prayer while awaiting the parousia: "The end of all things is near. Therefore be clear minded [*sōphronēsate*] and self-controlled [*nēpsate*] so that you can pray." Moral clarity assists prayer's effectiveness just as godly domestic relationships empower petition in 3:7.[30]

Both Jesus and Paul similarly emphasized the centrality of prayer to righteous perseverance (Mark 14:38; Luke 18:1–8; 21:36; 22:39–46; Eph. 6:18; Phil. 4:6–7; Col. 4:2). Moreover, Paul's intercessory prayers demonstrate that traits such as wisdom, knowledge, and insight provide the discernment essential to spiritual longevity (Phil. 1:9–10; Col. 1:9), especially when confronting the temptations of this evil age (Eph. 6:18). First Peter 5:8 underscores the same concern by offering a similar warning: "Be self-controlled [*nēpsate*] and alert. Your enemy the devil prowls around like a roaring lion looking for someone to devour." Clearheadedness and self-control must characterize any and every disciple hoping to withstand temptation and evade spiritual defeat. On this score the New Testament speaks with one voice; all believers are vulnerable to supernatural, immoral assault best negotiated prayerfully by those who keep their minds spiritually alert, focused on the things of God.[31]

A brief survey of 1 Peter's vocabulary demonstrates that both of the key words in 4:7, *clear-mindedness* and *self-control*, are consistently used throughout the New Testament to describe (1) the maintenance of personal holiness (*sōphronein* and related words in Rom. 12:3; 2 Cor. 5:13; 2 Tim. 1:7; *nēphein* and related words in 1 Thess. 5:8; 1 Tim. 3:2, 11; Titus 2:2; 1 Pet. 1:13; 5:8) while (2) persevering to the final judgment (*sōphronein* and related words in Titus 2:12; 1 Pet. 4:7; *nēphein* in 1 Thess. 5:6; 2 Tim. 4:5; 1 Pet. 4:7). Paul and Peter also speak with one

29. I am indebted to Johnston's "Does James Give Believers?" for prompting me to pursue this line of thinking. Karris, "Some New Angles," 215–16, credits a similar argument to Bottini, *La preghiera di Elia*. See also Warrington, "Significance of Elijah."

30. J. Elliott, *1 Peter*, 749.

31. Even though it lacks this eschatological dimension, 2 Cor. 2:5–11 is another example of Paul's conviction that withholding forgiveness (e.g., unconfessed sin within the family of God) creates an opening for satanic disruption of the community.

voice, at least on this: clear-mindedness and self-control are essential to successful discipleship in these last days because they enable God's children to discern when, where, and how to pray for the right things, in the right way, at the right time, making their petitions effective and their discipleship secure.[32]

Wisdom is first acquired by prayer and then serves to direct those same prayers more effectively. Personal petition and spiritual maturity coexist in an ongoing reciprocal relationship, each complementing and sustaining the other like two dancers gliding harmoniously across life's dance floor. First, we pray to gain wisdom and grow; then our wisdom and growth (re)direct our prayers. Petition steps forward into deeper spiritual insight. Spiritual insight reciprocates by moving petition closer to the selfless embrace of God's glory. Eventually, whether in this life or the next, the twin forces of petition and spiritual alertness become inseparably intertwined in the living experience of a saint (like Peter) whose lone remaining request is to see that "in all things God may be praised through Jesus Christ. To him be the glory and the power for ever and ever. Amen" (1 Pet. 4:11).

The final group of eschatological prayer texts comes from the Apocalypse. Thus far all the New Testament instruction about the role of prayer in perseverance has come from the temporal side of the eschatological divide. Now three passages from the book of Revelation depict the heavenly side of the tension, offering a glimpse of how petitionary prayer is received by God:

> And when he had taken [the scroll], the four living creatures and the twenty-four elders fell down before the Lamb. Each one had a harp and they were holding golden bowls full of incense, which are the prayers of the saints. (5:8)

> When he opened the fifth seal, I saw under the altar the souls of those who had been slain because of the word of God and the testimony they had maintained. They called out in a loud voice, "How long, Sovereign Lord, holy and true, until you judge the inhabitants of the earth and avenge our blood?" Then each of them was given a white robe, and they were told to wait a little longer, until the number of their fellow servants and brothers who were to be killed as they had been was completed. (6:9–11)

> Another angel, who had a golden censer, came and stood at the altar. He was given much incense to offer, with the prayers of all the saints, on the golden altar before the throne. The smoke of the incense, together with the

---

32. *Eis proseuchas* (1 Pet. 4:7) is a purpose clause: "in order that you will be able to properly attend to prayers."

prayers of the saints, went up before God from the angel's hand. Then the angel took the censer, filled it with fire from the altar, and hurled it on the earth; and there came peals of thunder, rumblings, flashes of lightning and an earthquake. (8:3–5)

Commentators generally agree that these three passages revisit the same heavenly scene, each providing a subsequent snapshot of God's response to the same set of prayers from the saints.[33] All three scenarios refer to a similar assortment of temple paraphernalia—golden furnishings (5:8; 8:3), incense bowls (5:8; 8:3–4), altar (6:9; 8:3–4)—indicating the same setting for each passage. The idea that God's throne is located in an eternal heavenly temple has its roots in the Old Testament (Hab. 2:20; Ps. 18:6; *Testament of Levi* 3.4–6; 5.1; 18.6) and is consistent with the idea of human prayer rising to heaven like incense from the altar (Ps. 141:2; Rev. 5:8; 8:3).[34] This collection of heavenly temple artifacts, together with the continual singing provided by the four living creatures, the twenty-four elders, and the angelic hosts (5:8–14; 7:11–12), portrays the heavenly temple as it conducts cultic service similar to the work that once transpired in the Jerusalem temple (Exod. 30:1–10; 1 Kings 6:20–22; 1 Chron. 6:31–32, 49).[35] John's temple visions, however, not only unveil heavenly worship; more important, they depict God's ongoing preparations for the last judgment. These prayers advance the unfolding plot of divine judgment at successive stages of world history.

The prayers in Rev. 5 are coordinated with the Lamb's acceptance of the scroll bearing seven seals, seals that are broken by the Lamb who has conquered through death (5:6, 9–10, 12–13). This is a crucial association: the first appearances of the saints' prayers are linked with the first appearance of the Lamb who was slain. "The Lamb" is the favorite title throughout the Apocalypse for the resurrected, ascended Jesus, providing an effective way to combine the images of leadership and sacrifice in a single symbol.[36] This is the slaughtered Lamb who is also a Lion (5:5); the suffering Victor who is "worthy to take the scroll / and to open

33. R. Mounce, *Revelation*, 182; Bauckham, *Climax of Prophecy*, 53, 55, 82; Heil, "Fifth Seal," 224–25, 232, 242; Aune, *Revelation*, 494–95, 512–13, 515; Beale, *Revelation*, 357, 455–57; and Osborne, *Revelation*, 259, 345.

34. Though Aune, *Revelation*, 511, notes that "there is never any hint in the OT or in early Jewish literature that a counterpart to conventional sacrificial practice was carried out in the heavenly world. Rev. 8:3–5 and 9:13 are the only passages in Jewish apocalyptic literature known to me in which either the incense offering or the golden altar of incense is mentioned."

35. R. Mounce, *Revelation*, 157, 181; J. Charles, "Apocalyptic Tribute to the Lamb"; and Aune, *Revelation*, 356–57, 405–6, 511.

36. See Aune, *Revelation*, 351–53, 367–73, who provides the biblical background for "Lamb" designating either "ruler" or "sacrifice." The title appears in Rev. 5:6, 8, 12, 13;

its seals, / because [he was] slain" (5:9). The prayers of God's people are received by the Savior-King who achieved victory through death.

The prayers themselves are symbolized by the incense rising from golden bowls carried by twenty-four elders offering worship to the Lamb (4:4; 5:9–10), indicating that the prayers of the saints are a priestly activity contributing to heavenly adoration. Even though there is no consensus on the elders' identity, there is a long-standing tradition, particularly in Jewish apocalyptic literature, of various heavenly figures mediating the prayers of God's people.[37] Since burning incense was a priestly responsibility, the elders are functioning as priestly intermediaries before God's throne.

The opening of the fifth seal in Rev. 6 reveals the content of the prayers from Rev. 5. They are cries for justice from Christian martyrs, "those who had been slain because of the word of God and the testimony they had maintained" (6:9). It is not uncommon for God's oppressed people to cry out impatiently, "How long, O Lord?" and to ask for vindication (Pss. 6:3–4; 13:1–2; 35:17; 74:9–10; 79:5; 80:4; 89:46; 90:13; 94:3; Hab. 1:2). The martyrs of Revelation do the same, and now the petitions of slain believers come before the slain Lamb.[38] The saints of Rev. 5 have metamorphosed into "souls under the altar" because their shed blood has become an acceptable sacrifice on heaven's altar. The imagery of God receiving Christian suffering as an acceptable sacrifice appears elsewhere in the New Testament (2 Cor. 4:11; Phil. 2:17; Col. 1:24; 2 Tim. 4:6), but Revelation offers a particularly graphic elaboration: the martyrs' lifeblood is running down the sides of the altar (compare Lev. 17:11, 14: "the life of a creature is in its blood") and accumulating at God's feet. It is a poignant image of suffering leading to security, for the pathway of bloody execution has brought these men and women to the only place where they can be eternally secure, intimately protected by the Savior for whom they died.[39] Their petitions for justice and vindication against their oppressors are the postmortem equivalent of the widow's pleas for justice in Luke 18:3, so it is not surprising to read God's similar response. In effect, the Lord replies to these martyrs as the judge replies to the widow: "Soon, but not yet." Whereas, Jesus's parable challenges

6:1, 16; 7:9, 10, 14, 17; 12:11; 13:8; 14:1, 4 [twice], 10; 15:3; 17:14 [twice]; 19:7, 9; 21:9, 14, 22, 23, 27; 22:1, 3.

37. See Aune, ibid., 287–92, for a survey of the many possibilities regarding the elders and their role in heaven.

38. Whether there is an intermediate state in which dead martyrs continue to pray is unclear. Perhaps the scene is symbolic, not of prayer continuing after death, but of the perpetual efficacy of prayers offered in life.

39. R. Mounce, *Revelation*, 157–58; Aune, *Revelation*, 404–6; and Beale, *Revelation*, 391, discuss the most likely backgrounds to these conflated images of (1) suffering souls under the altar and (2) protected souls under the throne.

its audience to persevere in the face of apparently unanswered prayer, the souls in Rev. 6 are those who did exactly that and met with death because of their faithfulness (Luke 18:8).[40]

Awarding each soul a white robe (Rev. 6:11) connects this group in Rev. 6 with the unnumbered multitude "from every nation, tribe, people and language, standing before the throne in front of the Lamb" in 7:9–17. Their robes have been "washed . . . white in the blood of the Lamb" (7:14), meaning that their suffering has been a participation in the Lamb's suffering. Yes, Christ's shed blood provides their atonement, but in this context it was, more important, their model for living—and dying (compare 12:11).[41] Consequently, even though their vindication is delayed, God now "spread[s] his tent over them" (7:15), providing eternal solace for his faithful children. Never again will they need to tighten their belts or bolster frayed nerves as they confront new hardships. Their vindication must wait, but their comfort has already begun as "God . . . wipe[s] away every tear from their eyes" (7:17).

The difficulty of God's response to his martyrs' prayers is compounded by the reason for his delay. Their vindication must wait "until the number of their fellow servants and brothers who were to be killed as they had been was completed" (6:11). God will execute justice for all of his martyrs simultaneously, so he waits for their total complement to be fulfilled. Revelation is not alone in this idea. Several Jewish apocalypses, nearly contemporaneous with the book of Revelation, agree that a predetermined number of martyrs must die before God will implement his final judgment: "'How long are we to remain here? And when will the harvest of our reward come?' And the archangel . . . answered and said, 'When the number of those like yourselves is completed; . . . he will not move or arouse them until that measure is fulfilled'" (2 Esdras [= 4 Ezra] 4:35–37 NRSV; see also *1 Enoch* 47; *2 Baruch* 23.4–5). The implications are clear. Suffering is a necessary component of redemptive history. Far from hindering the next stage in God's plan, Christian suffering is essential to history's progress toward the end. In a similar vein, the apostle Paul wrote, "I am happy about my sufferings for you, for by means of my physical sufferings I am helping to complete what still remains of Christ's sufferings on behalf of his body, the church" (Col. 1:24 TEV). God has predetermined a certain measure of suffering to be

40. See R. Charles, *Revelation*, 1.175–76; Aune, *Revelation*, 407, 411; and Osborne, *Revelation*, 286. While commentators observe the parallel between Luke 18 and Rev. 6, it is usually explained in terms of contrast; that is, Luke 18 shows God changing his mind, whereas in Rev. 6 he will not. The problem here is the mistaken interpretation of Jesus's parable; see chapter 4.

41. Aune, *Revelation*, 474–75.

experienced by his people, and he awaits its fulfillment before closing the curtains on history's final act.

Yet, God will not wait forever. The end will come. His people's prayers will be answered. Revelation 8:3–5 revisits the scene of prayers rising like incense into the heavenly temple one last time, only now they are described as the prayers of "all the saints" (8:3). No longer the prayers of martyrs alone, now they are the petitions of all God's people, including the faithful who have persevered and suffered in many ways but were fortunate enough to escape the pain of martyrdom.[42] Death is not the only sacrifice acceptable to God, nor is it the only way for the faithful to suffer.[43] The waiting is finally over for everyone, regardless of individual circumstances.

The vision in Rev. 7, intervening as it does between the prayers of Rev. 6 and Rev. 8, represents (both in structure and narrative) the outcome of God's delay: the full number of martyrs is made complete.[44] The last judgment can begin. Consequently, the censer that previously held the martyrs' prayers is now "filled . . . with fire from the altar and hurled . . . on the earth" (8:5).[45] The censer's dual purpose—first holding the prayers that ascend to heaven, then holding the coals thrown down to earth—highlights the intimate connection between the prayers and God's eventual response. God finally acts, not simply because it is time, but because he is moved by his people's requests. The coals of fire, causing "peals of thunder, rumblings, flashes of lightning and an earthquake" (8:5; compare 11:19; 16:18), symbolize God's final judgment against the wicked, a judgment that comes in response to the church's petitions.[46] This is also why the final prayer passage is connected to the seventh

42. Aune, ibid., 440–48, argues convincingly that the 144,000 (Rev. 7:1–8; 14:1–5) is a subset drawn from the ranks of the "great multitude" (7:9). The 144,000 are not martyrs, but the multitude includes all of God's people, martyrs and nonmartyrs alike. While all of God's people suffer, not all die a martyr's death. Consequently, there is room for an expansion of these prayers from (a) the petitions of martyrs (Rev. 5–6) to (b) the petitions of all God's suffering saints (Rev. 8).

43. Beale, *Revelation*, 455, offers an important pastoral perspective on this issue.

44. Bauckham, *Climax of Prophecy*, 55; and Lambrecht, "Opening of the Seals," 202, 210–11. Even though Bauckham, unlike Aune, understands the 144,000 to be the full complement of martyrs, the distinction between this group and the unnumbered multitude still allows additional martyrs to be added to the final gathering of God's people. In other words, Rev. 7 can function similarly in either interpretation.

45. I suspect that this explains the separation of the incense from the prayers in 8:4. In 5:8 the incense bowls are full of incense, "which are the prayers of the saints." The separation in 8:4, "the smoke of the incense, together with the prayers of the saints," allows the censer's incense to be replaced by fiery coals without suggesting that there can be no more prayer.

46. R. Mounce, *Revelation*, 182; Heil, "Fifth Seal," 230, 232; Lambrecht, "Opening of the Seals," 214; and Aune, *Revelation*, 494–95, 516–18, 545–46.

seal, for with the removal of the last seal, the seven trumpets of judg-ment—eventually leading to the seven bowls of wrath (Rev. 16)—can begin (8:6–9:21; 11:15–19); the scroll is finally opened, and the sequence of events leading to the end of the world begins to unfold. If the prayers associated with the fifth seal teach the church to be patient and to trust in God's timing, then the prayers linked to the seventh seal remind the church never to give up, for their prayers *do* matter to God; they *do* move him; he *will* respond, eventually. The prayers of the church have a bearing on the day of Christ's coming.

The petitionary prayers in John's Apocalypse create the same fun-damental theological tensions encountered repeatedly throughout this study. First, God has sovereignly determined a plan for salvation-history, and he waits for the indeterminate choices of human decision-making to move history toward his final destination. Second, when God does decide to act, it is according to his own purposes, but his actions simultaneously arise in response to the prayers of his people. Finally, the Father's timing always remains his own, but his willingness to act at any given moment remains pliable, always susceptible to the pleas of those he loves.

Summary

The General Letters and Revelation reiterate previously examined aspects of petitionary prayer while also introducing important new per-spectives not found elsewhere.

First, several writers insist that prayer has the potential for mov-ing God to respond in ways determined by our requests. Petitionary prayer can truly be impetratory prayer: Heb. 13:18–19; James 4:2–3; 3 John 2; and Rev. 8:3–5 all variously reflect the belief that asking makes a real (not just an apparent) difference in what happens. God not only acts in history, but at certain points his actions, on whatever scale, large or small, cosmic or individual, are the direct result of someone's prayer request. Once again, there are never any guarantees, nor are there universal cause-and-effect equations that would allow an investigator to reliably retrace all the connecting threads between any event X and all petitions Y. The New Testament never supplies a code-breaker to decipher the many mysteries inherent to human conversation with God. We are, however, given the promises (1) that God always hears and (2) that he acts in direct response often enough that the New Testament writers continually assume that their prayers can shape the future, making it different than it would have been had they not prayed at all. There is reciprocity in the divine-human relationship—give and take, ask and answer, solicit and respond. It works both ways. God has genuinely invited us to become his partners in shaping the future.

Second, as in Paul's letters, intercessory prayer serves to unite the body of Christ across space and time (Heb. 13:18–19; James 5:13–18; 3 John 2). The age, gender, and even the spiritual maturity of those who pray are irrelevant to the efficacy of their petitions when they pray faithfully for brothers and sisters in need. Intercession for the health and well-being of others who live to serve the Father will always find ready access to the throne.

Third, prayer in and of itself can supply whatever resources we need to persevere, even when the heavens seem shut against us and our petitions apparently fall lifeless to the ground (Heb. 5:7–8; James 4:2–3; 1 Pet. 4:7; Rev. 5:8; 6:9–11; 8:3–5). Whether those resources entail wisdom, comfort, clear-mindedness, deliverance from guilt, personal assurance, renewed community, or a deepened awareness of the Father's love, every believer is given the opportunity to share in Jesus's own experience of reaching out to the Father in a moment of desperation and receiving the strength necessary to faithfully stay the course. Although these authors are never as explicit as Paul in promising that prayer alone (quite apart from any particular answer or response) can produce "a divine peace transcending all human understanding that will guard your hearts and minds" (Phil. 4:6–7, my translation), a similar conviction implicitly underscores several of these passages. Sometimes our prayers influence God's future plans, but *every time* they provide an avenue for God's good gifts to be poured into the lives of his children.

Fourth, by detailing the various constraints that can inhibit prayer's effectiveness, the General Letters and Revelation make a distinctive contribution to any study of New Testament petition. Before itemizing these constraints, however, we first need to remember that they are restrictions within the realm of personal relationship; they are not mechanical or even natural laws about prayer per se. Prayer is not a natural process built into the fabric of the universe, subject to study and analysis like the laws of thermodynamics. Prayer is not spiritual chemistry. Adding elements X, Y, and Z will not catalyze God's responsiveness to yield a more immediate result; neither will the presence of components A, B, and C predictably retard God's reaction, as if his movements were the sum of a properly balanced equation. Rather, prayer is conversation, a conversation between two persons—you and God. As in any personal relationship, certain attitudes and behaviors are more or less conducive than others to open communication. God in his goodness has decided that, rather than give us the silent treatment and leave us to work out for ourselves why certain prayers are less likely to be answered than others, he will tell us in advance how and why he is more or less inclined to respond to certain types of communication. Whatever consistencies may appear are not due to the so-called laws of prayer but to the faithfulness and consistency of the Father's personality. Just as my children know that their father is never sympathetic to pouting or tantrums, so God's children can know that certain types of prayer are best kept to themselves.

Unlike the apostle Paul, who tends to focus on the superlative, positive dimensions of spiritual blessing available to every believer in every moment of prayer, the General Letters and Revelation identify at least six factors that may severely limit the effectiveness of our communication with God.

The first limiting factor is the failure to ask. James 4:2–3 is very clear. God is willing to do certain things if and when we ask, but until then these gifts are withheld. James does not elaborate on what these things might be, neither does he explain what might inhibit our requests, but the solution to both issues is crystal clear: ask! Whatever stifles my willingness or ability to come before God in prayer needs to be seriously addressed, resolved, and eliminated.

Second, God will not bless selfishness. James could not be any clearer. The Father considers the motives behind every request, and the reasons for our asking factor into how he eventually responds. Of course, if we had to bottle up every petition until absolutely certain that it was motivated exclusively by pure, sanctified, selfless desires, few (if any) of us would ever pray again. But it does not take a spiritual giant to sort out the differences between the mixed motives of a repentant sinner sincerely seeking God and the unadulterated competitiveness of spiritual hedonists who think that God exists only to satisfy their every whim. God tells us that he eagerly responds (in his wisdom) to all repentant sinners, however confused their prayers may be, but he remains unmoved by selfishness, no matter how emphatically it is launched heavenward.

Third, God warns that he will not affirm foolish prayer any more quickly than selfish prayer. James urges prayer for wisdom so that we may gain the wisdom to know how to pray. Peter similarly insists that truly effective prayer is offered by those who self-consciously cultivate spiritual alertness. Apparently, learning to pray effectively is something that can be developed in tandem with other aspects of spiritual maturity. Perhaps the implication is that perennially unanswered requests need to be reconsidered; God's repeated no may be more instructive than his periodic yes. Believers intent upon cultivating clear-mindedness and spiritual alertness should learn to discern the emerging patterns of wisdom and foolishness arising from long-term habits of prayer.

Fourth, because effective prayer ultimately remains subject to God's will, any petition rooted in disobedience will never receive a positive response. Granted, not every disobedient request arises from deliberate rebelliousness. Oftentimes, a devoted believer prays in ignorance completely unaware of just how wayward a petition may be. Yet, this is precisely why effective petitions are consistently described as prayers of the righteous, the reverent, those with faith, people who lack doubt, who ask in the name of the Lord. In one way or another, each of these epithets describes a prayer whose request concludes in exactly the same way: "Nevertheless, Father, not my will but yours be done."

Fifth, the General Letters and Revelation revisit Jesus's concern with the power of broken relationships to hinder a disciple's relationship with God. Whether addressing the nuclear family (1 Pet. 3:7) or the body of Christ (James 5:13–18), the message remains the same: persistent mistreatment of brothers and sisters in Christ inhibits our ability to communicate with the Father, and this Father never turns a blind eye to domestic abuse. Until the perpetrators repent and seek the necessary reconciliation, their petitions will remain ineffective. Perhaps ongoing self-examination offers the surest safeguard against this particular danger. It would certainly be disheartening to imagine that none of my petitions have any hope of ever being heard by God until every aspect of all my relationships are put in perfect working order. If that were the case, all petition becomes hopeless again! Fortunately, by revisiting the original contexts we are reminded that the New Testament writers were addressing deliberate, persistent misbehavior. The sinner refuses to change despite (a) the sin having been openly confronted and (b) the necessary correction having been explained and then ignored. Consequently, because the culprit willfully ignores God's word, the Father may choose to ignore his or her prayers.

Finally, every divine response to every human petition is always subject to the sovereignty of God's timing for salvation-history. Sometimes the Father may answer immediately. At other times, the response comes much more slowly, if at all. Both Jesus in Gethsemane (the Lamb about to be slain) and the host of martyred saints who litter history's brutal stage are told to wait. The timing of their requests was not quite right. God will respond, and he will respond in ways that make our paltry expectations appear pathetic in comparison to the unimagined, unimaginable grandeur that the Father intends to wrap around his precious children. Only, not right now, not just yet. In any case, whatever the timing of God's eventual answer, the faithful, like Jesus, will continue to pray and to wait.

14

Petition, the Hiddenness of God, and the Theology of the Cross

A small, single-engine plane carrying a young missionary and her infant daughter is shot down by a government fighter jet over the South American jungle because military radar mistook it for a flight of drug runners. The mother and baby are killed, with no drugs on board.

Two engaged college students take a break from their summer jobs as Christian camp counselors to hike along an isolated West Coast shoreline. During the night an unknown assailant shoots them both and disappears without a trace into the midnight fog. The murders remain unsolved.

What kind of God allows such horrific tragedies to screech their unkempt nails across the cosmic blackboard? According to the news reports covering both stories, it is the Christian God who sovereignly ordained both tragedies for his own good purposes. I watched several television conversations with various family members connected to both events who not only confessed their continuing faith in God, but insisted that their son's, daughter's, or spouse's untimely death was, in fact, a perfectly timed piece of God's plan.

I am acquainted with two fathers who have recently spent long, sleepless nights in the hospital wondering if their sons will ever walk again. One young man, brimming with overconfidence, made a foolish move while climbing and suffered a gruesome fall down a mountainside. By all rights he should have died, yet his physical therapy is progressing nicely, and it is only a matter of time before he climbs another mountain. The other boy obediently adhered to every safety rule insisted on by his parents when riding four-wheelers across the dunes, but one mishap, which at the time did not seem terribly threatening, has put him in a wheelchair for life.

Why?

Is there any rhyme or reason to the discordant notes and garbled syllables spat out at us by this occasional nightmare called life? Some, such as the men and women of faith mentioned above, are somehow able to hold firm to a remnant of trust in the goodness of their loving heavenly Father. Others, however, find it a much more tenuous proposition; holding onto faith becomes an exercise in (metaphorically) gripping a heavily greased pig. Except that slippery pork on the hoof feels more substantial than faith in a God who not only allows but purposefully plans murder and mayhem for the lives of his children.

How can anyone honestly pray to such a God in a world like ours? Arriving at satisfactory answers to questions about the nature and efficacy of petitionary prayer requires that we simultaneously formulate some perspective on the nature of God and divine providence. Can prayer make a difference to God? to the world? If it does, precisely what *kind* of difference can one expect? Such questions are as old as religion itself.

Third-century church father Origen composed one of the earliest commentaries on the Lord's Prayer and used the introduction to address similar questions raised by his friend, Ambrose: "First, if God foresees everything that will happen, and these things must happen, prayer is useless. Second, if everything happens according to the will of God, and His decisions are firm, and nothing that He wills can be changed, prayer is useless."[1] Origen—and many others since—firmly believed that there are good answers to these questions, answers that not only salvage a legitimate place for petitionary prayer but maintain a worthwhile personal relationship between the person who asks and the God who hears. Yet, experiencing personal trauma often has a way of upending life's apple cart and forcing us to reexamine the very foundations of our faith. At times the bedrock can begin to crumble.

There is a Grand Canyon–sized difference between theological answers that satisfy intellectually and a living faith that sustains a broken heart long after all sense and sensibility have evaporated from a tear-stained life. In the best of situations, theology and faith intertwine into an unbreakable cord of Christian perseverance. But, for many, the questions

---

1. Origen, *Prayer* (trans. J. J. O'Meara; New York: Newman, 1954), 30.

left unanswered, or unanswerable, are simply too overwhelming. If all spinal-cord injuries, unsolved homicides, car collisions, drownings, fatal illnesses, and other freakish events are each foreordained by God, what good does it do for parents to pray for the safety of their children? What good does it do to pray about anything at all? And, please, do not presume to counsel a distraught family by insisting that prayer remains good *for them*, since one's own personal well-being is the farthest thing from a parent's mind when a child lies dying and God appears to have taken an unscheduled vacation. The unavoidable question remains, what petitionary, or impetratory, force does prayer exercise in the world? Can our petitions actually influence God's course of action? That is the pressing question.

Having examined all the New Testament material pertaining to petitionary prayer, it is time to draw out the various threads discovered in this study and see what kind of theological fabric is woven when they all are brought together. What perspectives on the possible relationships between petition, providence, and the nature of God are most amenable to the evidence assembled here? Is there any evidence that prayer actually changes things? If so, then why does it so often appear ineffective? Before answering these questions, however, I should briefly touch on two more introductory notes that explain how my theological presuppositions influence my answers to these questions.

When Dorothy first confronts the Wizard of Oz, with her ragtag company of fellow travelers, she is thoroughly intimidated by what she sees—an august, larger-than-life figure barking commands through an eerie haze of smoke and flames, hardly an inviting figure that anyone would long to revisit. Yet, revisit she does, and when Dorothy finally returns victorious with the witch's charred broomstick, her dog Toto proves that canines sometimes have a gift for sniffing out the difference between wizardry and chicanery. Toto discovers that the real wizard is not the grandiose image revealed on the big screen but a forlorn snake-oil peddler who calls himself "the professor" hiding behind a side curtain.

What does the Wizard of Oz have to do with New Testament prayer? Just this. How we pray is largely determined by what we believe about the God who hears us. Christians learn about their God's true identity by reading the Old and New Testaments. I read these texts as divine revelation, which means that I approach them believing that the true God revealed himself truly in their pages and the history they record. The God and Father of our Lord Jesus Christ is not like the Wizard of Oz. He does not project a false image of himself onto the big screen of revelation while hiding his true identity behind some cosmic curtain. The reality of God's person and the particulars of his self-disclosure correspond to each other in such a way that a true understanding of his revelation leads the reader to a true understanding of God. This is not to suggest that the Father's revelation is always exhaustive or that the revelatory significance of every salvation-historical event is always self-evident. At this point, Martin Luther's emphasis on the "hiddenness of God" in the cross of Jesus Christ is significant.[2] Sometimes—perhaps, even most of the time—neither God's revelation nor the divine character discovered there is anything like what we expected to find. The suffering, failure, and abandonment exhibited at Calvary is the quintessential instance of a revelation wherein God is most magnificently unveiled while remaining utterly hidden. God is hidden in the cross, not because the crucifixion falsifies or obscures any part of his character, but because the truth revealed in a crucified Savior is inaccessible to anyone who will not look through the eyes of faith. Faith alone is able to perceive the truth lodged in this apparent contradiction, not because it believes the irrational but because it is willing to yield before the unexpected, to surrender to the unacceptable.

We must hold on to both of these convictions simultaneously. First, the Scriptures can always be trusted to show us the truth about God. Suggesting that he sometimes gives false information does not leave us waiting for a more congenial problem-solver to step out from behind the heavenly drapes (in this respect, we are not at all like Dorothy); it either leaves us wondering whether we should ever believe anything he says or devising highly subjective means of distinguishing the believable from the unbelievable.

Second, the God we discover in Scripture will sometimes be a Father who hides himself, his purposes, and his answers to prayer in events that strike us as shockingly contradictory and counterintuitive. An irony of divine revelation is the regularity with which it challenges our faith in revelation, for all divine self-disclosure ultimately portrays a God whose thoughts are never our thoughts, whose ways are never our ways (Isa. 55:8–9). Consequently, we must anticipate that faithful interpretation will be as discomfiting as reassuring, as disconcerting as encouraging, casting a new shadow with each new moment of illumination, raising another unexpected question with every startling new answer.

My final introductory point concerns the priority of biblical interpretation in establishing the proper parameters of Christian theology. When I use the term "New Testament theology," I mean to refer to those beliefs about God professed (either explicitly or implicitly) by the New Testament authors as reflected in their writings. If the New Testament is

2. See Grislis, "Martin Luther's View of the Hidden God"; Gerrish, "To the Unknown God"; and McGrath, *Luther's Theology of the Cross*, esp. chaps. 5–6. I am not referring to Luther's notion of God hidden *behind* his revelation (which does strike me as similar to the Wizard of Oz) but of God hidden *within* his revelation.

accepted as divine revelation, then the theology it contains is essential to Christian confession. Yet the correspondence between biblical teaching and Christian theology is not always obvious. Therefore, I find it helpful to distinguish between two distinct levels of theological discourse: the more fundamental level is one of *biblical necessity*; the more derivative level is that of *theological possibility*.

Biblical necessity encompasses the theological concepts conveyed in Scripture. They are the basic ingredients of biblical theology. For example, I would insist that believing that the preexistent Son of God entered human history as Jesus of Nazareth and that the one God eternally exists as Father, Son, and Holy Spirit are both biblically necessary beliefs to be accepted by any Christian claiming to take the New Testament seriously.

Theological possibility, on the other hand, describes the various heuristic, explanatory models devised by Christian thinkers in order to account coherently for the many theological claims of Scripture. These models begin with the biblical information, but they must eventually move well beyond that testimony, since the Scriptures rarely attempt thoroughgoing explanations of how or why theology works the way it does. The extent to which these models move beyond the biblical witness is the extent to which they show themselves to be possibilities rather than necessities. For instance, the historical debates surrounding the ideas of hypostatic union, Monophysitism, homoousia, theotokos, and Nestorianism (to name only a few) explored various theological/philosophical attempts to explain the inner workings of the incarnation. Each model has been offered by someone as a possible explanation of what it means for Christ to be God in the flesh, simultaneously divine and human. Historically, the church favored some possibilities over others, insisting that they are more faithful to the biblical evidence. Yet, the historic divergence between the theologies of the Eastern and Western churches testifies to the uncertainty endemic to this level of theological discourse and illustrates why such models can never become anything more than *possibilities*. The New Testament simply does not bother to explain how it is ontologically possible for Christ to be fully human and fully divine, or how these two natures can coexist metaphysically within the one human being. Each model attempts a possible explanation; some may be more consistent with Scripture than others, but they all extrapolate beyond the biblical data to such an extent that none of them can make any claim to *necessity*. New Testament theology must necessarily affirm that our Savior is the eternal Son of the Father who became fully human in Jesus of Nazareth, but the various explanatory models (whether incarnational, trinitarian, etc.) explored throughout church history ought never to claim more than they can deliver, and what they deliver are options, not certainties.[3]

It follows that theological possibility alone can never be used to distinguish orthodoxy from heresy; only necessary truths can draw that line, and necessary truths are born of exegesis, not philosophy.[4] Theology in all its forms does a grave disservice to the church and to its ability to conduct healthy theological discussion when we forget this distinction. There is sometimes a tendency for the defenders of different theological possibilities to greedily insist upon the privileges of biblical necessity, declaring that adherents of this or that theological suggestion fall outside the circle of authentic Christian faith simply because they do not adhere to the currently preferred model of orthodoxy. Yet, to speak in this way of orthodox possibilities is an oxymoron that can lead only to senseless splintering within the body of Christ.

With this in mind, what follows is my attempt to summarize the New Testament teaching on petitionary prayer. In observing the distinction between what it is necessary to affirm and what are the possibilities of elaboration, I believe that I have laid out the minimal parameters of an orthodox theology of Christian prayer. I have tried to limit my assertions to conclusions plainly discernable from the biblical text, however paradoxical they may appear. One result of this method is that possible answers to many outstanding questions about divine foreknowledge, providence, immutability, and how these divine qualities interact with free will, human petition, and historical contingency are left for others to work out in greater detail. Whatever possibilities others may offer in answer to these questions, I am convinced that the most legitimate theological possibilities will identify themselves by remaining true to the biblically necessary framework provided here. Perhaps more than one possibility exists for resolving these questions. I do not know. The New Testament has, however, laid down the outer boundaries of our

3. Of course, there is no agreement on all aspects of New Testament interpretation, so questions of biblical necessity can also be quite controversial. The difference, however, is that this debate is primarily a matter of interpretation, focusing on a shared collection of texts. The parameters of the discussion are more easily delineated, although it must be admitted that the variety of opinion may be no less diverse. Bultmann's New Testament theology did not insist that Jesus's bodily resurrection was a biblical necessity, yet his existentialist paradigm of human existence certainly was! I am not so naïve as to believe that my distinction between biblical necessity and theological possibility will resolve all theological disagreements. But I do believe that more debates would be characterized by patience, tolerance, and charity if the fundamental distinction between scriptural evidence versus theological/philosophical evidence were respected.

4. In my opinion, it is one of the great tragedies of church history, and much contemporary debate as well, that these words—orthodoxy and heresy—have been used far too promiscuously, causing much unnecessary division within the church.

playing field; any ball crossing the divinely inspired chalk lines is out of play. But, as long as we stay inside these margins, we may be able to devise any number of equally legitimate theological "games" in answer to our questions about the best way to enjoy the grassy field of petitionary prayer given to us by God. These boundary lines are drawn by five conclusions resulting from this study.

We Pray to a Personal God

Petitionary prayer is evidence of a personal relationship with a personal God. Admittedly, there is nothing particularly new or revolutionary about this conclusion. This most fundamental of all truths about prayer is, however, always worth repeating, not only because it is the foundation of all Christian hope but because of the many subtle ways that both academic and popular theology find to assent to the idea while undermining the reality. The importance of petitionary prayer as real, personal conversation with God can be highlighted by briefly mentioning three common mistakes.

First, the God of the Bible is best conceived as the supreme *person*, not the supreme *being* found in so much Christian theologizing. The New Testament describes our heavenly Father as a supremely personal deity who freely acts to carry out his purposes (both historical and eternal) for the people he loves, and he does so by finding ways to accomplish his plans while simultaneously enlisting the free actions and responses of those who love him.[5] This is the biblical portrait of a personal God entering into personal relationship. Unfortunately, a long-standing preoccupation with the philosophical issues surrounding the nature of the supreme being have historically pushed Christian thinkers toward discussions of the nature of causation and of God's "becoming," concerns that are quite foreign to biblical literature. Grappling with the idea of supreme personhood leads to a far more biblically coherent view of prayer as personal conversation between earth and heaven, where the only thing being "caused" is personal engagement with the three-in-one eternal person.

The great-grandfather of the comparative-religions study of prayer, Friedrich Heiler, once wrote: "Rational philosophical thought destroys the essential presuppositions of a simple prayer. These are: faith in the anthropomorphic character of God, in His real presence, in His change-

---

5. Brümmer's *Speaking of a Personal God* was particularly helpful in my thinking about the question of a personal God and what we are doing when we describe God as a person.

ability, and the reality of personal communion with Him."[6] Despite certain Christian traditions disputing this claim, I believe that our study demonstrates that Heiler's fundamental insights into the nature of world religions are equally true for biblical religion. New Testament petition is thoroughly tied to precisely these faith commitments. God is anthropomorphic in the sense that our relationship with him is best understood by way of analogy with human relationships, relationships that enjoy a certain measure of symmetry, as opposed to the asymmetrical quality of impersonal relationships.[7] We are quite correct in believing that God cares for us, that he makes plans concerning us, that he exercises personal decision and enters into true reciprocity with us in such a way that he allows himself to be affected by our words and decisions. Christian petition requires believing that the Father is honestly listening, is willing to be influenced, and is thus engaged in authentic two-way communication with the one who prays.

The New Testament is strewn with evidence testifying to the reality of petition as personal interaction: Jesus's own probing at Gethsemane into the flexibility of the Father's plan; the New Testament's repeated insistence that intercession makes a real difference in the lives of others; the apostolic requests for intercession about specific travel arrangements; the fact that certain personal sins prohibit positive answers to our requests or that some available gifts are never received simply because we never think to ask; and the extravagance of Paul's petitionary optimism, rooted as it is in the love of the Father, combined with the apostle's habit of repetition, urgency, and hopeful insistence. All of this evidence, and more, points to a God of profound intimacy, personally available to hear and to respond to each individual's requests in a two-way relationship of personal give and take. Granted, others find reason to read the evidence differently, taking particular offense at the implication that such conclusions make God and/or his purposes subject to change, and since neither the sovereign God nor his eternal plans may ever change, this particular relational view of petitionary prayer must be out of the question. Nevertheless, I suggest that these objections merely disguise a Neoplatonic theological prejudice that substitutes the Wizard for the Lord God, the land of Oz for the church, philosophical smoke and mirrors for the truth plainly revealed in Scripture.[8]

6. Heiler, *Prayer*, 98.
7. Lucas, *Freedom and Grace*, 16–19; and Brümmer, *What Are We Doing?* 46–47.
8. Lucas's observations are typical of the protests of many others who similarly insist that "the changelessness of God is not to be naturally read out of the Bible, but rather was read into it in the light of certain philosophical assumptions about the nature of God" (see *Future*, 215). If we begin with the premise that God is conceived as absolute being, then God cannot be associated with change, for change entails becoming. Becoming has

Second, an even more common—common in the sense of popular, but also in the sense of less academic—way of subverting the personal dimension of petitionary prayer is to quietly replace the dynamics of personal relationship with the expectations of causal relationship while failing to admit, or even to recognize, that a dastardly substitution took place. For instance, embracing references to "the power of prayer" or "steps to effective prayer" subtly—perhaps unwittingly but nonetheless truly—replaces the complexity of personal engagement with the perceived predictability of mechanistic cause and effect. Titles such as *The Prayer Matrix: Plugging into the Unseen Reality*, complete with a cover picture of a clockwork gear mechanism and the reminder that God "hard-wired the universe" to operate according to "the principles" of prayer,[9] reflect a worldview in which prayer is less personal conversation than it is mastery of impersonal forces. We simply need to learn the proper methods of "plugging in" to the heavenly power source; prayer is about learning to cause the right things to happen by mastering proper technique. Unfortunately, many people pray in precisely this manner without realizing what has happened. Believing that their concentration on proper method (praying in "the right" way) honors the New Testament's desire for mountain-moving faith, they allow an unrecognized mechanistic view of petition to replace their sometimes unpredictable personal God with a predictable cosmic machine. While talking the talk of personal relationship, they pray the prayers of impersonal causation.

Rick Ostrander's *Life of Prayer in a World of Science* offers a fascinating account of how the roots of this tendency to mechanize petition traces its heyday to the apologetics of nineteenth-century fundamentalism, which viewed petitionary prayer as the principal means of refuting modernist scientific attacks against the historic Christian faith. In deflecting the rationalistic assaults of empirical science, fundamentalism believed it had found firmer ground for defending God in the unassailable fortress of personal experience. Numerous volumes were produced in a genre of

---

no part in absolute being because being does not "become" anything; it already exists as pure actuality. If such language sounds foreign to readers of the Bible, it does so for good reason. K. Barth refers to this exchange as "the horrible confusion of God with that immovable idol" (*Church Dogmatics* §3.4.53.3). Perhaps *the* great irony of the history of Christian theology is the way in which the most marginal of theological possibilities (i.e., classical theism derived from Neoplatonic and Aristotelian philosophy) was construed as orthodox necessity by so many for so long. That many modern protagonists continue to demand adherence to this particular view of God demonstrates how far the church has yet to go in allowing careful exegesis and biblical theology to shape the authentic core of our necessary ecumenical beliefs. The importance of allowing Scripture to speak *on its own terms* simply cannot be overemphasized.

9. D. Jeremiah, *The Prayer Matrix: Plugging into the Unseen Reality* (Portland: Multnomah, 2004), 44.

devotional literature known as answered-prayer narratives. Titles such as *Getting Things from God, How I Know God Answers Prayer, Prayer and Its Remarkable Answers*, and *The Wonders of Prayer: A Record of Well Authenticated and Wonderful Answers to Prayer* proliferated widely, cataloging story after miraculous story of dramatic, divine intervention in response to Christian petition.[10] Prayer would prove what science now thought it could disprove: not only did God exist, but he intervened in people's lives.

Needless to say, many skeptics remained unconvinced, suggesting that for every apparent miracle there were many more instances of abandonment, death, and disappointment. Unanswered prayer was, in fact, the norm. How could Christian faith account for all those whose suffering was never relieved? whose rescue never appeared?

The authors of answered-prayer narratives had a ready reply: the disappointed were never fully surrendered. The "fully surrendered" were all those who had completely abandoned their wills, hearts, and minds to Christ in total submission. Without absolute surrender, a person's prayers could not be answered because they were too superficial. In order to see miracles, the fully surrendered saint petitioned fervently, repeatedly, with complete earnestness, never giving up, never yielding to doubt, always believing without hesitation in God's promise to do whatever is asked in faith. As the devotional classic *The Christian's Secret of a Happy Life* says, "'According to our faith' is always the limit and the rule."[11]

Unfortunately, fundamentalism's sincere attempt to defend the faith left a crippling legacy to large sectors of the church. It is not hard to uncover the circular reasoning or the damaging spiritual consequences now deeply embedded within the evangelical/fundamentalist traditions as a result of these misguided efforts to turn prayer into a science. The biblical testimony to earnestness, repetition, and persistence does not describe limiting factors waiting to be quantified, as this literature insists; it offers passionate expressions of intimacy and devotion, evidence of personal conversation between the Father and trusting people who believe that they commune with the Creator of the universe. We ought not to confuse either divine faithfulness or the longevity of personal passion with the measurements and forecasts of empirical method. There is a world of difference between the qualities of spiritual eagerness and the quantification of spiritual earnestness. The New Testament readily demonstrates the former, but the latter is nowhere to be found.[12] This

10. This sample of titles only scratches the surface of a long list of examples; see the discussion of answered-prayer narratives in Ostrander, *Life of Prayer*, 39–55.

11. Hannah Whitehall Smith, *The Christian's Secret of a Happy Life* (London: Nisbet, n.d.), 53.

12. K. Barth provides a pertinent discussion in *Church Dogmatics* §3.4.

Knocking on Heaven's Door

study clearly demonstrates that measures of faith or the volume of repetition (the two most common *amoral* considerations; see "Theological Reflections on Prayer in the Synoptic Gospels," pp. 90–94 above) have no bearing whatsoever on the Father's responsiveness to petitionary prayer. The only qualifications attached to our petitions are the *moral* concerns arising from the interpersonal nature of prayer itself (chapter 13).

Third, prayer as silent meditation is a noticeably elusive creature in the pages of the New Testament. From a biblical perspective, wordless prayer—not to be confused with silent prayer—is a contradiction in terms. Even glossalalia is prayer in an unknown heavenly *language* subject to interpretation (1 Cor. 14:1–19)! New Testament prayer is always an act of communication, an act requiring words. Whether run silently through the mind or whispered faintly on the lips, something is always being spoken because prayer is always a matter of personal expression. Even when the apostle Paul admits his ignorance of how or what to pray, it is the Holy Spirit, not Paul, who utters inarticulate groans to the Father. Paul wrestles with prayer while realizing that his fumbling quest for the proper words is simultaneously reinterpreted according to the Father's will by both the Spirit who dwells within and the Son enthroned above, so that his inadequate attempts at conversation with God are integrated into the ongoing conversation between the Father, Son, and Holy Spirit. Thus New Testament prayer is not only verbal, it is supremely aware of both the centrality of Christ as mediator and the work of the Spirit in making conversation with the Father a possible impossibility.

While the many ancient meditative traditions that arose throughout church history may certainly have their own spiritual benefits, they fall short of the biblical qualifications of true prayer whenever they either fail to remain Christocentric or forget that the Spirit enables *conversation* with our Abba, Father. Self-focused wordless concentration on such things as purification, emptiness, cleansing, stillness, oneness, self-control, or the cultivation of an inner life may have spiritual value (although a few of these objectives are highly debatable), but it is not anything that the New Testament writers would recognize as prayer. While mystical prayer occurs in both Jewish and Christian tradition, it is most noticeable by its absence from New Testament religion.[13] Although

13. This is not to suggest that there is no mysticism of any sort in the New Testament. In rejecting the impersonal elements of Heiler's definition of mysticism, Schweitzer's analysis of Pauline theology in *Mysticism of Paul the Apostle* is one of the most insightful works on Paul ever written. My point is simply that, while the Christian may be a "mystic," Christian prayer requires Christ-focused verbal communication with the Father. For a helpful appreciation of Schweitzer's work, see E. Sanders, *Paul and Palestinian Judaism*, 434–35, 438–42.

his arguments are rooted more in theological conviction than in biblical exegesis, K. Barth is absolutely correct when he insists:

> If by devotion we mean an exercise in the cultivation of the soul or spirit . . . then it is high time we realized that not merely have we not even begun to pray or prepared ourselves for prayer, but that we have actually turned away from what is commended us as prayer. This type of exercise . . . can perform a useful function as a means of psychical hygiene, but it has nothing whatever to do with the prayer required of us. Prayer begins where this kind of exercise leaves off.[14]

Prayer is an act, not a state; a deliberate articulation, not a frame of mind. Certainly, there are profound spiritual, existential benefits to all prayer. The New Testament does not divorce communication with God from one's own personal transformation. Far from it! But the individual development depicted in the New Testament occurs first through *conversation* with God and then through others *conversing* with God on our behalf.

A Personal God Is Willing to Be Moved

Second, if we accept the biblical testimony to a genuinely personal God, then we can also accept that conversing with the supreme person means that while God can never be coerced, he may honestly be influenced by our prayers. We may not be able to twist God's arm, but we can catch his eye and prompt a reply. The New Testament makes no secret that the Father has a definite purpose that he intends to accomplish through world history, both cosmically as he finally restores creation in the new heaven and the new earth and individually as he guides his children to realize his purposes for their lives. Whether we read about prayers for guidance in the ministry of Jesus, Paul, and the leaders of the early church or recall the apocalyptic goals of the book of Revelation, there can be no doubt about the Creator's sovereignty over the growth of his church and the course of salvation-history. The numerous instances where it is apparent that the Father chooses to respond negatively to a request—whether it is Jesus asking for his cup of suffering to be removed in Gethsemane, Paul asking the Roman church to pray for his deliverance from his opponents in Jerusalem, or martyred saints pleading for divine vengeance before God's throne—also make it crystal clear that the Father always reserves the right to answer any prayer in his own time, in his own way. No amount of repetition, no increase in angst or

14. K. Barth, *Church Dogmatics* §3.4; see also §3.3.

emotional fervor, no special vocabulary, no volume of repeated phrases, no particular physical location or bodily posturing can ever cause the Father to do something contrary to his intentions. We must forever be on guard against the sly shape-shifting that transforms prayer into magic, which is precisely what happens whenever we assume a direct causal relationship between God's action (or our interpretation of *an* action) and the particular manner of our petition. Such assumptions are, unfortunately, all too common and so very wrong.

Acknowledging the priority of divine sovereignty and the human inability to coerce God does not, however, answer every question about the relationship between human requests and divine response. The New Testament makes it equally clear that the sovereign Lord does some things precisely *because* we pray for them; furthermore, had we not prayed as we did, God would not have acted as he did. Some possibilities remain unrealized because they are never requested. The Father's unfolding plans for the world, and our part in those plans, may develop *in more than one direction* depending, in part, on how we pray. Whereas certain events are necessary occurrences, others never move beyond the realm of possibility. The future has options.[15] The New Testament insists that God is sovereign in the sense that the "game" of history never spins outside his control, never veering from his final goal, but he makes no claim to sovereignty in the sense that every individual event (or every play in the game) always occurs exactly as he willed or foreordained.[16] This is

15. Affirming that God's plan makes room for different future possibilities depending on human responsiveness (or lack thereof) says nothing, in and of itself, about one's relationship to the theology of God's "openness." Views of flexible providence have a lengthy history that antedate and develop quite independently of the current openness controversy. What I am affirming is different from the position typically affirmed by open theists who are distinguished by their commitment to three fundamental tenets—(1) presentism (God lacks foreknowledge), (2) libertarian human freedom, and (3) divine temporality—none of which is essential to my argument. For advocates of divine openness, see Rice, *Openness of God*; Pinnock et al., *Openness of God*; Basinger, *Case for Freewill Theism*; J. Sanders, *God Who Risks*; G. Boyd, *God of the Possible*; and Sanders and Hall, *Does God Have a Future?*

16. Deut. 32:39; 1 Sam. 2:6–7; Job 1:21; 2:10; Eccles. 7:14; Isa. 45:7; Lam. 3:38; and Amos 3:6 have long served as classic texts regularly used in arguments to the contrary. Lindström, *God and the Origin of Evil*, however, carefully analyzes each of these passages and convincingly demonstrates that none of them expresses anything like omnicausality or pancausality. Each text must be read within its salvation-historical context, not as a theological abstraction. I share Lindström's frustration in commenting on those who use these passages as handy proof-texts for divine determinism: "Not a single drop of ink is sacrificed to the problems presented by the different genres of these texts nor to their dates or intentions in their existing contexts. . . . The brutal fact is that in the Old Testament we have no text whatsoever which, read on normal exegetical lines, can be taken to mean that a popular conception of divine pancausality existed" (209). The current debate over the openness of God is producing another collection of books defending classical theism by

so, not because God's foreordination is subject to human sabotage, but because he has decided not to micromanage human history. Neither the Old Testament nor the New Testament requires Christian faith to confess that God wills, intends, plans, or predestines every unsolved homicide, every senseless act of violence, and all incurable disease. The Bible never demands that we embrace such pancausality.[17] While it is true that Paul recognized his own thorn in the flesh as a sovereignly bestowed "satanic messenger" (2 Cor. 12:7), thereby making it clear that God can and sometimes does employ evil circumstances to accomplish his purposes, knowing that divine sovereignty has the power to use evil is a far cry from insisting that divine sovereignty causes or determines all evil. Whatever the wickedness of Paul's thorn, his awareness of its origin arose as a personal insight granted by the Holy Spirit through his own prayerful turmoil. It is not a universal explanation of every evil ever experienced by God's people.

It is also worth noting that Paul's thorn was not God's punishment for a lack of faith or prayer. Just as some theologies mistakenly assert that all tragedy is a part of God's design, others insinuate that suffering is the result of someone's failure to pray. In other words, if those affected by tragedy had only prayed more faithfully, disaster could have been averted.

---

relying on these same texts, yet they typically fail to offer any perspective on the history of interpretation and never perform any serious grammatical-historical exegesis. For instance, none of the following works critical of the openness view appear to have any awareness of Lindström's research or the interpretive issues he addresses: see Geisler, *Creating God in the Image of Man?*; Ware, *God's Lesser Glory*; Frame, *No Other God*; and Piper, Taylor, and Helseth, *Beyond the Bounds*. Frame (89) makes one passing reference to Lindström, but his use of the Old Testament shows no awareness of the substance of Lindstöm's work. I can only conclude that a vast gulf continues to separate the understanding of exegesis among systematic theologians from that current among biblical scholars.

17. For example, compare Spear, *Theology of Prayer*, 20, who says, "Prayer to God recognizes him as the ultimate cause of all events." Spear represents the classic Reformed view of providence articulated by thinkers such as Calvin: "Nothing at all in the world is undertaken without his determination" (*Institutes of the Christian Religion* §1.16.6); "God's will is the highest and first cause of all things because nothing happens except from his command or permission" (§1.16.8); "God's providence exercised authority over fortune in directing its end. The same reckoning applies to the contingency of future events" (§1.16.9); "What for us seems a contingency, faith recognizes to have been a secret impulse from God" (§1.16.9); "In a wonderful and ineffable manner nothing is done without God's will, not even that which is against his will. For it would not be done if he did not permit it; yet he does not unwillingly permit it, but willingly" (§1.18.3). Unfortunately, Calvin's use of Scripture in these chapters of the *Institutes of the Christian Religion* falls far short of what we would normally expect from an exegete of his caliber. Furthermore, despite the nuance distinguishing God's decretive (antecedent) will from his permissive (consequent) will, what God determines versus what God allows, Calvin finally fails to account coherently for the place of a believer's personal disobedience in his scheme of providence. Though some may insist that Calvin did not teach pancausality, the term seems most apt to me.

On the surface, James's insistence that "you have not because you ask not" might appear to leave this door ajar. While James insists that God may withhold some blessings because we fail to ask, there is no New Testament evidence, however, to indicate that God sends disaster because we fail to pray sufficiently for deliverance. James says, "You do not have something good because you did not ask for something good." He does not say, "You were given something hurtful because you did not ask for something better." It is dangerous to assume that any single solution can be universally applied to any and all comparable circumstances. I can no more assume that disaster strikes because someone failed to pray than I can assume that all disaster is the will of God. Neither life nor the Bible can be interpreted so simplistically. We must wean ourselves of the compulsion to load up with silver-bullet solutions to life's difficult questions. Such responses regularly misfire. There is no such thing as a one-size-fits-all answer in life, apart from the continual confession of faith in our Father's faithfulness. Admittedly, faith may never explain everything, but it is always able to console. Explanation, whether simple or sophisticated, rarely comforts as meaningfully as does confidence in God's never-ending embrace.

In any event, the New Testament is much more nuanced and complex in its portrait of the historical relationship between (a) God's rock-solid constancy and (b) the contingency that fluidly ebbs and flows between God and humanity. O. Cullmann provides a more biblically astute description of the relationship between personal experience and God's design:[18]

> Contingency belongs to the manner in which God's plan develops. In the Bible the movement and purposes of the plan are revealed at the start but not the particular stages in it. They are disclosed for the first time in the events as they occur. The continuing execution of the divine plan, and its association with contingency, lapses, and detours, is expressed in the Portuguese proverb . . . "God writes straight, but with crooked lines."

God spontaneously incorporates human decision-making into his plans, not as the one who controls every personal decision, but as the one who possesses an all-powerful ability to seamlessly weave each successive new thread into his ancient pattern. The New Testament insists that petitionary prayer, including the complex interplay between personal obedience and disobedience, between faithfulness and rebelliousness, has a necessary role in the unique unfolding of God's plan, a plan that continually recombines the old with the new, the most desirable with the second best. There are certain points at which the specific natures

18. Cullmann, *Salvation in History*, 124.

of our petitions—hopeful, fearful, visionary, or nearsighted as they may be—all conspire to urge the Father toward using us in particular ways, to develop particular courses of action unique to particular situations. God's willingness to collaborate with his children like this is not due to any weakness or fallibility on his part. Far from it. It is simply his preferred means of operation; by grace he has chosen to make us partners in the fulfillment of his purposes. Certainly, any God powerful enough to create the universe from nothing is free to limit himself in whatever way he sees fit in order to provide enough space for his children's cooperation on the project of salvation-history.[19] A crucified Savior compellingly articulates God's ability to conceal himself in the oddest of places, fulfilling his purposes with his hands, if not tied behind his back, then nailed firmly to a cross.

Granted, certain theological traditions soundly reject such conclusions while purporting to maintain the integrity of petition, but it is a sleight of hand that ultimately fails. Perhaps the best-known argument was offered by Thomas Aquinas, who famously insisted: "We do not pray in order to change the decree of divine providence, rather we pray in order to impetrate those things which God has determined would be obtained only through our prayers" (*Summa theologiae* 2a2ae Q. 83.2).[20] In other words, when petitionary prayer does influence God, it does so because the prayers themselves were predestined. God predetermined that he would take certain actions as predestined responses to predestined prayers. While Thomas is correct in what he denies, he is wrong, however, in what he affirms. True, petitionary prayer can never alter the tiniest detail of God's providential decree. But how extensive is God's decree? Is it universally inclusive of everything that ever happens everywhere at all times? According to this logic, when the letter of James insists that there are some things "[we] do not have, because [we] do not ask God" (4:2), Thomas would have us believe that God predestined our failure

---

19. McGrath puts it well in *Mystery of the Cross*, 123: "If God *is* omnipotent, he must be at liberty to set that omnipotence aside, and voluntarily to impose certain restrictions upon his course of action—to put it dramatically, but effectively, he must be free to have his hands tied behind his back. The *Christian* understanding of the omnipotence of God is that of a God *who voluntarily places limitations upon his course of action*. The God of classical theism contemplates possibilities which always remain open precisely because he never does anything: the 'crucified and hidden God' acts—and by acting eliminates possibilities which would otherwise be open" (emphasis original). For similar views, see Lucas, *Freedom and Grace*, 38–40; Baelz, *Does God Answer Prayer?* 25–28; Davis, *Logic and the Nature of God*, 70–73; Tupper, "Providence of God," 589; Polkinghorne, *Science and Providence*, 98; and idem, *Work of Love*, 90–106.

20. Quoted in T. Flint, *Divine Providence*, 212. For a good introduction to this idea of petitionary prayer as one of the divinely ordained secondary causes to the fulfillment of God's predetermined purposes, see Tiessen, *Providence and Prayer*, 196–202.

to pray, that he predetermined withholding certain spiritual benefits by predestining that we not ask for them! But if this is the plain-sense meaning of James 4:2, then theology has turned Bible reading into non-sense. Thomas's single-minded commitment to divine changelessness turns the Creator into "a celestial Henry Ford, offering us a car of any colour provided it is black."[21] This is not the God of the Bible. We can never allow such philosophical prejudice to gag Scripture.

According to the Bible, prayer makes sense only in a certain kind of universe with a certain kind of God; and however else they may be described, God is not a fatalist and the cosmos is not a mechanism. Different thinkers have devised alternative pictures attempting to describe this God in a universe where prayer makes a difference. Most famously, P. Geach devised the well-known analogy of God as the Grand Chess Master supremely aware of the infinite variety of moves available to every opponent at all times. While the cut and thrust of history's game is real, and our moves are truly our own, the Master's final victory is never in doubt.[22]

Because every metaphor has its own strengths and weaknesses, there is plenty of room for a variety of images to illustrate a point, all of which complement each other while remaining within the necessary bounds of God's theological playing field. Perhaps I may be forgiven then for offering one more analogy: the life of prayer is like the Iditarod.

Every winter dozens of dogsled teams prepare themselves for the Iditarod—a grueling two-week race from Anchorage to Nome, Alaska, mushing their dogs over ice and snow, through blinding blizzards and subzero temperatures, over mountain passes and frozen tundra, all for the love of huskies, racing, endurance, and wilderness. Each team must begin and end at the same locations. Check stations are scattered along the 1,150-mile course, and each sled must pass sequentially through every station in order to remain a qualified contestant. It is what the racers do between the check stations that dramatically tells the story of strategy, performance, risk, and endurance. How each team's members choose to get from station to station is entirely up to them. Do they trust the weather to hold while they risk a rugged shortcut over a mountain pass?

21. Polkinghorne, *Science and Providence*, 72.
22. Geach, *Providence and Evil*, 58. Hasker, *God, Time, and Knowledge*, 195–96, takes Geach's metaphor and further elaborates the imagery. Lucas, *Freedom and Grace*, 39, suggests an analogy to Persian rug-making, where the experienced artisan sits at the loom opposite a novice child while both weave simultaneously toward the center. Though the apprentice inevitably makes mistakes, the artisan's mastery of weaving is such that he or she can always make whatever adjustments are necessary to maintain the beauty and balance of the intended pattern. Gorringe, *God's Theatre*, 79–82, prefers the metaphor of God as divine director overseeing history's stage, "wooing" from us the responses and actions most suitable to his production.

Or do they play it safe by taking a longer route that is less likely to present a white wall of snow when the storm finally hits? All the racers are free to plot their own courses as long as they eventually funnel through the predetermined checkpoints. The winner is the driver who responds best to changing weather conditions and implements the shrewdest strategy while remaining within the race's predetermined boundaries of check stations and finish line.

Life is like the Iditarod. The sovereign Lord has predetermined that certain events must occur in order to advance his plans for salvation-history, culminating in the final redemption of his chosen people. The promises to Abraham, Israel's possession of Canaan, the return from exile, the birth of Jesus, his death, resurrection, and ascension—to touch on only a few of the highest peaks in salvation-history—were all redemptive moments assured by divine promise. The same promissory dynamics hold true for every believer. Although there is no contemporary prophetic voice to render God's verdict on every choice here and now, we can at least rest assured of the Father's love, our eventual sanctification, and the guarantee of a final hope. The Father has promised to complete the good work he begins in each of his children (Rom. 8:29–30; Phil. 1:6; Heb. 7:25).

Between those moments of divine faithfulness, however, are innumerable occasions of human unbelief and failure that have as little to do with providence as holiness does with sin. God did not predetermine Israel's stubbornness or its rejection of the prophets, nor does he foreordain my disobedience, my willfulness, or my failure to trust him fully. Yet these threads of human depravity stand side by side with the Father's commitment to accomplish his goals in creation. Yahweh promised Israel the land of Canaan, but the people had a choice in how rapidly and thoroughly that promise was fulfilled. Jesus was assured all the hopes of every messianic promise, but he also made a myriad of daily decisions about how best to submit before the Father in each new moment. In similar fashion, God predetermined certain events for all of his people, but getting from check station to check station is an exercise in choosing among options, many of which are equally viable, some wise, some foolish, a few faithful, many self-destructive. Prayerful conversation with God becomes the wisest strategy for finding the best among many possible routes through life's Iditarod. God has not set us on a path predetermined in all its details from beginning to end, complete with every success and every trauma we will ever experience. He has sovereignly determined some things, especially the gift of a beginning and a final hope, but the greater remainder is left for us to negotiate by faith, depending on how willing we are to believe that God still works, to trust his promises, to keep our eyes on Jesus, and, most of all, to persevere in prayer without giving up (Luke 18:1–8).

Several unresolved theological issues have a bearing on whether a person will be sympathetic to this Iditarod analogy. Questions of immutability, omnipotence, omniscience, foreknowledge, timelessness, and free will all have a place in the conversation. Furthermore, it must be acknowledged that at any given moment we may never know whether we are praying for something that God has foreordained or imploring for something that can yield to our petitions. We may never know whether a particular course of action is one of life's divine checkpoints or an opportunity to freely strategize about the wisest option. But knowing the answers to these kinds of questions, whether theological or pragmatic, is not the crucial concern, at least not for biblical theology or faithful discipleship. What matters in this regard is the simple act of praying through life and living through prayer. This disposition is not a matter of knowing but of believing, not of understanding but of trusting, trusting that the Father who always loves us always hears our prayers and always responds in the best of all possible ways, at the best of all possible times.

Prayer Can Change Those Who Pray

Third, while prayer can at times change God, it should always change the one who prays. Though we may never know which petitions engage providence and which initiate possibility, we can know that every prayer brings a needy person before a need-meeting God (Phil. 4:19). Whether a petition impetrates a divine response, whenever a sinner implores the Savior, a two-way street is opened between heaven and earth, and the Father's generosity is ready to pour out more than we can ask or imagine (Eph. 3:20). Some call this the therapeutic sanctifying value of prayer.[23] The praying person receives an overflow of spiritual benefits that surpass, or even appear totally unrelated to, the specifics of any request. Prayer becomes a resource for meeting the existential necessities of strength, peace, solace, faith, direction, and contentment.

Historic advocates of prayer's therapeutic value comprise an odd fraternity, with members' views ranging from the protoclassical orthodoxy of St. Augustine to the purely rationalistic religion of Immanuel Kant. What these curious bedfellows have in common is a shared emphasis on prayer's therapeutic benefits as its *sole* spiritual achievement. Prayer can change us, but it never changes God, either because he remains

---

23. See the survey in Brümmer, *What Are We Doing?* 16–28.

immoveable, is impersonal, or does not exist. Thus Neoplatonist St. Augustine could write: "God does not need to have our will made known to him—he cannot but know it—but he wishes our desire to be exercised in prayer that we may be able to receive what he is preparing to give" (*Letter to Proba* 17).[24]

John Calvin provides an especially ardent exposition of petition's purely therapeutic powers when he defends the importance of praying to an all-knowing sovereign Lord because "he ordained [prayer] not so much for his own sake as for ours" (*Institutes of the Christian Religion* §3.20.3).[25] Any apparent impetratory effects are merely illusory misinterpretations of providence.

Kant insisted that true religion rejected the "fetish faith" that believed prayer might actually influence God. Mature, rational faith understood that genuine prayer looked inward, taking ethical concerns and clothing them "in words and formulas [that] can, at best, possess only the value of a means whereby that disposition within us may be repeatedly quickened."[26] Prayer is religious self-talk. Of course, Augustine and Calvin would have been appalled at Kant's development of their perspectives, but it is not hard to see how Kant understood himself to be standing on their shoulders.

In any case, the question needs to be asked: must all theological options remain mutually exclusive in this way? Are the answers necessarily limited to prayer *either* changing God *or* changing us? Of course not. The New Testament clearly indicates that not only *can* prayer change God, but it most certainly *ought* to be changing anyone who prays. No one can encounter the supreme person and remain unaffected by their time together. So it goes without saying that prayer should always transform the person praying, assuming of course that a real meeting has transpired. Naturally, this is simpler to profess than it is to prove or to create. How can anyone guarantee an encounter with God? For many people, prayer *can* begin to feel like an exercise in self-hypnosis or wishful thinking. The sense of actually meeting with something or someone, of experiencing a power outside oneself, or of receiving a message from heaven is as foreign as it is infrequent. Persistent prayer becomes the supreme act of faith because the Christian life slowly evolves into a spiritual wasteland waiting to be refreshed by a watering can with no holes in it and noth-

24. Quoted by Brümmer, *What Are We Doing?* 23.

25. This section is Calvin's introduction to the Lord's Prayer. According to Calvin, the importance of the Lord's Prayer is found in the way that it reorients the believer's mind and heart. Unfortunately, this therapeutic tradition eventually makes way for the final distortion of prayer by deistic and atheistic thinkers, who will continue to defend prayer's personal, existential value while eliminating God from the picture altogether.

26. Immanuel Kant, *Religion within the Limits of Reason Alone*, trans. T. M. Greene and H. H. Hudson (New York: Harper, 1960), 184.

ing inside. We can wait for so very, very long and still see so very little evidence that anyone is paying attention. In cases like this, what can it possibly mean to insist that prayer changes the person praying? Can it do anything more than turn the hopeful into the forlorn? Even Kant's solution begins to ring hollow.

The problem is that we tend to assume that legitimate change always involves an emotional component. We know we have been changed when we *feel* different, and not just any kind of "different," but different in a way that is inexplicable apart from miraculous intervention. Yet, this becomes our problem precisely because it is not what the New Testament offers us in the way of change. Scripture insists that conversation with the Father can affect us in two ways: it can help to clarify God's will for our lives, and it can provide comfort and encouragement in times of need. Yet neither offer necessarily involves the type of experiential transformation that answers most requests for God to "change me" in the twenty-first century.

God offers transformations of the understanding and the will, changes that *may* entail the emotions but ultimately supersede emotionalism. Visions and ecstatic experiences are not necessarily transformational, but the supernatural reinforcement of firmly held convictions may one day help to change the world. Scripture offers precious little encouragement for those who approach God anticipating a fresh mountaintop experience with every new "amen." The occasional miraculous encounters recorded there are few and far between, the exceptions that prove the rule. More typically, New Testament encounters with God highlight faith and ethics over fervor and feelings, but learning to be content with such observations presumes less narcissism and more self-forgetfulness among the prayerful.

First, God has already revealed the greater portion of his will for every one of his children. And second, every Christian's greatest need is the faithfulness necessary to always do what is right. As surprising as it may seem, the New Testament gives little attention to mundane concerns such as personal health, family problems, employment, or finances (the kinds of issues that tend to preoccupy modern Western prayers). Such concerns are not totally absent from Scripture; they do occasionally arise, but when they do it is invariably because they pose some threat to the mission of the gospel. God's will is, first and foremost, that all believers live for his glory in whatever situation they find themselves, to sincerely pray "your kingdom come, your will be done" while searching for opportunities to live out the truth of the gospel in the simplest tasks of daily life. Those who insist that this is not specific enough direction, that they need a more detailed outline of God's plan, or that prayer must offer more nuanced answers to life's unexpected developments fail to grasp the mind of the New Testament. For the New Testament writers, "to live is Christ and to die is gain" (Phil. 1:21). Simply knowing that God hears our requests and is faithful in doing whatever is right was more than enough to assure them of "the peace of God, which transcends all understanding" (4:7). *This* is the change that prayer works in God's people: to transform the inwardly focused into the outwardly concerned, to turn the service of our heavenly Father into life's highest priority, to replace the worry of this world with utter confidence in the next.

None of this automatically excludes the possibility of direct super-natural "nudges" or "bumps" from the Holy Spirit. Those who have prayed long enough, looked for the possibilities hard enough, and been willing to risk looking foolish enough have their own stories to tell about how they once simply "knew" what to do and where to go or how the Spirit surprisingly "led" them in a new, unexpected direction. Just as Jesus received guidance in his selection of the Twelve (Luke 6:12–16) and Paul was redirected from Asia into Macedonia (Acts 16:6–10), so the Holy Spirit may continue to give specific answers to prayer today. But we do well to remember that the more likely candidates for such mystical leadings are those whose lives are first surrendered to the service of God's kingdom.

We Pray between the Times

The preceding discussion about the ways in which prayer changes us has already introduced the fourth observation: while Christian prayer occurs in this life, its priorities and values are dictated by the next. Grasping this fact is key to understanding prayer's mysteries. New Testament petition is indelibly shaped by the peculiarities of biblical eschatology, specifically the "already/not yet" tension inaugurated by Jesus's introduction of the kingdom of God. Eschatology is the grammar of prayer. Prayer is the language of eschatology.

Three issues in particular can be properly understood only from this vantage point: (1) why we pray for God to accomplish his will; (2) why New Testament petition is principally focused on spiritual concerns; and (3) why intercession has such a prominent place in New Testament prayer.

First, why does Jesus teach the disciples to pray, "Father, your kingdom come, your will be done, on earth as it is in heaven"? Why do we need to ask an all-powerful sovereign to do what he already wants to do with his own creation? What purpose is served by praying for the inevitable, unless we believe that God's will may fail? A variety of answers have been offered to this question, most of which finally reduce themselves to the ancient tonic of therapeutic change: we are instructed to pray this way because it attunes us to the Father's plans, making us more suitable servants. God's plan will not fail, but by praying for the accomplishment of his will, we obey the Father's instructions and thereby align our wills with his.

Yet, as vitally important as this answer is, to stop here ignores the obvious: when Jesus tells us to pray for God's will to be done, he makes it plain that God's will is not being done completely and that his kingdom is not now fully established.[27] The life and ministry of Jesus carved out a beachhead for the kingdom's arrival, and the history of the church advanced God's offensive against the realm of darkness, but there are many battles yet to be fought. While only the Father can bring the kingdom (hence, the request), our prayers can hone us into sharper instruments in God's hands.[28] Of course, this once again assumes that our petitions can make a real difference to God, but that seems to be Jesus's point! In fact, he once explained a temporary demonic victory over the disciples as a direct result of their failure to pray (Mark 9:28–29). Luke's Gospel makes it clear that the disciples' abandonment of Jesus on the night of his arrest was also due to their prayerlessness (Luke 22:31–46). God's kingdom is still coming. Though its final victory is assured, the final contours of its progress have yet to be determined. Both the degree of our personal involvement in the King's future victories and the course of the kingdom's encroachment over the cosmos will be shaped in part by the content and the faithfulness of our petitions.

Second, we have seen that Paul's obsession with the last day leads at least one scholar to suggest that we dare not look to the apostle as a sane model for Christian petition today. Yet, this is exactly the wrong conclusion. The exemplary value of Paul's prayer life is due to the clarity of his eschatological vision. The church inhabits the end of time. The old has gone; the new has come. In the next instant, in the twinkling of an eye, the Lord may appear like the proverbial thief in the night hunting for the family jewels. What is he likely to find?

New Testament petition has a laser-like focus on the things that matter for eternity. Physical health is temporary. No one evades decrepitude or the grim reaper indefinitely, but prayerfully cultivating a grace-filled life in the face of disappointment, pain, and mortality reaps a harvest of eternal fruit that will feed more hungry souls than we can ever imagine, in more ways than we will ever know this side of paradise. Not only does

27. Baelz, *Does God Answer Prayer?* 25.
28. Any suggestion that our behavior can ever "bring in the kingdom" is seriously misguided. The kingdom is God's alone to bring; its arrival is a thoroughly apocalyptic event. As members of God's kingdom, disciples are to live out kingdom values, thereby serving as salt and light to the world, but we should not confuse which is the cart and which is the horse.

that kind of sustenance last forever, but one day all physical illness will be eradicated; every devouring germ, virus, bacterium, and mutation will be banished from existence; and the Father will permanently replace sickness with the wholeness of what was meant to be. This is not "pie in the sky, by and by." It is Christian faith. Consequently, the apostle Paul intercedes for such gifts as grace, blamelessness, purity, endurance, holiness, confidence, and wisdom with all knowledge and depth of insight into the infinite goodness of God. Becoming this type of person while living a life such as ours is prayer's ultimate accomplishment. Certainly, there is plenty of biblical precedent for prayers motivated by life's worries (Matt. 6:11; Rom. 15:30–32; 2 Cor. 1:8–11; Eph. 6:18; Phil. 4:6), but life in Christ means that "our light and momentary troubles are achieving for us an eternal glory that far outweighs them all. So we fix our eyes not on what is seen, but on what is unseen. For what is seen is temporary, but what is unseen is eternal" (2 Cor. 4:17–18).

Ultimately, only the heavenly minded can be of any earthly good. The universe is our Father's good creation, but it is a distorted product, a cosmos groaning, waiting for release. Its final redemption occurs in a great conflagration. This world is not our final home. There is a tension here to be tightly grasped. Biblical eschatology never demands that we ignore life's injustices or withdraw from its painful realities. Loved ones will die, and we are right to grieve. Tragedy strikes, and we ought to pray for God's deliverance while doing everything we can to bring relief. Biblical eschatology does, however, require God's people to radically reprioritize their passions. Though we live in this world, any prayer life preoccupied with the concerns of this world is a life that has lost its way.

Third, the church is our Father's eschatological community, his new temple, a family of faith where brothers and sisters hold each other's best interests at heart even if we occasionally lose sight of what is best for ourselves. Thus the overwhelming majority of New Testament prayers are intercessions for the spiritual development and perseverance of family members. Of course, this raises an obvious question: if it is God's will to sanctify his people, why do we need to pray for anyone else's spiritual growth? Are we not asking for the inevitable? Would not a good God accomplish this anyway?

Once again, the biblical answer moves beyond the predictable therapeutic assurances. The New Testament is clear that, although God promises to complete every project he begins, some projects reach completion more readily than others; crossing life's finish line is a cooperative effort with no guarantees as to how rapidly or impressively anyone completes the race. Even the great apostle to the Gentiles apprehensively admitted the possibility of running in a way that was less than his best (1 Cor. 9:24–27; Gal. 2:2; Phil. 2:16). So, he consistently interceded for others and frequently asked others to intercede for him that they would all finish strong, confidently running toward the judgment seat of Christ where they would hear the verdict, "Well done, good and faithful servants." The conclusion is inescapable: intercessory prayer makes a real difference to the spiritual lives of others. Perhaps the greatest gift we can offer anyone is the prayer we make for their encouragement, guidance, patience, faith, peace of mind, conviction, repentance, or spiritual renewal.

Every believer is embedded within a transcontinental, transcendent web of spiritual connectedness called the body of Christ. No one's spiritual survival is totally dependent on intercession alone, and only God can retrace the complex threads of petitionary connectedness woven among all the interceding saints who love each other across time and space, but the benefits of intercession are as real as the kingdom's coming. No Christian ever succeeds alone. We are all carried in a collective net of innumerable prayers cast our way. Whether our accomplices have familiar faces or are distant strangers, whether they intercede sympathetically according to our requests or hammer out unsolicited pleadings contrary to our foolish desires, every Christian is buoyed on the intercessions of brothers and sisters in Christ.[29]

Power Appears through Suffering

The fifth and final observation also follows from the eschatological insights of the previous point: while miracles are still possible, suffering remains the norm for God's people. One distinguishing feature of Christian faith is the conviction that "with God all things are possible" (chapter 1). This is no less true in the twenty-first century than it was in Jesus's day; the same God and Father continues his work in this world. Therefore, faithful prayer will not hesitate to ask for miracles. The notoriety of television shysters and church charlatans can never diminish the reality of God's power or his willingness to share it with his children. I am convinced, for example, that I have experienced a number of miracles—events that are inexplicable apart from God's doing something out of the ordinary—in my own life. The challenge of mature Christian faith, however, is finding the faithful balance between believing in God's power, on the one hand, while participating in the foolishness of the cross, on the other.

The New Testament offers no predictable relationship between faith and miracle (chapter 2); neither is there any quantitative correlation

29. The idea of "double agency" found in Lucas (*Freedom and Grace*, 2–19) and then elaborated by Brümmer (*What Are We Doing?* 64–69; *Speaking of a Personal God*, 108–27) provides a very helpful tool for thinking about the different ways in which God's work and human action may cooperate as complementary "causes" in achieving God's will.

between measures of faith, fervency, or persistence and the likelihood of miraculous answers to prayer (chapters 3–4). In fact, miracles are most noticeable by their absence outside the Gospels and Acts. Jesus makes a few comments on the relationship between the two; the book of Acts describes several miraculous events that occur in response to the church's prayers; but praying for miracles vanishes from the remaining pages of the New Testament. This observation is rarely made, much less given the weight that it deserves. What do become quite frequent, and occupy a prominent place in the Gospels and Acts as well, are repeated prayers for endurance in the midst of trials, tests, temptations, persecutions, groanings, tears, rejection, suffering, and impending death. True, Paul had his own miracle stories: rescue from a Philippian jail (Acts 16:22–34), healing of a poisonous snake bite (28:1–6). But he told many more tales of "hardships . . . beyond [his] ability to endure" (2 Cor. 1:8–11), of his life "given over to death for Jesus' sake" (4:7–12), including beatings, imprisonments, hunger, bandits, and fleeing from threats under cover of darkness (6:3–10; 11:23–33).

How can we account for this trend in the biblical evidence? Once again, the answer is *eschatology*. Initially, Jesus's inauguration of the kingdom and the fulfillment of his intentions for the early church called for visual demonstrations of the Spirit's power. Consequently, there was an outbreak of the miraculous testifying to the truth of the gospel. But, as history proceeds, the miraculous "already" must exist within the confines of an incomplete "not yet." We still await the completed kingdom. This, too, is a piece of God's plan, to raise up his praying people in a time of eschatological tension, a time where miracles and disappointment coexist side by side.

What bearing does biblical eschatology have on praying for miracles?

Even though suffering is not the exclusive antithesis of miracle, it is safe to say that the majority of prayers for divine intervention are motivated by a desire to avoid unhappy circumstances. Therefore, suggesting that miracles may occur less frequently than we would hope implies that suffering will be more frequent than we might like. Equating prayer with power is a serious mistake, principally because we tend to misconstrue the New Testament meaning of power. God never promised to cloth his people in a miracle bubble protecting them from the trials and tribulations of life in a fallen world. Christians share in the daily turmoil of creation's frustrated groaning. The principal evidence of God's power is not seen in deliverance from discomfort, but in our Spirit-inspired ability to call him Abba and to know "that our present sufferings are not worth comparing with the glory that will be revealed in us" (Rom. 8:15–18). The ultimate manifestation of powerful prayer is Paul's hope, expressed while imprisoned, that we "may have power, together with all the saints, to grasp how wide and long and high and deep is the love of Christ, and to know this love that surpasses knowledge" (Eph. 3:18–19). If God in his wisdom has decided that life's greatest lessons are about his love and grace and that these lessons are best learned through suffering, then true prayer rebukes the mere power of miracle and embraces the authentic miracle of power in the cross (1 Cor. 1:18–25).

God's power most often hides in suffering. Understanding the power of prayer, therefore, demands that we first make peace with the hiddenness of God. Just as the Father revealed himself most beautifully while remaining hidden in the darkness of Calvary, so his power to answer prayer works most spectacularly in those saints who share in "the fellowship . . . of [Christ's] sufferings, becoming like him in his death" (Phil. 3:10). The Father's power is most clearly revealed as he hides himself in our most faithfully endured discomforts. To demand that he behave otherwise is to prefer the grandiose smoke and mirrors of a bogus wizard over the God who suffers with us behind Christ's tears.

The death and resurrection of Christ mean that it is always dangerous to equate answered prayer with apparent displays of power, for it implies that weakness is evidence of unanswered prayer (if not divine impotence). Aside from the childish assumption that God's answers will always give us what we want, this gross misunderstanding of the place of weakness in God's world creates a mindset that is both simplistic and un-Christian. A truly biblical theology of prayer will always remain rooted in the theology of the cross. We cannot infer God's apparent intentions from the raw experience of suffering. We can only interpret our suffering in the light of what we know about God's intentions.[30] Christian prayer will make sense over a lifetime only if we keep our eyes riveted on the man hanging from a cross.

By faith we know that the Father's intentions for us, as for Jesus, are always and only good. By faith we can rest assured that our Father always answers every prayer, however unexpected or even unwanted the reply may be. By faith we believe, as Jesus believed, that the plan of God can reshape the ugliest of life's experiences—the ones from which prayer does not deliver us, the ones that prayer delivers us into—by transforming them into redemptive moments we would never trade away. These are the lessons of the cross, and the cross was the fruit of Christ's prayer life, not just in Gethsemane, but in every moment where he surrendered, saying, "Father, not my will, but yours be done." It is in prayers such as these that the Christian path is illuminated as we experience a miraculous life of joy in this world and blessed hope in the next.

30. See Brümmer's helpful insights into interpreting God's intentions in *What Are We Doing?* 86–98.

Bibliography

Achtemeier, P. J. *1 Peter*. Philadelphia: Fortress, 1996.

———. "The Lucan Perspective on the Miracles of Jesus: A Preliminary Sketch." *Journal of Biblical Literature* 94 (1975): 547–62.

———. "Miracles and the Historical Jesus: A Study of Mark 9:14–29." *Catholic Biblical Quarterly* 37 (1975): 476–82.

Arndt, W. F. *Luke*. St. Louis: Concordia, 1956.

Arnold, C. *Ephesians, Power, and Magic: The Concept of Power in Ephesians in Light of Its Historical Setting*. Cambridge: Cambridge University Press, 1989.

Artz, P. "The 'Epistolary Introductory Thanksgiving' in the Papyri and in Paul." *Novum Testamentum* 36 (1994): 29–46.

Attridge, H. W. *The Epistle to the Hebrews*. Philadelphia: Fortress, 1989.

Aune, D. *Revelation*. 3 vols. Dallas: Word, 1997–98.

Baelz, P. *Does God Answer Prayer?* London: Darton, Longman & Todd, 1982.

Bahr, G. "The Use of the Lord's Prayer in the Primitive Church." *Journal of Biblical Literature* 84 (1965): 153–59.

Bailey, J. A. *The Traditions Common to the Gospels of Luke and John*. Leiden: Brill, 1963.

Bailey, K. E. *Poet and Peasant: A Literary-Cultural Approach to the Parables in Luke*. Grand Rapids: Eerdmans, 1976.

———. *Through Peasant Eyes: More Lucan Parables*. Grand Rapids: Eerdmans, 1980.

Baldwin, E. S. G. "Gethsemane: The Fulfillment of a Prophecy." *Bibliotheca Sacra* 77 (1920): 429–36.

Barb, A. A. "The Survival of Magic Arts." Pages 100–125 in *The Conflict between Paganism and Christianity in the Fourth Century*. Edited by A. Momigliano. Oxford: Clarendon, 1963.

Barr, J. "'*Abba*, Father' and the Familiarity of Jesus' Speech." *Theology* 91 (1988): 173–79.

———. "'*Abbā* Isn't Daddy." *Journal of Theological Studies*, n.s., 39 (1988): 28–47.

Barrett, C. K. *A Commentary on the Epistle to the Romans*. New York: Harper, 1957.

———. *A Critical and Exegetical Commentary on the Acts of the Apostles*. 2 vols. Edinburgh: Clark, 1994–98.

———. *The Gospel according to St. John: An Introduction with Commentary and Notes on the Greek Text*. London: SPCK, 1967.

———. "Light on the Holy Spirit from Simon Magus (Acts 8,4–25)." Pages 281–95 in *Les Actes des Apôtres: Traditions, rédaction, théologie* by J. Kremer et al. Leuven: Leuven University Press, 1979.

Barth, K. *Church Dogmatics*. Translated and edited by G. W. Bromiley and T. F. Torrance. 5 vols. Edinburgh: Clark, 1936–77.

Barth, M. *Ephesians: Introduction, Translation, and Commentary*. 2 vols. New York: Doubleday, 1974.

Basinger, D. *The Case for Freewill Theism: A Philosophical Assessment*. Downers Grove, IL: InterVarsity, 1996.

Bauckham, R. *The Climax of Prophecy: Studies on the Book of Revelation*. Edinburgh: Clark, 1993.

Bauer, W., W. F. Arndt, F. W. Gingrich, and F. W. Danker. *A Greek-English Lexicon of the New Testament and Other Early Christian Literature*. 3rd edition. Chicago: University of Chicago Press, 2000.

Beale, G. K. *The Book of Revelation: A Commentary on the Greek Text*. Grand Rapids: Eerdmans, 1999.

Beasley-Murray, G. R. *Jesus and the Kingdom of God*. Grand Rapids: Eerdmans, 1986.

———. *John*. 2nd edition. Nashville: Nelson, 1999.

Benjamin, D. C. "The Persistent Widow." *Bible Today* 28 (1990): 213–19.

Best, E. *A Critical and Exegetical Commentary on Ephesians*. Edinburgh: Clark, 1998.

Betz, H. D. "Magic and Mystery in the Greek Magical Papyri." Pages 244–59 in *Magika Hiera: Ancient Greek Magic and Religion*. Edited by C. A. Faraone and D. Obbink. Oxford: Oxford University Press, 1991.

Betz, H. D., ed. *The Greek Magical Papyri in Translation: Including the Demotic Spells*. Chicago: University of Chicago Press, 1986.

Bigg, C. *A Critical and Exegetical Commentary on the Epistles of St. Peter and St. Jude*. Edinburgh: Clark, 1901.

Black, D. A. *Paul, Apostle of Weakness: Astheneia and Its Cognates in the Pauline Literature*. New York: Peter Lang, 1984.

Black, M. "The Cup Metaphor in Mark xiv.36." *Expository Times* 59 (1947–48): 195.

Blaising, C. A. "Gethsemane: A Prayer of Faith." *Journal of the Evangelical Theological Society* 22 (1979): 333–43.

Blass, F., A. Debrunner, and R. W. Funk. *A Greek Grammar of the New Testament and Other Early Christian Literature*. Chicago: University of Chicago Press, 1961.

Bloesch, D. G. *The Struggle of Prayer*. San Francisco: Harper & Row, 1980.

Blomberg, C. L. *Interpreting the Parables*. Downers Grove, IL: InterVarsity, 1990.

———. "The Miracles as Parables." Pages 327–59 in *The Miracles of Jesus*. Edited by D. Wenham and C. Blomberg. Gospel Perspectives 6. Sheffield: JSOT Press, 1986.

Bolt, J. "The Relation between Creation and Redemption in Romans 8:18–27." *Calvin Theological Journal* 30 (1995): 34–51.

Bottini, G. G. *La preghiera di Elia in Giacomo 5,17–8: Studio della tradizione biblica et giudaica*. Jerusalem: Franciscan Printing House, 1981.

Bovon, F. "Apocalyptic Traditions in the Lukan Special Materials: Reading Luke 18:1–8." *Harvard Theological Review* 90 (1997): 383–91.

Bowker, J. W. "'Merkabah' Visions and the Visions of Paul." *Journal of Jewish Studies* 16 (1971): 157–73.

Boyd, G. *God of the Possible: A Biblical Introduction to the Open View of God*. Grand Rapids: Baker, 2000.

Boyd, R. F. "The Work of the Holy Spirit in Prayer." *Interpretation* 8 (1954): 35–42.

Boyle, J. L. "The Last Discourse (Jn 13,31–16,33) and Prayer (Jn 17): Some Observations on Their Unity and Development." *Biblica* 56 (1975): 210–22.

Brettler, M. Z. "Biblical History and Jewish Biblical Theology." *Journal of Religion* 77 (1997): 563–83.

Brown, R. E. *The Death of the Messiah, from Gethsemane to the Grave: A Commentary on the Passion Narratives in the Four Gospels*. New York: Doubleday, 1994.

———. *The Gospel according to John*. 2 vols. New York: Doubleday, 1966–70.

———. "The Passion according to Mark." *Worship* 59 (1985): 116–26.

———. "The Pater Noster as an Eschatological Prayer." *Theological Studies* 22 (1961): 175–208.

Bruce, F. F. *The Book of the Acts*. Revised edition. Grand Rapids: Eerdmans, 1988.

———. *The Epistle to the Hebrews*. Grand Rapids: Eerdmans, 1964.

———. *1–2 Thessalonians*. Waco: Word, 1982.

Brümmer, V. *Speaking of a Personal God: An Essay in Philosophical Theology*. Cambridge: Cambridge University Press, 1992.

———. *What Are We Doing When We Pray? A Philosophical Inquiry*. London: SCM, 1984.

Buchanan, G. W. "Symbolic Money-Changers in the Temple?" *New Testament Studies* 37 (1991): 280–90.

Bultmann, R. *The Gospel of John: A Commentary*. Translated by G. R. Beasley-Murray. Philadelphia: Westminster, 1971.

——. *History of the Synoptic Tradition*. Translated by J. Marsh. Oxford: Blackwell, 1963.

——. "Is Exegesis without Presuppositions Possible?" Pages 145–53 in *New Testament and Mythology and Other Basic Writings*. Edited by S. M. Ogden. Philadelphia: Fortress, 1984.

——. *The Johannine Epistles*. Translated by R. P. O'Hara, L. C. McGaughy, and R. W. Funk. Philadelphia: Fortress, 1973.

——. "Πιστεύω." Vol. 6 / pp. 171–228 in *Theological Dictionary of the New Testament*. Edited by G. Kittel and G. Friedrich. Translated by G. W. Bromiley. Grand Rapids: Eerdmans, 1968.

——. *Theology of the New Testament*. Translated by K. Grobel. 2 vols. New York: Scribner, 1951–55.

Bundy, W. E. *Jesus and the First Three Gospels: An Introduction to the Synoptic Tradition*. Cambridge: Harvard University Press, 1955.

Burney, C. F. *The Poetry of Our Lord: An Examination of the Formal Elements of Hebrew Poetry in the Discourses of Jesus Christ*. Oxford: Clarendon, 1925.

Caird, G. B. *New Testament Theology*. Completed and edited by L. D. Hurst. Oxford: Clarendon, 1994.

Calvin, J. *Institutes of the Christian Religion*. Edited by J. T. McNeil. Translated by F. L. Battles. 2 vols. Philadelphia: Westminster, 1960.

Cameron, P. S. "Lead Us Not into Temptation." *Expository Times* 101 (1990): 299–300.

Carson, D. A. *A Call to Spiritual Reformation: Priorities from Paul and His Prayers*. Grand Rapids: Baker, 1992.

Catchpole, D. R. "Q and 'The Friend at Midnight' (Luke xi.5–8/9)." *Journal of Theological Studies* 34 (1983): 407–24.

——. "The Son of Man's Search for Faith (Luke xviii 8b)." *Novum Testamentum* 19 (1977): 82–104.

Charles, J. D. "An Apocalyptic Tribute to the Lamb (Rev. 5:1–14)." *Journal of the Evangelical Theological Society* 34 (1991): 461–73.

Charles, R. H. *A Critical and Exegetical Commentary on the Revelation of St. John*. 2 vols. Edinburgh: Clark, 1920.

Charlesworth, J. H. "A Caveat on Textual Transmission and the Meaning of Abba: A Study of the Lord's Prayer." Pages 1–14 in *The Lord's Prayer and Other Prayer Texts from the Greco-Roman Era*. Edited by J. H. Charlesworth, M. Harding, and M. Kiley. Valley Forge, PA: Trinity, 1994.

——. "Jewish Prayers in the Time of Jesus." *Princeton Seminary Bulletin*, n.s., 13 (1992): 36–55.

Charlesworth, J. H., ed. *The Old Testament Pseudepigrapha*. 2 vols. Garden City, NY: Doubleday, 1983–85.

Chase, Frederic Henry. *The Lord's Prayer in the Early Church*. Cambridge: Cambridge University Press, 1891.

Chilton, B. *God in Strength: Jesus' Announcement of the Kingdom*. Freistadt: Plöchl, 1979.

———. *Pure Kingdom: Jesus' Vision of God*. Grand Rapids: Eerdmans, 1996.

Chilton, B., and J. I. H. McDonald. *Jesus and the Ethics of the Kingdom*. Grand Rapids: Eerdmans, 1987.

Collins, J. J. *Jewish Wisdom in the Hellenistic Age*. Louisville: Westminster John Knox, 1997.

Conzelmann, H. *A Commentary on the Acts of the Apostles*. Translated by J. Limburg, A. T. Kraabel, and D. H. Juel. Philadelphia: Fortress, 1987.

Cook, J. *The Structure and Persuasive Power of Mark: A Linguistic Approach*. Atlanta: Scholars Press, 1995.

Cooper, R. M. "Leitourgos Christou Iesou: Toward a Theology of Christian Prayer." *Anglican Theological Review* 47 (1965): 263–75.

Craddock, F. B. *Luke*. Louisville: John Knox, 1990.

Cranfield, C. E. B. *A Critical and Exegetical Commentary on the Epistle to the Romans*. 2 vols. Edinburgh: Clark, 1975–79.

———. "The Cup Metaphor in Mark xiv.36 and Parallels." *Expository Times* 59 (1947–48): 137–38.

———. *The Gospel according to Saint Mark*. Cambridge: Cambridge University Press, 1959.

———. "The Parable of the Unjust Judge and the Eschatology of Luke-Acts." *Scottish Journal of Theology* 16 (1963): 297–301.

Crossan, J. D. *The Historical Jesus: The Life of a Mediterranean Jewish Peasant*. New York: HarperCollins, 1991.

Crump, D. *Jesus the Intercessor: Prayer and Christology in Luke-Acts*. Grand Rapids: Baker, 1999.

———. "The Virgin Birth in New Testament Theology." Pages 65–92 in *Chosen by God: Mary in Evangelical Perspective*. Edited by D. F. Wright. London: Marshall Pickering, 1989.

Cullmann, O. *Christ and Time: The Primitive Christian Conception of Time and History*. Translated by F. V. Filson. Philadelphia: Westminster, 1964.

———. *Prayer in the New Testament*. Translated by J. Bowden. Philadelphia: Fortress, 1995.

———. *Salvation in History*. Translated by S. G. Sowers. London: SCM, 1967.

Cunningham, G. *Religion and Magic: Approaches and Theories*. New York: New York University Press, 1999.

D'Angelo, M. R. "*Abba* and 'Father': Imperial Theology and the Jesus Traditions." *Journal of Biblical Literature* 111 (1992): 611–30.

———. "Theology in Mark and Q: *Abba* and 'Father' in Context." *Harvard Theological Review* 85 (1992): 149–74.

Dalman, G. *Die Worte Jesu: Mit Berücksichtigung des nachkanonischen Jüdischen Schriftttums und der Aramäischen Sprache*. Leipzig: Hinrichs, 1898.

———. *The Words of Jesus: Considered in the Light of Post-Biblical Jewish Writings and the Aramaic Language*. Translated by D. M. Day. Edinburgh: Clark, 1909.

Danker, F. W. *Jesus and the New Age*. Revised edition. Philadelphia: Fortress, 1988.

Daube, D. "A Prayer Pattern in Judaism." *Studia Evangelica* 1 (1959): 539–45.

Davids, P. *The Epistle of James: A Commentary on the Greek Text*. Grand Rapids: Eerdmans, 1982.

Davies, W. D., and D. C. Allison Jr. *A Critical and Exegetical Commentary on the Gospel according to Saint Matthew*. 3 vols. Edinburgh: Clark, 1988–97.

Davis, S. T. *Logic and the Nature of God*. Grand Rapids: Eerdmans, 1983.

De Boer, W. P. *The Imitation of Paul: An Exegetical Study*. Kampen: Kok, 1962.

Derrett, J. D. M. "The Friend at Midnight—Asian Ideas in the Gospel of St. Luke." Pages 78–87 in *Donum Gentilicium: New Testament Studies in Honour of David Daube*. Edited by E. Bammel, C. K. Barrett, and W. D. Davies. Oxford: Clarendon, 1978.

———. "Law in the New Testament: The Parable of the Unjust Judge." *New Testament Studies* 18 (1971–72): 178–91.

———. "Sleeping at Gethsemane." *Downside Review* 114 (1996): 235–45.

Di Sante, C. *Jewish Prayer: The Origins of the Christian Liturgy*. Translated by M. J. O'Connell. New York: Paulist Press, 1991.

Dickie, M. W. *Magic and Magicians in the Greco-Roman World*. New York: Routledge, 2001.

Dodd, C. H. *The Epistle of Paul to the Romans*. London: Hodder & Stoughton, 1932.

———. *Historical Tradition in the Fourth Gospel*. Cambridge: Cambridge University Press, 1963.

Donin, H. H. *To Pray as a Jew: A Guide to the Prayer Book and Synagogue Service*. New York: Basic Books, 1980.

Donn, T. M. "Our Daily Bread." *Evangelical Quarterly* 21 (1949): 209–18.

Dowd, S. E. *Prayer, Power, and the Problem of Suffering: Mark 11:22–25 in the Context of Markan Theology*. Atlanta: Scholars Press, 1988.

———. "Toward a Johannine Theology of Prayer." Pages 317–35 in *Perspectives on John: Method and Interpretation in the Fourth Gospel*. Edited by R. B. Sloan and M. C. Parsons. Lewiston, NY: Mellen, 1993.

Drane, J. W. "Simon the Samaritan and the Lucan Concept of Salvation History." *Evangelical Quarterly* 47 (1975): 131–37.

Dunn, J. D. G. *Romans*. 2 vols. Dallas: Word, 1988.

Eddy, G. E. G. "Transformed Values of Honor and Shame in Luke 18:1–14." *Proceedings of the Eastern Great Lakes and Midwest Biblical Societies* 12 (1992): 119–25.

Edwards, J. "The Most High a Prayer-Hearing God." Vol. 6 / pp. 498–511 in *The Works of President Edwards*. Edited by E. Williams and E. Parsons. New York: Franklin, 1968.

Edwards, J. R. "Markan Sandwiches: The Significance of Interpolations in Markan Narratives." *Novum Testamentum* 31 (1989): 193–216.

Ellingworth, P. *The Epistle to the Hebrews: A Commentary on the Greek Text*. Grand Rapids: Eerdmans, 1993.

Elliott, J. H. *1 Peter: A New Translation with Introduction and Commentary*. New York: Doubleday, 2000.

Elliott, S. M. "John 15:15 . . . Not Slaves But Friends." *Proceedings of the Eastern Great Lakes and Midwest Biblical Societies* 13 (1993): 31–46.

Eppstein, V. "The Historicity of the Gospel Account of the Cleansing of the Temple." *Zeitschrift für die Neutestamentliche Wissenschaft* 55 (1964): 42–58.

Evans, C. A. "Jesus' Action in the Temple: Cleansing or Portent of Destruction?" *Catholic Biblical Quarterly* 51 (1989): 237–70.

———. "Jesus' Action in the Temple and Evidence of Corruption in the First-Century Temple." Pages 522–39 in *Society of Biblical Literature Seminar Papers* 28. Atlanta: Scholars Press, 1989.

———. "Jesus and the 'Cave of Robbers': Toward a Jewish Context for the Temple Action." *Bulletin for Biblical Research* 3 (1993): 93–110.

———. *Mark 8:27–16:20*. Nashville: Nelson, 2001.

Fee, G. D. *The First Epistle to the Corinthians*. Grand Rapids: Eerdmans, 1987.

———. "John 14:8–17." *Interpretation* 43 (1989): 170–74.

Feldkämper, L. *Der betende Jesus als Heilsmittler nach Lukas*. Bonn: Steyler, 1978.

Finkel, A. "The Prayer of Jesus in Matthew." Pages 131–70 in *Standing before God: Studies on Prayer in Scriptures and in Tradition with Essays in Honor of John M. Oesterreicher*. Edited by A. Finkel and L. Frizzell. New York: Ktav, 1981.

Fitzmyer, J. A. "Abba and Jesus' Relation to God." Pages 15–38 in *À Cause de L'Évangile: Études sur les Synoptiques et les Actes*. Cerf: Saint-André, 1985.

———. *The Acts of the Apostles: A New Translation with Introduction and Commentary*. New York: Doubleday, 1998.

———. *The Gospel according to Luke*. 2 vols. Garden City, NY: Doubleday, 1981–85.

———. *Romans: A New Translation with Introduction and Commentary*. New York: Doubleday, 1993.

Fitzmyer, J. A., and D. J. Harrington. *A Manual of Palestinian Aramaic Texts*. Rome: Pontifical Biblical Institute Press, 1978.

Flint, T. P. *Divine Providence: A Molinist Account*. Ithaca: Cornell University Press, 1998.

Flint, V. "The Demonization of Magic and Sorcery in Late Antiquity: Christian Redefinitions of Pagan Religions." Pages 279–348 in *Witchcraft and Magic in Europe: Ancient Greece and Rome*. Edited by B. Ankarloo and S. Clark. Philadelphia: University of Pennsylvania Press, 1999.

Frame, J. M. *No Other God: A Response to Open Theism*. Phillipsburg, NJ: P&R, 2001.

Freed, E. D. "Parable of the Judge and the Widow (Luke 18.1–8)." *New Testament Studies* 33 (1987): 38–60.

———. "Psalm 42/43 in John's Gospel." *New Testament Studies* 29 (1983): 62–73.

Fridrichsen, A. "Exegetisches zum Neuen Testament." *Symbolae Osloenses* 13 (1934): 38–46.

Garland, D. E. "The Lord's Prayer in the Gospel of Matthew." *Review and Expositor* 89 (1992): 215–28.

Garrett, S. R. "Exodus from Bondage: Luke 9:31 and Acts 12:1–24." *Catholic Biblical Quarterly* 52 (1990): 656–80.

Gärtner, B. *The Temple and the Community in Qumran and the New Testament: A Comparative Study in the Temple Symbolism of the Qumran Texts and the New Testament*. Cambridge: Cambridge University Press, 1965.

Gaventa, B. R. "To Speak Thy Word with All Boldness, Acts 4:23–31." *Faith and Mission* 3 (1986): 76–82.

Geach, P. *Providence and Evil: The Stanton Lectures, 1971–2*. Cambridge: Cambridge University Press, 1977.

Geddert, T. J. *Mark*. Scottdale, PA: Herald, 2001.

Geertz, H. "An Anthropology of Religion and Magic, I." *Journal of Interdisciplinary History* 6 (1975): 71–89.

Geisler, N. L. *Creating God in the Image of Man? The New "Open" View of God— Neotheism's Dangerous Drift*. Minneapolis: Bethany, 1997.

George, A. R. *Communion with God in the New Testament*. London: Epworth, 1953.

Gerhardsson, B. "The Matthean Version of the Lord's Prayer (Matt 6:9b–13): Some Observations." Vol. 1 / pages 207–20 in *The New Testament Age: Essays in Honor of Bo Reicke*. Edited by W. C. Weinrich. Macon, GA: Mercer, 1984.

———. *The Mighty Acts of Jesus according to Matthew*. Lund: Gleerup, 1979.

Gerrish, B. A. "'To the Unknown God': Luther and Calvin on the Hiddenness of God." *Journal of Religion* 53 (1973): 263–92.

Goetz, R. "On Petitionary Prayer: Pleading with the Unjust Judge?" *Christian Century* 114 (Jan. 29, 1997): 96–99.

Goldingay, J. "The Logic of Intercession." *Theology* 101 (1998): 262–70.

Gorringe, T. J. *God's Theatre: A Theology of Providence*. London: SCM, 1991.

Goshen-Gottstein, M. "Tanakh Theology: The Religion of the Old Testament and the Place of Jewish Biblical Theology." Pages 617–44 in *Ancient Israelite Religion: Essays in Honor of Frank Moore Cross*. Edited by P. D. Miller et al. Philadelphia: Fortress, 1987.

Graf, F. *Magic in the Ancient World*. Cambridge: Harvard University Press, 1997.

————. "Prayer in Magic and Religious Ritual." Pages 188–213 in *Magika Hiera: Ancient Greek Magic and Religion*. Edited by C. A. Faraone and D. Obbink. Oxford: Oxford University Press, 1991.

Graubard, B. "The *Kaddish* Prayer." Pages 59–72 in *The Lord's Prayer and Jewish Liturgy*. Edited by J. J. Petuchowski and M. Brocke. New York: Seabury, 1978.

Grayston, K. "The Decline of Temptation—and the Lord's Prayer." *Scottish Journal of Theology* 46 (1993): 279–92.

Green, J. B. *The Death of Jesus: Tradition and Interpretation in the Passion Narrative*. Tübingen: Mohr, 1988.

————. *The Gospel of Luke*. Grand Rapids: Eerdmans, 1997.

————. "Jesus on the Mount of Olives (Luke 22:39–46): Tradition and Theology." *Journal for the Study of the New Testament* 26 (1986): 29–48.

————. "Persevering Together in Prayer: The Significance of Prayer in the Acts of the Apostles." Pages 183–202 in *Into God's Presence: Prayer in the New Testament*. Edited by R. N. Longenecker. Grand Rapids: Eerdmans, 2001.

Greeven, H. *Gebet und Eschatologie im Neuen Testament*. Gütersloh: Bertelsmann, 1931.

Grislis, E. "Martin Luther's View of the Hidden God: The Problem of the *Deus Absconditus* in Luther's Treatise De Servo Arbitrio." *McCormick Quarterly* 21 (1967): 81–94.

Guelich, R. A. *The Sermon on the Mount*. Waco: Word, 1982.

Gundry, R. H. *Mark: A Commentary on His Apology for the Cross*. Grand Rapids: Eerdmans, 1993.

Haenchen, E. *The Acts of the Apostles: A Commentary*. Translated by B. Noble and G. Shinn. Oxford: Blackwell, 1971.

————. *John 2: A Commentary on the Gospel of John Chapters 7–21*. Translated by R. W. Funk. Philadelphia: Fortress, 1984.

Hagner, D. A. *Matthew*. Dallas: Word, 1993.

Hamilton, N. W. "Temple Cleansing and Temple Bank." *Journal of Biblical Literature* 83 (1964): 365–72.

Hammer, R. *Entering Jewish Prayer: A Guide to Personal Devotion and the Worship Service*. New York: Schocken, 1994.

Hammond, D. "Magic: A Problem in Semantics." *American Anthropologist* 72 (1970): 1349–56.

Harner, P. B. *Understanding the Lord's Prayer*. Philadelphia: Fortress, 1975.

Harris, O. G. "Prayer in Luke-Acts: A Study in the Theology of Luke." Ph.D. dissertation, Vanderbilt University, 1967.

Hartman, L. "'Into the Name of Jesus': A Suggestion concerning the Earliest Meaning of the Phrase." *New Testament Studies* 20 (1974): 432–40.

Hasker, W. *God, Time, and Knowledge*. Ithaca: Cornell University Press, 1989.

Hawthorne, G. F. *Philippians*. Waco: Word, 1983.

Hayden, D. R. "Calling the Elders to Pray." *Bibliotheca Sacra* 138 (1981): 258–66.

Hays, R. B. *The Faith of Jesus Christ: The Narrative Substructure of Galatians 3:1–4:11*. 2nd edition. Grand Rapids: Eerdmans, 2002.

Hedrick, C. W. *Parables as Poetic Fictions: The Creative Voice of Jesus*. Peabody, MA: Hendrickson, 1994.

Heil, J. P. "The Fifth Seal (Rev 6,9–11) as a Key to the Book of Revelation." *Biblica* 74 (1993): 220–43.

Heiler, F. *Prayer: A Study in the History and Psychology of Religion*. Translated by S. McComb. London: Oxford University Press, 1932.

Heinemann, J. "The Background of Jesus' Prayer in the Jewish Liturgical Tradition." Pages 81–89 in *The Lord's Prayer and Jewish Liturgy*. Edited by J. J. Petuchowski and M. Brocke. New York: Seabury, 1978.

———. *Prayer in the Talmud: Forms and Patterns*. Berlin: de Gruyter, 1977.

Held, H. J. "Matthew as Interpreter of the Miracle Stories." Pages 165–299 in *Tradition and Interpretation in Matthew*, by G. Bornkamm, G. Barth, and H. J. Held. London: SCM, 1963.

Hemer, C. "Ἐπιούσιος." *Journal for the Study of the New Testament* 22 (1984): 81–94.

Hengel, M. *The Charismatic Leader and His Followers*. New York: Crossroad, 1981.

———. *The Son of God: The Origin of Christology and the History of Jewish-Hellenistic Religion*. Philadelphia: Fortress, 1976.

Herzog, W. R. *Parables as Subversive Speech: Jesus as Pedagogue of the Oppressed*. Louisville: Westminster John Knox, 1994.

Hicks, J. M. "The Parable of the Persistent Widow (Luke 18:1–8)." *Restoration Quarterly* 33 (1991): 209–23.

Hiers, R. H. "Purification of the Temple: Preparation for the Kingdom of God." *Journal of Biblical Literature* 90 (1971): 82–90.

Hodge, C. *Commentary on the Epistle to the Romans*. 1886. Revised edition. Reprinted Grand Rapids: Eerdmans, 1947.

Hoffman, L. A. *The Canonization of the Synagogue Service*. Notre Dame: Notre Dame University Press, 1979.

Holleran, J. W. *The Synoptic Gethsemane: A Critical Study*. Rome: Gregorian University Press, 1973.

Holtz, T. "Paul and the Oral Gospel Tradition." Pages 380–93 in *Jesus and the Oral Gospel Tradition*. Edited by H. Wansbrough. Sheffield: JSOT Press, 1991.

Hooker, M. D. *The Gospel according to Saint Mark*. Peabody, MA: Hendrickson, 1991.

———. "Traditions about the Temple in the Sayings of Jesus." *Bulletin of the John Rylands Library* 70 (1988): 7–19.

Houk, C. B. "*Peirasmos*, the Lord's Prayer, and the Massah Tradition." *Scottish Journal of Theology* 19 (1966): 216–25.

Hultgren, A. J. "The Bread Petition of the Lord's Prayer." *Anglican Theological Review* 72 (1990): 41–54.

Hunter, W. B. *The God Who Hears*. Downers Grove, IL: InterVarsity 1986.

Janowitz, N. *Magic in the Roman World: Pagans, Jews, and Christians*. New York: Routledge, 2001.

Jeremias, J. "Abba." *Theologische Literaturzeitung* 79 (1954): 213–14.

———. "Abba." *Zeitschrift für die Neutestamentliche Wissenschaft* 45 (1954): 131–32.

———. *Abba: Studien zur neutestamentlichen Theologie und Zeitgeschichte*. Göttingen: Vandenhoeck & Ruprecht, 1966.

———. *The Central Message of the New Testament*. London: SCM, 1965.

———. "Kennzeichen der ipsissima vox Jesu." Pages 86–93 in *Synoptische Studien Alfred Wikenhauser zum siebzigsten Geburtstag*. Edited by J. Schmidt and A. Vögtle. Munich: Zink, 1953.

———. *New Testament Theology: The Proclamation of Jesus*. Translated by J. Bowden. New York: Scribner, 1971.

———. *The Parables of Jesus*. Translated by S. H. Hooke. Revised edition. New York: Scribner, 1963.

———. *The Prayers of Jesus*. Translated by J. Bowden and J. Reumann. London: SCM, 1967.

John, J. "Anointing in the New Testament." Pages 46–76 in *Oil of Gladness*. Edited by M. Dudley and G. Rowell. London: SPCK, 1993.

John, M. P. "Give Us This Day Our . . . Bread." *Bible Translator* 31 (1980): 245–47.

Johnson, A. F. "Assurance for Man: The Fallacy of Translating *Anaideia* by 'Persistence' in Luke 11:5–8." *Journal of the Evangelical Theological Society* 22 (1979): 123–31.

Johnson, L. T. *The Gospel of Luke*. Collegeville, MN: Liturgical Press, 1991.

———. *The Letter of James: A New Translation with Introduction and Commentary*. New York: Doubleday, 1995.

Johnson, N. B. *Prayer in the Apocrypha and Pseudepigrapha: A Study of the Jewish Concept of God*. Philadelphia: Society of Biblical Literature and Exegesis, 1948.

Johnston, W. G. "Does James Give Believers a Pattern for Dealing with Sickness and Healing?" Pages 168–74 in *Integrity of Heart, Skillfulness of Hands*. Edited by C. H. Dyer and R. B. Zuck. Grand Rapids: Baker, 1994.

Juel, D. "The Lord's Prayer in the Gospels of Matthew and Luke." Pages 56–70 in *The Lord's Prayer: Perspectives for Reclaiming Christian Prayer*. Edited by D. L. Migliore. Grand Rapids: Eerdmans, 1993.

———. *Messiah and Temple: The Trial of Jesus in the Gospel of Mark*. Missoula, MT: Scholars Press, 1977.

Jülicher, A. *Die Gleichnisreden Jesu*. 2 vols. Tübingen: Mohr, 1899.

Kalimi, I. "History of Israelite Religion or Old Testament Theology? Jewish Interest in Biblical Theology." *Scandinavian Journal of the Old Testament* 11 (1997): 100–123.

Karris, R. J. *Prayer and the New Testament: Jesus and His Communities at Worship*. New York: Crossroad, 2000.

―――. "Some New Angles on James 5:13–20." *Review and Expositor* 97 (2000): 207–19.

Käsemann, E. *Commentary on Romans*. Translated by G. W. Bromiley. Grand Rapids: Eerdmans, 1980.

―――. *Perspectives on Paul*. Philadelphia: Fortress, 1971.

Kee, H. C. "Magic and Messiah." Pages 121–41 in *Religion, Science, and Magic: In Concert and in Conflict*. Edited by J. Neusner, E. S. Frerichs, and P. V. M. Flesher. Oxford: Oxford University Press, 1989.

Keener, C. S. *A Commentary of the Gospel of Matthew*. Grand Rapids: Eerdmans, 1999.

Kelber, W. H. "Mark 14:32–42: Gethsemane, Passion Christology, and Discipleship Failure." *Zeitschrift für die Neutestamentliche Wissenschaft* 63 (1972): 166–87.

Kelly, J. N. D. *A Commentary on the Pastoral Epistles*. London: Black, 1963.

Kiley, M. "'Lord, Save My Life' (Ps 116:4) as Generative Text for Jesus' Gethsemane Prayer." *Catholic Biblical Quarterly* 48 (1986): 655–59.

―――. "The Lord's Prayer and Matthean Theology." Pages 15–27 in *The Lord's Prayer and Other Prayer Texts from the Greco-Roman Era*. Edited by J. H. Charlesworth, M. Harding, and M. Kiley. Valley Forge, PA: Trinity, 1994.

Kio, S. H. "A Prayer Framework in Mark 11." *Bible Translator* 37 (1986): 323–28.

Kittel, G. "Ἀββᾶ." Vol. 1 / pp. 5–6 in *Theological Dictionary of the New Testament*. Edited by G. Kittel and G. Friedrich. Translated by G. W. Bromiley. Grand Rapids: Eerdmans, 1968.

Klauck, H.-J. *Magic and Paganism in Early Christianity: The World of the Acts of the Apostles*. Translated by B. McNeil. Minneapolis: Fortress, 2003.

Knight, G. W. *The Pastoral Epistles: A Commentary on the Greek Text*. Grand Rapids: Eerdmans, 1992.

Kolenkow, A. B. "A Problem of Power: How Miracle Doers Counter Charges of Magic in the Hellenistic World." Pages 105–10 in *Society of Biblical Literature 1976 Seminar Papers*. Edited by G. MacRae. Missoula, MT: Scholars Press, 1976.

Kotansky, R. "Incantations and Prayers for Salvation on Inscribed Greek Amulets." Pages 105–37 in *Magika Hiera: Ancient Greek Magic and Religion*. Edited by C. A. Faraone and D. Obbink. Oxford: Oxford University Press, 1991.

Kuhn, H. W. *Enderwartung und Gegenwärtiges Heil: Untersuchungen zu den Gemeindeliedern von Qumran*. Göttingen: Vandenhoeck & Ruprecht, 1966.

Kuhn, K. G. "New Light on Temptation, Sin, and Flesh in the New Testament." Pages 94–113 in *The Scrolls and the New Testament*. Edited by K. Stendahl. New York: Crossroad, 1992.

Kümmel, W. G. *Promise and Fulfilment: The Eschatological Message of Jesus*. Translated by D. M. Barton. London: SCM, 1957.

Kysar, R. *John: The Maverick Gospel*. Louisville: John Knox, 1993.

Ladd, G. E. *The Presence of the Future: The Eschatology of Biblical Realism*. Grand Rapids: Eerdmans, 1974.

Lambrecht, J. "The Opening of the Seals (Rev 6,1–8)." *Biblica* 79 (1998): 198–220.

Lane, W. A. *Hebrews*. 2 vols. Dallas: Word, 1991.

Latourelle, R. *The Miracles of Jesus and the Theology of Miracles*. New York: Paulist Press, 1988.

Laws, S. *A Commentary on the Epistle of James*. San Francisco: Harper & Row, 1980.

Leaney, R. "The Lucan Text of the Lord's Prayer (Lk. xi 2–4)." *Novum Testamentum* 1 (1956): 103–11.

Levenson, J. D. "Why Jews Are Not Interested in Biblical Theology." Pages 281–307 in *Judaic Perspectives on Ancient Israel*. Edited by J. Neusner, B. A. Levine, and E. S. Frerichs. Philadelphia: Fortress, 1987.

Levinson, N. "Importunity?" *Expository Times* 9 (1925): 456–60.

Lieu, J. *The Gospel of Luke*. Peterborough: Epworth, 1997.

Lincoln, A. T. *Ephesians*. Dallas: Word, 1990.

———. "God's Name, Jesus' Name, and Prayer in the Fourth Gospel." Pages 155–80 in *Into God's Presence: Prayer in the New Testament*. Edited by R. N. Longenecker. Grand Rapids: Eerdmans, 2001.

———. *Paradise Now and Not Yet*. Cambridge: Cambridge University Press, 1981.

———. "Paul the Visionary: The Setting and Significance of the Rapture to Paradise in 2 Corinthians 12:1–10." *New Testament Studies* 25 (1979): 204–20.

Lindström, F. *God and the Origin of Evil: A Contextual Analysis of Alleged Monistic Evidence in the Old Testament*. Lund: Gleerup, 1983.

Linnemann, E. *Parables of Jesus: Introduction and Exposition*. Translated by J. Sturdy. London: SPCK, 1975.

Lohmeyer, E. *The Lord's Prayer*. Translated by J. Bowden. London: Collins, 1965.

Lohse, E. "Miracles in the Fourth Gospel." Pages 64–75 in *What about the New Testament? Essays in Honour of Christopher Evans*. Edited by M. Hooker and C. Hickling. London: SCM, 1975.

Longenecker, R. N. "Prayer in the Pauline Letters." Pages 203–27 in *Into God's Presence: Prayer in the New Testament*. Edited by R. N. Longenecker. Grand Rapids: Eerdmans, 2001.

Losie, L. A. "The Cursing of the Fig Tree: Tradition Criticism of a Markan Pericope (Mark 11:12–14, 20–25)." *Studia biblica et theologica* 7 (1977): 3–18.

Lucas, J. R. *Freedom and Grace*. Grand Rapids: Eerdmans, 1976.

———. *The Future: An Essay on God, Temporality, and Truth*. Oxford: Blackwell, 1989.

Lüdemann, G. "The Acts of the Apostles and the Beginnings of Simonian Gnosis." *New Testament Studies* 33 (1987): 420–26.

Lundström, G. *The Kingdom of God in the Teaching of Jesus: A History of Interpretation from the Last Decades of the Nineteenth Century to the Present Day.* Translated by J. Bulman. Edinburgh: Oliver & Boyd, 1963.

MacRae, G. "A Note on Romans 8:26–27." *Harvard Theological Review* 73 (1980): 227–30.

Madigan, K. "Ancient and High-Medieval Interpretations of Jesus in Gethsemane: Some Reflections on Tradition and Continuity in Christian Thought." *Harvard Theological Review* 88 (1995): 157–73.

Manson, T. W. "The Cleansing of the Temple." *Bulletin of the John Rylands Library* 33 (1951): 271–82.

———. *The Gospel of Luke*. London: Hodder & Stoughton, 1930.

———. "The Lord's Prayer." *Bulletin of the John Rylands Library* 38 (1955–56): 99–113, 436–48.

———. *The Teaching of Jesus: Studies of Its Form and Content*. Cambridge: Cambridge University Press, 1939.

Marshall, C. D. *Faith as a Theme in Mark's Narrative*. Cambridge: Cambridge University Press, 1989.

Marshall, I. H. *Acts: An Introduction and Commentary*. Grand Rapids: Eerdmans, 1980.

———. *The Epistles of John*. Grand Rapids: Eerdmans, 1978.

———. *1 and 2 Thessalonians*. Grand Rapids: Eerdmans, 1983.

———. *The Gospel of Luke: A Commentary on the Greek Text*. Grand Rapids: Eerdmans, 1979.

Martin, B. *Prayer in Judaism*. New York: Basic Books, 1968.

Martin, R. P. *2 Corinthians*. Waco: Word, 1986.

———. *James*. Waco: Word, 1988.

Mawhinney, A. "God as Father: Two Popular Theories Reconsidered." *Journal of the Evangelical Theological Society* 31 (1988): 181–89.

McGrath, A. E. *Luther's Theology of the Cross: Martin Luther's Theological Breakthrough*. Oxford: Blackwell, 1985.

———. *The Mystery of the Cross*. Grand Rapids: Zondervan, 1988.

Meeks, W. A. "Simon Magus in Recent Research." *Religious Studies Review* 3 (1977): 137–42.

Meier, J. P. *A Marginal Jew: Rethinking the Historical Jesus*. 3 vols. New York: Doubleday, 1991–2001.

Menzies, R. P. *The Development of Early Christian Pneumatology with Special Reference to Luke-Acts*. Sheffield: JSOT Press, 1991.

Metzger, B. M. "How Many Times Does '*Epiousios*' Occur outside the Lord's Prayer?" *Expository Times* 69 (1957): 52–54.

———. *A Textual Commentary on the Greek New Testament*. 2nd edition. New York: United Bible Societies, 1994.

Meyer, B. F. "A Caricature of Joachim Jeremias and His Scholarly Work." *Journal of Biblical Literature* 110 (1991): 451–62.

Meyer, M., R. Smith, and N. Kelsey, eds. *Ancient Christian Magic: Coptic Texts of Ritual Power*. San Francisco: Harper, 1994.

Michaels, J. R. *1 Peter*. Waco: Word, 1988.

Mitton, C. L. *The Epistle of James*. Grand Rapids: Eerdmans, 1966.

———. *The Epistle to the Ephesians*. Oxford: Clarendon, 1951.

Moessner, D. P. "'The Christ Must Suffer': New Light on the Jesus–Peter, Stephen, Paul Parallels in Luke-Acts." *Novum Testamentum* 28 (1986): 220–56.

Moore, G. F. *Judaism in the First Centuries of the Christian Era: The Age of the Tannaim*. 3 vols. Cambridge: Harvard University Press, 1954.

Morgan, M. A. *Sepher ha-Razim: The Book of the Mysteries*. Chico, CA: Scholars Press, 1983.

Moule, C. F. D. "An Unsolved Problem in the Temptation-Clause in the Lord's Prayer." *Reformed Theological Review* 33 (1974): 65–75.

———. "'As We Forgive . . .': A Note on the Distinction between Deserts and Capacity in the Understanding of Forgiveness." Pages 68–77 in *Donum Gentilicium: New Testament Studies in Honour of David Daube*. Edited by E. Bammel, C. K. Barrett, and W. D. Davies. Oxford: Clarendon, 1978.

Mounce, R. H. *The Book of Revelation*. Grand Rapids: Eerdmans, 1977.

Mounce, W. D. *Pastoral Epistles*. Nashville: Nelson, 2000.

Mullins, T. Y. "Paul's Thorn in the Flesh." *Journal of Biblical Literature* 76 (1957): 299–303.

Murphy-O'Connor, J. *Paul: A Critical Life*. Oxford: Oxford University Press, 1997.

Murray, J. *The Epistle to the Romans*. 2 vols. Grand Rapids: Eerdmans, 1968.

Naveh, J., and S. Shaked. *Amulets and Magic Bowls: Aramaic Incantations of Late Antiquity*. Jerusalem: Magnes, 1987.

———. *Magic Spells and Formulae: Aramaic Incantations of Late Antiquity*. Jerusalem: Magnes, 1993.

Neirynck, F. "Paul and the Sayings of Jesus." Pages 265–321 in *L'Apôtre Paul*, by A. Vanhoye et al. Leuven: Peeters, 1986.

Neusner, J. "Money-Changers in the Temple: The Mishnah's Explanation." *New Testament Studies* 35 (1989): 287–90.

Newsom, C. A. "Songs of the Sabbath Sacrifice." Pages 28–32 in *Prayer from Alexander to Constantine: A Critical Anthology*. Edited by M. Kiley. London/New York: Routledge, 1997.

Neyrey, J. "The Absence of Jesus' Emotions—the Lucan Redaction of Lk 22,39–46." *Biblica* 61 (1980): 153–71.

———. *The Passion according to Luke: A Redaction Study of Luke's Soteriology*. New York: Paulist, 1985.

Nickelsburg, G. W. E. *Jewish Literature between the Bible and the Mishnah*. Philadelphia: Fortress, 1981.

Nicol, W. *The Sēmeia in the Fourth Gospel: Tradition and Redaction*. Leiden: Brill, 1972.

Nineham, D. E. *Saint Mark*. Philadelphia: Westminster, 1963.

Nisbet, P. "The Thorn in the Flesh." *Expository Times* 80 (1969): 126.

Nolland, J. *Luke*. 3 vols. Dallas: Word, 1989–93.

Nygren, A. *Commentary on Romans*. Translated by C. C. Rasmussen. Philadelphia: Muhlenberg, 1949.

Obeng, E. A. "The Reconciliation of Rom. 8.26f. to New Testament Writings and Themes." *Scottish Journal of Theology* 39 (1986): 165–74.

———. "The Spirit Intercession Motif in Paul." *Expository Times* 95 (1984): 360–64.

O'Brien, P. T. *Colossians, Philemon*. Waco: Word, 1982.

———. "Divine Provision for Our Needs: Assurances from Philippians 4." *Reformed Theological Review* 50 (1991): 21–29.

———. *Introductory Thanksgivings in the Letters of Paul*. Leiden: Brill, 1977.

———. "Prayer in Luke-Acts." *Tyndale Bulletin* 24 (1973): 112–27.

———. "Thanksgiving within the Structure of Pauline Theology." Pages 50–66 in *Pauline Studies*. Edited by D. Hagner and M. Harris. Grand Rapids: Eerdmans, 1980.

O'Connor, E. D. *Faith in the Synoptic Gospels: A Problem in the Correlation of Scripture and Theology*. Notre Dame: University of Notre Dame Press, 1961.

Oesterreicher, J. M. "'Abba, Father!' On the Humanity of Jesus." Pages 123–34 in *The Lord's Prayer and Jewish Liturgy*. Edited by J. J. Petuchowski and M. Brocke. New York: Crossroad, 1978.

Omanson, R. L. "The Certainty of Judgement and the Power of Prayer." *Review and Expositor* 83 (1986): 427–38.

Omark, R. E. "The Saving of the Savior: Exegesis and Christology in Hebrews 5:7–10." *Interpretation* 12 (1958): 41–43.

O'Neill, J. C. "The Lord's Prayer." *Journal for the Study of the New Testament* 51 (1993): 3–25.

Orchard, B. "The Meaning of *ton Epiousion*." *Biblical Theology Bulletin* 3 (1973): 274–82.

Osborne, G. R. *Revelation*. Grand Rapids: Baker, 2003.

Osiek, C. "Paul's Prayer: Relationship with Christ?" Pages 145–57 in *Scripture and Prayer*. Edited by C. Osiek and D. Senior. Wilmington, DE: Glazier, 1988.

Ostrander, R. *The Life of Prayer in a World of Science: Protestants, Prayer, and American Culture, 1870–1930*. Oxford: Oxford University Press, 2000.

Pao, D. W. *Thanksgiving: An Investigation of a Pauline Theme*. Downers Grove, IL: InterVarsity, 2002.

Park, D. M. "Paul's Σκόλοψ τῇ Σαρκί: Thorn or Stake?" *Novum Testamentum* 22 (1980): 179–83.

Parry, D. T. N. "Release of the Captives—Reflections on Acts 12." Pages 156–64 in *Luke's Literary Achievement: Collected Essays*. Edited by C. M. Tuckett. Sheffield: Sheffield Academic Press, 1995.

Phillips, C. R. *"Nullum crimen sine lege*: Socioreligious Sanctions on Magic." Pages 260–76 in *Magika Hiera: Ancient Greek Magic and Religion*. Edited by C. A. Faraone and D. Obbink. Oxford: Oxford University Press, 1991.

Pinnock, C. H., et al. *The Openness of God: A Biblical Challenge to the Traditional Understanding of God*. Downers Grove, IL: InterVarsity, 1994.

Piper, J., J. Taylor, and P. K. Helseth. *Beyond the Bounds: Open Theism and the Undermining of Biblical Christianity*. Wheaton, IL: Crossway, 2003.

Plummer, A. *A Critical and Exegetical Commentary on the Gospel according to St. Luke*. Edinburgh: Clark, 1896.

Polkinghorne, J. *Science and Providence: God's Interaction with the World*. Boston: Shambhala, 1989.

———. *The Work of Love: Creation as Kenosis*. Grand Rapids: Eerdmans, 2001.

Pool, D. De Sola. *The Kaddish*. 3rd edition. Jerusalem: Sivan, 1964.

Powell, W. "Lead Us Not into Temptation." *Expository Times* 67 (1956): 177–78.

Price, R. M. "Punished in Paradise (an Exegetical Theory on 2 Corinthians 12:1–10)." *Journal for the Study of the New Testament* 7 (1980): 33–40.

Pulleyn, S. *Prayer in Greek Religion*. Oxford: Oxford University Press, 1997.

Purdy, A. C. "The Epistle to the Hebrews." Vol. 11 / pp. 577–763 in *The Interpreter's Bible*. Eited by G. A. Buttrick. New York: Abingdon Cokesbury, 1951.

Reicke, B. *The Epistles of James, Peter, and Jude*. New York: Doubleday, 1964.

———. *Re-examining Paul's Letters: The History of the Pauline Correspondence*. Harrisburg, PA: Trinity, 2001.

Reid, B. E. *Choosing the Better Part? Women in the Gospel of Luke*. Collegeville, MN: Liturgical Press, 1996.

———. "A Godly Widow Persistently Pursuing Justice: Luke 18:1–8." *Biblical Research* 45 (2000): 25–33.

Reif, S. C. *Judaism and Hebrew Prayer: New Perspectives on Jewish Liturgical History*. Cambridge: Cambridge University Press, 1993.

Rendtorff, R. "The Future of Biblical Theology: A Jewish and Christian Interpretation." *Toronto Journal of Theology* 5 (1989): 280–92.

Reumann, J. "How Do We Interpret 1 Timothy 2:1–5 (and Related Passages)?" Pages 149–57 in *One Mediator, the Saints, and Mary*. Edited by H. G. Anderson, J. F. Stafford, and J. A. Burgess. Minneapolis: Augsburg, 1992.

Rice, R. *The Openness of God: The Relationship of Divine Foreknowledge and Human Free Will*. Nashville: Review & Herald, 1980.

Richardson, A. *The Miracle-Stories of the Gospels*. London: SCM, 1941.

Rickards, R. R. "The Translation of Luke 11.5–13." *Biblical Translator* 28 (1977): 239–43.

Roberts, C. H. *Manuscript, Society, and Belief in Early Christian Egypt*. London: Oxford University Press, 1979.

Robin, A. De Q. "The Cursing of the Fig Tree in Mark xi: A Hypothesis." *New Testament Studies* 8 (1962): 276–81.

Robson, J. "The Meaning of Christ's Prayer in Gethsemane." *Expository Times* 6 (1894–95): 522–23.

Rordorf, W. "The Lord's Prayer in the Light of Its Liturgical Use in the Early Church." *Studia Liturgica* 14 (1980–81): 1–19.

Rowland, C. *The Open Heaven: A Study of Apocalyptic Judaism and Early Christianity*. London: SPCK, 1982.

Runnalls, D. "The King as Temple Builder: A Messianic Typology." Pages 15–37 in *Spirit within Structure*. Edited by E. J. Furcha. Allison Park, PA: Pickwick, 1983.

Sabbe, M. "The Cleansing of the Temple and the Temple Logion." Pages 331–54 in Sabbe's *Studia Neotestamentica: Collected Essays*. Leuven: Leuven University Press, 1991.

Sanday, W., and A. C. Headlam. *A Critical and Exegetical Commentary on the Epistle to the Romans*. Edinburgh: Clark, 1902.

Sanders, E. P. "Defending the Indefensible." *Journal of Biblical Literature* 110 (1991): 463–77.

———. *Jesus and Judaism*. London: SCM, 1985.

———. *Judaism: Practice and Belief, 63 BCE–66 CE*. Philadelphia: Trinity, 1994.

———. *Paul and Palestinian Judaism: A Comparison of Patterns of Religion*. Philadelphia: Fortress, 1977.

Sanders, J. *The God Who Risks: A Theology of Providence*. Downers Grove, IL: InterVarsity, 1998.

Sanders, J., and C. A. Hall. *Does God Have a Future? A Debate on Divine Providence*. Grand Rapids: Baker, 2003.

Sanders, J. A. *The Dead Sea Psalms Scroll*. Ithaca: Cornell University Press, 1967.

———. *The Psalms Scroll of Qumrân Cave 11 (11QPsᵃ)*. Discoveries in the Judaean Desert of Jordan 4. Oxford: Clarendon, 1965.

Schäfer, P. "Jewish Magic Literature in Late Antiquity and Early Middle Ages." *Journal of Jewish Studies* 41 (1990): 75–91.

Schiffman, L. H., and M. D. Swartz. *Hebrew and Aramaic Incantation Texts from the Cairo Genizah*. Sheffield: JSOT Press, 1992.

Schmid, Josef. *The Gospel according to Mark*. Translated by K. Condon. Staten Island, NY: Mercier, 1968.

Schnackenburg, R. *The Gospel according to St. John*. Translated by D. Smith and G. A. Kon. 3 vols. New York: Crossroad, 1980–82.

———. *The Johannine Epistles: Introduction and Commentary*. Translated by R. Fuller and U. Fuller. New York: Crossroad, 1992.

Scholem, G. *The Messianic Idea in Judaism and Other Essays on Jewish Spirituality*. New York: Schocken, 1971.

Schottrof, L. *Lydia's Impatient Sisters: A Feminist Social History of Early Christianity*. Louisville: Westminster John Knox, 1995.

Schubert, P. *Form and Function of the Pauline Thanksgivings*. Berlin: Töpelmann, 1939.

Schuller, E. "The Psalm of 4Q372 1 within the Context of Second Temple Prayer." *Catholic Biblical Quarterly* 54 (1992): 67–79.

Schürmann, H. *Praying with Christ: The "Our Father" for Today*. Translated by W. M. Ducey. New York: Herder & Herder, 1964.

Schwartz, J. W. "Jesus in Gethsemane." *Lutheran Quarterly* 22 (1892): 267–71.

Schweitzer, A. *The Mysticism of Paul the Apostle*. Translated by W. Montgomery. London: Black, 1931.

Schweizer, E. *The Good News according to Mark*. Translated by D. H. Madvig. Richmond: John Knox, 1970.

———. *The Good News according to Matthew*. Translated by D. E. Green. Atlanta: John Knox, 1975.

———. *The Letter to the Colossians*. Translated by A. Chester. Minneapolis: Augsburg, 1976.

Scott, B. B. *Hear Then the Parable: A Commentary on the Parables of Jesus*. Minneapolis: Fortress, 1989.

Seeley, D. "Jesus' Temple Act." *Catholic Biblical Quarterly* 55 (1993): 263–83.

Sellew, P. "Interior Monologue as a Narrative Device in the Parables of Luke." *Journal of Biblical Literature* 111 (1992): 239–53.

Senior, P. *The Passion Narrative according to Matthew: A Redactional Study*. Gembloux: Leuven University Press, 1975.

———. *The Passion of Jesus in the Gospel of Matthew*. Wilmington, DE: Glazier, 1985.

Sharot, S. *Messianism, Mysticism, and Magic: A Sociological Analysis of Jewish Religious Movements*. Chapel Hill: University of North Carolina Press, 1982.

Shogren, G. S. "Will God Heal Us—A Re-examination of James 5:14–16a." *Evangelical Quarterly* 61 (1989): 101–7.

Smalley, S. S. *1, 2, 3 John*. Waco: Word, 1984.

———. "The Spirit, Kingdom, and Prayer in Luke-Acts." *Novum Testamentum* 15 (1973): 59–71.

Smillie, G. R. "Ephesians 6:19–20: A Mystery for the Sake of Which the Apostle Is an Ambassador in Chains." *Trinity Journal* 18 (1997): 199–222.

Smith, G. "The Function of 'Likewise' (ὡσαύτως) in Romans 8:26." *Tyndale Bulletin* 49 (1998): 29–38.

Smith, M. *Jesus the Magician*. London: Gollancz, 1978.

Smith, N. G. "The Thorn That Stayed: An Exposition of 2 Cor 12:7–9." *Interpretation* 13 (1959): 409–16.

Snodgrass, K. "*Anaideia* and the Friend at Midnight (Luke 11:8)." *Journal of Biblical Literature* 116 (1997): 505–13.

Spear, W. *The Theology of Prayer: A Systematic Study of the Biblical Teaching on Prayer*. Grand Rapids: Baker, 1979.

Spittler, R. P. "The Limits of Ecstasy: An Exegesis of 2 Corinthians 12:1–10." Pages 259–66 in *Current Issues in Biblical and Patristic Interpretation*. Edited by G. F. Hawthorne. Grand Rapids: Eerdmans, 1975.

Stagg, F. "Luke's Theological Use of Parables." *Review and Expositor* 94 (1997): 215–29.

Stanley, D. M. "'Become Imitators of Me': The Pauline Conception of Apostolic Tradition." *Biblica* 40 (1959): 859–77.

———. *Boasting in the Lord: The Phenomenon of Prayer in Saint Paul*. New York: Paulist Press, 1973.

Stein, R. H. "The Cleansing of the Temple in Mark (11:15–19): Reformation or Judgment?" Pages 121–33 in Stein's *Gospels and Tradition: Studies on Redaction Criticism of the Synoptic Gospels*. Grand Rapids: Baker, 1991.

———. *Luke*. Nashville: Broadman, 1992.

———. *The Synoptic Problem: An Introduction*. 3rd edition. Grand Rapids: Baker, 2000.

Steinsaltz, Adin. *A Guide to Jewish Prayer*. Translated by R. Toueg. New York: Schocken, 2000.

Stendahl, K. "Paul at Prayer." *Interpretation* 34 (1980): 240–49.

Strecker, G. *The Johannine Letters: A Commentary on 1, 2, and 3 John*. Translated by L. M. Maloney. Minneapolis: Fortress, 1996.

Stuckwisch, D. R. "Principles of Christian Prayer from the Third Century: A Brief Look at Origen, Tertullian, and Cyprian with Some Comments on Their Meaning for Today." *Worship* 71 (1997): 2–19.

Swete, H. B. *The Gospel according to St. Mark*. London: Macmillan, 1898.

Swetnam, J. "The Crux at Hebrews 5,7–8." *Biblica* 81 (2000): 347–61.

Tannehill, R. C. "Israel in Luke-Acts: A Tragic Story." *Journal of Biblical Literature* 104 (1985): 69–85.

Taylor, V. *The Gospel according to St. Mark*. London: Macmillan, 1953.

Telford, W. R. *The Barren Temple and the Withered Tree: A Redaction-Critical Analysis of the Cursing of the Fig-Tree Pericope in Mark's Gospel and Its Relation to the Cleansing of the Temple Tradition*. Sheffield: JSOT Press, 1980.

Thomas, J. C. "The Devil, Disease, and Deliverance: James 5.14–16." *Journal of Psychology and Theology* 2 (1993): 25–50.

Thompson, G. H. P. "Thy Will be Done in Earth, as It Is in Heaven (Matthew vi.11)." *Expository Times* 70 (1959): 379–81.

Thompson, M. M. "Intercession in the Johannine Community: 1 John 5:16 in the Context of the Gospel and the Epistles of John." Pages 225–45 in *Worship, Theology, and Ministry in the Early Church: Essays in Honor of Ralph P. Martin*. Edited by M. J. Wilkins and T. Paige. Sheffield: JSOT Press, 1992.

Thrall, M. E. *A Critical and Exegetical Commentary on the Second Epistle to the Corinthians*. 2 vols. Edinburgh: Clark, 2000.

Thurston, B. *Spiritual Life in the Early Church: The Witness of Acts and Ephesians.* Minneapolis: Fortress, 1993.

Tiede, D. L. *Luke.* Minneapolis: Augsburg, 1988.

Tiessen, T. *Providence and Prayer: How Does God Work in the World?* Downers Grove, IL: InterVarsity, 2000.

Trites, A. A. "The Prayer Motif in Luke-Acts." Pages 168–86 in *Perspectives on Luke-Acts.* Edited by C. H. Talbert. Danville, VA: Association of Baptist Professors of Religion, 1978.

Tupper, E. F. "The Providence of God in Christological Perspective." *Review and Expositor* 82 (1985): 579–95.

Turner, M. M. B. "Prayer in the Gospels and Acts." Pages 58–83 in *Teach Us to Pray: Prayer in the Bible and the World.* Edited by D. A. Carson. Grand Rapids: Baker, 1990.

Twelftree, G. H. *Jesus the Exorcist: A Contribution to the Study of the Historical Jesus.* Tübingen: Mohr, 1993.

Van Der Loos, H. *The Miracles of Jesus.* Leiden: Brill, 1968.

Van Roon, A. *The Authenticity of Ephesians.* Leiden: Brill, 1974.

Van Straten, F. T. "Gifts for the Gods." Pages 65–151 in *Faith, Hope and Worship: Aspects of Religious Mentality in the Ancient World.* Edited by H. S. Versnel. Leiden: Brill, 1981.

VanGemeren, W. "Abba in the Old Testament?" *Journal of the Evangelical Theological Society* 31 (1988): 385–98.

Vermes, G. *The Complete Dead Sea Scrolls in English.* 3rd edition. New York: Penguin, 1997.

———. *Jesus the Jew.* London: SCM, 1983.

Versnel, H. S. "Some Reflections on the Relationship Magic-Religion." *Numen* 38 (1991): 177–97.

Via, D. "The Parable of the Unjust Judge: A Metaphor of the Unrealized Self." Pages 1–32 in *Semiology and Parables: Exploration of the Possibilities Offered by Structuralism for Exegesis.* Edited by D. Patte. Pittsburgh: Pickwick, 1976.

Waetjen, H. C. "The Subversion of 'World' by the Parable of the Friend at Midnight." *Journal of Biblical Literature* 120 (2001): 703–21.

Wahlde, U. C. von. "The Theological Assessment of the First Christian Persecution: The Apostles' Prayer and Its Consequences in Acts 4,24–31." *Biblica* 76 (1995): 523–31.

Wainwright, G. "Praying for Kings: The Place of Human Rulers in the Divine Plan of Salvation." *Ex auditu* 2 (1986): 119–22.

Walker, W. O. "The Lord's Prayer in Matthew and in John." *New Testament Studies* 28 (1982): 237–56.

Wall, R. W. "Successors to 'the Twelve' according to Acts 12:1–17." *Catholic Biblical Quarterly* 53 (1991): 628–43.

Ware, B. A. *God's Lesser Glory: The Diminished God of Open Theism.* Wheaton, IL: Crossway, 2000.

Warrington, K. "The Significance of Elijah in James 5:13–18." *Evangelical Quarterly* 66 (1994): 217–27.

Wedderburn, A. J. M. "Romans 8.26—Towards a Theology of Glossolalia?" *Scottish Journal of Theology* 28 (1975): 369–77.

Weima, J. A. D. *Neglected Endings: The Significance of the Pauline Letter Closings.* Sheffield: JSOT Press, 1994.

Weiss, J. *Jesus' Proclamation of the Kingdom of God.* Translated and edited by R. H. Hiers and D. L. Holland. Philadelphia: Fortress, 1971.

Wenham, D. *Paul: Follower of Jesus or Founder of Christianity?* Grand Rapids: Eerdmans, 1995.

———. "Paul's Use of the Jesus Tradition: Three Samples." Pages 7–37 in *The Jesus Tradition outside the Gospels.* Edited by D. Wenham. Gospel Perspectives 5. Sheffield: JSOT Press, 1985.

Werline, R. *Penitential Prayer in Second Temple Judaism: The Development of a Religious Institution.* Atlanta: Scholars Press, 1998.

Westcott, B. F. *The Epistle to the Hebrews: The Greek Text with Notes and Essays.* Reprinted Grand Rapids: Eerdmans, 1984.

———. *The Gospel according to St. John.* London: Murray, 1909.

White, J. L. *The Form and Function of the Body of the Greek Letter: A Study of the Letter-Body in the Non-literary Papyri and in Paul the Apostle,* Missoula, MT: Society of Biblical Literature, 1972.

Wiles, G. P. *Paul's Intercessory Prayers: The Significance of the Intercessory Prayer Passages in the Letters of St. Paul.* Cambridge: Cambridge University Press, 1974.

Willis, G. G. "Lead Us Not into Temptation." *Downside Review* 93 (1975): 282–83.

Wilson, R. M. "Simon and Gnostic Origins." Pages 485–91 in *Les Actes des Apôtres: Traditions, rédaction, théologie* by J. Kremer et al. Leuven: Leuven University Press, 1979.

Windisch, H. *The Meaning of the Sermon on the Mount: A Contribution to the Historical Understanding of the Gospels and to the Problem of Their True Exegesis.* Translated by S. M. Gilmour. Philadelphia: Westminster, 1951.

Witherington, B. *The Acts of the Apostles: A Socio-Rhetorical Commentary.* Grand Rapids: Eerdmans, 1998.

Woods, E. J. *The "Finger of God" and Pneumatology in Luke-Acts.* Sheffield: Sheffield Academic Press, 2001.

Wright, N. T. *The Letter to the Romans.* New Interpreter's Bible Commentary 10. Nashville: Abingdon, 2002.

Wu, J. L. "The Spirit's Intercession in Romans 8:26–27: An Exegetical Note." *Expository Times* 105 (1993): 13.

Young, B. H. *The Jewish Background of the Lord's Prayer.* Austin: Center for Judaic-Christian Studies, 1984.

———. *The Parables: Jewish Tradition and Christian Interpretation*. Peabody, MA: Hendrickson, 1998.

Zahavy, T. *Studies in Jewish Prayer*. New York: University Press of America, 1990.

Zeller, D. "God as Father in the Proclamation and in the Prayer of Jesus." Pages 117–29 in *Standing before God: Studies on Prayer in Scriptures and in Tradition with Essays in Honor of John M. Oesterreicher*. Edited by A. Finkel and L. Frizzell. New York: Ktav, 1981.

Zerwick, M. *Biblical Greek, Illustrated by Examples*. Rome: Pontifical Biblical Institute Press, 1963.

Subject Index

abandonment 59
abba 98–99, 102, 104n29, 204–6, 209
abiding 161, 162–63, 167
Achtemeier, P. 53
Acts, as golden age of church 179–80
Adam, fall of 200–201
adoption 106, 107, 199, 205, 207, 208
a fortiori logic 70–71, 73, 80
already/not yet 37, 124n30, 129, 133, 165,
   173, 199, 241, 251, 299, 303
Ambrose 279
Amidah 110
amoral conditions 91, 288
amulets 176, 177
anaideia 65–70, 82–83
Ananias 193
anguish, in prayer 75
anointing 171, 266
answered prayer 162, 167
antecedent will 291n17
antichrist 152
Antiochus IV Epiphanes 130
anxiety 149
apatheia 54n47
apathy 215
Apocalypse. *See* Revelation
apologetics 286–87
apostasy 144, 262, 267
apostolic church
   mission 227, 242
   prayer habits 179–96
application 18
Aquinas, Thomas 293

Aramaic 111
Aristotelian philosophy 286n8
Arndt, W. F. 88n19
asking 72, 115, 276
atheism 297n25
Augustine 296–97
Aune, D. 270n34, 273n42
awakenings 60

Babylonian exile 111
Babylonian Talmud 109, 146
Bailey, K. E. 69, 82n7
banquet 150
Barnabas 188–89
Barr, J. 104n29
Barrett, C. K. 192
Barth, K. 286n8, 289
Barth, M. 237
Bauckham, R. 273n44
Beasley-Murray, G. R. 124n29, 136n6
becoming 284, 285–86n8
benedictions 112, 231n1
Benjamin, D. C. 88n20
ben Sira 138, 142
berakhot 112
Bible
   authority 114
   interpretation 17
biblical necessity 282–83
biblical realism 124n30
biblical theology 282
Blaising, C. A. 55n47
blamelessness 301

love 86
mercy 137
name 115–20
not bound by prayer 223
omnipotence 293n19
openness 290n15
ordains prayer 129
as personal 284–86
power to do impossible 32, 33, 35, 37,
    56–57, 58–59, 302
purposes 59
as redeemer 101
revelation 14, 280–81
slowness 85
sovereignty 16, 44n10, 45, 74, 81n4, 121,
    130, 146, 182–83, 196, 209, 274, 290,
    295
timing 84, 86, 93, 274, 277
wisdom 72–74, 223
wrath against sin 57n58
godliness 216
Gordon, S. D. 62
Gorringe, T. J. 294n22
gospel 242
grace 225, 242, 301
Grand Chessmaster analogy 294
gratitude 215, 242. See also thanksgiving
Graubard, Baruch 107
Greek philosophers 135
Gregory of Nyssa 136n7, 149n33
groaning 200–204, 251, 301, 303
guarantees, in prayer 36–38, 274
guidance 302
guilt 75
Gundry, R. H. 50n30

healing 21–24, 42, 264
health wish 253
heaven and earth 126–28
heavenly mindedness 301
Hebrews 253–55
Heiler, Friedrich 284–85, 288n13
Heinemann, J. 58n63, 111
Held, H. J. 43n5, 46n18, 49n27
Hengel, M. 119n14
Herod Agrippa I 192
Herod Agrippa II 189
Herzog, W. R. 88n20
Hezekiah 57n59
Hicks, J. M. 83n10
hiddenness of God 281, 304

high priestly prayer 164, 237
historical-critical principles 91
Hoffman, L. A. 111n53
holiness 216, 250, 268, 301
Holy Spirit. See Spirit
honor 82–83, 86
human decision and God's sovereignty 75,
    189, 210n23, 274
human frailty 14, 203–4, 245
humility 15
husbands 261
hyperbole, in Paul 244

Iditarod metaphor 294–96
idolatry 27
immutability 283, 296
impetratory prayer 219, 274
incantations 175, 177, 178. See also magic
incarnation 92
incense 271, 273n45
individualism 175
inner life 288
insight 268, 301
intercalation 25–28, 32
intercession 188, 218, 219, 225–29, 299,
    301–2
Israel
    apostasy 267
    stubbornness 295

James, Epistle of 153, 262–68
Jeremias, Joachim 96n2, 98–99, 100n14,
    101n19, 102n22, 104n29, 105n30, 111,
    132–33, 139n12, 149, 152
Jesus
    acting of Father 43, 160–62
    cursing of fig tree 24–28
    death 57, 257–58, 272, 304
    divinity 58n62, 282
    as enabler of prayer 181
    faith, faithfulness 49–51, 53, 58
    humanity 58n62, 258–59, 260, 282
    inaugurated kingdom 37, 119–20, 303
    intercession 164
    lordship 125
    as magician 172
    as mediator 164, 174
    miracles 44, 45
    as model of prayer 181, 195, 217–18,
        255–56
    obedience 55–56, 59, 144–46, 259–60

Index of Scripture and Other Ancient Writings